"Everything is sad," wrote the Ancient poets. But is this sadness merely a human experience, projected onto the world, or is there a gloom attributable to the world itself? Could the universe be forever weeping the "tears of things"?

In this series of meditations, Dominic Pettman and Eugene Thacker explore some of the key "negative affects" – both eternal and emergent – associated with climate change, environmental destruction, and cosmic solitude. In so doing they unearth something so obvious that it has gone largely unnoticed: the question of how we should feel about climate change. Between the information gathered by planetary sensors and the simple act of breathing the air, new unsettling moods are produced for which we currently lack an adequate language. Should we feel grief over the loss of our planet? Or is the strange feeling of witnessing mass extinction an indicator that the planet was never "ours" to begin with? *Sad Planets* explores this relationship between our all-too-human melancholia and a more impersonal sorrow, nestled in the heart of the cosmic elements.

Spanning a wide range of topics – from the history of cosmology to the "existential threat" of climate change – this book is a reckoning with the limits of human existence and comprehension. As Pettman and Thacker observe, never before have we known so much about the planet and the cosmos, and yet never before have we felt so estranged from that same planet, to say nothing of the stars beyond.

Sad Planets

Sad Planets

Dominic Pettman and Eugene Thacker

polity

First published in 2024 by Polity Press

Polity Press
65 Bridge Street
Cambridge CB2 1UR, UK

Polity Press
111 River Street
Hoboken, NJ 07030, USA

ISBN-13: 978-1-5095-6235-0
ISBN-13: 978-1-5095-6236-7 (pb)

A catalogue record for this book is available from the British Library.

Library of Congress Control Number: 2023942110

Typeset in 10.5 on 13pt Palatino
by Cheshire Typesetting Ltd, Cuddington, Cheshire
Printed and bound in Great Britain by CPI Group (UK) Ltd, Croydon

For further information on Polity, visit our website:
politybooks.com

Contents

Preface

In recent years, a host of official terms have emerged which attempt to grapple with a new kind of sorrow: "climate anxiety," "climate angst," "environmental grief," "eco-grief," "eco-guilt," and "solastalgia," to name but a few. While they differ in their specifics, what these and similar terms have in common is a reckoning with the limits of human existence vis-à-vis the planet on which we are but temporary residents. Never before have we known so much about the planet; never before have we felt so estranged from that same planet – to say nothing of the wider cosmos.

From a certain perspective, the awareness of global climate change seems to have been primarily scientific, evidenced by the now routine articles, news reports, and media coverage on the topic, themselves backed up by a plethora of research data. However, what the data reveals are not only changes to atmospheric conditions but a range of "existential threats" that are as much philosophical as they are political, social, economic, and ecological. Again and again, climate change documentaries have collated the science into a cautionary tale about the precarious relationship between human beings and planet Earth. A whole "climate culture" has emerged, one that includes everything from corporate "off world" initiatives, to climate activism, to the latest Hollywood disaster film.

In the maelstrom of big data, media coverage, and public opinion, something else has emerged, something so obvious that it has, perhaps, gone unnoticed: the question of how one should *feel* about climate change. "Climate" is, after all, a strange entity, ambient but palpable, diffuse yet tangible, something abstract that is also felt, in the way that heat, cold, humidity, air pressure, and the weather are felt. Climate is as vast as the sky and as minuscule as particles of air. It floats above us and moves through us, and in scale it renders human existence insignificant at the same time that it is judiciously measured, predicted, debated, and even engineered. In the process a new "we" is produced, one that is still vaguely defined, at once inclusive and exclusive, divergent and convergent, fractured and holistic, human and non-human. Between the data generated by a vast array of planetary sensors and the simple act of breathing the air, there are emergent emotions, affects, and moods for which we perhaps lack an adequate language.

A host of questions emerge. Should we feel grief over the loss of our planet, or is the strange feeling of planetary sorrow an indicator that the planet was never "ours" to begin with? Hovering in the background of such ruminations is the specter of human extinction, the thought of which seems both unacceptable and inevitable. Is human extinction some far-off and remote event, or is it in fact already happening? How should one mourn the death of a species? And who – or what – will be left to mourn the end of humanity?

There is a sense in which even beginning to address such questions is both daunting and presumptuous. Traditional forms of thinking and writing will not do; and a single, linear, totalizing argument would seem to lack an appreciation of the indistinctness of both climate and affect. Therefore, this book is organized differently, centered around a series of micro essays of sorts. These in turn have been constellated into "Sequences" based on overlapping themes and their variations. While there is a linear flow to each sequence, each of the micro-essays can also be read on its own.

New York, Summer 2023

Sequence 1

In Space No One Can Hear You Weep

Opportunity Knocked

"My battery is low. And it's getting dark." Many of us felt a heart-spasm when we first read these words – the last transmission from the Opportunity robot, stranded on the surface of Mars. A diligent non-human NASA employee, which had been doing its job so conscientiously for fifteen years, was now succumbing to a kind of mechanical mortality. The pathos was pure, even if the rover's last words were condensed for poetic effect. The robot, also known as Opportunity – or "Oppy," for short – surprised its makers in terms of its resilience on the red planet, so far from home, as well as for its work ethic. Long after scientists assumed it would have succumbed to rust, radiation, or some other interstellar malady, Oppy continued to forage, explore, sample, and send missives home. It was like some kind of plucky character from a Pixar movie. Except it was real. In the end, a massive dust storm was the thing that did the rover in. As Abigail Fraeman, one of the project managers, explained: "By Thursday, we knew that it was bad. And then, by Friday, we knew it was really bad, but there was nothing we could do but watch. And then it was Sunday, we actually got a communication from the rover and we were shocked . . . It basically said we had no power left." Apparently Oppy was overcome with a kind of awe at the sight of the approaching wall of rust-colored dust, about to engulf all its sensors like a sublime tsunami. Indeed, the rover's last words essentially said, "the skies are incredibly dark

. . . no sunlight is getting through. It's night time during the day."[1] Before its battery died, Opportunity managed to send back a last image, a distorted and grainy image of shadowy gray, half-truncated as the transmission was cut off.

Is the pang many of us felt at this story merely a viral case of the pathetic fallacy, so potent that even scientists were not immune from it? Or is there something *objectively sad* about a machine with a purpose, left to face its end on its own, perhaps the only moving thing on the planet – exposed to the alien elements in a way, and on a scale, that no human has yet to experience? No doubt, the philosophers can argue about whether the pathetic fallacy is in fact a fallacy or not until philosophy itself faces the same entropic fate as the Mars rover. But we would submit that there is indeed something powerfully poignant about such a scenario as this, not isolated to – or explained away by – the eye of the human beholder. Perhaps there is a seam of sorrow threaded through the universe to which humans may be the most sensitive – or maybe not – but in any case affects the universe in different ways, even where, and when, life is absent. (Perhaps partly *because* of this absence.) Creatures no doubt experienced sad situations long before there were humans around to witness or record them. Trees, after all, certainly fell in the forest many millions of years before *Homo sapiens* came along to question the sound that these timber giants most definitely made. Who are we to presume that trees don't mourn the collapse of one of their neighbors? (After all, we've only recently discovered the extent to which trees communicate and cooperate through "the world wood web.") Perhaps it's a form of arrogance to assume that only humans can experience what Spinoza called "the sad passions" and what Virgil called "the sadness in things." Perhaps even a courageous laborer, made of the world's most expensive nuts and bolts, is imbricated in an affective atmosphere as much as an elemental one.

Then Again

Then again, we could just as well propose the opposite hypothesis. That the cosmos is not a cold and sorrowful void but an inviting plenum on which glittering jewels of possibility are scattered across the heavens like warming embers. This would be the true pulse of the universe that the mystics attempt to find and channel through their ecstatic whirling or their immobile meditation. This is the subterranean ocean of tranquility beneath all our suffering and sadness: a wretchedness that, these same mystics insist, is just an illusion (from one view), or (from another) a series of necessary tests, on the path out of Saṃsāra to Nirvana. Melancholia would then, contrary to the alchemical or astrological tradition, be unconnected to the motion or music of the spheres and instead be a slimy film that humans alone leave in their wake – viscous evidence of their heavy and gloomy passage through this world. Human sadness as material excretion, manifest in our poetry as much as in our plastic, and in our sparkling new mega-churches or supermarkets as much as in our ruins. This heavy psychic, or even spiritual, baggage marks our species in sharp contrast to all the other creatures, who flow through life "like water in water,"[2] and who only know sadness when humanity introduces it to them. (An introduction no living thing can now fully avoid, given our genius for leaving the calling card of our own misery inside every crevice and infusing our own bitter tears into every toxic droplet.)

An Inventory of Affects

Climate seems at once distant or remote and at the same time the most intimate and immediate. The vast weather systems that form hurricanes, wildfires, or tsunamis operate at a scale beyond the comprehension of the individual human beings, and yet it is individuals that are also directly impacted by such events. A downstream effect occurs as those of us not directly impacted bear witness to the effects of extreme weather and are in turn affected indirectly. The experience of climate events – at whatever level – then opens onto other, more abstract, more ambivalent dispositions. As instances of climate migration increase around the planet, at what point will human beings find themselves exiled from the planet itself? Behind the climate event lurks the specter of human extinction, the haunting image of an uninhabitable Earth, a planet indifferent to the human inhabitants that have occupied it for a comparably brief moment in deep time. A rift begins to grow between the planet and its now temporary human inhabitants.

A culture of climate, a confusion of affects. Is it going to happen soon or is it happening now? To feel climate and to feel about climate. The weather "out there" and the weather right here, at my doorstep. The devastation wrought by extreme weather events – themselves becoming more regular, more normalized – cannot but produce emotional and affective responses. At the same time it can be difficult to know how or what to feel about something that operates at a scale that so far exceeds that of the individual human being. No doubt this is why, in recent years, a new vocabulary has emerged in the public discourse surrounding climate change. Psychologists discuss "eco-grief," the grieving expressed by those directly impacted by climate events. This is often distinguished from "environmental grief," or the indirect grief felt by those of us who witness the devastation of climate events for human beings, but also for animal and planetary life as well (the term has also been applied to the mourning of the loss of species). The plethora of information about the near-term impacts of climate change has also had an impact on our relationship to the future and our ability (or inability) to plan for it, given the unstable and tenuous character of climate events themselves. This has led psychiatrists to talk about "climate anxiety," the feeling of uncertainty and instability linked to climate change, which in some cases may inhibit an individual's ability to make future life decisions at all. Related to this is what journalists sometimes call "climate angst," or the frustration felt by individuals at the inertia and apathy of political leaders and government organizations to adequately respond to the "existential threats" of climate change. The troubling sense of the inevitability of it all is linked to what philosophers and sociologists have termed "solastalgia," or the irretrievable sense of a loss of home, be it one's actual home, one's place of residence, or one's country – in some cases scaled up to the planet itself.

In short, a new affective vocabulary concerning climate change has emerged, existing in the shadows of the more official, more public discourses of science, policy, and politics. While each of these terms is different from the others, they all bear witness to a unique emotional terrain for which there may not be adequate words. Not yet, that is. It will likely be a matter of time before this new vocabulary enters the official, institutional taxonomy of the Diagnostic and Statistical Manual (DSM). Many of these unofficial diagnoses take terms usually applied to individuals ("anxiety," "grief") and apply them to the species as a whole, terms denoting something about the planet that so far exceeds the individual we can only use generalities ("climate," "ecology," "environment"). Are we already witnessing a near future in which doctors can diagnose patients with "climate anxiety" or "geotrauma"? What are the treatment options for "climate angst," much less a pandemic of "solastalgia"?

Perhaps, before rushing headlong into classifying – and pathologizing – these ambivalent affects, it's worth pausing in order to acknowledge their diffuse, nebulous, and shadowy contours. The range of emotions, affects, and moods surrounding climate change are arguably of a different sort. They are negative affects: affects that point to a sense of helplessness and hopelessness, and in so doing they raise deeper, "existential" questions about the particular being that has had the provenance to name itself a human being. These are also negative affects in the sense that they index the horizon of our ability to have a relation to something as devastatingly impersonal as a hurricane, a wildfire, a flood, an earthquake. How should we relate to something as diffuse and ambient as the weather, as climate? The question is almost an elemental one. Wind, fire, water, ice. Negative affects reside at the liminal edges of the more accepted, more "healthy" affects, but, because of this, perhaps they also reveal more. Perhaps they also reveal the limits of our species-specific attitudes, orientations, and dispositions towards "our" planet. Perhaps what they reveal is a gulf between our habitual, human-centric beliefs towards the planet and the difficult-to-accept notion of the planet in itself, indifferent to our varied fears and desires.

The Weeping Animal

Nietzsche understood that the animals judge us for our histrionic ways and for being the drama queen of the animal kingdom. "I fear that the animals see man," he wrote, "as a being like them who in a most dangerous manner has lost his animal common sense – as the insane animal, the laughing animal, the weeping animal, the miserable animal."[3] This is an intriguing reversal of the humanistic assumption that it is our own kind who, exceptionally, are the rational ones. Nietzsche makes this observation in his great attempt to construct a "gay" or "joyful" science (*fröhliche Wissenschaft*), rising like a phoenix out of the ashes of the dismal archive of most human thought and endeavor. (At least, that is, since Socrates showed up and poisoned the well with his sanctimonious talk of goodness, morality, truth, and reason.) Despite his contempt for modern man, Nietzsche retained a faith in our latent potential to transcend our own resentments and the attendant passive-aggressive sharing of negativity that so often goes under the cloak of culture, society, and so on. Indeed, only someone who felt the weight of the world so heavily could understand the stakes in forging a more lighthearted orientation towards being – in saying "Yes" to existence, despite the profound insecurity of fleeting mortality. (And, in this Zarathustran project, Nietzsche would enlist many animals as totem or spirit guides.)

Of course, the wrong people listened to the wrong parts of Nietzsche, and took it the wrong way. Hitler believed the *Übermensch* would climb ever upwards on the charred bones of lesser men, while Ayn Rand – not quite so extreme – used the philosopher's words as an alibi to promote the kind of self-defeating cynical solipsism that officially informs much of our current anti-social society.

Rather than humbly ask the animals for advice on drying our neurotic tears, we slaughtered them for sport and status, destroyed their habitats, drove them to extinction, and imprisoned the remaining ones for our civic edification. When the Tove Jansson-like character, from Jansson's short story "The Wolf," visits a forsaken zoo on an abandoned island in mid-winter, she is overcome with sadness when she sees the eponymous creatures in their snowy cage. "The wolves' ceaseless pacing struck her as appalling. It was timeless. They loped back and forth behind their bars week after week and year after year, and if they hate us, she thought, it must be a gigantic hate! She felt cold, suddenly, terribly cold, and she started to cry."

The weeping animal indeed. Seeking forgiveness from a creature that howls at the moon. But does the wild wolf – free and far from the human stench – howl at the moon out of joy or from a purer sadness, moved by the pack perception of lunar beauty and the reflective illumination it provides?

We Need Not Decide

We need not decide – at this early point in our consideration of such key matters – whether humans are merely the most sensitive species when it comes to absorbing ambient and universal sorrow, or whether it is humans themselves who funk up the cosmos with their own woeful stench. (Forever lamenting their fallen state, as part of the world, but not truly *of* it.) Is the human mind, and its subsequent arts and sciences, a prism reflecting an ubiquitous sorrow, saturated into the marrow of Things? Or is it a powerful projection mechanism, using ever more powerful optical technologies to beam our own wan inadequacies onto the panoramic widescreen of the night sky. The quantum aspect of existence means both could be equally true. Or equally false.

These two alternatives, however, should be kept in mind – along with the tension created between them – as we explore the interstellar terrain of sad planets.

Earthshot

In October of 2021, in the midst of the Coronavirus pandemic, Prince William announced the launch of a new initiative, the Earth Shot Prize – "a new global prize for the environment," valued at £5 million annually, and "designed to incentivize change and help to repair our planet over the next ten years." Motivated by an increasingly rare sense of *noblesse oblige*, the then second-in-line to the English throne noted, in an interview with the BBC: "We are seeing a rise in climate anxiety; young people are now growing up where their futures are basically threatened the whole time." William went on to sympathize with the plight of those unfortunate enough to be born outside of Buckingham Palace – or, failing that, the English aristocracy – stopping short, of course, of calling for a dissolution of the monarchy and the redistribution of wealth, lands, and resources. Channeling the struggling classes as best he could, the prince concedes, "You've got to worry about a job, you've got to worry about family life, you've got to worry about housing, you've got to worry about all these things. Then you put the climate – the very thing we live, breathe, and walk around on – on top of that? So no wonder we're having a lot of mental health concerns and challenges coming along."[4]

Perhaps the likely future king is right, and anxiety is the dominant mood of the times. Others may nominate anger, or indignation, as the signature affect of our age. Certainly, social media, and the echo chamber of public life, seem custom-designed to fan the flames of both fear and fury. We however, have chosen to focus on sadness in the following pages, for several related reasons. First, sadness is a sibling to anxiety, angst, and anger, but is what remains when the energy or passion of the latter burn away. In that sense, sadness seems more of an underlying condition, foundation, or given. Sadness is, we submit, the natural tone of things once all the other cacophonous sounds die away. As such – and this brings us to the second reason – sadness (along with its close cousins melancholy, sorrow, despair, gloom, grief, and so on) is somewhat taboo in our relentlessly upbeat, frozen grimace, "have a nice day," motivational poster-plastered culture. To feel down, bereft, wan, or low is akin to blasphemy in an age that asks us to sacrifice everything but our optimism and hope, both of which – famously, cruelly, masochistically, and stubbornly – spring eternal. (Cioran: "One is and remains a slave as long as one is not *cured* of hoping." Which may explain why Prince William is so keen to reward those who continue to toil in the increasingly fallow fields of such faith.) Sadness is both timely and timeless in its response to each poignant scene or situation with which we find ourselves confronted each day; and also, in its more profound and universal understanding of the futility of action, the vanity of plans, and inevitable passing of all that is precious. (Including the cold comfort of sadness itself.)

What the Earth and all of its inhabitants are enduring at present – including insentient elements such as landscapes and habitats – is a scandal and a shame. What's more, we are ashamed that we are the main source of the scandal, as much as some of us still try to deny it. Clearly the world is becoming a sadder place to live in, if only because the extinction rate is accelerating exponentially for our fellow living beings (even as those animals that call themselves humans are multiplying at an alarming rate). Even those people who sit right at the top of Maslow's hierarchy of needs – adjusted to include fast wi-fi, prestige brand clothing, and cold-pressed juice bars – feel the sadness that washes all around them, like a rising tide. (For, as much as the economically comfortable try to deny it, happiness is a collective resource and cannot be hoarded without great psychic cost.)

The end looms – through floods, famine, fire, plague, or nuclear winter. And yet we no longer have faith in the kind of existential consolation that the idea of the apocalypse or the End Times used to bring. We suspect and understand that the earthly story, along with its pathetic human drama, will limp along even after things have completely fallen apart. No rapture awaits. No kingdom of heaven. But rather struggle, improvisation, conflict, and sheer persistence for its own tenacious sake. Yes, we have a right to be angry, given how callously those self-nominated to be our stewards act and obtain. Yes, we have a right to be fearful, given how close we sail daily to the figurative cliff. But sadness, we feel, is the pulse of the matter, even as it forms the conditions for those precious and fleeting efflorescences of joy to which even the most miserable of souls is prone, despite their – our – commitment to a sense of infinite resignation.

When it comes to an existential inventory of the affects, this book could certainly be the first volume in a series – including *Mad Planets, Scared Planets, Scarred Planets, Charred Planets,* and so on. (Even *Glad Planets,* if we're feeling foolishly optimistic.) . . . But sadness seemed the right affect for the times, as well as for the timeless human condition itself. (And, by extension or association, the world, the planet, the solar system, and beyond.)

Ecce Kosmos

We all have at least one. A moment in which the scales finally fall from our eyes and we look around us as if suddenly reborn, seeing the world – nay, the universe! – afresh. Seeing beyond the horizon of the familiar is an uncanny feeling; a cosmic feeling – to realize, not only mentally, but *viscerally* – that we are but fleeting creatures, clinging to a rock that is somehow both spinning and hurtling through the endless inky darkness of space. This epiphany can be either terrifying or wondrous, or a stirring combination of both. For at least one person, it happened during a rather epic excursion to Cappadocia, in Turkey; a strange lunar landscape of caves and human ant-hills that once concealed entire subterranean towns of persecuted Christians. Today, it plays host only to tourists and the occasional nomad or wandering ascetic. Climbing to the top of one of the tallest of these sandy peaks at sunset, this person suddenly discovered the glowing, golden orb of the sun to their left and the rising, silver full moon to their right. For one prolonged and breathless twilight moment, these two heavenly bodies appeared the same size, and the heaven-struck one stretched out their arms as if they could catch hold of both of them, as if they were suddenly a kind of phoenix – stretching their wings – in the midst of an allegorical, Vitruvian tableaux. *Ecce homo. Behold the human.*

Or, at least, behold this one human – one of several billion, whiling away their allotted time on this sad planet. See how small this person is – how foolish – stretching their arms like a faded wax miniature, perched atop a dry and long-stale wedding cake. See how they channel their sense of cosmic insignificance into its inverse, by virtue of an astronomical fluke. (Had this person lingered a little longer during that last gas station rest stop, they would surely have missed this particular angle on the spectacular sunset.) The humanist double-gesture *par excellence*: to acknowledge the accident of our own existence, and then to swiftly turn this contingency into some kind of epic necessity.

Once upon a time we explained away the fact that there is something rather than nothing – especially the "something" that is ourselves – by virtue of theological necessity. ("He is the image of the invisible God, the firstborn of all creation . . . He himself is before all things, and in him all things hold together.")[5] Today the operation is more nuanced, though no less self-aggrandizing. On some level we understand, and even admit, the profound absurdity of our own existence – the fact that all of our moods, experiences, efforts, hopes, toils, and troubles are but the haphazard end point of a 13 billion-year concatenation of mysterious quantum dominoes. Despite this, we remain egocentric enough to feel that we were also somehow inevitable, if not decreed. In public, we admit that our dentist bills, or latest opera – and everything else that takes up our sphere of attention – are but the continuing aftershocks of the Big Bang, and a mysterious cocktail of particles, energies, forces, genetic sequencing, and animating affects. In private, however, we can't but help pat ourselves on the back (or, alternatively, wring our hands in lamentation) that we ourselves – this unique individual that carries the burden of our name – are more than just a brief sneeze in God's great handkerchief; we are a singular witness to the infinite miracle of existence, with all the agency and existential privilege this entails.

You Are Here

"Planet Earth is blue and there's nothing I can do," sings Major Tom (aka David Bowie). A preemptive epitaph for our species? In this age of climate strife and planetary catastrophe – all bundled up in the catch-all phrase "the Anthropocene" – our cosmic dilemma takes on a special significance. In contrast to other secular epochs, in which a certain human continuity was taken for granted, we now have a new and keen appreciation of our situatedness and accompanying fragility. The human race can suddenly see an unexpected finishing line looming ahead of us, and yet it cannot slow down the pace in a bid to keep the marathon going. We live in a neo-millenarian age, except this time the prophets of doom are not preachers describing fire and brimstone from the pulpit but scientists describing "cataclysmic events" with detailed graphs and charts from the Senate room floor or the UN assembly. Who can we turn to, now that God is dead to our institutions, if not to our atavistic hearts? Who can we appeal to for salvation, other than ourselves? (A terrifying scenario, since we are not at all convinced that we are worth saving.) Without a divine overseer or benign alien intervention, we either sink into a kind of fatalistic gloom or displace such helpless feelings onto adolescent fantasies of interstellar colonization. "Planet Earth is blue and there's nothing I can do," sings the human choir, their tear-stained cheeks smudged with ashes. "There is nothing they can do," echoes the Greek chorus of these apathetic End Times.

Historians and philosophers alike fetishize the moment we saw our own Earth from a distance not through the prism of the imagination but through an actual camera (either hitched to a satellite or operated by an astronaut). Martin Heidegger famously talks of "the age of the world picture" – a modern upheaval in which our rather abstract and numinous "world" is reduced to an objective "factual" representation of the planet. With the advent of satellite photography, "the world" suddenly becomes conflated with, or reduced to, "the Earth" – representable, analyzable, parsable; reduced to an object of positivist, scientific knowledge. The dark irony here is that the moment we see the world as a unified visual, cognitively graspable object, we lose the capacity to really think about *the world* (and thus we lose the capacity to think the world into being, anew). Henceforth, we can only approach it instrumentally, as something to manipulate, conquer, control, terraform.

Seeing the Earth trapped within the frame of representation can be reassuring to those minds who feel more confident when they have maps to help orient themselves. (Indeed, what is more grounding than those maps that confidently assert, "You are here"?) And yet "here" is never self-evident or easily given. Less literal minds find the iconic image of our planetary home to be alienating, disorienting, and reductive. For how can one really reconcile all those billions and billions of lives – of which humans are only a fractional, albeit consequential, instance – with such a flat, remote image? What knowledge or wisdom is gained by seeing the material foundation of our collective being in a single selfie? Assuredly, the scientific gaze tells us as much about the world as the male gaze tells us about women.

Pale Blue Dot

Emerging from the techno-cultural matrix that gave us the first photographs of Earth is also the figure of the benign astronomer, embodied most famously in the soothing voice of Carl Sagan. His rousing speech about the "Pale Blue Dot" is indeed a moving piece of rhetoric, which continues to make many an eye misty as it circulates in pirated versions on YouTube. In this speech, Sagan wrestles with what we might call "the enabling trauma" of being suddenly alienated from our own spiritual homeland through the blunt rendering of its actual cosmic situation – its isolated spatial location.

> Look again at that dot. That's here. That's home. That's us. On it everyone you love, everyone you know, everyone you ever heard of, every human being who ever was, lived out their lives. The aggregate of our joy and suffering, thousands of confident religions, ideologies, and economic doctrines, every hunter and forager, every hero and coward, every creator and destroyer of civilization, every king and peasant, every young couple in love, every mother and father, hopeful child, inventor and explorer, every teacher of morals, every corrupt politician, every "superstar," every "supreme leader," every saint and sinner in the history of our species lived there – on a mote of dust suspended in a sunbeam. . . . The Earth is a very small stage in a vast cosmic arena. Think of the rivers of blood spilled by all those generals and emperors so that, in glory and triumph, they could become the momentary masters of a fraction of a dot. Think of the endless cruelties visited by the inhabitants of one corner of this pixel on the scarcely distinguishable inhabitants of some other corner, how frequent their misunderstandings, how eager they are to kill one another, how fervent their hatreds. . . . Our posturings, our imagined self-importance, the delusion that we have some privileged position in the Universe, are challenged by this point of pale light. Our planet is a lonely speck in the great enveloping cosmic dark. In our obscurity, in all this vastness, there is no hint that help will come from elsewhere to save us from ourselves. . . . The Earth is the only world known so far to harbor life. There is nowhere else, at least in the near future, to which our species could migrate. Visit, yes. Settle, not yet. Like it or not, for the moment the Earth is where we make our stand. . . . It has been said that astronomy is a humbling and character-building experience. There is perhaps no better demonstration of the folly of human conceits than this distant image of our tiny world. To me, it underscores our responsibility to deal more kindly with one another, and to preserve and cherish the pale blue dot, the only home we've ever known.[6]

With this stirring invocation, Sagan describes "the local sublime," rousing us to feel a kind of global pride in embracing our own *outré* status as conscious beings who find themselves in a far-flung corner of the void. The mystery remains, he argues, as does the dilemma. But this new awareness of our pale blue precarity allows us – for the first time in our species' history – to truly acknowledge the fragility of our conditional existence. The resulting hope is thus that we shall be more respectful of one another through such knowledge, gained through an unprecedented estrangement from ourselves.

Billions and Billions

Astronomers are indeed nothing if not optimistic, forever on the lookout for new bodies, new orbits, new portals to new dimensions. Yet they are also inherently melancholic, inventing larger and more powerful telescopes every few years in order to peer further and further into the abyss. Their charge, in the modern era – in contrast to more enchanted times, in which the skies were vast scrolls containing the fates and fortunes of Men – is to make increasingly exquisitely detailed maps of the Infinite and Expanding Nothingness, to make recordings of the vast and intimidating heavenly silence. (Though we must also accept that this scenario is only depressing for biocentric people – that is to say, people with a disproportionate investment in the notion of life.) But the universe is weird. It is somehow *both* mind-bendingly empty and host to multitudes. It is a plenum set into a glittering void. It contains countless bodies, but these bodies are forever out of reach, winking at one another across quantum ballrooms of unfathomable distances. (Recall that, before TripAdvisor, one of the most popular travel guides was called *Lonely Planet*.)

"Billions and billions" is the astronomer's mantra. There are billions of stars out there, we are assured, some of which must surely nurture life of some description. But while the math is heartening, the signs are not. (Or, rather, the lack of signs are not.) Telling humans that there are billions and billions of stars out there is about as helpful as reminding a poor farmer in Ecuador that there are billions and billions of dollars out there. It's a verifiable fact, but not of any relevance in this case – and indeed not great for morale. To realize the intense and inexplicable "state of exception" in which terrestrial life subsists is to experience a cosmic version of "sonder": the sudden realization that other people have as deep and complex lives as you do. Except, in this case, the feeling is inverted and reversed. It is the sudden, sinking understanding that we earthlings are the only creatures at least within thousands, perhaps millions, of light-years. The consequences of this negative epiphany – psychic, social, scientific, ethical, metaphysical, and so on – have yet to be fully grasped.

Indeed, it's probably an act of self-preservation to *avoid* grasping this knowledge fully. Lonely, yes. Though we have invented a dizzying variety of ways to distract ourselves from this loneliness. (Art, media, gossip, alcohol, money, love, sport . . . the list is nearly endless.) Indeed, who is to say we would be any less lonely if a fleet of friendly aliens suddenly arrived in our skies. No doubt they would just be one more form of difference to become aggravated or threatened by – yet another opportunity to indulge in xenophobia.

The Last Dog

The first female in space was not, as commonly considered, Valentina Tereshkova, in 1963, but Laika the dog, nearly six years earlier. We tend to forget this detail, even as Laika herself has become a tragic near mythical figure, embodying the ambitions and follies of the Cold War space race. (Notably, all space dogs in the Soviet program – of which there were dozens – were female, since there was no room in the nose-cone of the rocket ships for male dogs to lift their leg up and relieve themselves.) Laika herself was sourced, like all her other canine cosmonaut comrades, from the streets of Moscow. Scientists, armed with tape measures, poached amiable strays and brought them to the Institute of Aviation Medicine. After distinguishing herself in training, Laika was ultimately chosen not only for her cool temperament under pressure but for her photogenic visage and pleasing silhouette. (A different dog, Albina, actually performed better in most tests leading up to the launch but was not deemed as attractive. The space race was, after all, just as much an artifact of marketing and propaganda as of astrophysical achievements.)

Laika was chosen to orbit the Earth in Sputnik 2 – a larger and more ambitious satellite than the unmanned one which had shot across the headlines of the world less than a month earlier (giving the Soviets first blood when it came to the conquest of space). As a result, the Western media initially nicknamed Laika "Muttnik." Under pressure to ensure this second launch was timed to coincide with the fortieth anniversary of the Russian Revolution, short-cuts were made. And while there was no expectation, from the beginning, that Laika would survive the journey, she was supposed to be spared too much trauma on her heroic flight, designed to pave the way for human space travel soon after.

Sputnik 2 launched successfully on November 3, 1957, and official Soviet news outlets reported a healthy passenger for the first few days. Decades later, we would learn that these were in fact lies, and that poor Laika perished around seven hours after lift-off after enduring terrible stress and unbearable temperatures (the latter due to a known issue with the thermal insulation). As a result, this first creature to leave the Earth's orbit, presumably in the history of the planet, circled the globe as a singed corpse for five long months before finally receiving an organic cremation when Sputnik 2 disintegrated on re-entering the Earth's atmosphere on April 14, 1958 (after circling the Earth 2,570 times). The English newspapers called Laika "the fuzziest, loneliest, unhappiest dog in the world." After she was pronounced dead by Soviet officials, her demise was framed as a noble "sacrifice" towards a more glorious, interplanetary future. Indeed, Laika was not the first of such sacrifices, and it is estimated that at least fifteen dogs died during suborbital launch experiments in the 1950s. (Though accurate figures are hard to come by, even today, due to the intense state secrecy around the space program.)

While the reaction in the West was mostly one of outrage, fanned by the growing animal rights movement, the US did not exactly have firm footing on the moral high ground, as several species of chimp and monkey died during experiments and test flights on the American side of the space race. (Indeed, as recently as 2019, NASA euthanized twenty-seven monkeys in a single day at one of their research facilities.)[7] Dogs were preferred to chimps in the USSR because simians – like humans – required more training and vaccines. Additionally, primates were deemed "emotionally unstable and fidgety" by the Soviet scientists in charge of animal discipline. (The celebrated figure of Pavlov, and his behaviorist experiments with canines, was also a likely influence concerning the preference.)

We might pause, then, to consider what it really means that the first living being to reach outer space was, on the one hand, not human and, on the other hand, not truly cognizant of her mission. Today, our sentimental hearts spasm at the thought of an adorable, innocent animal, strapped into a capsule and roasted alive to better pave the way for human space flight. The Soviet scientists at the time, however, considered dogs as quasi-comrades: fellow pioneers and willing allies for the glory of all humankind. This did not prevent, however, belated remorse. (As Oleg Gazenko, a medical officer involved in the program, noted, "The more time passes, the more I'm sorry about it. We shouldn't have done it. We did not learn enough from the mission to justify the death of the dog.")[8] It is a question of perspective, then, whether these dogs were merely fulfilling their deeper evolutionary mission, as our obedient "best friends," or if they were hoodwinked from the beginning: doomed as soon as the first wolf crept too close to the primal human fire.

Remarkably, animals were involved in experiments, with space travel in mind, conducted as early as 1897. Konstantin Tsiolkovsky, for instance, known as "the father of the cosmonaut program," managed to increase the mass of a chicken by a factor of ten, while simulating intense gravitational forces, using a centrifuge of his own invention. (The chicken survived.) But why involve non-humans at all? Why scoop them up and strap them down in the rickety manifestation of our own pathology, our own misguided passion for a cosmic escape plan? On what grounds can we justify sending up fuzzy surrogates to test the temperature of the astral waters, even when – as in the happier case of Belka and Strelka – the four-legged cosmonauts return alive and in one piece? Surely this is little more than cowardice. Ignoble, in any case.

Non-human cosmonauts and astronauts complicate the image of ourselves as the lone star-faring species, at least potentially speaking. And this glitch in our own self-image can occasionally happen in public, as when Yuri Gagarin followed the initial trajectory of Laika to become the first human to leave the Earth's atmosphere (orbiting the planet only a single time). Upon his return to terra firma, he is said to have joked, "Am I the first human in space, or the last dog?"

A Mir Formality

When heading out into space, you cannot count on things being the same when you return. So learned the Russian engineer and cosmonaut Sergei Konstantinovich Krikalev, after blasting off to spend a planned five months in the Mir Space Station, which circled the Earth from 1986 to 2001. Krikalev arrived in orbit safely, via a Soyuz rocket, in May 1991, and promptly began running various experiments, safety checks, and maintenance routines. No doubt the cosmonaut experienced cold feet about heading into the heavens when events were so uncertain on the ground, especially in his native Russia. For the past eighteen months – since the fall of the Berlin Wall – the various countries comprising the Soviet Union were falling to revolutions, and other upheavals, like dominos. The entire Eastern bloc was in tumult. As a model citizen, however, Krikalev put on his space suit and set forth for the Mir: a tangible reminder of the supremacy with which the Soviets had helped initiate the space race.

When October arrived, and when Krikalev should have been strapping in to return to his loved ones on terra firma, he was surely perturbed to learn that his orders had changed. Even more disconcerting, Krikalev found no clarity around who was in charge anymore, and thus who was authorized to issue orders in the first place. The world's first "spaceport" – the Baikonur Cosmodrome, from which the Soyuz rockets came and went – was based in Kazakhstan, which had recently gained independence. The fate of his mission – indeed the fate of the space station itself – was suddenly anything but certain. As a result, Krikalev was obliged to bide his time after the rest of the crew had left and continue to maintain the Mir – an endearingly messy vessel, which several cosmonauts, in contrast to the pragmatic Americans on the International Space Station nearby, considered a living organism, like a kind of metal maternal womb. Thankfully food supplies, while flavorless and modest, were not yet an issue, and Krikalev spent his time talking to amateur radio enthusiasts back on Earth who had recently learned how to patch in to his satellite communications system. One person in particular – the pilot, folk dancer, polyglot, literacy consultant, and amateur radio enthusiast Margaret Iaquinto – kept Krikalev company over the ham channel; records show that he chatted with her almost every day for a year. We can only imagine how Krikalev felt when, the day after Christmas, the Soviet Union was formally dissolved.

After 311 days, however – twice as long as his planned mission – Krikalev finally touched down back on Earth after an international team of scientists secured his safe return. Given the fact that this hardy cosmonaut left the surface during one historical epoch and came back during another, Krikalev is sometimes referred to as "the last Soviet citizen." (Though this description might best be reserved for Vladimir Putin, who seems to think the KGB is an ongoing concern.)

Less fortunate than Krikalev are the astronauts ejected into orbit by an exploded rocket in Ray Bradbury's evocative short story "Kaleidoscope." The tale opens with the disaster: "The first concussion cut the rocket up the side with a giant can opener. The men were thrown into space like a dozen wriggling silverfish. They were scattered into a dark sea; and the ship, in a million pieces, went on, a meteor swarm seeking a lost sun." In the following pages, we eavesdrop on the panicked conversation of these temporary survivors – still connected for the moment by the communication system in their space suits – but now orphaned from the mother ship and floating alone according to whatever helpless trajectory the explosion had reserved for them. "The components of the brain which had worked so beautifully and efficiently in the skull case of the rocket ship firing through space were dying one by one; the meaning of their life together was falling apart."

Bradbury's economical language manages to capture the pettiness and resentment that can persist even in existential emergencies such as this, as the men lurch from bickering, to vain boastfulness, to choked-up reminiscence, to raging against the dying of the light, to mortal resignation.

> They were all alone. Their voices had died like echoes of the words of God spoken and vibrating in the starred deep. There went the captain to the Moon; there Stone with the meteor swarm; there Stimson; there Applegate toward Pluto; there Smith and Turner and Underwood and all the rest, the shards of the kaleidoscope that had formed a thinking pattern for so long, hurled apart.[9]

One by one the voices cease, like stars winking out. "The many good-bys. The short farewells," notes the narrator. "And now the great loose brain was disintegrating."

One of the doomed astronauts, Hollis, has the perhaps comforting honor of heading directly back towards Earth and begins feeling the gravitational tug of the outer atmosphere. In a twist on so many "killer comet" scenarios, Hollis finds himself in the position of hurtling towards the surface. "He fell swiftly, like a bullet, like a pebble, like an iron weight, objective, objective all of the time now, not sad or happy or anything, but only wishing he could do a good thing now that everything was gone, a good thing for just himself to know about." Falling, a thought occurs to him: "When I hit the atmosphere, I'll burn like a meteor."

Down on Earth, at precisely the same moment, a mother and her child are watching the night sky. "Look, Mom, look!

A falling star!" says the boy. "Make a wish," says his mother. "Make a wish."

Where No Man Has Gone Before

Two decades after the Mir Space Station was called back home, to disintegrate in the Earth's atmosphere and scatter into the Southern Pacific Ocean, three billionaires were sublimating primal phallic urges into a new space race for the world's richest citizens. In 2021, Jeff Bezos, Elon Musk, and Richard Branson all launched private vessels into the upper atmosphere in a bid to reboot the golden age of space exploration, but now with a strident entrepreneurial bent, favoring rich tourists over highly trained cosmonauts.

Jeff Bezos' vessel – Blue Origin – was notable for one of its four passengers: William Shatner, the actor who played the captain of the starship Enterprise in the original *Star Trek* series. In a supremely Baudrillardian moment, television and actuality fused into a nostalgic hyperreality, as if, since Regan perhaps, we need the blessing of an avatar of the Spectacle in order to make any aspirationally historic scenario *feel* real. For his part, Shatner – a long-time self-parodying figure of ironic camp and high kitsch, surfing the long wave of the *Star Trek* franchise into his nineties – seemed genuinely shaken on his return; not mentally prepared for confronting the Real that extends forever beyond both the domesticated "reality" of terrestrial life and the false bubbles of pseudo-reality that flicker on our TV screens. "The covering of blue," he said, at the post-landing press conference. "This sheet, this blanket, this comforter that we have around. We think, 'Oh, that's blue sky.' Then suddenly you shoot through it all of a sudden, as though you're whipping a sheet off you when you're asleep, and you're looking into blackness, into black ugliness."

Shatner – for all the world an aged Captain Kirk – departed from his famous character in being visibly haunted by the brute fact of "having gone where (almost) no man has gone before." He groped for the words to convey his existential vertigo. "You look down," he added. "There's the blue down there . . . comforting Mother Earth . . . and then . . . the black up there." Shatner looked around the room, his eyes trying to adjust to the enclosed space, having just lost a staring competition with infinity. He then asked the assembled reporters, as if hoping for an answer:

"Is that death? . . . I don't know."

Stranger Danger

Today we tend to think of alienation as a historical phenomenon, in large part to the ongoing influence of Karl Marx. According to this famous critic of capital, it is the march of modernity, and the accelerating distance between people and their own products, destinies, and gestures, that leads to a profound sense of estrangement from what Marx called our "species being" (i.e., our own human *raison d'être*). In other words – and to simplify a great deal – we were, once upon a time, intimately connected with our own actions, minds, intentions, communities, and so on. With the arrival of capitalism, however – which introduced an insatiable, systemic appetite for profit, along with all sorts of coercive techniques to maximize the efficient extraction of such – we started upon the extended devolution into neurotic, organic robots of our own making. Since the Industrial Revolution, we have been estranged from our sense of self, since we have been obliged to work for the benefit of others, and to be badly treated and compensated into the bargain.

A century after Marx introduced this particular notion of alienation – for which communism and an egalitarian share in "the mode of production" is the antidote – the French intelligentsia were experimenting with an even more formidable strain of the problem: not just a social form of estrangement but a metaphysical one. Jean-Paul Sartre's classic novel *Nausea*, for instance, speaks of the alienation that sensitive souls suffer from merely being conscious subjects thrust into an absurd and pedantic world. While it is true that we cultural creatures have *always* been obliged to juggle various roles in order to get by – parent, teacher, diplomat, lover, and so on – the modern individual has so many masks to wear, codes to master, and expectations to navigate that we find it increasingly difficult to separate the performance from the performer. As a result, we begin to question not only our sense of purpose or identity but even our most fundamental existential orientation in the world. We become alienated from not only our own motivations and desires but from the entire surreal enterprise of being a legible human among others. For, if God is dead, then what narrative frame, or transcendent authority, is left to provide a much needed sense of validation and meaning? (The existentialists would eventually propose a kind of auto-validation process, where humanity must legitimize itself anew in a deliberate secular key, and for our own collective well-being rather than for the glory of an elusive Big Other.)

Interestingly, "alienation," as a term, first occurs in English with early editions of the Bible, describing the terrible distress visited upon our kind when we became estranged from God. In a late fourteenth-century version of the Old Testament, for example, we are told, "Alienacioun of God is to men worchynge wickidnesse." While in the anonymous fifteenth-century *Speculum Sacerdotale*, Eve is blamed for breaking up the beautiful friendship between Maker and made, for "Sche made alienacion and partynge bitwene God and man." Alienation – derived from the Latin word *alienus*, meaning "foreign, or belonging to another" – thus has a long history of describing not only a constant and categorical state of difference (itself measured by a perceived norm) but also a sudden rift, an unanticipated distance, or a lurching change in perspective. A perplexing moment of defamiliarization can, it seems, happen at any moment. And while aliens are usually people from "out there," who occasionally show up "over here," their very presence – whether real or imagined – threatens our (preferably unreflective) sense of coherence, belonging, and purpose. (Xenophobia means "fear of foreigners" – a definition that neatly demonstrates the way that the aperture of common-garden racism can simply be widened to preemptively include any and all visitors from another world. There is, in other words, no gradation to the category of alien. It simply begins beyond one's front door, city gates, or national border and can theoretically extend to the end of the universe.) Aliens from without can be discouraged, screened, quarantined, chased away. The alien *within*, however, is much harder to deal with. For how does one deport an essential part of oneself?

All these layers of what we might call "the alien effect" are suggestively present in two singular films, made nearly four decades apart but which work together as a resonant double feature: Nicolus Roeg's *The Man Who Fell to Earth* (1976) and Jonathan Glazer's *Under the Skin* (2013). Both feature an alien, disguised as a human, sent to Earth on a mission. And in both cases the visitor is obliged to deal with the strange humans who presume, at least at first, there is nothing untoward about the stranger. Both movies attempt to convey the alienation inevitably experienced by aliens themselves.

In *The Man Who Fell to Earth*, the titular "man" (played by David Bowie) is one of the last members of an extraterrestrial race who have driven themselves to the brink of extinction through a reckless misuse of resources. Specifically, they are running desperately out of water. This strange being lands in North America and, thanks to a disguise, manages to "pass" as an eccentric English entrepreneur calling himself Thomas Jerome Newton. Here he patents the advanced technology from his home planet to accumulate the capital to build a spaceship capable of freighting water back home. (Raising the possibility that Elon Musk is in fact an alien, whose enthusiasm for colonizing Mars is a deliberate ruse to get himself back there.) As Newton's ambitious plans coalesce, he has a rather passive intimate relationship with an alcoholic drifter, Mary-Lou (played by Candy Clarke), and – through her – learns many of the alien customs of the Americans. Through a swift flashback, however, we learn that Newton has a family back on his home planet. It is thus a combination of loneliness, isolation, guilt, and stress that nudges him towards becoming addicted to alcohol, as well as to the narcotic effects of television. Newton starts to accumulate a dozen or more television sets, watching them all at once as he waits for his spaceship to be built, his sanity fraying at the edges ("Get out of my head," he screeches at one point – though he never simply turns them off). Meanwhile, Newton's main assistant becomes increasingly suspicious of not only his boss's behavior but also his origins, and manages to take a clandestine X-ray of the ersatz Englishman, revealing him to indeed be an extraterrestrial. Now that the jig is up, Newton also reveals his true form to his lover, Mary-Lou, who understandably freaks out. (Though how she didn't notice anything untoward during their frequent sexual encounters is anyone's guess.) The feds are soon involved, and Newton becomes the subject of cruel experiments, soon losing his sight. Clearly, he failed his mission and will never see his family again. In addition to this personal tragedy, the unhappy visitor must live with the knowledge that, on his account, his people will expire for lack of liquid. Talk about sad planets!

Roeg's film, based on the novel by Walter Tevis, has become a cult classic of 1970s art cinema. The editing is erratic, the visual design stylized, and the story told in elliptical loops. The director is interested more in conveying a mood than in simply presenting the events of a science fictional narrative or trying to present events in a realistic way. Through a series of meta neo-Brechtian anti-conventions – intrusive music, epileptic montages, unexpected camera angles, and so on – Roeg initially alienates the audience, but in a way that mirrors the fractured experience of Newton himself, and thus eventually creates a paradoxical identification with the protagonist. In other words, it's a pretty hip film, designed to appeal to people usually more interested in Andy Warhol than Arthur C. Clarke.

Under the Skin, by contrast, is also made for the "art" crowd but maintains a slow and steady pace, featuring long shots, gradual takes, and an unsettling ambient score. In this scenario, the alien – played by Scarlett Johansson – touches down in Scotland. She is similarly disguised as an earthling and interacts exclusively with lonely men, mostly from the driver's seat of her van. (Some of the scenes were filmed, candid-camera style, with oblivious members of the public.)

The unnamed alien lures several men into a run-down house on the outskirts of Glasgow, where they are horrified to discover they are now trapped in some kind of "liquid abyss": a viscous black pool, awaiting God knows what. After conducting a number of abductions, the alien starts to show signs of – if not remorse – then at least curiosity about the species she is impersonating. In one memorable scene she visits a country tea room and orders some cake. After a single bite, however, she coughs it back up on the plate (to the disgust of the other patrons). She also seems to experiment with the local mating rituals, visiting a nightclub and even kissing a man in his humble home. This experience prompts her to examine "her own" genitals with a lamp – this anatomy being in fact a prosthetic effect of her human-suit – and she seems so traumatized by what she sees that the possibility of sex seems off the menu from then on.

All these moments, once again, produce an alienation effect in the viewer, amplifying the unease we all feel, to a varying extent, with being embodied intellects, obliged to haul a fleshy envelope around with us wherever we go. Perhaps having a body is *already* an alien experience. Moreover, given Johansson's semiotic force as one of our most conspicuous objects of desire, the film quietly provokes a series of half-articulated questions around sex, gender, desire, empathy, (self-)identification, alterity, estrangement, and embodiment. One critic, Ara Osterweil, even described the film as "one of the most important feminist interventions in recent cinematic history," though its feminist message – if it has one – is both ambiguous and ambivalent. Johansson's character, after all, is burnt to death by a predatory man: hardly the climax of an empowering narrative. (Of course a feminist film should not automatically have a feel-good resolution; but it does, in this case, beg the question.) In any case, Glazer provides enough room – both visually and sonically – for the audience to come up with their own interpretations of the possible equations between the low-key hunt of the alien and her all-too human – indeed all-too female – demise. What happens to our own sense of compassion (itself considered a key aspect of our species-being) when we are the initial quarry? How does the classic science fiction script flip when the frightening alien figure looks like a young, conventionally attractive woman rather than a reptile–squid hybrid? How does the *Predator* template create new affective responses in the audience when the hunter presents as a seemingly conflicted woman from the United States? Finally, what does the title tease for us in terms of coming to terms with difference? (The phrase "under the skin" usually being deployed as a rhetorical device to shame superficial, epidermal bigotry.)

While *The Man Who Fell to Earth* relies on a jazzy psychedelic kind of maximalism, *Under the Skin* proceeds according to a muted, post-rock minimalism. The former adds layer upon celluloid layer, while the latter almost subtracts each scene from the screen until there is nothing left but the enigma. (A deliberate decision by the director, since the book on which it was based, written by Michel Faber, is more forthcoming about the alien, her mission, and her thoughts.) Despite their aesthetic differences, however, both films effectively capture and convey the profound sadness that the alien experiences in a new environment so far from home. (David Bowie, of course, made a stellar career out of playing forsaken star-men in his songs, lost and adrift in space.) One wonders, however, about the granular nature of experience in such encounters. After all, Mary-Lou – no matter her faults – was a warm welcoming party for Newton. And the unnamed alienness in *Under the Skin* found glimpses of friendly intimacy to trouble her own non-relationship with humans. Was the problem that they both touched down on Earth during an especially alienated age? (So to say, in post-Fordist US, or post-Thatcher UK?) Would they have had less occasion to feel depressed if they had arrived in, say, Egypt during the time of Cleopatra; or in the antipodes, pre-European invasion; or in Morocco during the height of the Islamic Empire? Would Newton have had a nervous breakdown in front of a giant stained-glass window in Notre Dame Cathedral, as he did in front of a pyramid of television sets? Would Johansson's character have learned more rewarding things about her own kind if she had been seduced by an Aztec priest?

Such hypotheticals again return us to the key question of alienation, and whether it can be traced back to a social or metaphysical source. Can we really agree with the utopian thinkers who believe that our sense of existential unease can be dispelled by a more humane way of organizing our needs, institutions, and relations? Or is that itself a fantasy – a symptom of our own alienation, trying to dream up a solution to itself? Indeed, can *any* self-reflexive creature avoid becoming alienated, since sentience involves a meta-layer of thinking, initially designed to help with decision-making but inevitably leading to second-guessing, doubt, and crises of confidence? (By such logic, it is even just a matter of time before advanced AI systems have a mental breakdown.)

Final Contact

Historically, the science fiction genre has been wary of the alien, too often portrayed as either suspect visitor or invading other. (No doubt this is partly the reason why aliens are so commonly represented as vaguely reptilian or insectoid "colonies.") Enmity, conflict, war, the struggle for dominion. *War of the Worlds*. But there is also the inverse of this, in which the alien other is neither alien nor other at all but simply another kind of human, a cipher for equally conflicted and agonistic relations between humans, from the sweeping, epic melodrama of Olaf Stapledon's *Last and First Men*, to Isaac Asimov's *Foundation* series, to the many incarnations of the *Star Trek* franchise. Conflict, enmity, and war, but also diplomacy, communication, and the political dream of universal community. The alien as human, or the alien as the opposite of the human.

These two tendencies perhaps reached their extreme in 1982, the year that two films featuring aliens were released: Steven Spielberg's *E.T. the Extra-Terrestrial* and John Carpenter's *The Thing*. The alien as friendly, peace-loving visitor, by turns a childhood imaginary friend, a dress-up doll, a domestic pet, and a wizened old sage; the alien who shows us, through healing and humbleness, that the real threat is not aliens but human beings. Or the alien as malevolent and inhuman, as viral contagion, so distant from human comprehension that it has no form, no shape, no body, except through its unnerving capacity to infect, possess, and ceaselessly recombine the other life forms that it absorbs. The alien that displays more humanity than humans themselves. Or the alien that is so "other" that it is quite literally nothing in itself, the alterity of some nebulous "thing" towards which no relation is possible – until it's too late.

As different as they are, these two aspects of alien otherness – the alien as another kind of human and the alien as the horizon of the human – both presume there is something "out there" that one recognizes, identifies, and confronts as other. A different perspective, however, is given in "The Architects of Fear," an episode of *The Outer Limits,* which originally aired in 1963. In the midst of the Cold War, the secret government organization United Labs conducts an experiment to actually transform a human being into an alien. Giving a new meaning to the idea of "deep cover," the agent who volunteers for the procedure must undergo a series of radical surgical modifications (until, presumably, he looks appropriately alien to "pass"). He – or it – is placed in a spacecraft and sent into orbit, whereby the craft circles back and "invades" the Earth. The hope is that this faked alien invasion will prompt unification among divided Cold War nations. (It doesn't. The mission goes awry, leading only to the tragic death of the "alien.") A variant on the "enemy of my enemy is my friend" motif, the episode points back to earlier science fiction by authors such as Alice Bradley Sheldon (James Tiptree Jr.), Ray Bradbury, and Kurt Vonnegut and formed a substantial part of Alan Moore and Dave Gibbons's graphic novel *Watchmen.*

The "architects of fear" are also, of course, the architects of both alienness and alienation, and the implication is simple: there is no alien, only the human. Put differently, the alien is a projection of the human, an incarnation of the fear or dread of a human-made planet slowly rotating in a remote region of space, burdened with the absence of any other form of life that would ratify its existence. Embedded in "first contact" is its inverse – the impossibility of contact other than as a tragic-comedic projection of the human; an encounter in which first contact is also a final contact.

Loving the Alien

The figure of the alien in our creative thinking can be traced back to Lucian of Samosata and his second-century novella, the ironically titled *A True Story*. Given the slim percentage of surviving works from antiquity, we can confidently presume that other proto-science-fictional stories pre-dated this fanciful description of travels through outer space and encounters with extraterrestrials. As long as we have gazed up at the moon or peered at nearby planets through telescopes, we have entertained ourselves with the prospect of finally meeting our reclusive celestial neighbors. Aliens in film and literature are thus a mirror of our own ambient alienation from the cosmos: a symptom of our unease at seemingly being the only technically advanced creatures around. They also serve as ciphers of our relationship to Otherness in general – especially embodying our bad faith and conscience concerning the history of colonialism. (As well as Europe's ongoing desire to keep the human legacies of that history at bay.) As science fiction has evolved as a genre, the alien has gone from trickster space pixies, to fearsome invaders, to benevolent demi-gods, to flawed and confused beings in their own right. They form an index of our own comfort level – or, rather, discomfort level – with our current behavior, as well as our own fragile sense of place and belonging. (It is thus useful to remember that, according to the increasingly legitimate *panspermia* theory of life, we are indeed *all* aliens, the building blocks of our ancestors arriving on this planet from the Great Beyond, courtesy of a wayward comet.)

Life, from our painfully limited perspective, seems to be a cosmic anomaly. No matter its actual distribution, however, throughout the universe – something we'll simply never know – life is strangely *both* the site of a kind of natural flourishing and the space where such vitality begins to question itself. Life is perhaps an endless dialectic between "merely being" and "being bummed out by having to be." We could call it Hamlet's Paradox. Life is the source and medium of various affects, as well as the generator of disaffection. George Bataille once described the experience of animals as being "water within water." This lovely phrase describes a consciousness that has no split or internal difference with which to torture itself; no troubling addiction to hypotheticals or "what ifs" or symbolic reflections. Animals simply *are*. Their ontology is pure. Recent animal studies, however, puts the lie to this romantic notion, which casts humans as the only creatures smart enough to torture themselves with their own minds. Nevertheless, whether animals can be alienated is an interesting question. It is clear, however, that indeed they can, especially when coming into contact with humans – wrenched from their habitats, families, rhythms, comforts, etc. Domesticated pets, for instance, are alienated animals that have largely made peace with that fact for the compensation of regular meals. Zoo animals, much less so. Indeed, today – when natural ecosystems are disappearing fast – alienation is no longer a perverse human privilege but, rather, an inevitable undertone of all life. (Including trees and plants.)

Hence the new craving for higher connection: whether this be through meditation, or yoga, or religion, or exercise, or drugs, or music, or whatever technique one can find for accessing "the oceanic feeling" that allows us complicated apes – us overthinking machines – to shut the fuck up for a while and simply *be*: to simply experience the non-experience of forming part of the continuous, unreflective universe. Sadly, the only way to really achieve this state, as Bataille well knew, is to let go of consciousness altogether: that is, to die and return to brute matter. But then there's nothing left to experience a cosmic communion. Ironically, then, the idea of a perfect elemental intimacy is the kind of idea that could only be dreamed up by a life-form that is constituently incapable of accessing such a state. (At least, not for more than the duration of your average magic mushroom trip, or love-making session, or Pink Floyd album.) We are constantly being crotch-blocked by our own restless minds. Alienation thrives in this knowledge of our own mortality and trajectory. And yet our most inspiring and fulfilling moments are when we – temporarily, it must be admitted – build bridges across the void to encounter one another (and encounter the self in the other). From this perspective, human civilization itself, taken as a whole, is simply what we *do* with our unfortunate birthright of alienation. Art, culture, love, knowledge, enterprise . . . these are all ways that we attempt to counter our primal estrangement. And yet these pursuits have become so privatized, professionalized, and reified that they are more likely to be the *source* of spiraling insecurity than a way to gain any significant relief from the same.

The lesson delivered by the figure of the alien is therefore as crucial as it is blunt. We are all aliens. We are all strangers in a strange land; interlopers in our own lives; imposters in our own minds; and visitors from another timeline. A certain measure of alienation is inevitable as soon as we have the capacity to ask ourselves: "What the heck am I doing?" Modern philosophy, via Descartes, is built upon such a bottomless doubt, as well as the dubious Jedi mind tricks used to find a firm footing. ("I think therefore I am . . . I think.") This curse is also a blessing, however, because everything we cherish and value stems from the attempt to process and metabolize this default sense of estrangement. The *real* problem arrives when the wider society abandons all the ways in which we used to help each other navigate the perplexing facticity of life – what Cioran called "the trouble with being born."

Pre-modern cultures invented all sorts of rituals, stories, and creative mechanisms for feeling at home in this world. Indeed, they *invented* worlds, in collaboration with the Earth, which made living more meaningful, and sensory. Today we have forsaken these humane technologies of orientation and coherence. Moreover, we have rather masochistically leaned into disaffection. We have engineered environments, economies, experiences, and exigencies that maximize the distance between ourselves and our bodies, our work, our sense of purpose, and our fellows. Nicolas Roeg and David Bowie were both on the vanguard of avant-garde movements that were experimenting with a new type of artistic alchemy: turning the intensified alienation of postmodern life into a new romantic cult. While the original Romantics sought to return to fragrant pagan meadows, these new romantics believed the only way to avoid the numbing and gnawing of life is to go forward: to embrace the sterile machine, to speed up the beat, to multiply the input channels of stimulation. Today, both strategies are bankrupt. Going backwards is impossible, and going forwards is a nightmare. Which leaves us meta-alienated: alienated from even former modes of alienation. (Forms that today appear to us as the functional equivalent of being affirmed, harmonized, reconciled.)

In the mid-1980s – the point at which alienation first became not only a life-style choice but a government policy – Bowie wrote a song entitled "Loving the Alien." While not as musically inspired as some of his previous hits, the title alone seems to summarize his whole schtick: that is, his postmodern pastiche of exchangeable personae; his performative alienation from himself – the humble and unremarkable English boy from Bromley, in Kent. Through a parade of Hollywood movies, we have indeed learned to love the alien, even if that alien is trying to skin us for sport. Moreover, thanks to such diabolical new inventions, like social media, we have even learned to love alienation; for it serves as the alibi for peevish tweets that, if composed in such a way to flatter the algorithm, promise to provide a micron of endorphins when a specific combination of pixels signify the fact that your complaint was not only registered but "liked" by a stranger. (A process that itself undermines the very meaning of what it means to like something.)

If animals, since the emergence of life on Earth, have been water-within-water, then we humans have increasingly arranged things to ensure that we are well out of our element: a species splashing self-consciously around in puddles of digital feces.

Ego Bruises

Any attempt to confront the void will be inadequate and traumatic. Truth be told, it often feels as if we have yet to recover from the numerous ego bruises that humankind has inflicted on itself since the so-called Enlightenment, when we started to question the lovely – albeit rather fearful – lullaby of monotheism. Starting with a keen-eyed astronomer by the name of Copernicus, we were suddenly jolted from the absolute epicenter of Things to the cosmic equivalent of an off-off-Broadway show. A mere four centuries later, a natural scientist by the name of Charles Darwin boldly asserted that we were not in fact the noble descendants of Adam and Eve but, rather, the upstart progeny of jungle monkeys (and thus belonging to the same extended family that could be seen throwing their own feces at the London Zoo). While still reeling from this biological bombshell, a pioneering cartographer of the mind by the name of Sigmund Freud pulled the fading Persian rug from under us even further by claiming that most of our words, thoughts, and actions were unconscious, misrecognized, and even subversive of our own personal autonomy. Less than a century later, cybernetic systems – such as the Deep Blue supercomputer – were placing the last nail in the coffin of humanist self-respect, showing how sophisticated cognitive calculations could not only be replicated by a machine but accelerated exponentially. Thus, within half a short millennium, humanity went from wise and divinely ordained cosmic protagonist to random, parochial, marginalized, neurotic simian simpleton.

No wonder the twentieth century was an abattoir, as humanity lashed out against itself in a blind fury. And no wonder we have seen a resurgence in futurist *machismo* as a compensatory coping mechanism, especially in the form of neo-Promethean tech-bros reading Ayn Rand, building phallic rockets, smothering every human interaction in code, and blithely geo-engineering a brighter tomorrow (or certainly a warmer one). Atlas shrugged indeed! But we should see the Silicon Valley booster for what he is – the symptomatic flipside of a profound sadness, or even an "infinite resignation," regarding the future of not only the human race but the grim trajectory of the entire planet. (Or at least of all those who call the planet home, since the geology of this place has shrugged off greater disasters than this one.) Techno-optimism is the metallic silver frosting on the deep-baked cake of sadness on which we chew like a cud in a doomed bid to ignore the loudly howling void.

Being an earthling in the present moment is an intrinsically sad proposition; arguably even sadder than previous incarnations due to the social dimension of disaster, hastening an already too fleeting finitude. In simpler terms, it did not need to be like this. Humans did not need to trash the planet. They – we – could have lived in a more mindful, respectful, sustainable relationship with it. Rather than treating the planet like a rented Airbnb, we could have recognized it as a beautiful, living home: one with which we have been briefly entrusted and feel a pride in passing on in good condition. But of course we did not. (We moderns, that is. Indigenous people the world over understood the stakes in scaling and speeding things up and put various checks and balances in place to avoid this scenario. And for this far-sighted wisdom they were treated as "backward" or "savage" by supposed advanced civilizations, who were too boorish to see the limits upon which they trampled.)

Extreme Weather

Ecostress

NASA has already provided a succinct and evocative name for the anxiety we feel in the face of climate fears: "ecostress." Rather than applying the term to humans, however, these scientists are focusing on plants, since the vegetal kingdom forms a living index of fluctuations in the environment, from the tolerable to the fatal. NASA's new ECOSTRESS project monitors the water levels in the Earth's remaining flora, from forests to farmer's fields, and asks how "changes in diurnal vegetation water stress impact the global carbon cycle." For just as human life is threatened by an increase in what's known as "the wet bulb temperature," plants too need moisture in order to regulate their response to the planet's rising mercury. NASA anticipates that such monitoring will help create an "Evaporative Stress Index" that will more reliably predict hotspots most vulnerable to drought, and thus hopefully lead to action that mitigates the effect (for instance, in California, which in mid-2021 was suffering the worst drought in at least 1,200 years). Like most initiatives today, however, ECOSTRESS seems more engaged with the real-time *visualization* of disaster than in implementing any necessary preemptive changes that might help avoid the need for such diagnostic tools in the first place.

Sequence 2
Dark Star

A Sad Planet (I)

In the autumnal dawn of September 2017, a small spacecraft some 900 billion miles away followed its final orbit around Saturn. It made several passes through the gap between the planet and its innermost rings before then descending towards the planet itself, where it was inexorably vaporized by the extreme pressures of the planet's atmosphere, leaving only the faintest traces of its long journey. The NASA Cassini spacecraft had been orbiting Saturn for some twenty years before its planned "grand finale." In that time, it had explored Saturn's atmosphere, the planet's many moons, and of course the extensive ring system that has become synonymous with the planet itself. While Cassini's destruction had been planned by NASA scientists, it was, nevertheless, difficult for those involved in the project not to sense a twinge of sorrow at the solitary spacecraft's final orbit, almost as if it had been compelled by strange and unknown forces to make one final and fatal pass, closer to Saturn than any spacecraft had ever been – a kind of suicide orbit that would be at once the culmination of decades of data-gathering as well as the final obliteration of the closest we as human beings have ever been to the enigmatic ringed planet, so often linked in the history of myth and astronomy to melancholy and sorrowful moods. The last images reportedly sent from Cassini as it neared Saturn's atmosphere were those of the planet's solstice, which occurs every fifteen years, rare images saturated in the colors of decay – mottled oranges, dirtied yellows, withering greens.

From the Cassini mission data, a number of discoveries were made, particularly regarding the mysterious and iconic ring system. One such discovery is that the rings of Saturn are gradually disappearing and will eventually – meaning in around 300 million years – vanish entirely. The rings themselves have been the subject of ongoing research and speculation, and nearly everything about them – how they formed, how old they are, what purpose they serve – has remained opaque. Everything that is, except for the ring shapes themselves, which were studied as early as the 1650s, when the Dutch scientist Christiaan Huygens observed the thin, flat, elliptical rings using a refracting telescope. Huygens's treatise *Systema Saturnium* (1659) provided details of Saturn's rings, including its relation to Saturn's orbital path.

Though rooted in empirical observation, Huygens was wary that his findings would seem improbable to those in the scientific community: "I believe that I should take a moment to respond to the objections of those who will find it strange that I should assign to one of the celestial bodies a form the likes of which has not, up until now, been observed before." In spite of this, Huygens asserts his position, noting "that I place this solid and permanent ring (for such I consider it) about Saturn, without any links or chains," which "remains at a uniform distance on every side," moving in harmony with the planet. The spherical form is, he would argue, the only one capable of accommodating this enigmatic conjunction of planet and ring system, noting that "there is no reason why it should not be possible for some celestial body to have this form, which . . . is as well adapted to circumcentral motion as the spherical form itself." And yet, among the numerous pages of observations, measurements, and diagrams, there is something else Huygens finds compelling about Saturn and its rings, something about a planet solitary, spherical, remote, and darkly haloed by invisible forces. It's a kind of sentiment Huygens expresses only in rare passages: "Certainly, it is less surprising that such a form should be given to a celestial body of this kind, as opposed to another form ill-fitted to the harmony of planetary orbits."[1] A shape abstract and remote, at once cosmic and elemental, the shape of sorrow, the shape of beauty.

A Sad Planet (II)

Huygens was known to have struggled with periodic bouts of depression throughout his life, and it is perhaps no accident that he devoted himself to the study of the planet that had been associated, at least since the Middle Ages, with a tendency towards a melancholic disposition. Some thirty years after his work on *Systema Saturnium*, Huygens found himself exiled from the intellectual and scientific circles of Paris, the victim of political circumstance. A period of inertial depression followed, in which he seemed unable to do anything, even daily tasks. And then, as if obeying some secret law of planetary orbits, he suddenly threw himself into an ambitious, difficult-to-categorize project of speculative astronomy, which he titled *Cosmotheoros*. Not published until after his death in 1698, *Cosmotheoros* is striking in its metaphysical optimism; it utilizes the scientific theories of his day to postulate the possibility of life on other planets, as well as providing speculative descriptions of how extraterrestrial gravity and atmospheric composition might determine different kinds of life forms that could exist on other planets.

Huygens was not the only one to leverage the knowledge of the Scientific Revolution in this way; such examples of speculative science (one is tempted to say, proto-science fiction) were also to be found in other works of the period, including Johannes Kepler's *Somnium* (1634), John Wilkins's *The Discovery of a World in the Moone* (1638), and Athanasius Kircher's *Itinerarium exstaticum* (1656). But *Cosmotheoros* is perhaps unique in that its scientific optimism was curiously counter-balanced by its theological pessimism. If the universe is so bountiful and brimming with life on other planets, why have we as Earth-bound, terrestrial humans not yet encountered it? Perhaps there were other worlds, and perhaps there was life on those worlds, but could it be that they were intentionally placed so far apart from one another so as to never come into contact? Whether it be by divine design or the deterministic laws of the universe, it seemed to Huygens that there was something about life on a cosmic scale that was irrevocably linked to its finitude, its mortality, its sense of metaphysical and even existential alienation.

Indeed, what we know today about Saturn's rings itself seems to evoke a mood of melancholy and its strange allure of mortality. The rings, composed primarily of water, ice, and rock particles, are thought to have been produced by micrometeorites entering the planet's magnetic fields, where trace elements of solar radiation allow them to gather around the planet's gravitational pull. Once entranced by Saturn's invisible forces, the particles enter into the slow cadence of elliptical drifting that forms the elaborate ring system. Some of the particles may stray from the ring system, perhaps due to weakened radiation, and will then circle closer and closer to the planet itself, where they will be vaporized in its atmosphere. In a phenomenon scientists call "ring rain," space dust cascades down from distant orbital rings in a misty landscape of somber gray and black. There is speculation that this same process may also be the origin of the ring system itself, though on a larger scale. According to one hypothesis, one of Saturn's moons, having drifted imperceptibly nearer to the planet itself, had been pulverized into a thousand particles, arrayed outwards across gravitational fields, swirling into its now familiar elliptical paths. At the outer edges of astrophysics is the possibility that, in fact, there is no planet Saturn with its rings, as if the two could be separated. The more research is produced about Saturn from the Cassini mission, the more it seems plausible that the cadence of ring rain and the slow dissipation of the ring system is in fact normal and not an anomaly. The planet, its moons, its ring system, all of them form a slow and heavy dance of disintegration. Perhaps that's what Saturn is, a massive planetary vortex of cosmic matter – moons, meteorites, ice particles – mysteriously drawn inward towards their own obliteration by the inevitable forces of deep time.

A Star and a Sorrow

The history of Saturn – the planet, the god, the mood – is as convoluted and polarized as the melancholic dispositions with which it has often been associated. The Saturn–melancholy conjunction traces a thin, vaporous line that runs through ancient sources, including Greek myth, Arabic astrology, and Hippocratic medicine, in addition to Neoplatonism, Christian mystical theology, and Renaissance occult science. Before melancholy and melancholia become maladies of the soul, imbalances in mood, or the curse of poets, Saturn is this uncanny conjunction between a planet and a mood, a star and a sorrow. A cold and heavy planet slowly hangs in heavy space at the farthest reaches of the cosmos. Turgid, remote rays of distant stars that suddenly seem more intimate than one's own inner states. The mysterious link between Saturn and melancholy stretches back to Babylonian myths of fatalistic night skies and forward to modern clinical psychiatry, astrology podcasts, and the latest advances in computer-designed pharmaceuticals.

Ovid, Tertullian, and Macrobius write of the Roman god Saturn, god of the fields, of agriculture, of crops and harvests, and the Saturnalia festivals that follow. Saturn is also the guardian of wealth and abundance, of calculation and coins. But behind these aspects of Saturn are more shadowy ones. Saturn the persecuted, Saturn the exiled. One finds linkages between Saturn and the figure of Kronos (*Κρόνος*) of ancient Greece. Attested to in the works of Hesiod and Homer, Kronos is a god of contrasts, a polarized god. There is Kronos the elemental god, born of the primordial forces of earth (Gaia) and sky (Uranus). Like many of the gods, Kronos is fundamentally of the elements – earth, sky, fire, water, weather. There is also Kronos the personified Titan, the father of Zeus, Poseidon, Hades. A pantheon is born. The world begins to look more familiar, more human. The planet begins to look more familiar too, a place, an abode, a planet "out there."

There is also Kronos the cursed god, the one who dethrones his father and is in turn dethroned by his son. Goya's famous painting *Saturn Devouring His Children* (c.1819–23) gives us perhaps the most grotesque and deranged image of Kronos, the one who challenges fate, even at the cost of infanticide. In the works of later Roman authors, Kronos would overlap with Chronos, the god of time, change, and mortality, resulting in a contradictory image of a god of abundance, harvests, and the Saturnalia, but also the god dethroned, the dweller of the underworld, the brooding and futile god, time devouring generations of the living.

Everything Kronos does to outwit the cosmic order of things proves to be futile. It is a motif that appears repeatedly in Greek tragedy. The attempt to gain mastery of a wider, cosmic order that always seems to be a few steps ahead. The attempt to gain a hold on a cosmos (*κόσμος*) that always threatens to turn into chaos (*χάος*), a cosmos that not only envelops us but of which we can only guess, an order of things of which we only dimly intuit the faintest traces. Kronos the god of dejection, despair, futility, exiled into the sorrowful abyss of Tartarus.

By the time the Elizabethan era rediscovers the ancients, the alliance between Saturn and melancholy dispositions had long been forged. Authors like the playwright Robert Greene could produce idiosyncratic works such as his *Planetomachia* (1585), where entire cosmic dialogues ensue between the planets, each with their affective quirks and dispositions. Both Venus and Mars take turns describing Saturn in less than flattering ways: "Claudius Ptolomeus and Galen call the star of Saturne intemperate, infortunate, and ill affected, perhaps for the melancholy humor which with a secret violence doth rage and reign in human bodies, procuring by his Saturnine influence, both cold and dryness."[2] Because of this, Saturn is said to be the domain of "crabbed Philosophers, who hated love, and fed upon gall and melancholy."[3]

The barest forms of a tragic tale emerge. Saturn as of the Earth and yet apart from the Earth. Reigning over the planet and then engulfed in a chthonic pit of sorrow. Dominion and despondency. Born of the elements, we are forever trying to separate ourselves from them in order to enact a ritual forgetting that seems commensurate with human consciousness itself. And yet, "it" is still "us," if only in the most distant, Saturnine sense.

The Gift of Sorrow

But this wandering line connecting a planet, a god, and a mood is also part of what melancholy and its attendant affects have become – an indistinct impression whose history is itself indistinct, as if generations of philosophers, physicians, theologians, and astrologers have done nothing but trace vanishing figures in the sand. It would take centuries of forgetting and remembering to resurrect the figure of Saturn in the Renaissance. There, the syncretic influences of medicine, astrology, and mythology would enact a shift in Saturn, from the deity to the planet, from allegory (myth) to analogy (astrology), from the macrocosm of the cosmos to the microcosm of the human being. But at the root of this transformation is the same concern: the conjunction of a mood with the stars.

In a letter to a friend, Marsilio Ficino – Renaissance physician, Platonist, priest, and astrologer – writes of his own experience with melancholy. Even when offering encouraging words of consolation to others, Ficino finds himself constantly drawn into a somber mood. "I accuse a certain melancholy disposition, a thing which seems to me to be very bitter unless, having been softened, it may in a measure be made sweet for us by frequent use of the lyre."[4] For Ficino the physician it is often music and poetry that makes for the best medicine. And yet, an inescapable sense of being destined for melancholy turns Ficino outwards towards the stars. "Saturn seems to have impressed the seal of melancholy on me from the beginning: set, as it is, in the midst of my ascendant Aquarius, it is influenced by Mars, also in Aquarius, and the Moon in Capricorn."[5] Is it something that comes from within or that comes from without? Is it a blessing or a curse? Is the capacity that allows for the construction of knowledge and its shimmering systems of totality the same capacity that also allows for suspicion, doubt, and a pervasive sense of the tragic futility of human endeavor? It is a question, Ficino notes, that reaches back to the ancients. And it prompts him to, in effect, lean into Saturnine melancholy even more: "I shall seek a shift . . . if it should be necessary that it does issue from Saturn, I shall, in agreement with Aristotle, say that this nature itself is a unique and divine gift."[6] The gift of sorrow.

Sadness is a Planet

As a committed humanist, Ficino's primary concern was to transform suffering into human well-being using the tools at hand, be it Neoplatonic theology, Renaissance medicine, or the latest developments in post-Copernican astronomy. The priest in him wants to alleviate suffering in the world, but the physician in him knows that, to some extent, this is futile – the world is indifferent. The astrologer in him is keen to transform the understanding of the rotation of the planets into practical, even therapeutic advice for human living. But the astronomer in him knows, deep down, that the planets don't care, and at best we limited, finite human beings are helpless before the cosmic forces of the infinite.

It is for this reason that the relationship between the microcosm and macrocosm is at the core of so much of Ficino's writing. The culture in which Ficino is working is one of a refinement of the disciplines but also a syncretic culture, where the disciplines criss-cross each other, that gray zone where astrology and astronomy seamlessly overlap. Ficino resurrects the kaleidoscopic tradition of Greek and Roman myth, which, through its narrative devices, implies a fundamental link between the world of human affairs and the larger cosmos within which human affairs have meaning. In addition to this, he draws on the long history of ancient Greek medicine, giving him the humoral framework in which the human body is intimately connected to an elemental earth. Finally, advances in the sciences – particularly cosmology – allow Ficino to concretize the already prevalent notion that the positions of distant stars have an impact on both the climate and our own affective dispositions.

This syncretism allows Ficino to talk about medicine in astrophysical terms while also reframing astronomy as a kind of anatomy of the cosmos. In the *Three Books on Life* (*De vita libri tres*, 1489) this involves a basic premise about the self–world relationship, a relationship so central to the Western philosophical tradition: that the world shapes the self as much – and possibly more – than the self shapes the world. And it does so in ways of which we are not fully aware, as well as at distances and scales of time that lie outside the scope of human experience.

Immediately astrology, medicine, and myth are brought to bear on the problem: "In the main, three kinds of causes make learned people melancholics. The first is celestial, the second natural, and the third human."[7] The rays of stars, as well as the humors of the body, earth, and climate, are for Ficino as intimately interwoven into human consciousness as the cultural psychology of long-standing myths and their archetypes. What is internal is also external. Adopting the perspectives of analogy and correspondence – rooted in Renaissance traditions of "natural magic" – Ficino can elaborate this self–world relationship from the macrocosm of distant planets such as Saturn to the microcosm of sorrow and despondency in the individual human being.

A whole paradigm emerges, where a particular conjunction of one planet with others, the shifting seasons and climate, the shifting physiology of the body – all conspire to produce moods and affects that freely circulate between body, planet, and cosmos. And at the center of his studies is melancholy, both the planet and the mood, that indistinct yet palpable affect that, as the Aristotelian sources tell him, is both blessing and curse. A planet cold and remote linked to melancholic withdrawal and estrangement. A planet far from the sun moving heavy and slow, a temperament of lethargy and inanimateness. Winter. Rain. Low light. Sleep or sleeplessness.

Astral Melancholy

The "star medicine" of Ficino's *Three Books on Life* triangulates these influences – mythology, cosmology, medicine – into what is really a theory of moods. Saturn the deity, Saturn the planet, the Saturnine mood or disposition. What results is an "astral melancholy" that is as physical as it is metaphysical, both disease and disposition, an individual feeling and an impersonal mood, that which is both sacred and cursed, elevated but outcast. Ficino is already outlining a proto-Romantic myth: melancholy as a brooding mood born of its own capacity for reflection, an atmosphere of listless thought ruminating on the constraints of human self-awareness. Ficino often returns to a phrase borrowed from Christian mythical theology: *vita contemplativa*. The contemplative life, emblem of a higher state of human consciousness, can also be the occasion for the deepest sorrow, the *gravitas* of despondency and a bewildering sense of the infinite. In fact, Ficino opens his treatise by wondering why writers, artists, and those who are engaged in studies, or who generally overthink things, are so often prone to melancholy (evidenced by chapter titles such as "How Black Bile Makes People Intelligent").

Many of these themes would be given structure in Albrecht Dürer's famous engraving *Melencolia I* (1514) – an image that for many has come to encapsulate early modern attitudes towards melancholy. While the number of interpretations of *Melencolia I* is so overwhelming as to itself induce a bout of melancholia, one particular aspect of the image is noteworthy, and that is the way Dürer's engraving suggests a dual aspect to melancholy: a brooding figure at once immersed in and yet detached from intellectual endeavor, portrayed here in the various tools, the mathematical "magic square," and the enigmatic polyhedron which has puzzled so many scholars and art historians.

In their classic study *Saturn and Melancholy*, Raymond Kilbansky, Erwin Panofsky, and Fritz Saxl suggest that, in addition to its many densely layered symbols, the main effect of *Melencolia I* is "to characterise Melancholy as Geometry, or Geometry as Melancholy."[8]

Geometry, considered by Dürer the science of sciences, expanded knowledge of the world with mathematical precision at the same time that it revealed how limited human knowledge was with regard to the boundaries of space and time. This duplicity haunts *Melencolia I*. A sigh of fatigue, the tools are set aside, the head slightly bowed in resignation, a brooding, ruminative stare into a space beyond space – the same ruminative stare of inquiry that prompts one to once again take up the tools.

Oscillating between melancholy and geometry lies Saturn, the planet, the disposition, the quasi-medical heaviness of black bile, at once mood and measurement, the source of intellectual creativity and the futility of that endeavor. Ficino also notes this correspondence between the remoteness of the planet Saturn and the tendency of contemplative, ruminating melancholics to remove themselves from the world and human society. And, it seems, the more one tries to repress or resist this tendency, the worse it gets:

> For just as the sun is hostile to nocturnal animals, but friendly to the diurnal, so Saturn is hostile to those people who are either leading publicly an ordinary life or even to those fleeing the company of the crowd but not laying aside their ordinary emotions. For Saturn has relinquished the ordinary life to Jupiter; but he claims for himself a life sequestered and divine.[9]

For Ficino, the consciousness that binds us to the planet is also that which estranges us from it. The "divine contemplation" of human finitude, that is also its curse, set against the backdrop of a cosmic order that ceaselessly intersects human self-awareness with its "rays of stars."

Perhaps this is why "Dürer's fusion of the notion of Melancholy, Saturn and 'Artes Geometricae'" has produced such a shadowy and conflicted visage that appears in *Melencolia I*. Melancholy disposition tends towards the visionary but also the delusional. Is the shooting star in the background an omen, a prophecy, or simply an astrological reminder of the ephemeral quality of all things? "A being under a cloud . . . a being whose powers of invention are limited to the realms of visibility in space . . . and whose prophetic gaze can see only menacing catastrophes of nature . . . a being, finally, who is darkly aware of the inadequacy of their powers of knowledge."[10]

Rays of Sorrow

There is something about the Saturn–melancholy conjunction that involves a kind of planetary dysphoria, a detachment from the human world of everyday concerns, a sense of being out of orbit that produces both an insight and a disposition. It is what the desert monastics of early Christianity called *acedia* (ἀκηδία), the sense of being listlessly cast adrift in a planetary wasteland, estranged from humanity, abandoned by God – the stark apprehension of a planet without people. One senses this being out of orbit in the deserts of fourth-century Egypt, where Antony undertakes his famous reclusion into an enigmatic "inner desert," itself modeled on the Gospel tradition of Jesus' paradigmatic forty days in the desert. It is also there in the "desert theology" of Evagrius Ponticus and John Cassian, both of whom describe *acedia* as "the sorrow of the world," linking it to the ambivalent spiritual terrain of remote deserts, mountains, and forests.

It would take generations of poets to put the final – and most lasting – touches on this paradigm, as the fascination with melancholy itself spread northward, to such a degree it was often simply dubbed "the Elizabethan malady." It is Hamlet's forever sullen equivocation "O that this too solid flesh would melt, / Thaw, and resolve itself into a dew!"[11] It is also the conjunction of deep time and mortality that marks the Shakespearean sonnet: "In me thou see'st the twilight of such day / As after sunset fadeth in the west, / Which by and by black night doth take away, / Death's second self, that seals up all in rest."[12] It is found in the many expressions of melancholy emergent in the early Renaissance, with its evocations at once naturalistic and cosmic. Petrarch's mournful "No lovely stars that roam through limpid skies," hovering around "groundless and unstable thoughts," leading to the dim apprehension of "stars conspired to impoverish me."[13] Gaspara Stampa's torrential and ambivalent appeal "to fall into a sea of tears."[14] Climates of despair, affects almost elemental, as the baroque "fires of night" described by Luis de Góngora, which precariously glimmer on a world cast in our own image, inevitably fade and flicker: "buried in themselves / their limbs, crumbled into ash, / on their own graves are the stones."[15]

This tendency in lyric flows through the weather-saturated love poems of Alain Chartier to Milton's ruminative *Il Penseroso*, with its calls to "divinest Melancholy," "too bright / To hit the sense of human sight; / And therefore to our weaker view, / O'er-laid with black, staid Wisdom's hue."[16] We are just steps away from the Graveyard School, the *Weltschmerz* of early German Romanticism, Baudelairean *ennui*, and the mournful modernism of overgrowth and decay found in poets such as Giacomo Leopardi, José Asuncíon Silva, Yevgeny Baratynsky, Chūya Nakahara, Alfonsina Storni, Noh Cheonmyeong. No stranger himself to the effects of Saturn, Paul Verlaine's 1866 volume *Poèmes saturniens* offers to us a series of lush and mournful "sad landscapes" (*paysages tristes*): "Melancholy lulls / My heart with soft songs / As it drifts off / With setting suns."[17]

It is, arguably, in the poetics of melancholy that a kind of alchemy takes place between interiority and exteriority, a morphology in which the affect, the planet, and the cacophony of gods obtain a tenebrous isomorphism. The poets show us that the link between Saturn and melancholy is a slow, uneven, and gradual process that is the product of classical Greek medicine, Arabic astronomy, early Christian theology, Renaissance occult science, and an assortment of myths that in some cases stretch back to the Babylonians. The link – however fanciful it may seem to us today – refutes any notion that affects such as sadness or melancholy are simply personal feelings, felt by individual human beings living in a world that seems to perpetually occlude the planet. If the poets teach us anything, perhaps it is this suggestion that melancholic moods are in some way deeply correlated to climate, planet, and the movements and rotations and positions of distant stars. In the variegated history of melancholy in the West, the proposition of Renaissance thinkers such as Ficino is deceptively simple: that sadness not only occurs on the planet, but that sadness is a planet itself.

Nietzsche, jubilant as ever, reminds us that "night is also a sun."[18] A sentiment echoed a century later, in the title of the book by the Argentine poet Olga Orozco: "Darkness is a different sun." The microcosm is the macrocosm, the personal is the impersonal. Sorrow externalized. There are planets within.

Saturnalia

Given the long tradition in the West of associating Saturn with melancholy, it is remarkable how often Saturn – the deity and the planet – is also associated with revelry, festivity, and an almost Dionysian exuberance. In the hands of authors such as Tertullian and Ovid, the Roman god Saturn becomes an emblem of the fecundity of crops and harvest time and, by association, a god of wealth, bountifulness, and in some cases the god of coins, counting, and measurement. The heaviest planet is also the planet of levity; the planet most distant and cold is also a planet of dancing efflorescence. Saturn is also the Saturnalia, a bountiful planet, the winter solstice, a green planet. Nowhere is this more evident than in Macrobius' *Saturnalia*, the fifth-century work that contains a series of dialogues that take place during the Roman festival in December. With little structure and almost no narrative, the *Saturnalia* as a work contains seemingly endless digressions and diversions, from conversations about the origin of the Roman calendar, to enumerations of sensual pleasures, to the undisputed virtues of Virgil's poetry, to opinions on Roman sumptuary laws.

At its core, however, is an attempt to square the angst-ridden, melancholic Saturn (the Greek god Kronos) with the

Saturn of harvest and festival, much of which turns on the agrarian cycles of the seasons: "It is said that Saturn used to swallow his children and vomit them forth again, a myth likewise pointing to an identification of the god with time, by which all things in turn are created, destroyed, and brought to birth again."[19]

As one of the discussants observes, "Kronos (Saturn) then is held to be the son of Heaven, and he, as we said a moment ago, is Time."[20] Saturn is not just time itself but the passing of time, the ebb and flow of terrestrial time and the multitude of what ebbs and flows on the planet, from organic and mineral life to the geological time of the planet itself. Even at the peak of planetary bountifulness there is something passing away, a melancholy seeded in the soil itself.

While parts of Macrobius' work have been lost, what remains of the *Saturnalia* seems to mime the fecundity and excess of the Saturnalia festival itself. The elite, over-educated discussants gathered together seem to engage less in actual conversation than in rapid-fire proclamations, generously infused with quoted words of wisdom from classical authors. It's as if the discussants themselves are not the ones really talking, as if the fecundity of culture is brimming at the surface, overflowing in a deluge of self-reflexive opinions, references, and quotations. It's as if the discussants are anxious to keep things light and cheerful, perhaps in order to ward off thinking about the coming "winter blues." While the *Saturnalia* contains little in the way of in-depth reflections on the melancholy side of Saturn, what it performs is a kind of excess that strangely borders on sorrow, perhaps in the same way that the fullness of crops lead to their harvest, the planetary cycle of growth and decay beginning again.

Planetary Ennui

The heaviest and the lightest, the lunar and the solar, excess turning to sorrow and back again. These seemingly contradictory aspects of Saturn are found in *Micromégas*, a short narrative prose piece by Voltaire, published around 1752. Cited by many scholars as an early example of proto-science fiction, *Micromégas* is ostensibly a travel narrative in outer space. However, instead of human beings traveling into outer space, in *Micromégas* an alien visitor – named Micromégas (literally, "small-large") – comes to Earth from a distant planet orbiting the star Sirius. No doubt Voltaire's inversion of the travel narrative was intended to satirize the presumptuousness of the many expeditions at the time, laden as they were with the conceits of imperialist expansion and the possibility of colonial occupation. The outsider's perspective of Voltaire's visitor from Sirius allows us to ridicule what passes as normal among "Enlightened" society of eighteenth-century Europe.

However, on the way to Earth, Micromégas first makes a brief stop at Saturn. There we are introduced to the inhabitants of Saturn and the world in which they live. Quickly the differences between their worlds are apparent. The planet that Micromégas is from is millions of times larger than Saturn. Micromégas is a hundred thousand feet tall, has over a thousand different senses, and will live for ten million years. By contrast, the Saturnians are a fraction of the size, they have only seventy different senses, and their planet is a mere speck in the cosmos. In spite of these differences, however, they find common ground. One of the Saturnians laments: "Our imagination transcends our wants; for, with these seventy-two senses, our five moons and our ring, we find ourselves very much restricted; and, notwithstanding our curiosity, and the no small number of passions that result from our seventy-two senses, we have still time enough to suffer from *ennui*."[21] The Saturnians seem infused with a palpable sense of the insufficiency of terrestrial existence, on whatever planet it may be. Micromégas replies in sympathy: "I can readily believe it . . . for, though in our globe we have near a thousand different senses, there still remains a certain vague desire, an unaccountable quietude, which incessantly makes us aware of our own insignificance, and that there are other beings much more perfect."[22]

Discovering an alliance rooted in their shared melancholy, Micromégas and one of the Saturnians decide to travel together to Earth, where further revelations of sorrow and the absurd await them. In addition to the varieties of strange customs that compose earthly (and, specifically, European) life, what Micromégas and his companion discover is the relativism of this sense of terrestrial insufficiency. A kind of existence in which the planet is never enough. A terrestrial malaise, a planetary ennui – of which the planet itself knows nothing, blissfully indifferent to the leaden insufficiencies born of consciousness.

Rings of Saturn

If the convoluted threads that link Saturn and melancholy reveal anything, perhaps it is the furtive acknowledgement that we are but the after-effects of cosmic forces that seem to constantly recede into the blind spot of limited human cognition. There is sadness on a planet, bearing witness to the ephemeral coming-to-be and passing-away of all things. But there is also the notion that sadness is a planet, the nebulous influences of the planets that serve as a constant reminder of just how little we still understand of cause and effect. A melancholy emerges from within the interiority of the self, at the same time that melancholy always seems to come from without, seemingly without cause or origin, leaving only the weather, a landscape, an impression, a jumbled array of dimly intuited thoughts and vague recollections, themselves inflected through environmental and even cosmological conditions that we struggle to delineate. Signs rise and descend, intersect and diverge. Saturn conjuncts Jupiter. Saturn returns.

These themes are interwoven throughout W. G. Sebald's *The Rings of Saturn*, a book whose form itself recapitulates the drifting, wandering aspects of Saturnine melancholy. Part travelog, part essay, and part memoir, *The Rings of Saturn* follows a series of long walks by the author (or someone we assume is the author) along the eastern English coastline. But the apparently neat linearity of the book stops there. While each of Sebald's walks does technically have a beginning and an end, the account in *The Rings of Saturn* is much more preoccupied with a sense of directionlessness and a poetics of drifting. This is the case both in Sebald's actual walking journey as well as in the happenstance, free-associative ruminations that themselves form another, parallel journey. A rest on the hillside by an empty overcast beach near Southwold will occasion reflection on an earlier era where the waters were populated by the destruction of maritime battles between English and Dutch ships, which then turns to the author's recollection of a trip to the Netherlands a year previously, when he sat on a not dissimilar beach, looking at the same body of water, which then leads to reflections on the hagiography of Saint Sebolt, the Anglo-Saxon missionary said to have descended from a Danish king, which then leads to an almost delirious, dreamlike recollection of a plane which leaves Schiphol on its return trip back to Norwich:

> No matter whether one is flying over Newfoundland or the sea of lights that stretches from Boston to Philadelphia after nightfall, over the Arabian deserts which gleam like mother-of-pearl, over the Ruhr or the city of Frankfurt, it is as though there were no people, only the things they have made and in which they are hiding. One sees the places where they live and the roads that link them, one sees the smoke rising from their houses and factories, one sees the vehicles in which they sit, but one sees not the people themselves. And yet they are present everywhere upon the face of the earth, extending their dominion by the hour, moving around the honeycombs of towering buildings and tied into networks of a complexity that goes far beyond the power of any one individual to imagine . . .[23]

And, from this hallucinatory episode, we are back to the author resting on the Southwold beach. We have traveled extensively, but the author hasn't taken one step. In this and other examples, Sebald evokes a sense of being without direction, a sense of directionlessness that – avoiding that cliché of clichés – is neither simply journey nor destination. It is the same place but a different time (a once lavish seaside hotel now dilapidated and in ruins). Or it is the same time but a different place (a year ago I was looking at this same scene from the other side, in a different country). There is a sense of never quite being where or when you are, a sense of perpetual displacement, of an ongoing estrangement from the very landscape that one is traversing, a kind of geological dysphoria whose topography forms the terrain of melancholy around which Sebald's writing constantly revolves.

The Rings of Saturn is not simply about the state of being lost, nor is it about any romantic evocations of straying from the straight and narrow path. The state of actually being lost is a matter of calibration; it presumes an arrow pointing to a definite destination that has somehow become misaligned. Being lost in this sense is always subordinated to getting back on track. Consult the map, double back, check your phone. The romantic inverse of this, embedded in the sense of travel itself, is the sense of adventure, perhaps of escape or abandon, casting oneself into the unknown, in a desperate grasping for that diffuse thing called "freedom."

But it doesn't last. It can't. There is a sullen core to even the most exuberant, most despairing acts of launching oneself "out there." It's there in John Clare's haunting perambulations across the vanishing Northborough countryside, evidenced in his final poems, where he finds himself on the threshold of delusion, walking across an already dead Earth. It's there in Gérard de Nerval's drifting prose narratives, with their nocturnal vistas that arc across wild woods and cobblestoned streets, culminating in hallucinations of all times compressed into a single place, a single landscape, a single Earth. And it's there in Matsuo Bashō's late travel diaries, where the encounter with the cycles of transient climate and autumnal withering find poetic expression in the acute awareness of passing time, imprinted in stray "records of a weather-worn skeleton."

Even the wildest, most mystical sense of abandon still heads out in a direction, even if it is a negative direction, a direction away from some place: into the desert, the mountains, a remote cave, the wide open sea, deep space. And, beyond it, something else entirely – oblivion, annulment, the still point of non-existence, a sense that every direction is, in the end, the same.

Every Direction is the Same

The sense of directionlessness in *The Rings of Saturn* might be more accurately described as dereliction. Dereliction is being cast adrift, moving this way or that according to non-human forces at the limits of one's comprehension. This can take several forms. There may have been a destination, but that has now been lost, perhaps irretrievably lost. But one keeps on walking. There is no doubling back, retracing one's steps. Directionlessness is no longer having a direction – but one keeps on walking. Directionless because direction makes little sense in a landscape where everything is overgrown, fecund with the melancholy of natural history:

> Everything is on the point of decline, and only the weeds flourish: bindweed strangles the shrubs, the yellow roots of nettles creep onward in the soil, burdock stands a whole head taller than oneself, brown rot and greenfly are everywhere, and even the sheets of paper on which one endeavors to put together a few words and sentences seem covered in mildew.[24]

Not to regain a new direction and neither to be finally liberated from all direction. There is nothing heroic or tragic about it. Every locale Sebald visits, whether it be a deserted overcast shore or an equally deserted town, seems to inhabit this nebulous gray zone, as if an entire landscape or terrain were hovering in a strange non-time of nostalgic calm at once mundane and melancholic. A hallucinatory quality saturates even the simplest scenes. In one walk, near Lowestoft, an abandoned beach reveals only a series of small tents, evenly spaced from each other in a row, each with a tiny fishing pole cast out into the meandering sea. The occupants do not leave their shelters, they do not talk to each other, and no one catches any fish. Perhaps, the author imagines, "they just want to be in a place where they have the world behind them, and before them nothing but emptiness."[25]

It is no accident that one finds numerous examples of dereliction in the mystical literature of medieval Christianity. Attentive to the long literary and mythological traditions of journeying, Christian mystical texts often allegorized wandering, drifting, and dereliction as a crucial part of religious experience. The mystical itineraries of Angela of Foligno, Hadewijch, Methild of Magdeburg, the *Theologia Germanica*, John of the Cross (not to mention Pascal, Simone Weil, or Georges Bataille) all contain a sense of dereliction at their core. Many of them point back to the Gospel tradition and its depictions of religious doubt, the sense of having been abandoned by God, of faith wavering in despair and confusion, of the harrowing possibility of living a life utterly bereft of order, meaning, purpose. This condition – of being without direction, and yet one keeps on walking – is so central to Christian mysticism that it forms an entire tradition itself, often known as the *via negativa*, a negative path that leaves itself no other option than to reduce the human being to its absolute minimum, shorn of all presuppositions, all expectations, all of the hubris that comes with being human. And then, at this zero-point, what is left?

Ruinous Time, Incessant Decline

In dereliction, the human subject recedes into the background until it is nothing more than an ephemeral and happenstance indicator of the passage of deep time. In a sense, *The Rings of Saturn* inverts the modern genre of travel writing. The "lonely planet" is not there to be peopled by the human provenance of adventure, the planet as background for the quite literal, pictographic foregrounding of us human tourists, evolutionary interlopers to a planet that we are but visiting. This is undoubtedly why much of the description in *The Rings of Saturn* is of unpopulated landscapes, town squares, buildings, as if these ruins are the only reminders that there were ever humans here to begin with:

> Through Brundall, Buckenham and Cantley, where, at the end of a straight roadway, a sugar-beet refinery with a belching smokestack sits in a green field like a steamer at a wharf, the line follows the River Yare, till at Reedham it crosses the water and, in a wide curve, enters the vast flatland that stretches southeast down to the sea. Save for the odd solitary cottage there is nothing to be seen but the grass and the rippling reeds, one or two sunken willows, and some ruined conical brick buildings, like relics of an extinct civilization.[26]

In these solitary moments, it's as if Sebald's perambulations suddenly take on the quality of a post-apocalyptic movie: a single figure, bewildered and in disarray, stumbling across a derelict landscape now eerily unpeopled. The planet itself suddenly transformed into a cosmic, orbiting ruin, an interzone where the ephemera of human history and the processes of natural decay secretly overlap. "With decay, and with it alone, historical occurrence shrinks and withdraws into the setting."[27] This is Walter Benjamin, in his dense, drifting, and sullen treatise on baroque tragedy, a literary tradition which not only illuminates the hubris of human agency but does so against a planetary backdrop suffused with decay, decline, and time in ruin. "In the ruin, history has passed perceptibly into the setting. And so configured, history finds expression not as process of an eternal life but as process of incessant decline."[28]

Both background and foreground, the ruin is not only the setting, the environment, in which tragic drama takes place; it is also, in a way, the entirety of tragedy condensed into imperceptibly withering rock and stone. In this way, the ruin is, in Benjamin's own condensed prose, the "allegorical physiognomy of natural history." And, in the context of tragic theater, it is but a short step from thinking about the ruin to the more harrowing, more unsettling notion that thinking is a ruin itself. All systems, all structures, all axioms, elegies and testimonies, they all quietly crumble in the patient gravity of ruinous time.

If this kind of literature serves a purpose, it is less to uphold fragile and dissipative ideals about heroic humanity and more to serve as a reminder of the transience of a world arrayed around human exceptionalism. The result, for Benjamin, is an affect that is specific to the ruin – mourning. "Mourning (*Trauer*) is the disposition in which feeling, as though masked, reanimates the emptied-out world, so as to have an enigmatic satisfaction at the sight of it."[29]

On the furthest tip of the beach near Orford, we find, again, Sebald's nameless wanderer, having discovered half-submerged, otherworldly, concrete bunkers which serve as a reminder of lost time:

> I imagined myself amidst the remains of our own civilization after its extinction in some future catastrophe. To me too, as for some latter-day stranger ignorant of the nature of our society wandering about among heaps of scrap metal and defunct machinery, the beings who had once lived and worked here were an enigma, as was the purpose of the primitive contraptions and fittings inside the bunkers, the iron rails under the ceilings, the hooks on the still partially tiled walls, the shower heads the size of plates, the ramps and the soakaways.[30]

Extreme Weather

Wet Bulbs

The wet-bulb temperature describes the lowest degree that can be attained by the evaporation of water. This is especially important for living organisms who depend on evaporation to regulate their own temperatures. For human beings, a wet-bulb temperature of 32 °C / 90 °F (equivalent to a heat index of 55 °C / 130 °F) is the absolute upper limit of physical tolerance. Above this, the body begins to overheat and expire. When it comes to somewhat lower wet-bulb thresholds, other factors come into play, such as physiological tolerance, topographical context, and cultural experience. Clearly someone who grew up in the Middle East can "survive" extreme heat with more aplomb than someone who spent their entire life in, say, Helsinki. But this should not be taken to mean that the former are somehow more "hardy" or can "handle it." In any case, the people more adapted to cooler climes will need to adapt quickly to rising temperatures and be aware of wet-bulb conditions, given the speed with which the entire planet is heating up. (And given the fact that even the Arctic Circle itself can register more than 30 degrees centigrade these days.) In the summer of 2021, for instance, even famously cool and damp Portland, Oregon, faced an unprecedented heatwave of 113 °F – the result of a rare "heat dome," trapping high pressure and holding it fast over the city. Even this scenario, however, is preferable when compared to the recent experience of the inhabitants of Jacobabad, Pakistan, who were obliged to contend with 52 °C / 126 °F this same year – a reading tickling the wet-bulb temperature in which humans begin to cook like lobsters in their own skin. Few buildings have air-conditioning in Jacobabad, and even the ones that do are beset by frequent electrical blackouts. As a result, the hospitals are well acquainted with the symptoms of extreme heat stroke. And, as one resident noted: "When it gets that hot, you can't even stay on your feet."

Sequence 3

Planetary Sorrow

Alien Stupidity

Most of us are familiar with the ongoing search for alien life, even if we have little sense of its methods or various authorities. The acronym SETI stands for the Search for Extraterrestrial Intelligence – a loose, quasi-official network of governmental and corporate attempts to scan the silent skies for even a distant sneeze, if not an alien radio station. Programs have even been developed where any random civilian could "donate" part of their own personal computer's processing power to help crunch through gigaflops of raw data, as part of the global search for patterns that perhaps promise some kind of intent to communicate.

Such an endeavor raises many questions, of course. What counts as a pattern? What medium is the most likely to yield positive results? What frequency? How to distinguish random patterns that are "natural" – say the pulse of a rotating star – from those that are the result of xeno-technics? What, moreover, if alien intelligence is characterized by the ability to evade our attempts at detecting presence or communication, like a cunning operator, who knows how to fly under the radar? Questions such as these have been asked over the past century by different experts in different fields in the collaborative attempt to refine the approach.

But what about alien stupidity? Why are we so quick to assume that aliens are smarter than us? No doubt a steady diet of science fiction has played its part, along with the logical deduction that any extraterrestrial life-form that can contact us from beyond our own parochial planet must by default be more "advanced" than we are. (As if there is a single telos, and line of development, from primitive single-celled organism to space-faring star-warrior.) Aliens, however, may well be able to build and navigate spaceships while also being stupid. After all, we do the same with our cutting-edge fighter jets and moon rockets. Stupidity, in other words, is not the opposite of intelligence but, rather, its residue or by-product. We may even posit a universal rule: the more intelligent something becomes, the greater its capacity for stupidity.

This should be obvious from the history of imperialism and colonization. The world's indigenous societies were never under any illusion that the newcomers were more intelligent than them – merely more aggressive. Certainly, they may have more effective weaponry and tools. But these could only be classed as more "intelligent" within a world-view that perceived the world a certain way – for conquering, reshaping, exploiting. Sophistication has many modes, just as there are many different types of intelligence (as the Nobel Prize committee well knows, if lacking the street smarts needed to survive outside academia).

As we write, several almost literal clowns control, or recently controlled, some of the world's most powerful nations. Buffoonery today seems to be the modus operandi of an uncannily effective political strategy and intelligence. It's as if Machiavelli belatedly realized that the jester would be a more effective sovereign than the prince. And, thus, we propose NASA launch a parallel program – SETS – the Search for Extraterrestrial Stupidity, which would comb the background noise of the ongoing echoes of the Big Bang for xenological chatter equivalent to our own Fox News or *New York Times* editorial.

The Grass is Greener

When you were a kid, prone to contemplating the bigger mysteries, you would sometimes be struck by the miraculous luck of being born on such a hospitable planet. "Imagine being born on Venus!" you would say to your sister, as you both ate your tinned spaghetti on toast in front of the TV. "Or even worse – Mercury! . . . We'd melt away." It would take an embarrassing amount of years to truly appreciate the fact that your birth on Earth was not a lucky break but a direct result of the biological fluke of our chemical legacy (itself at least partly a result of being in the so-called Goldilocks zone of our own solar system: not too close to the sun, and not too far from it either). Certainly, it is a miracle that we get to experience this weird thing called life. But it's not exactly a coincidence that this is happening here on Earth, given that this is one of the few astral bodies we know capable of sustaining life. (Even as we have yet to come up with a very convincing definition of life, either as scientists or philosophers.)

Now, however, we are told that there is another planet in our general cosmic neighborhood perhaps *even more* conducive to biological exuberance than Earth. An article in *Wired* magazine from 2015 explains that, "A new index has been devised to help researchers select which exoplanets are most likely to harbour life." According to this new metric, "the Earth is assigned a habitability rating of 0.829 – slightly lower than that of Kepler-442b, a recently discovered planet about 1,100 light years away, which is rated 0.836." How are we to take such news? Indeed how are we supposed to avoid the sense that the grass may well be greener on this slightly superior doppelganger of our own home? Had we been fortunate enough to be born on Kepler-442b, might we have had a somewhat more fulfilling life – a better job, a healthier, more gravity-defiant body, a more exotic sex life? After first assuming that Earth was the center of the universe, and then fearing we are the only instance of an inhabited planet in the universe, we now discover we may be living on a second-rate space-rock? At least compared to the xeno-Joneses.

"There is no Planet B," insist the ecological activists. And of course they are right. But the pedantic astronomers will remind us that there is Planet 442b, which enjoys the right conditions to sustain liquid water and is even one-and-a-half billion years younger. No matter that we will never be able to figure out how to travel across such a vast distance in one piece, let alone settle there. Yet knowing such an uber-Earth exists, taunting us with its theoretically technical perfection across the Milky Way, raises the strange possibility that we may be living on the planetary equivalent of Pepsi, after all.

Belated Lives

We are told – by rather malicious, scientifically minded pedants – that the stars we see in the night sky are "already dead . . . already gone." And, as children, we eventually learn that the light from different stars takes so long to get to us that the source is extinguished before their radiant aftermath reaches us. Given the new and insistent presence of mortality bequeathed to us by the pandemic, it's tempting to think regretfully of our fellow humans as stars in this sense. Even as someone nods hello – or simply saunters by in the street, without noticing us at all, like a shooting star – we have the morbid feeling that they are already deceased, and we are just seeing the belated signals of their fleeting existence. (A feeling that becomes increasingly distressing the more we care about the person in question, and the more we attend to their gestures with a rising, sickening feeling of preemptive loss.) But then, through an act of will, we can shift the sails in our mind around and tack in a different direction. Deep down, of course, we refuse to really believe the astronomers and their bleak insistence that the stars we see twinkling above us are just a trick of the space–time continuum. Likewise, we refuse to believe that the people around us – so animated by life and by the twitching demands of embodiment – will ever really pass away. As one especially poetic astronomer once famously said, "we are all made of star-stuff." The carbon atoms that make up our soft bodies have already circled around the universe many times, over and over, for the past 11 billion years or so. We are just an infinitesimal moment in the wriggling astonishment of a vast cosmic recycling program. Which means that everything we encounter (including ourselves) is always already dead but also constantly transformed and reanimated. The lights that guide us – or at least guided our ancestors – are, from a certain dominant perspective, an optical illusion. But then how to explain that we can still see them? An extinguished source does not mean the end of its "life." So, just as a long-vanished star can persist, as a beam of bright light, so can the people who are no longer with us continue to glimmer and shine, as long as there are pathways to illuminate.

Phoning Home (but Being Left on Hold)

How might the classic science-fiction "first contact" scenario change if the aliens – whether friendly visitors or hostile invaders – gave us fair warning of their arrival? After all, in most of the canonical tales of this genre – *The War of the Worlds, The Day the Earth Stood Still, Close Encounters of the Third Kind, Arrival*, and so on – the extraterrestrials tend to show up on our doorstep, and only then do we scramble to survive, adapt, fight back, or assemble a passable welcoming party. Cixin Liu's cult novel *The Three-Body Problem* (the first book in the trilogy *Remembrance of Earth's Past*) proposes the jarring possibility that we may receive advance notice from interstellar visitors – a scenario that would unquestionably mess with our limited human minds. The reader learns quite early, along with the main characters, that extraterrestrials are planning to visit Earth. In contrast to other sci-fi writers, however, Liu takes into account the long distances involved, whereby the technologically advanced aliens travel according to the physical limits of light years. As a result, the date is set 450 years into the future. Preparations will thus be a multigenerational affair. How might humanity respond to such elongated, unprecedented anticipation?

First contact, in *The Three-Body Problem*, occurs one fateful night in the life of Ye Wenjie – an astrophysicist – who works, rather against her will, at a secretive government facility dedicated to searching for evidence of extraterrestrial life. On that same night, she is startled to receive an unmistakable message from the dark abyss above. The message is a warning, in fact, sent by a conscientious citizen of the planet Trisolaris, cautioning the recipient to abandon all attempts to make contact, since to hail aliens – such as his own kind – is to invite merciless invasion. Ye, traumatized by China's violent cultural revolution, and now misanthropic to a frightening degree, ignores this warning and responds to the message, thereby deliberately betraying the existence, and whereabouts, of the vulnerable Earth, as well as setting in motion the interstellar imperial fleet.

Some time passes, and Ye finds herself surrounded by the rich and powerful of the planet. They are all in on the secret, which becomes less exclusive with every pair of loose lips. Soon enough hundreds are involved. Indeed, Ye finds it necessary to "bring in" dozens upon dozens of people to prepare for the fateful moment, each of whom – as fractures appear between the stakeholders; must decide to which faction they will pledge their allegiance. The very idea of looming "first contact" serves as an X-ray to starkly reveal different – entrenched and intractable – political, philosophical, and ideological divisions – especially concerning the capacities, and even purpose, of humankind.

A certain utopian cast of mind is prone to think that if, or even when, we discover that we are indeed not alone in the universe, then this new knowledge – this miraculous confirmation – would lead to a new global accord. Gone would be our petty squabbles, and the narcissism of minor differences, as we acknowledge our species solidarity as the foundation of interacting with the alien newcomers. Liu's story, however, is not so rosy:

> Naïve, idealistic hopes had been shattered. Scholars found that, contrary to the happy wishes of most people, it was not a good idea for the human race as a whole to make contact with extraterrestrials. The impact of such contact on human society would be divisive rather than uniting, and would exacerbate rather than mitigate the conflicts between different cultures. In summary, if contact were to occur, the internal divisions

> within Earth civilization would be magnified and likely lead to disaster.[1]

Proving the scholars right, the general population in Liu's story shakes out into three main groups: the Adventists, the Redemptionists, and the Survivors. The Adventists are disillusioned post-humanists, who believe our species has lost its way and is in dire need of some serious alien life-coaching if we – and the planet – are to survive. They initially believe in a "pan-species communism." As time proceeds, however, and as human folly multiplies and causes further harm, the Adventists become increasingly pessimistic and start to resemble the (real-life) Voluntary Human Extinction movement. The Redemptionists, by contrast, are more optimistic and start to think of the arriving aliens in New Age messianic terms: as saviors. "Gradually," we are told, "as fantasies about that distant civilization grew more and more elaborate, the Redemptionists developed spiritual feelings towards Trisolaran civilization. Alpha Centauri became Mount Olympus in space, the dwelling place of the gods; and so the Trisolaran religion – which really had nothing to do with religion on Trisolaris – was born." The Redemptionists are thus not a universe away from Scientologists. The third faction, known as the Survivors, is essentially a group of well-funded "preppers," reminiscent of the Silicon Valley billionaires who are already building bunkers in New Zealand to somehow wait out the End Times. As the book summarizes the differences between these three sects: "The Adventists would like to destroy the human race by means of an alien power; the Redemptionists worship the alien civilization as a god; the Survivors wish to betray other humans to buy their own survival."[2]

What is striking about Liu's highly complex literary game of *The Sims* is the way that humanity's deepest insecurities and hopes are magnified and refracted through the approaching prism of not quite imminent alien contact. The actual moment of encounter eventually arrives, elliptically, in subsequent books. In the meantime, however, weird interstellar and trans-temporal scenarios are nested inside each other – virtual worlds embedded within actual ones, and vice versa – like devious and intertwined . . . well . . . Chinese boxes. As the first volume in the series, *The Three-Body Problem* has much to say beyond the pages of the book about the strange liminal space in which humanity finds itself today – still living with the rotting, partially reanimated corpse of various Gods, while also contending with scientific forecasts that are increasingly dire with each new environmental study. How to go on when there is no *deus ex machina* to save us from our own inventions but ones that we try to manufacture ourselves? (And as such, inevitably exacerbate the problem.) As one lapsed xeno-biologist, and now converted zealot, explains, in the novel: "Human society can no longer rely on its own power to solve its problems. It can also no longer rely on its own power to restrain its madness. Therefore, we ask our Lord [i.e., the Trisolarians] . . . to carry out this divine punishment: the destruction of all humankind."[3] Here, the Christian eschatological belief in a Second Coming is conveniently projected onto aliens. Other responses, however, are no less saturated in older modes of conceptualizing and symbolizing our predicament, along with our shortcomings. Are we even worth protecting from would-be invaders? Will we find ourselves waiting for a much needed extraterrestrial intervention forever, like forsaken characters in a Samuel Beckett play? Should we embrace the knowledge that we would indeed, as the musician Perry Farrell insisted, "make great pets" for the aliens?

Given the fact that the universe contains "billions and billions" of stars, each of which may host its own solar system any of which may contain a planet that hosts intelligent life – why is it that we have not yet been definitively visited by aliens? The conundrum underlying this question now has an official name in the scientific literature: the Fermi Paradox. (A formal phrase based on a casual outburst by the Italian-American physicist Enrico Fermi during a high-powered lunch: "But where is everybody?" he exclaimed, after his lunch-mates insisted on the likelihood of other inhabited planets like ours, out there, among the stars.)

Certainly, our lack of visitors has not been for want of trying. We have sent constant radio signals out into space for a century now: some targeted and deliberate, most just leaking out of the atmosphere and continuing on their merry way. We even sent out some very expensive messages in a bottle – the Voyager 1 and 2 satellites – including golden records engraved with welcoming images of our waving anatomy and cosmic maps detailing just where to find us. Some, however, are beginning to express serious reservations about this practice, along with our neighborly impulse to encourage intergalactic folks to "come on by." No lesser figure than Stephen Hawking publicly discouraged attempts to make contact with ETs, fearing this is the equivalent of a bunch of field mice waving a giant flag to attract the attention of the local owl population. Any prospective alien visitors, Hawking believed, "will be vastly more powerful [than us] and may not see us as any more valuable than we see bacteria": a fear deeply rooted in our own human history, of course – specifically that the brutality of European "expansion" may be visited upon the species as a whole in a kind of cosmic form of karma.

This possibility is being debated by scientists who are now wondering if we should pivot from SETI (the *Search* for Extraterrestrial Intelligence, via eavesdropping on signals from space) to METI (*actively messaging* ETs, with powerful broadcast technologies). Those who believe the latter to be a foolish and dangerous venture have borrowed the title of Liu's final book in the trilogy – *Dark Forest* – to supplement the Fermi Paradox. For these concerned citizens of Earth, the Dark Forest theory names the prudence with which we should actively avoid alerting other intelligent life to either our presence or our location. The stakes are too high, they argue, to yoo-hoo into the Milky Way and hope for the best. Some even suggest that *the reason* we find no evidence of life anywhere other than Earth is that evolved intelligences know better than to make themselves conspicuous, while we humans wave and shout out into the void, like drunken lugs at a baseball game. As *The Washington Post* reports:

> One vocal critic of the idea of reaching out to aliens proactively – astronomer John Gertz of SETI – has developed proposals to move toward more inclusive public consideration of these activities. What we need, he suggests, are laws and international treaties to govern more explicit contact attempts. Without prior broad agreement from some globally representative body, Gertz says, contacting extraterrestrials should be considered "as the reckless endangerment of all mankind, and be absolutely proscribed with criminal consequences, presumably as exercised at the national level, or administered through the International Court of Justice in The Hague."[4]

While there is no concrete, verified proof of alien visitation, there is also no shortage of eye-witness accounts, from UFO sightings in the sky to harrowing tales of abduction and experimentation. Aliens certainly stalk our collective psyche, if not our actual lives. (Or at least not unless you have those truth-revealing sunglasses from *They Live*.) Area 51 notwithstanding, however, the invading alien will continue to be a figure of intense cathexis and projection: revealing our troubled conscience, inherited from the past; our seething resentments, rooted in the present; and our profound anxieties about the increasingly uncertain future. What if the aliens arrive too late to save us and find only cockroaches and orphaned Roombas and Teslas roaming the planet? What if there is a *Star Trek*-style Inter-Galactic Federation out there, and we are left here, in the cosmic boonies, fending for ourselves like a bunch of ignorant backwater dwellers?

The debate continues, however, in scientific circles as much as in science fiction stories. Meanwhile, the jury is still out about whether we should be assembling NASA's equivalent of a HELP sign made of stones on the beach, or whether we should be very careful about continuing to send sophisticated smoke signals up into the skies in the hope of attracting attention, lest we become the slaves, or even the dinner, of some unknowable, predatory alien species.

The Bringer of Old Age

Jupiter is the least lugubrious of the planets. Or so the composer Gustav Holst would lead us to believe. In his suite of orchestral "mood pictures," *The Planets* (1914–17), which depicts the great bodies of our solar system, Jupiter is described as "the bringer of jollity." Holst was interested in astrology and struck upon the idea of distilling the primary affect of each of our local planets down to their putative essence. It is not clear why he associated this particular massive sphere of swirling gas with mirth and happiness, though the zodiac often equates Jupiter with good fortune, abundance, and generosity. (All of which certainly help in raising the spirits.) Some of the other planets are more clearly pinned to their traditional cultural symbolism, such as Mars for war, Mercury for messages, and Venus for peace. (Love may have been the most obvious association for Venus, but the suite was written during the First World War, which likely explains the emphasis on harmony.) Saturn is also, unsurprisingly, the most melancholy of the movements, and Holst's composition summons the sad undertones accompanying the passage of time: this planet is described as "the Bringer of Old Age." Writing several decades after the first performance of this popular work, Holst's daughter noted that the assembled audience drooped under the weight of this movement's passage: "In Saturn," she wrote, "the isolated listeners in the dark, half-empty hall felt themselves growing older at every bar."

Notably, Earth is not sonically represented in Holst's arrangement: a planet too compromised by its most ambitious inhabitant, perhaps, to distil into one mood. As the viewing platform for the other astral bodies, our own planet enjoys the privilege of being a "structuring absence": the figure missing from the picture, because *someone* has to take the photograph of all the others. Notable also is the fact that Pluto does not make the cut, since this far-flung member of the solar circle was not officially recognized as a planet until 1930. As a consequence, the last portrait in the suite is Neptune, "the Mystic": a gentle, pulsing piece that ends with a rather eerie chorus, becoming fainter and fainter, until the listener – along with the symphony itself – seems to leave the relatively warm embrace of the solar system and dissolve into the chilly silence of infinite space.

The belief that our own moods and blood-tides are influenced by different stars and planets is the basis of astrology – a practice with many different faces and facets over the centuries. Astrological projections have themselves influenced the decisions of great empires as much as the humble choices of any given perplexed soul, hungry for guidance. Adorno spoke for millions of contemporary skeptics, however, when he scoffed at modern astrological claims: for him, astrology was a cynical superstition for an age yearning naively for a more enchanted experience. For this notorious snob, it was the comfort of the "semi-erudite" – people who had read just enough to enjoy hermeneutic patterns but who preferred narcissistic validation from the cosmos rather than the (admittedly rather joyless) secular perspective. In other words, Adorno believed astrology to be astronomy for people who can't get beyond the self. No condemnation, however, exhausts the condemned, and even a persuasive critique can miss, or at least understate, the way that vestigial practices – no matter how dubious – can also be a symptom of a healthy interest in movements and machinations beyond our own minds, and beyond our personal (even terrestrial) – spheres. Astrology, after all, can be a gateway drug to imaginative and creative triumphs, such as Holst's planetary suite, that allow the sublime "in through the back door," as it were. (A point that still stands, even if Adorno winced his way through this particular symphony and considered it closer to kitsch.)

To consult with "authentic" star-readers from centuries past would be, one imagines, a jarring experience. Their language, their advice, their assumptions, their solicitations, and so on, would be a world away from the breezy, prosaic info-dumps of today's forecasts. But it is likely a historical constant that we consult such figures in times of uncertainty and doubt. We seek from them clarity and counsel. Surely our fate or fortune cannot rest solely on our own shoulders? Surely the heavens – from which everything came, and to which we shall one day return – have plans, or at least pathways, in store for us? Similarly, we all know people who seem to have been "born under a bad star," and no matter what sage decisions they make – and no matter how much they deserve a better deal – they bring with them nothing but woe and adversity. How do we account for those who lose out, far beyond the laws of probability? (Even considering all the "intersectional" disadvantages that most struggle against, to differing degrees.) Of course it's foolish to blame Saturn or Mercury for such problems, as if a distant ball of swirling hydrogen has any influence over our job prospects or love lives. But there is something about the divination process that can reveal various impasses or issues that we would not otherwise intuit.

Today, astrology is a loose constellation of inherited ideas: a sprawling attic filled with dusty semi-recognizable shapes and glittering figures, evoking ancient emotions, passed down through generations. It can be as banal as a daily text message from a zodiac-themed app or as enigmatic as a new, avant-garde tarot deck, conceived by an elusive artist who has communed – ironically or not – with the spirits, as well as several exclusive neural networks. Astrology is above all an *archive*, which helps us orient our discussions about ourselves, and one another, through shared motifs and symbols. (Not unlike psychoanalysis, or pop culture in general.) People tend to drift towards astrology, as already mentioned, when they are troubled or seek relief from sadness. (Seldom will a joyful person rush to check their horoscope, since such an action seems redundant at such times.)

The notion of Saturn being an especially "sad planet" is a cultural belief, not an astrophysical one. Sadness, however, is not merely a subjective illusion – completely divorced from the fabric of the space–time continuum – but itself part of the texture of the natural world. So insisted great philosophers, such as Spinoza and Schelling, extending back also to many of the pre-Socratics, who believed that it is a fundamental error to drive a metaphysical wedge between our own experiences and the material world. For where did we come from – along with all our fibrillating emotional climates – if not the latter? (Even the Hebrew God made us out of clay.) If sadness is an exclusive property of intelligent life, then this phenomenon is still an emergent property of the atomic matrix – albeit to a second degree. This understanding is summarized by Cicero, when he wrote:

> If flutes playing tunefully were sprouting on an olive-tree, you would surely have no doubt that the olive-tree had some knowledge of flute-playing; again, if plane-trees bore lutes playing in tune, you would likewise, I suppose, judge that plane-trees were masters of the art of music. Why then is the universe not accounted animate and wise, when it brings forth from itself creatures which are animate and wise?[5]

By the same token, why then is the universe not accounted sad when it brings forth from itself creatures which are sad?

A valid research question, then: not so much the problem of origin, when it comes to sadness, but its formal properties, composition, extent, location, valences, and so on. Is the quantity of cosmic sorrow always the same, for instance, yet unevenly distributed, like energy? Or is it running out, like helium? Is it compressed, like Saturn or Jupiter? Or is it stretched across the universe, like the cosmic microwave background? Or perhaps sadness is compounding and accumulating, like carbon particles in the Earth's atmosphere? Such questions may be the purview of a new science: melanchology. Or acediatrics. We can imagine, then, the press conferences called by such wan-faced experts to announce an exciting find: a rare sad nebula in the Ursa Major star cluster, or a depressive vortex in the Tau Ceti system. A sadness several light-years across, and with a greater density than some black holes. (Indeed, this may be a partial explanation *for* black holes. To say nothing of dark matter.) Perhaps a new NASA – NASA 2 – will be founded: the National Astronomical Sadness Agency. And with special teleaffectoscopes, they will detect and explore a sadness so powerful that even a gray, rainy Sunday in England is not enough to contain it. A sorrow so intense that it has its own gravity, forging new planets like crystalline or mineral tears, suspended in space: planets such as WASP-76b – a globe roughly the size of Jupiter, 634 light-years from Earth, and apparently host to an endless rainstorm of iron ore.

We picture the fund-raising galas of NASA 2 – its scientists all dressed in formal black coats – nibbling on caviar canapes before attending a performance by the next Gustav Holst: a contemporary sonic mood-painter, who composes music in honor of the mournful force of such beautiful, yet forsaken, celestial bodies.

Impact Statement

"Sad Planets." What does this mean? What does it evoke? Is the conjunction between the two terms any more meaningful than Lautréamont's umbrella and sewing machine, finding themselves in random proximity on a dissection table? Or is there some kind of logic? A secret correlation?

Certainly, there is a long tradition, in many cultures, of linking our passions and emotions with heavenly bodies. Saturn, after all, is a melancholic god as well as a planet. And our moods are said to be heavily influenced by whether Mercury is in retrograde or not. But, in pushing these two words together today, we find a somewhat different, emergent resonance. We seem to be pairing an ancient science – astronomy – with a new field – affect theory. There is a telegraphic implication of entanglement, or even complicity. How does the contemporary understanding of "the planetary" impact our emotional landscape or affective weather? (And can we even consider a "vice versa" in this scenario, given the vast distances between astral bodies and terrestrial moods?) Moreover, the term "sad planets" signals a collapse of scales: the infinitely vast and numberless is suddenly saddled with a modest, introspective adjective. Are we only talking about the way planets make *us* feel – we moody humans? Or is there a sense in which the planets themselves may "catch feelings" (to use a recent colloquialism). After all, it seems far more likely that the famous "music of the spheres" is more attuned to Bruckner, Arvo Pärt, or The Cure than Handel, Gershwin, or The B-52's.

In any case, the assumptions – and potential projections – embedded in the phrase "sad planets" encourages reflection on the way that a cosmic perspective (or gesture, or frame), obliges us to face all those things from which modern culture is designed to distract us: futility, entropy, absurdity, death. The planetary aspect of sadness – in tandem with the sad aspect of planets – gives us a kind of existential vertigo, as we toggle our hearts and minds to account for *both* the astronomical and the personal, the objective and the subjective, the cold and indifferent and the warm and intimate. We humans are obsessed with accounting for "how things make us feel." But the very formulation presumes a pure passivity on our part: we are *made* to feel this way or that as a result of various psycho-social collisions. "How did this event impact you?" a therapist may ask us, as if – like the moon – we are simply exposed to random satellites that appear suddenly, out of the inky void, to plough into our face, our surface – the dark side of our psyche.

Sad Sacks

Sadness, it must be said, is not *always* sad. In the seventeenth century, Richard Burton classified many types of sadness, some of which – such as "love-sadness" – can provide a perverse kind of pleasure, in the bitter-sweet pulp of their dark fruit. "I miss the comfort of being sad," sang Kurt Cobain, who clearly had a very ambivalent relationship with the benefits of success. Melancholia itself can be considered an addiction to sadness, since it either has no clear source or object or, alternatively, it represents an ingenious strategy for holding on to something that once made one happy. (As with Miss Havisham, who wears her wedding dress decades after being abandoned at the altar, in order to keep an emotional connection to the promise of happiness that her fiancé failed to keep.) Around 2010, there was an explosion of "sad girls" online: a demographic that posted wan images on Tumblr, along with depressing quotes about loneliness or disappointment. Even happy and well-adjusted young women felt obliged to strike a sad pose on social media lest they be considered gauche or "basic." Sadness was in the atmosphere, and the pressure to perform it – especially for the young – was intense. "Emo" music provided the demoralizing soundtrack.

Of course, this is nothing new, as the young especially have always spent their relatively free time sighing and feeling sorry for themselves. Oh woe is me! What am I to do with this healthy, sap-filled body and its treacherous hormonal ocean currents? Can the muses help me distill this unique pain I feel into poetry or music? Or memes?

One of life's great pleasures can indeed be misting up on cue, listening to sad songs, or weeping openly at the end of tear-jerker films. Catharsis is a crucial part of our species-being, as the ancient Greeks knew well. (Just as Freud understood that human motivations go far "beyond the pleasure principle.") It is an intriguing question whether pathos, as a cultural pathology, describes an especially Western vice. Indigenous myths, for instance, may tell a sad story, but the narrative rarely seems to be an occasion or alibi for self-indulgent *wallowing*. More likely, it is an allegorical tale, or symbolic explanation, for the way things are and how they came to be. In any case, it is evident that the modern world has turned "being sad" into both a fine, bespoke art and an off-the-rack generic experience. So when we speak of "sadness" in the following pages, we do well to recall all the nuances and range involved. For intractable, "clinical" depression, grief, or anxiety can be tethered by the same word to the more wistful forms of sadness, such as sepia nostalgia, an *umami* melancholia, or even a creatively generative gloom.

Mono no aware

Mono no aware is a Japanese phrase often translated as "the sadness of things." The sadness in question derives specifically from "an awareness of the transience of things," as emphasized by Zen Buddhism. The most common example of *mono no aware* is the intense but fleeting cherry blossom season, which brings so much pleasure in such a compressed amount of time (usually around two weeks in any given locale).

This phrase brings two thoughts to mind: the first being a group of Zen refuseniks, who resist the temptation to surrender to the bittersweet, ephemeral nature of things in favor of making them last as long as possible. This band of sensualist aesthetes – committed to prolonging and sustaining pleasures far beyond their organic duration – would deliberately set up camp in the semi-tropical islands of southern Japan, in early spring, to catch the first fleshy petals that burst into pungent life on the cherry trees closest to the equator. This group would then essentially follow the wave of color as it rolls up the country in three months or so, flowing up the long and proud peninsula of Japan, as if they were surfers, riding a sublime explosion in slow motion, all the way to the last foam of the season, turning from magenta to rose to pink to faun to white to brown, on the northernmost cherry trees in the relatively isolated climes of northern Hokkaido.

The second thought is more of a question: what of the sadness of things that *persist*? What of spectacles that endure? Or entities that take longer than human timescales to fade? "This too shall pass," was the philosophical consolation of the ancient Persians, suggesting that any given trial or tribulation is surely a temporary state. (Including, of course, the trial of life itself.) Indeed, the Japanese may well have a word for the other side of the coin struck by *mono no aware*: a term that captures the pathos of persistence; of things that – from obscure internal motives or uncanny laws of physics – refuse to pass, like fixed furniture in the great passage of Time. The sadness of effectively permanent things. Of interminable conditions. The sadness of planets that are seemingly suspended in a silent void forever. Of mountains that are exposed to the sun, experiencing the same monotony as Sisyphus, who at least pushes a boulder across their cracked backs once a day; or of Prometheus, whose screams at least punctuate the otherwise timeless day, though they are eventually drowned out by the eagle's shrieks. *Mono no aware*: the sadness of the moon, whose inscrutable face has watched the Earth change color from bone to brown to green to blue – and back to a hazy desert-brown.

"What's the Point?"

So asks the young Alvie Singer in Woody Allen's most celebrated film, *Annie Hall*. The boy is slumped next to his worried mother in the office of an upbeat, cigarette-smoking pediatrician.

"Why are you depressed, Alvie?" asks the doctor.

"Tell Dr Flicker," insists the mother to her son. Then, turning to the expert in the room. "It's something he read."

After a desultory pause, the young boy answers: "The universe is expanding."

The doctor prompts his patient further, so Alvie continues. "Well, the universe is everything. And if it's expanding, some day it will break apart . . . and that will be the end of everything."

The mother – who has clearly heard this doleful little speech several times already – can't help but exclaim: "*What, is that your business*?!" Again, she makes a plea to the doctor. "He's stopped doing his homework."

"What's the point?" asks the boy.

"What has the universe got to do with it?" she screeches. "You're here in Brooklyn. Brooklyn is not expanding!"

The doctor rallies in support of the mother. "It won't be expanding for billions of years, Alvie." He smiles and puffs deep on his cigarette, just at the thought of this. "And we've gotta try to enjoy ourselves while we're here, huh? . . . Huh?"

But the boy is unmoved by this well-meaning Hippocratic suggestion.

Riding a Cannonball

As it turns out, Alvie shares a cosmic sensitivity with one of the protagonists of Ermanno Cavazzoni's charming little book *Brief Lives of Idiots*. This sensitivity, however, is inverted or reversed. The idiot in question – a Signore Vacondio, who lives in Turin – is in fact *soothed* by the vast spaces of nothingness stretched between planets, stars, and galaxies. "Distance in general," explains the narrator, "comforts him"; along with the fact that, "fortunately, the universe was still expanding." Why is Signore Vacondio in need of such comfort? And why does he consider the expansion of the universe to be fortunate? While Alvie feels universal entropy in his still growing bones, Signore Vacondio is afflicted with a different sensitivity; itself a kind of internalized knowledge. Namely, he cannot simply accept the fact that the Earth is rushing through space, while we proceed with our lives as if this isn't anything but terrifying.

> "Do you know how fast we're going?" he would say whenever anyone noticed his worried look. "108,000 kilometers an hour, do you realize?" Because of this, he said, he wasn't comfortable going on working while the Earth shot through space at such an insane speed with us here like a bunch of numbskulls at its mercy. He said that everyone, his coworkers first and foremost, acted irresponsibly. They'd go out dancing, or get married like it's nothing, all happy, as the Earth careens unchecked through space, and no one knows where it could wind up at any moment. . . . "We're riding a cannonball," he said, "with one, very simple, prospect; it's a matter of time, even hours or minutes."[6]

Hence the calming effect – once the idea eventually came to Signore Vacondio – of studying astronomical maps and realizing the "one, very simple, prospect" (i.e., a massive galactic collision) was not necessarily imminent, given the relatively fixed orbits of the solar system, the deep gravitational grooves of the galaxy, and the vast spaces of, well, space. No longer did he find himself clinging to his mattress in a cold sweat, eyes scrunched closed, waiting for the impending impact with some other fateful astral body – a giant car crash in the void.

Nevertheless (and, once again, like Alvie), Cavazzoni's idiot is not completely convinced by the reassurances of other people; people who, after all, by their very willingness to avoid dwelling upon disturbing scientific facts – particularly the fact that everything we know is smeared over the surface of a vast piece of grapeshot, fired at lightning speed into the Great Unknown by an equally enigmatic shooter (possibly with suspect aim) – disqualify the integrity of their own reassurances. Eventually, however, like the rest of us, Signore Vacondio learns to push this admittedly disconcerting cosmic knowledge down into the more muffled parts of his soul.

Having read this little fable, however, we can't help but wonder if *our own* teeth-grinding, or night sweats – or free-floating anxiety – aren't at least partly inspired by similar fears, even if these have been buried so deep in our psyche that we can no longer identify the source. Perhaps, on some level, we are *all* such overly aware idiots, "agonizing over the ever imminent possibility of colliding with wayward asteroids . . . or a toxic comet tail made up of cyanide with its characteristic bitter almond smell." (More marzipan, anyone?) Indeed, after watching Alvie's depression on screen – and after reading about Signore Vacondio's chronic panic – so to say, after being reminded of our profound existential precarity, in an inescapable, cosmic sense – our fears of universal expansion, or interplanetary impact, may also become conscious, manifest, and palpable. In which case, we would do well to channel the spirit of Alvie's exasperated mother and remind ourselves, *"what is that our business*?!"

A Gleaming Leprosy

Gustave Flaubert wrote for three very different audiences. The first was his close circle of friends. These he sometimes tested with epic readings of a manuscript in progress – on one occasion, eight hours a day for four straight days. Louis Bouilhet and Maxime du Camp, his two most patient chums, later described such a reading (in this case, of *The Temptation of Saint Anthony*) as "the most painful days of our lives." (Critics agree this is not his most accessible work.) Flaubert's second audience was the general reading public, a population that multiplied after the publication of his most famous work, *Madame Bovary*. The third audience, however, was harder to reach – the heavenly bodies, twinkling in the night sky – even as Flaubert sweated by candlelight, quill in hand, in the concerted effort to bend the French language into such intricate shapes that it would eventually affect them. "Language is like a cracked kettle," he wrote in his best-selling novel, "on which we beat out tunes for bears to dance to" (perhaps a fourth audience we neglected to mention before). All the while, he continues, "we long to move the stars to pity." An interesting ambition for a writer – to compose a story so affecting that even extraterrestrial bodies are moved. From Ruskin's perspective, this is the pathetic fallacy cranked up to the most pathetic ego-mania: an artist who not only believes in the emotional capacities of dead matter, but who also believes in his own capacity to affect them. Romantic hubris! (Of course we should not take Flaubert at his literal word, given this is literature, but consider such comments as a somewhat ironic statement, stitched into the logic of the narrative, about the cosmic ambitions of the aesthete, and thus making some gentle fun of himself.)

Across the border, in Germany, a different kind of writer – the formidable philosopher Georg Wilhelm Friedrich Hegel – expressed quite a different relationship with those luminous pin-pricks shimmering in the night sky. One mild summer evening, Hegel was dining with Heinrich Heine, his soon to be famous pupil. In his memoirs, the latter recalls: "One beautiful starry-skied evening, we stood next to each other at the window, and I, a young man of about twenty-two who had just eaten well and had good coffee, enthused about the stars and called them the abode of the blessed. But the master grumbled to himself: 'The stars, hum! Hum! The stars are only a gleaming leprosy in the sky.'" Apparently this anecdote perplexed men of letters for many years thereafter, to the extent that Hegel felt obliged to explain his disdain for such exulted astral companions: "It has been rumored round the town," he writes, in an addition to his *Encyclopaedia*, "that I have compared the stars to a rash on an organism where the skin erupts in a countless mass of red spots. . . . In fact, I do rate what is *concrete* higher than what is *abstract*, and an animality that develops into no more than a slime, higher than the starry host." In reversing the traditional hierarchy thus, Hegel concretizes his own key role in the European Enlightenment, with its emerging embrace of science, empiricism, and materialism. Heretical to both Platonism and monotheism, Hegel prefers not to gaze at the heavens but wrestle with the sludge in pursuit of an "absolute spirit" that is not numinous, and extraterrestrial, but firmly tethered to the worlding of the world (to use a somewhat later Germanic philosophical language).

Hegel died when Flaubert was just a boy of ten, scribbling juvenilia in Rouen. As a result, the two towering figures never had a chance to engage in a dialectical debate concerning the importance or influence of the stars on the great humanist adventure. We can only speculate who might win such a debate: the master of logic or the maestro of rhetoric. In any case, it is a discussion of no interest to that emerging type, the natural scientist, since it would not have concerned the stars themselves – their orbits, their size, their chemical compositions – but only involved their cultural resonance or symbolic utility. It is notable, however, that Hegel was not yet willing to entertain the idea of stars as being equally concrete as animals or slime, albeit harder to observe, and much, much farther away. Perhaps it was Flaubert – the indulgent fabulist, so willing to torture his fellow man through the medium of relentless self-expression – who paradoxically better understood the power of stars: their presence, their actuality, and their enigmatic participation in the wider cosmic spirit.

Seeds of Time

Airplanes are an actualization – a crystallization – of the *virtual* line that represents the shortest distance between two points, connecting, say, Paris and New York, or Dubai and Manila. An airplane – as the linguistic history of the word attests – manifests a "wandering plane" or section of air that has learned to move, like a piece of earth that has learned to launch itself into the sky, like self-folding origami. Following this perspective, *all* phenomena can indeed be understood as an emergent property – a kind of congealing, or materializing – of circumstantial nudges; of various objective "suggestions" made by the layout of the world; the givenness of the cosmos. A bridge, for instance, is thus the concrete expression that renders the whispering of two river banks into an enduring song. A frog is a convenient organic carry-pouch for water to explore the land. Likewise, we might think of love – or, indeed, hatred – as the manifestation of the potential resonance between two people; something that emerges in the contingent, geometric relation between bodies or souls. Humans themselves, viewed through the prism of this conceit, may be considered little more than an organic short-cut between the sea and the stars; a self-propelling vessel intent on bringing the ocean to the Milky Way via the inefficient medium of tears. In any case, it can be both helpful and humbling to remember that the things we take for granted as representing our own genius may well be but detours towards our own obsolescence. With this in mind, we might be more cautious about where we next fix our restless and covetous attention. As the polymath Vilém Flusser understood, "NASA already existed in germinal form within the first gaze directed at the Moon."[7]

The Forgetting of Stars

We are familiar with the notion of light pollution, even if we don't pay it as much mind as we do air, water, or even noise pollution. Yet the implications are profound, as Emanuel Jakob Auerbach-Baidani explains in his book *Astroloetheia* (first published in 2022 in a handsome and extremely limited edition of four letter-press copies). The increasing illumination of our cities – combined with smog, satellites, space junk (along with a generalized *looking down* into our phones) – has all but erased the stars from our skies, so that we are obliged to plan elaborate trips to the desert, or other under-populated places, in order to see the Milky Way or the Southern Cross with any kind of clarity. Auerbach-Baidani's book is dedicated to exploring not only "the forgetting of stars" but our ongoing indifference to the same. How can it be that the majestic intimacy of the heavens above – the map, scroll, and oracle of our species for tens of thousands of years – can be so casually dispensed with, so callously shrugged off? Not only are we forgetting the prophetic power, and orienting importance, of the firmament, but we have already forgotten to mourn its radical and sudden absence from our lives, minds, and hearts. "The stars are a relief from the horror of day," writes Auerbach-Baidani. But "what shall relieve us from the horror of a starless night." Moreover, "the stars are now the opposite of the sun: we can see the sun but cannot look at it, we can look at the stars but we cannot see them." *Astroletheia* is effectively a belated elegy for a now lost cosmic connection: a connection forged through the instinctive understanding of vast scales, distances, and time frames. Instead, we have blinkered and boxed ourselves in to tiny devices, routines, habits, and thought processes. Ironically, perhaps, the Enlightenment shone *so* bright that it blinded us, so that our eyes can no longer adjust to the shadows, the night, the darkness. The current cultural obsession with science fiction, according to this view, is thus a symptomatic desire to reconnect with astral bodies and stellar dispositions. Similarly, the constant zodiac-based chatter can be read according to this new, artificial light. For "what is astrology but the abreaction of a society which has repressed its relation to stars?"

Extreme Weather

The Fires This Time

Two months before Covid-19 was officially pronounced a global pandemic, the world's horrified attention was fixed on Australia, which had seemingly burst entirely into flames. "Bushfires" in the Great Southern Land are of course nothing new. But something about the scale and intensity of this particular conflagration felt of a different scale and order. Thousands of separate fires – some lit deliberately and others igniting through lightning strikes – combined into an inferno that terrorized country- and city-folk alike. Thousands of homes were lost, and hundreds of people were forced to flee to cinder-covered beaches or sooty football fields – some clutching keys for houses that no longer existed – in order to escape the voracious flames. Suddenly, global warming felt less like a tropical bath and more like a biblical kiln. A few dozen people died inside the furnace, condemned to the flames by hesitation, confusion, and capricious winds; while hundreds of others perished from breathing in the smoke that blanketed the land and obscured the sun for weeks. The real toll, however, was Australia's famous and unique wildlife. Scientists, surveying the scorched aftermath, estimated that at least a billion creatures had not been so lucky as most people, who had been airlifted to safety or shepherded onto naval vessels waiting offshore. This unthinkable reality prompted the teenage boy in Mike White's dark comedy *White Lotus* to acknowledge the tragedy, while eating breakfast with his family at a fancy Hawaiian resort: "A billion animals died in the fires in Australia," he says, in response to their petty squabbles. "A billion." The boy's parents, unsure how to respond to this sublime and horrible number, simply stare, numb to such statistics in the face of pragmatic parenting challenges. Receiving no sympathetic answer, the boy continues with a question far beyond his years, his expression pained, yet unreadable: "Where does the pain go?"

Sequence 4

Comets, Importing Change

No Safe Spaces in Space

Comets have historically been interpreted as a divine sign – an omen for mortals to embroider their own meanings upon. In earlier times, when astronomy was a handmaiden of theology, any such anomaly would be an occasion for fear and trembling, a portent that Judgment was at hand. Conversely, an opportunistic sovereign could pronounce the rare astral visitor a blessing from the gods concerning an already established plan of action here on Earth – a mandate to hasten the latest abuse of power.

In his documentary film *Fireball: Visitors from Darker Worlds*, Werner Herzog turns his characteristic Bavarian attention to those comets – or other significant space debris – that strayed so close to our atmosphere as to be captured by it. Such meteoric guests, crashing down onto the Earth, often leave a deep indexical imprint on the planet's surface, even as these have subsequently been covered by vegetation, forests, and even towns and cities. The biggest impact on the geologic record is, of course, the one that famously wiped out the dinosaurs – a massive meteor that struck the present-day Yucatán peninsula sixty-six million years ago (a catastrophe that has recently been described as "the single worst day for multicellular life on Earth").[1] Tiny particulates of this apocalyptic moment – which, had it been any bigger, could have snuffed out *all* life on our planet – continue to blow around our feet in the form of intergalactic dust. Herzog's film follows some amateur astro-sleuths, who use microscopes to identify traces of the original scene, intermingled among more banal and harmless extraterrestrial "guests" of our local and parochial gravity. ("Dust," says one enthusiast, "is the currency of the universe.") Herzog's film suggests that paying close attention to these strange and violent "visitors" is a powerful way of "looking eternity in the eye."

Through stories, paintings, songs, and so forth, *Fireball* traces the aftershocks of various meteor strikes, as well as the way they linger in the memory, many generations after the initial impact. The film is fascinated by the way meteor strikes oblige us to pay attention to the "darker worlds" far beyond our own sublunary concerns, since they remind us that we are essentially ant-like beings, clinging to the surface of a random rock, which itself is being constantly pelted by other rocks of various sizes and trajectories. The enduring figure of the "falling star" is thus a potent symbol of our own, all too often disavowed, cosmic *exposure*: to fate, to chance, to vengeful gods, to indifferent physics. The comet – even more than the lightning strike or the volcano – is a much more than human phenomenon that humbles us: a sublime reminder that this surreal sojourn in the land of the animate may end at any moment, and due to forces far beyond our control.

Supremely ironic, then, to realize (as the film also emphasizes) that the once eccentric *panspermia* theory – which holds that life was initially brought to this planet from elsewhere in the form of dormant biological building blocks, hitching a ride on a meteorite – is now becoming an increasingly orthodox hypothesis.

Comets give, and comets taketh away.

Ashes to ashes, and space dust to space dust.

Graduating from the Human Evolutionary Level

In the grand scheme of things, Halley's Comet can be considered a regular visitor to our night sky. It passes through our general neighborhood every seventy-five years and is visible to the naked eye, making it the only comet that may be experienced twice in a lifetime (memory cells permitting). Thankfully it is not on a collision course with Earth but, rather – like a good friend or relative – just passes through rather swiftly, without feeling the need to actually crash at our place. Indeed, I still remember excitedly pointing my home Celestron telescope towards Halley's Comet in 1986, hoping to see a flaming astral body, akin to the meteoric missiles that regularly pounded alien planets in the geeky science-fiction movie marathon that was forever playing in my teenage mind. Instead, however, I saw what amounted to a pale smudge, something that could just as easily have been left on the lens of my telescope by a wayward thumb rather than a proud satellite hurled by the Big Bang itself. This, in turn, served as a sobering reminder that even visitors from another part of the galaxy can be underwhelming, depending on expectation, proximity, and the tools at one's disposal.

My next indirect brush with a comet came eleven years later, as I sat cross-legged on a squeaky bed in a small hotel room in San Francisco, watching the breaking news story of the Heaven's Gate suicides. My emotional response to this bombshell was – I'm not proud to report – a kind of jet-lagged glee, as I found myself in the United States only because I had secured some modest travel funds to research my PhD on modern millenarian cults and cultures. Given the new millennium was looming, my funding proposal argued that something spectacular was surely brewing. And my hunch was – all things considered – that this *something* was most likely going to happen in California. Watching the live footage of thirty-nine bodies being removed from the cult's compound in San Diego, their famous Nike shoes poking out from the bottom of the blankets, vindicated my own prophecy and justified my research trip before it had even properly begun. Looking back from a more mature perch, I of course feel more muted emotions concerning the poor misguided souls who apparently truly believed a spaceship was traveling alongside the Hale–Bopp Comet – which had last been seen by humans in 2000 BC, back in the Bronze Age – ready to take them to the next dimension.

Missed Connections

In 1844, across New England, a millenarian cult known as The Millerites (after their charismatic leader, William Miller) prepared for the Rapture. Miller – who had grown up with the Book of Revelation open upon his knee – confidently communicated the date of March 21 as the great Day of Reckoning. Indeed, he had already interpreted the great comet of 1843 ("so huge and dazzling that it was visible in the daytime") as God's special signature, written across the heavens and confirming the Imminence of the End (along with the salvation of the righteous). Members of this distributed congregation even wore specially tailored "Ascension robes" to help them on their final journey, and – on the morning of the appointed day – climbed high up in the branches of apple trees to get closer to the God who was about to pluck them from the sinful Earth. One man even fastened turkey wings on his back and, "when the excitement was at a high pitch," leaped out of the tree and promptly broke his arm. Miller's prophecy, evidently, did not come true, consistent with every previous attempt to set a precise date for the End of the World. Indeed, one can only imagine the nettle sting of shame and disappointment in the heart of each individual Millerite when the breeze continued to blow, the birds continued to sing, and the sun completed its arc across the sky and slipped below the horizon. At such time, these aspiring angels were obliged to climb down from the trees and descend back to their abandoned fields, still wearing their now scuffed and soiled Ascension robes; some with hands still frozen into the shape of the branches they had been clinging to for so long, and with such fervor, in the late winter cold.[2]

X-Risk

In his recent book *X-Risk,* Thomas Moynihan argues that human extinction is a comparatively novel idea, "one that remained entirely unavailable for the greater part of our existence as a species." Asserting an epochal break around the turn of the twentieth century, Moynihan contrasts the historical –

even ancient – "sense of an ending" with the relatively recent "ending of sense." Religious apocalypse is, by this account, not at all analogous to the contemporary threat of secular extinction, since, in the case of the former, humanity always ends in concert with the World itself (in contrast to so many cli-fi scenarios of today, in which we ponder the very real possibility of "the world after humans"). Apocalypse, writes Moynihan, "is premised upon a projection of our values and a naive identification of those values with the universe at large." Thanks, however, to our new, profoundly Copernican understanding of our place – or placelessness – in the universe, the actual threat of human extinction frees us from our own former delusional hubris.

This massive shift in self-image – from tragic main character to fully disposable "non-player character" (to use video-game speak) – obliges us to reboot the relationship with our own species-being. The most important legacy of the Enlightenment, according to Moynihan, is to finally "understand ourselves as a biological species within a desacralized cosmos." "What other Earthborn species can think upon its own demise," he asks, "let alone take responsibility for it by using science to predict and perhaps prevent it? No other animal on the planet can assume liability for its own fate in this way." To which we might reply, what other animal fucking needs to?! The core claim of Moynihan's book – "that the discovery of human extinction may well yet prove to have been the very centerpiece of that unfolding and unfinished drama that we call modernity" – fails to take into account the extent to which indigenous and other non-modern cultures preempted and actively avoided the compulsively interventionist human exceptionalism that is directly leading to what we might paradoxically call "actually existing extinction." Moynihan is right to mark the profound fracture between theological and scientific anticipations of the end, even as there are some suggestive continuities as well. He is showing his neo-Promethean hand, however, when he claims that "discovering" our extinction was "an essential part of our assuming *maturity* as rational beings."

X-Risk, in other words, prescribes larger, and more frequent, doses of the same ideological antibiotics that wiped out our collective microbiome (and macrobiome) and led us to the brink in the first place. And, in doing so, it is trapped in the accelerationist Silicon Valley (il)logic of increasingly hi-tech solutions to exponentially volatile hi-tech problems – just as Monsanto's aggressively engineered monocrops require specific proprietary fertilizers and pesticides in order to grow. (Rather than, for instance, thinking systematically about the wisdom of diversifying, decelerating, and strategically tiptoeing back from the edge of the abyss through a less teleological, homogenizing, expansionist, and historically compromised project that still, rather embarrassingly, goes by the name of "modernity.") Moynihan's argument is not unaware of the stakes, for he states that, "in discovering our own extinction, we realized that we must think *ever better* because, should we not, then we may never think ever again." While the urgency of this imperative may indeed be true, thinking "ever better" need not be according to the same universalist, positivist values. Indeed, one may well wonder – after Hiroshima, Bhopal, Chernobyl, and Flint, Michigan – why anyone would be so confident that the only answer to our own perilous position is continuing further down the same path that got us to this point in the first place.

Excessive Egotism

In 1894, H. G. Wells published an essay entitled "The Extinction of Man," in which he begins by noting: "It is part of the excessive egotism of the human animal that the bare idea of its extinction seems incredible to it." Wells then goes on to detail some of the reasons why such faith in our long-term survival stands on shaky ground; specifically the ground in which the fossil record has retained compressed lessons for our species – lessons we tend to disavow. With the far-sighted provocation that served the writer so well in his popular fiction, Wells speculates that we humans are – like the dinosaurs that ruled the Earth at one moment and then apparently vanished from it the next – bound to succumb to the same fate as all previous apex species. And (he further surmises) even if our demise were not to be as sudden and spectacular as that of the "thunder lizards," we may well still find ourselves contending with new, evolved species, jealous of our status as "undisputed master" of the land: giant crustaceans, for instance, or some new kind of shark "that could raid out upon the land." Nor might our collective final breath be at the claws or jaws of so spectacular a beast as these. African ants, for example, could presumably overwhelm us, if and when they decide to band together in sufficient numbers, swamp our cities and transform them into so many vast ant-hills. "A world devoured by ants seems incredible now," Wells writes, "simply because it is not within our experience; but a naturalist would have a dull imagination who could not see in the numerous species of ants, and in their already high intelligence, far more possibility of strange developments than we have in the solitary human animal. And no doubt the idea of the small and feeble organism of man, triumphant and omnipresent, would have seemed equally incredible to an intelligent mammoth or a paleolithic cave bear."

Moving down the scale even further, Wells is especially attuned to the risk posed by viruses and bacteria, plotting their sinister coup beneath the cloak of invisibility. (And here, in the age of Covid, it is worth quoting the paragraph in full):

> there is [indeed] always the prospect of a new disease. As yet science has scarcely touched more than the fringe of the probabilities associated with the minute fungi that constitute our zymotic diseases. But the bacilli have no more settled down into their final quiescence than have men; like ourselves, they are adapting themselves to new conditions and acquiring new powers. The plagues of the Middle Ages, for instance, seem to have been begotten of a strange bacillus engendered under conditions that sanitary science, in spite of its panacea of drainage, still admits are imperfectly understood, and for all we know even now we may be quite unwittingly evolving some new and more terrible plague – a plague that will not

take ten or twenty or thirty per cent, as plagues have done in the past, but the entire hundred.

The moral of Wells's short essay is stated clearly in the conclusion: "man's complacent assumption of the future is too confident." Moreover, "[w]e think, because things have been easy for mankind as a whole for a generation or so, we are going on to perfect comfort and security in the future." Today, twelve decades after Wells wrote this essay – in an age when the mass-harnessing of electricity and atomic energy has let the capricious genie of possible extinction completely out of the bottle – we toggle between two extremes: deep complacency and existential dread, sometimes experiencing both modes at precisely the same time. But, like every Chicken Little on Twitter, who doom-post about this or that crisis in order to increase the possibility of experiencing the dark, faux-inoculating pleasure of being able to boast later, "I told you so," Wells can't help but anticipate his own bitterness at not being heeded in time. (In this case, because the average reader cannot discern the hard scientific facts that lie at the heart of his dizzying futuristic stories.) Wells thus insists, "if some poor story-writing man ventures to figure this sober probability in a tale" – that poor story-writing man being, of course, himself – all the naively jaded cosmopolitan reviewers will queue up to insist that human extinction is "utterly impossible."

Ironic, perhaps – or perhaps simply predictable – that a popular writer would be concerned more about not having his powers of prophecy acknowledged by the public than the fact that his nightmarish prophecy, of the end of our kind, might in fact come true.

Man Has Lived in Vain

Three years after speculating on the termination of our species, H. G. Wells published a short story, "The Star," about a cataclysmic comet. In the opening pages of this story, a prominent London newspaper reports "a planetary collision" observed by concerned astronomers. Soon enough, even the illiterate are well aware of the situation, since the massive meteorite heading for Earth is clearly visible in the daytime, like a second sun. And, in a kind of proto-montage, evoking those quick pans of a global situation in blockbuster movies, Wells writes, "And where science has not reached, men stared and feared, telling one another of the wars and pestilences that are foreshadowed by these fiery signs in the Heavens. Sturdy Boers, dusky Hottentots, Gold Coast Negroes, Frenchmen, Spaniards, Portuguese, stood in the warmth of the sunrise watching the setting of this strange new star."

Indeed, "The Star" now reads as a pulp literary prequel to the big budget disaster spectacles that would regularly populate the Hollywood release cycle from the middle of the twentieth century up to today. (Remembering also that "disaster" literally means "bad star.") Explosion-loving directors, like Roland Emmerich and Michael Bay, have collectively spent billions of dollars – and made back billions more – holding up a shimmering mirror to our own, possibly imminent, demise. The popularity of such scenarios certainly begs the question: why do we take such pleasure in watching cinematic depictions of extinction-event scenarios? Is it because we get to acknowledge various deep-seated or ambient fears, while simultaneously exorcising them in the form of a happy ending for the chosen few? (Among whom we all secretly consider ourselves.) Or is there something less therapeutic and more nihilistic going on? Do we glean some perverse glee in seeing everything we've accomplished, our so-called civilization, washed away in CGI tsunamis or explosions? Does this speak to a repressed guilt concerning our own presumed sovereignty over the Earth, our almost god-like status in our own minds? Moreover, is this auto-apocalyptic scopophilia a sign of the times or an ahistorical human quirk? (For Walter Benjamin, this phenomenon is intimately connected to troubled historical developments, such as media-savvy National Socialism. And, as he noted, in an especially well-known passage, humanity's self-alienation "has reached such a degree that it can experience its own destruction as an aesthetic pleasure of the first order.")

Wells's story is especially interesting for the way that it anticipates the forms of denial, or even indifference, that many feel, even when the prospect of extinction is staring us directly in the face (a motif most recently explored in dispiriting satirical detail by Adam McKay in *Don't Look Up*). "Pretty women, flushed and glittering, heard the news told jestingly between the dances, and feigned an intelligent interest they did not feel. 'Nearer! Indeed. How curious! How very, very clever people must be to find out things like that!'" When the rogue astral body crashes into Neptune, sending both hurtling towards Earth, the gig is clearly up. Nevertheless,

> use and wont still ruled the world, and save for the talk of idle moments and the splendor of the night, nine human beings out of ten were still busy at their common occupations. In all the cities the shops, save one here and there, opened and closed at their proper hours, the doctor and the undertaker plied their trades, the workers gathered in the factories, soldiers drilled, scholars studied, lovers sought one another, thieves lurked and fled, politicians planned their schemes.

As the deep impact looms, the "master mathematician," who has been tracking the disaster since initial detection, announces grimly to his circle, "It would seem, gentlemen, if I may put the thing clearly and briefly, that – Man has lived in vain." Earthquakes swallow up most of the human population, and massive tidal waves mop up many of the rest. But, at the last moment, the fatal star narrowly misses the Earth and heads towards the sun; leaving only a handful of people to do what they can to replenish the species.

As the tale concludes, Wells introduces us to some Martian astronomers, "for there are astronomers on Mars, although they are very different beings from men." Through their alien telescopes, trained on Earth, they had a box seat to witness the last-minute reprieve of their nearest neighbor. And as one such witness wrote in his journal:

> Considering the mass and temperature of the missile that was flung through our solar system into the sun . . . it is astonishing what a little damage the earth, which it missed so narrowly, has sustained. All the familiar continental markings and the masses of the seas remain intact, and indeed the only difference seems to be a shrinkage of the white discoloration (supposed to be frozen water) round either pole.

Wells's narrator cannot resist underlining the moral of the story, which concerns the inverse relationship between stakes and scale, when it comes to something as massive as the universe. So to say, such events reveal just "how small the vastest of human catastrophes may seem, at a distance of a few million miles."

Justine and Claire

"The Earth is evil," announces Justine, in Lars von Trier's film *Melancholia*. She makes this declaration to her sister, Claire, as a deadly rogue planet fills the sky, coming closer and closer each day. "We don't need to grieve for it," she insists, still meaning the Earth. "Nobody will miss it."

"There may be life somewhere else," counters Claire, herself many moons from being reconciled with the impending global apocalypse.

"There isn't," states her sister, flatly.

Claire is not confident enough to continue insisting otherwise, for Justine seems to *know* things, preternaturally. (For instance, the precise amount of beans in a jar.) Indeed, Justine seems to have some kind of cosmic connection with this killer comet, which has been given the strangely poetic name of Melancholia.

"I know things," continues Justine. "And when I say we're alone, we're alone. Life is only on Earth. And not for long."

After attempting various coping mechanisms – including, of course, denial – Claire is forced to face the fact that The End is indeed nigh. Her husband has already committed suicide rather than face the impact head on. So Claire is left with her sister and her son, with no instruction manual for how to prepare when it comes to an actual, imminent apocalypse. Nevertheless, she pleads: "I want us to be together when it happens . . . I want to do this the right way."

Justine, however, is not following the Hollywood script in terms of the proper affective response. She is not interested in "the right way." Having sabotaged her own wedding just a few days earlier, she now seems intent on resisting any kind of pat familial reconciliation before turning into ashes. Indeed, Justine seems to waver between an almost beatific kind of cosmic resignation and an active aversion to the well-meaning – but ultimately empty – gestures of her frightened sibling.

"Beethoven's Ninth?" suggests Justine sarcastically, "something like that? . . . light some candles? . . . gather on the terrace, drink a glass of wine? . . . sing a song?"

Claire nods in a tearful and helpless fashion.

"Do you want to know what I think of your plan?" continues her sister, cruelly. "I think it's a piece of shit." Then, adding for good measure, "Why don't we meet on the toilet?"

Of course, none of us can *really* know how we're going to act, or react, at the end of the world, unless we find ourselves in a situation that feels close to a sudden, extinction event. We may like to *think* we'll be brave, heroic, empathetic – noble. And, indeed, we may surprise ourselves by being so, if and when the moment comes. In the meantime, the end approaches at a pace that is either perceptible yet not pressing, or pressing and not (yet) universal. To paraphrase William Gibson, "the end is already here – it just isn't evenly distributed yet." Moreover, in the modern age, we don't have a secular equivalent of falling on our knees and praying for redemption and divine mercy. And in place of such essential instruction – in place of lessons concerning how to face death without meaning – we instead fall back on the rote and flimsy scenography of an Instagram commercial for some abstract lifestyle product or service. Food, wine, company, music, smiles. But, to quote the Peggy Lee song, "Is that all there is?"

The idea for the film *Melancholia* is said to have come to Lars von Trier during therapy sessions for chronic depression. His analyst told him that "depressive people tend to act more calmly than others under heavy pressure, because they already expect bad things to happen." Indeed, we saw plenty of anecdotal evidence of this during the first few months of Covid-19 lockdowns, as clinically anxious and depressed people tentatively expressed a sense of something resembling relief when the wheels suddenly fell off the whole human comedy. Suddenly everyone was now obliged to live in the same liminal affective space, marked by turmoil and held breath. Surprisingly, the arrival of an actual, objective, collective cataclysm made many people unclench a little. "You see," they said, "we told you so." The charade of treating life like a Pinterest picnic – when it is, in fact, a canvas by Hieronymus Bosch made flesh – had finally been exposed as so much bluff. Calling the angst of existential exposure what it is lifted the burden of trying to pretend that "everything is fine."

Justine certainly leans into her role as angel of death in von Trier's most elegantly understated film. And somehow her history of "episodes" and "scenes" prepares her – more than all the others on the estate – to welcome the end to all life in the universe. Apparently, to her mind, life is a cosmic aberration, which led to the anomalous evil of Earth. And now this mistake was going to be rectified by an astral body named after black bile. With a quiet kind of weary rapture, she stands poised, ready to be metabolized back into blank, inorganic matter.

Facing Fate

Remarkably, Lars von Trier's first listed film was made when he was the precocious age of fourteen, four decades before *Melancholia*. This short film was given a cheeky and unwieldy title that, nevertheless, foreshadowed one of the main preoccupations of his entire career: *Why Try to Escape from Which You Know You Can't Escape from? Because You Are a Coward.*

One can't help but note that there is something especially "white" about the world von Trier chooses to focus on in *Melancholia*. Justine's family is immensely wealthy, and thus – prior to the arrival of the killer comet – her problems could be filed under the general heading of "poor little rich girl." As the narrative unfolds, we are witness to the special kind of especially indignant pain the privileged feel when they are forced to remember the bare and exposed life they share with even the poorest and most "wretched of the earth." In his famous study of the latter, Frantz Fanon included some case studies of "mental disorders" created by colonial wars, such as the French–Algerian war with which he was so intimately acquainted. In such cases, Fanon identifies "the triggering factor" as principally "the bloodthirsty and pitiless atmosphere, the generalization of inhuman practices, and the firm impression that people have of being caught up in a veritable Apocalypse."[3] Up to our current moment in time – that is to say, in *human* time or memory – eschatology has arrived in fits and spurts. Countless cultures, peoples, languages, and ways of being have vanished off the face of the Earth, sometimes because of environmental conditions, sometimes because of war, and mostly because of colonial and/or genocidal conquest. From such a premise, we could say the apocalypse has been with us from the beginning and is merely moving from place to place, or unspooling very slowly. (At least according to our own temporality, since, from the perspective of evolution, human arrival and departure will of course be in the blink of a dusty eye; and even more so from the point of view of geology.)

The wealthy European can only imagine the end of his or her life-world on a cosmic register: either a killer comet, a nuclear war, or a collapse of the social structures due to climate change (within which we can include global pandemics). For those children of the slave trade, however, who are still living in the long shadow of its legacy, the apocalypse has already happened, and the contemporary world calls for post-apocalyptic survival skills. From this perspective, *Melancholia*'s troubled – but cosmically attuned – protagonist,

Justine, can see outside the *Umwelt* of her own privilege by virtue of her own "mental disorder," and is thus better prepared to see it burst.

Jim and Julia

For those who have already lived through the apocalypse, there can be something cleansing about the Last Days. Black Americans, whose ancestors were essentially kidnapped by aliens, have never been fully welcomed into the world of their former enslavers. Indeed, for many, the forms of slavery have simply adapted to the times, from the plantation to the private prison labor program. In a short story published in 1920, "The Comet," W. E. B. Du Bois depicts a New York City euthanized by the deadly gasses of a passing astral visitor. The narrative follows the two sole apparent survivors – a humble black messenger and a young white heiress – as they walk the stricken streets. Jim, the messenger, we learn immediately, never felt a part of the city in any case. "Few ever noticed him save in a way that stung. He was outside the world – 'nothing!'" Julia, the banker's daughter, lived a diametrically opposed life: privileged, validated, assimilated. Today, Du Bois's story evokes the oft-quoted formula that "it is easier to imagine the end of the world than the end of capitalism." Instead, it suggests that "It's easier to imagine the end of the world than the end of racial inequality." (Though both, of course, are intimately entwined.)

When Jim discovers Julia, crying for help outside a window on 72nd Street, they stare at each other across the racial divide, even as the culture which maintained the color line with such diligence now seemed to lie in ruins. Julia is especially jolted: "Of all the sorts of men she had pictured as coming to her rescue she had not dreamed of one like him. Not that he was not human, but he dwelt in a world so far from hers, so infinitely far, that he seldom even entered her thought." Given the situation, however, they work quickly to bridge the social chasm that separates them, as they face each other in a new context – the prospect of a new Edenic imperative nagging at the back of their minds. After all, if they are the only two humans left – as their city-wide search suggests – then it may indeed be incumbent on them to repopulate Earth. Indeed, as Jim and Julia drive through the city, the same taboo thought seems to nag at them: "All nature slept until – until, and quick with the same startling thought, they looked into each other's eyes – he, ashen, and she, crimson, with unspoken thought. To both, the vision of a mighty beauty – of vast, unspoken things, swelled in their souls . . ."

As they continue to pick through the corpse-ridden streets, Julia starts to see Jim as "very human – very near now." Indeed, she admits, "how foolish our human distinctions seem – now."

"Death, the leveler!" he muttered.

"And the revealer," she whispered gently . . .

Soon enough they see themselves, and each other, as archetypal: "primal woman" and "great All-Father of the race to be."

With impeccable timing, however, just as the Black Adam and the White Eve are about to consummate their sacred task, a car horn intervenes. In a ludicrous, but structurally necessary, plot twist, it is revealed that only New York was affected by the deadly comet tail. Indeed, Julia's father has somehow tracked his daughter down and found her just before she made an unforgivable mistake. Not only is Jim denied his Pharaonic moment, but he is instantly returned to his alienated place, through liberal use of the N-word. The final moments of the story are operatic in their overblown unlikelihood, as Jim clutches a tainted cash reward for "rescuing" Julia, just as his own wife finds him as well, sobbing in joy and relief. *Deus ex machina*. The social order is restored after the curtains parted on a more utopian possibility for one fleeting moment.

The reader can't help but wonder, however, if Du Bois would have been tempted to allow Jim and Julia to fulfill their divine mission, had the publishing climate of the day been even remotely tolerant of such a possibility. Or would he still find the lesson of the story to be more resonant, performing its own impotence in the face of the status quo, and the capacity of the latter to overwhelm even the utopian imagination?

Civilization is Back

An extended, and more complex, rendering of Du Bois's post-apocalyptic scenario can be found in Ranald MacDougall's compelling 1959 film *The World, the Flesh, and the Devil*. This story also takes place in the devastated streets of Manhattan; this time, however, they have been emptied due to a global nuclear accident – almost all forms of life extinguished by giant radioactive clouds. All the buildings still stand, and the cars sit abandoned, but there is no sign of organic activity. Not even pigeons. (How the filmmakers managed to make New York appear so utterly devoid of movement save that of the main characters is certainly one of its most remarkable achievements.) For the first third of the narrative, we follow the African-American miner Ralph Burton (Harry Belafonte), who – having survived underground, and ignorant of the terrible accident – begins to come to terms with being, very possibly, the last human alive. He commandeers a fancy car, peoples his equally fancy apartment with mannequins – in lieu of human company – and jerry-rigs a generator, so at night his building is the only honeycomb of light amidst the uncanny hive of a darkened and silent city. All things considered, he is holding up remarkably well.

Nevertheless, the loneliness begins to bite. So much so that – in a fit of frustration, provoked by the implacable smile of one of his store-dummy roommates – Ralph throws the grinning thing out the window, to crash on the road many stories below. This rash act prompts a sudden scream from outside, and Ralph is shocked to learn that another person survived the catastrophe. As it turns out, he has been followed – and spied upon – for several weeks. His cautious stalker turns out to be a young woman named Sarah Crandall (Inger Stevens), who – as in Du Bois's story – is white and (until recently) well-to-do. Sarah quickly admits that, in a brief moment of panic, she presumed that the mannequin – now lying askew and inert in the middle of the street – was Ralph himself. Once the confusion is cleared up, however – and the disorientation of relearning human interaction and conversation begins to fade – Ralph and Sarah set about making some kind of life among the well-preserved ruins.

The different color of their skins, however, complicates matters, even as there is no one else to judge them. Nor is there anyone to coerce them into former protocols of behavior. Nevertheless, Ralph is the very picture of a gentleman and insists Sarah live nearby, for safety, but in a different building, for decorum. (Apparently taking a different apartment in the same building would be too much temptation for the two survivors.) Their conversations are elliptical, always tiptoeing around the giant elephant in the room, since each is acutely aware of the fact that they are essentially living in a concrete New Eden and should probably start thinking about repopulating the Earth. (Moreover, both are healthy and attractive, so neither seems to have any complaints about the human specimen bequeathed to them in this unfortunate situation.) Indeed, the subtext of every idle comment seems to be a tentative testing of the waters in a way that would seem excessive and unnecessary had they both been white, or black.

Eventually, the elephant comes stampeding into the room. Ralph switches from a lifetime of biting his own tongue to giving the young woman a tongue-lashing for recently, and thoughtlessly, using the unfortunate expression (apparently common at the time): "I'm free, white, and twenty-one."

Sarah is pained by Ralph's rather tortured attempts to both acknowledge their differences while also smoothing over them. For her, any taboo around the possibility of an intimate relationship is preposterous in these new circumstances. But, for Ralph, a lifetime of habit, shame, and rage cannot be so easily transcended.

"Ralph," she cries, "what do I say, help me! I know you, you're a fine, decent man, what else is there to know?"

"That world that we came from," he replies, emphatically, "you wouldn't know that. You wouldn't even know me." Indeed, he continues, "Why should the world fall down to prove what I am, when there's nothing wrong with what I am?"

In one especially memorable scene, following this heated exchange, Ralph attempts to move beyond his misgivings and designs the perfect birthday party for Sarah. He forages an elegant evening dress for her, procures a luxurious gift (a diamond necklace), and secures the very best table in one of Manhattan's most exclusive restaurants (the Camel Oasis). He even goes to the trouble of printing a single newspaper to announce the occasion – "Sarah Crandall has birthday. New York City plans huge celebration. Come one, come all. . . . We regret to inform our readers that this is all the news there is." As Ralph juggles all these roles, however – journalist, event planner, chauffeur, maître-d', musician, and waiter – he finds it difficult to step into the role of romantic companion for the evening, despite her well-meaning flirtations.

As Ralph seats the guest of honor – and as Harry Belafonte's own voice croons in the background thanks to a salvaged record-player – Sarah says: "As soon as Mr Burton finishes his number, can you ask him to come sit with me?"

Ralph's face stiffens.

"Mr Burton is not allowed to sit with the customers," he tells the birthday girl.

Indeed, at that charged moment he is both the nuclear survivor within the film *and* the "colored" entertainer Harry Belafonte, who was obliged to carry a complex historical and semiotic burden throughout his life as a successful exception to the rule. Tactlessly reminding Sarah of the racist conventions of the Before-Times is something Ralph seems compelled to do, even as it stings her deeply and sours the occasion he planned so meticulously. Centuries of social asymmetry, it is clear, cannot simply be forgotten. At least, not by the one person present who suffered from that asymmetry.

After this awkward occasion, Ralph and Sarah grow clumsier around each other, even as they begin to fall more deeply in love. We get the sense, however, that things would eventually work themselves out, and this love would triumph, if given the time to flow into its own natural course between the sexes. A fly soon arrives in the ointment, however. Or, rather, two flies. The first comes in the form of a buzzing shortwave radio broadcast from France: one that Ralph picks up during his daily scan of the airwaves. While Ralph doesn't understand the French sentences coming through the speaker, almost buried under sonic clouds of static, he instantly perceives the implications. Thus his initial smile at learning other people survived turns swiftly to a scowl. "People," he mutters to himself, simply. Evidently, Eden is now vulnerable to interlopers. And, as he tells Sarah later that day, in an ominous tone: "civilization is back."

The second fly comes in the form of Benson Thacker (Mel Ferrer), a somewhat older white man who arrives by boat, in bad shape, but who is quickly nursed back to health. Triangular sexual tension wastes no time in asserting itself between them. Ralph steps performatively back from Sarah, deferring – not without observable bitterness – to the epidermal birthright of Benson. Sarah, for her part, is insulted by the Darwinian snarlings between the men and the presumption that she will settle for whomever turns out to be the alpha male. ("Why don't you flip a coin!" she yells, in vexation.) Nevertheless, she is fond of both these contrasting Adamites, despite their timeless posturings, and would seemingly prefer the three of them to get along without the complication of sex, as a friendly *communauté à trois*, than be forced to choose one over the other. And so they all stew in resentment and marinade in a kind of post-social impasse – the phantoms of racism still influencing the intimate possibilities inherent in the situation. Benson, driven almost mad with desire for Sarah's soft white skin, is the first to become animalistic, almost taking her against her will (though in truth, for a few fleeting moments she seems to sincerely encourage his passion). Benson then hands Ralph a loaded gun and gives him both a heads up and a head start, obliging Ralph to essentially fight to the death for the possession rights to this urbane Eve.

The climax of the film follows a shoot-out in the ruined streets of the Financial District. But, in the end, it turns out no one really wants to extinguish one-third of the current population with a single shot. Indeed, in a rare resolution to this age-old story of sexual rivalry, the three survivors link arms and stroll into an uncertain future together – as if the final script were a collaboration between Roger Corman, Tennessee Williams, and Ernst Lubitsch. As such, this is a much more utopian story than Du Bois's "The Comet," since there is hope for not only a more equitable "color-blind" future but even a new multiracial society, based on a founding polyamory. It is still notable, however, that such a provocative happy ending – let's remember this film was made in 1959, before Martin Luther and the civil rights movement hit the front pages – can only occur within the confines of an extreme "state of exception." That being the near-extinction of the entire human race.

Space is the Place

In retrospect, W. E. B. Du Bois could be considered one of the first adherents of "Afrofuturism" – at least if we focus on some of his more speculative or futuristic short stories. Indeed, there is a subterranean history of black Americans who employed science-fictional tropes, scenes, and scenarios in order to work through the profound and ongoing trauma of the Middle Passage – a specific sub-history that is only recently being excavated and assembled into a coherent story. (One that works in a different direction to the traditional search for "roots" and, rather, reaches out to find new pathways to the stars.) Most accounts of Afrofuturism, for instance, rightly acknowledge the eccentric musician Sun Ra as the pioneering crystallization of this technorganic style, which borrowed as much from the iconography of ancient Egypt as it did from ufology and B-movies about alien visitors.

Sun Ra himself never used the term "Afrofuturism" and preferred to talk in terms of "astro-black mythology." While he released over 120 albums of forward-looking space-jazz and soul, Sun Ra is best remembered for the 1974 film *Space is the Place*: a low budget mashup between *The Seventh Seal* and *Superfly*. In this film, Sun Ra plays himself – or, rather, plays the persona that he played in real life so well, and so earnestly – descending to Earth in a Moses-like mission to help fellow black people migrate to a more beautiful planet where they will not be subjected to the evils of racism. (Sun Ra insisted throughout his life that he was visited by aliens as a younger man – an experience that set him on the interplanetary path from which he never wavered – believing, among other things, that he was a messenger from Saturn.)

Sun Ra did not attempt to deny his gift for self-mythologizing. Indeed, this was a central part of his – well – mythos. "Am I real?" he asks some skeptical folks in a youth club in *Space is the Place*. "I'm like you, not real. If you were real, you'd have equal rights ... some status. We're both myths. ... Because that's what black people are. Myths." He goes on to insist on the false discontinuity between past and future, as if already wary of the moniker of "Afrofuturism," by adding: "I'm a present sent to you by your ancestors."

Sun Ra depicts himself as an enigmatic and messianic figure, sent to save people who are "out of tune with the universe," reduced to "a mass of writhing and sweating / melting and flowing mass of protoplasm."[4] Leaning into an estrangement at once racial and terrestrial, he asks, "I roam the cosmos / and I've never seen life of this kind – / do you really call this life?"[5]

His program was not explicitly political, in sharp contrast to much of black discourse at the time, when the Black Panthers were at the height of their influence. Instead, he preached a cosmic musical doctrine, one that would redeem lost souls through some kind of vibrational alchemical teleportation: "I'm glad this is not my planet / I'm so sorry that it is yours / why don't you leave here?"[6] A mass exodus was all the more urgent, since – as one of his collections states in the title – "this planet is doomed." (An assertion that stands, again, in stark contrast to a more political act, like that of Public Enemy, who pointed to the general "fear of a black planet" without seeking to literally abandon the latter.)

Indeed, it is in Sun Ra's poetry – even more so than in film – that we see the depths of his understanding of sad planets and the intensity of his melancholia, whereby the *blackness* of black bile is given a historical-tragic dimension rather than merely a humoral one – "I am the summation of everything black / in the entire universe." He declares, "I must nullify astrology / I must nullify all prophecies," a departure from a human-centered planet into a cosmos in which "the earth is a hole in space."[7]

Sun Ra's science fiction poems lurch between an ecstatic recognition of the restorative powers of interplanetary travel and a bitter reflection on the dark impasse of earthly existence, especially if obliged to navigate that existence while incarnated in a black body. Condemned to the fringes of society for losing the epidermal lottery, Sun Ra dreams of escaping and transcending identity itself, a strangely utopian zero-degree of anthropocentrism.

Sun Ra was nothing if not a visionary explorer: exploring the reaches of musical composition, cultural expression, historical resonance, affective ambivalence, and cosmic aspirations. His legacy is thus a bridge between Afrofuturism and Afropessimism – the latter being a school of thought that tarries consciously against and within the social, even ontological, negativity of blackness: "black is space / the outer darkness / the void direction to the heavens."[8] Unlike Moses – and perhaps closer to Benjamin's terrifying angel of history – Sun Ra arrives in our midst only when it's already too late: "I never visit a planet," he notes, "until there's no hope."

On Gloomth

Melancholia has little time for hope. It prefers to obsessively trace the intimate contours of hopelessness. Melancholia has been twinned with gothic themes and motifs for several centuries, consciously yoked together by writers such as Matthew Lewis, Horace Walpole, Mary Shelley, Charles Baudelaire, Edgar Allan Poe, and many others. Together, melancholia and the gothic evoke a heady and bittersweet flavor of seductive despair. On its own, the "gothic" signals many things: an ancient Germanic people, a medieval artistic genre, a pre-modern architectural style, a musical genre, a morbid sensibility, and a general affinity for all things shadowy and frightful. If we were to move a lens around the globe, like Van Helsing's late Victorian magnifying glass, we would note the way different places generate their own unique form of the gothic – the *terroir* of terror, one might say – such as Southern Gothic or Japanese folk gothic. No matter the geographic flavor, however, all such instances are connected by a taste for the macabre, the belated, the unsettling, and the damned.

The emergence of a "goth" subculture in the late 1970s, which crystallized around the music scene of the same name, borrowed its infamous maximalist aesthetic from the gloomiest of romantic poets and artists and the haunted characters depicted in their books or paintings. Strange, then, that – given their passion for all things black – most goths spent much of their time whitening already pale skin with even paler make-up (according to a style once called "necrophilic chic"). As a cultural critic and "purveyor of gloomth," Leila Taylor has noted, in her excellent book *Darkly*, goths love all things black. Except, that is, when it comes to skin. For there is a deeply Eurocentric sense of selfhood at the heart of its iconography: white bodies menaced, or tempted, by black forces.

Taylor – an African-American woman who grew up in the goth scene of 1990s Detroit – is especially attuned to this contradiction (or, rather, disavowal) at the heart of the subcultural code. Black people, she realized at the time, were not necessarily welcomed into the clubs and covens of middle-American alternative youth, since they were presumed to have no organic connection to "the gothic" sensibility (read: European; read: melanin-bereft). And yet, what could be more gothic than an actual black person, from a lineage that has had direct and long-lasting experience with horror and violent death? As Taylor notes, quoting an online phrase popularized by the illustrator Bianca Xunise, she was *so* goth that she "was born black."

What some might call the "Afro-gothic" today has a very different overall look and feel to Afrofuturism, although there is certainly some overlap in the Venn diagram. (An overlap captured by the imagery associated with Brooklyn's

"Afropunk" music festival.) Black goths in the 2020s may indeed take as much inspiration from *Black Panther* or *Blade* than from *Dracula* or The Cure. And, as with all youth movements today, things can fractalize into micro-niche scenes very quickly. (Themselves policed with the endless energy associated with "the narcissism of minor differences.") In short – and in tune with Taylor's book – there is something *especially* gothic about the black American experience, which taps into the infinite reservoir of sadness and despair created by centuries of slavery.

Taylor presents a simple formula for the gothic: melancholy + terror + the uncanny. And, according to this equation, we would be hard-pressed to find a more gothic song than Billie Holiday's version of "Strange Fruit," a chilling lament about the shockingly prosaic experience of lynching. Nor would we find a more gothic tale than Toni Morrison's *Beloved*, a wrenching story about an escaped slave woman who kills her own child rather than have her newborn dragged back onto the plantation. In contrast to the redemptive, or reparative, qualities of Afrofuturism, the black gothic "stays with the trouble" and "tarries with the negative" of the Middle Passage and its aftermath, even as it slowly works through the open wound of America's founding horror. Taylor's book offers the contemporary singer M Lamar as the self-stylized embodiment of a black gothic sensibility: a "NEGROGOTHIC devil-worshiping free black man in the blues tradition." Where Sun Ra sings of spaceships and aliens, M Lamar – a queer, histrionic figure with a fondness for "funeral doom spirituals" – sings of sadomasochism and zombies. And while it may have taken four decades or so for young "goths" to begin accepting black people as legitimate members of their overwhelmingly pale clan, figures such as M Lamar – as well as his fans of color – serve to remind us that the descendants of the enslaved have a much stronger claim when it comes to assembling identity around sorrow. Indeed, the tension for many white goths may have been an unspoken, and perhaps even unconscious, resistance to acknowledging sadness as something more than an individual affliction. The black goth can be an unwelcome reminder that the personal is political, and that sorrow can be collective, and historical. (Even as it is this extremely ambivalent semiotic burden – of being asked to represent that history while usually just wanting to dance like a vampire like everyone else – that *Darkly* describes so well.)

Just as there is a taboo against being black and angry (as President Obama clearly understood), there is also a taboo against being black and (visibly) sad. Taylor notes: "Blackness is often used as a metaphor for any number of social ills: poverty, crime, violence, drug use, promiscuity, broken families, ignorance," and so on. This helps explain why the sadness of the absinthe-addled Byronian romantic, the jaded Parisian *flâneur*, or even the wasted young mall goth, is a privilege that most black people do not get to exhibit or inhabit. (At least, not without compounded consequences.) Melancholy, on the whole, is the privilege of those with a melanin deficit (and, thus, less to be melancholic about). Black people are consistently reminded – by their own kin as much as hostile strangers – that they are not allowed to wallow in negative feelings. Weakness or fragility, as enacted by a subgroup of the enfranchised – such as the Romantics or the decadents – can be a kind of artistic critique of the status quo. Established members of the dominant order don't love it, but they will tolerate it when performed by an easily dismissed minority in the shadows. But weakness or fragility, as enacted by the dispossessed and marginalized, is a double-baked sin. The people in power don't want to be reminded of the historical violence underlying their position; nor do they want to be confronted with its palpable effects (especially when these manifest as *affects*). To self-reflexively perform melancholia, as a black person, as M Lamar does, is to break this taboo of showing the emotional impact of "structural racism": a rather technical term describing a violence that has been stretched out across the generations for so long that it has solidified into social infrastructure. "Owning" or "leaning into" sorrow – beyond that now neutralized form of expression known as "the blues" – politicizes affect beyond the mere feelings of an individual and taps into the experience of an entire people.

To be both black and melancholic – that is to say, to be Afro-gothic – is to consciously render oneself as a medium in the Victorian sense, channeling the unquiet voices of one's ancestors and actively encouraging "the return of the repressed" (itself a key gothic trope, as both Freud and Poe understood).

As Taylor again notes, "to be Black is to *be* the fear, to be the thing that goes bump in the night hiding under the bed." Indeed, "it is one thing to use literature and film to process social anxieties, but what do you do when *you* are the social anxiety? What do you do when the villagers with torches and pitchforks are coming after you?"

Extreme Weather

Armadillo Caravan

Just as great "caravans" of refugees have been increasing in the last few years, welling up from South and Central America in search of more merciful conditions up north, some native animals also seemed to take their chances by relocating to the United States. In the fall of 2021, a swarm of armadillos began making their way to higher latitudes, driven to this unprecedented migration pattern due to climate change. As one news outlet reported: "The armadillos give off a sort of loamy grey color at night." By November, these unusual creatures had reached North Carolina, creating problems for locals who preferred their manicured lawns unmolested by landscaping mammals. The analogy to refugees from Latin America could not be more obvious, as armed militia were soon called in to deal with the "situation." "It's like hunting aliens," noted one animal bounty hunter, who – as the reporter noted – was more used to hunting feral pigs. "We know nothing about them. We can't seem to kill them easily. They show up unexpectedly. And their numbers have just exploded." One may wonder if such bounty hunters see these new interlopers in the same light as the families looking for a better life in the so-called land of opportunity. "There's no malice on my part," noted one. "And there's no malice on the animal's part . . . They aren't doing anything wrong, they are just trying to eat and survive. But they are causing damage, so we have to remove them."

Sequence 5

Last Life

A Lump of Death, a Chaos of Hard Clay

In the winter of 1816, Lord Byron – adventurer, aristocrat, and paragon of British Romanticism – published the short poem "Darkness" in his collection *The Prisoner of Chillon and Other Poems*. In language infused with apocalyptic imagery, the poem describes an inexplicable darkness that covers the Earth and the eventual extinction of humanity that follows in its wake.

> The bright sun was extinguish'd, and the stars
> Did wander darkling in the eternal space,
> Rayless, and pathless, and the icy earth
> Swung blind and blackening in the moonless air;[1]

In the ominous darkening of the planet, a diffuse panic sets in among its human inhabitants, and everything is set ablaze in order to provide some light: watchtowers, houses, ships, forests, entire villages and cities:

> some lay down
> And hid their eyes and wept; and some did rest
> Their chins upon their clenched hands, and smil'd;
> And others hurried to and fro, and fed
> Their funeral piles with fuel, and look'd up
> With mad disquietude on the dull sky,
> The pall of a past world;[2]

But the fires die out, and the inevitable cooling of the embers reveal a different image of the planet, a planet soon pervaded by an all-encompassing stillness, infused with the silence of extinction. Humanity, now cut off from the sun, the moon, and the solar system, descends into the fanaticism of fevered prayer, sleepless vigils, and the slow preparation for extinction. "The world was void," the poem announces. "A lump of Death – a chaos of hard clay."[3]

By his own account, Byron wrote "Darkness" in June of 1816, while sailing with Percy Shelley on Lake Geneva. Dark clouds seemed inexplicably to cover the summer skies of Southern Europe, causing a dramatic drop in temperatures, which in turn affected agriculture, leading to food shortages and in some cases famine. Torrential rains, flooding, and freezing were reported in Northern Europe as well as in North America. Extreme weather, the dismantling of infrastructure, the migrations of people. The darkness that spread across the northern hemisphere in 1816, known as the "Year Without a Summer," was due to the volcanic eruption of Mount Tambora on the island of Sumbawa in Indonesia, then the Dutch East Indies. A series of eruptions had occurred a year earlier, by some estimates the most destructive volcanic eruption in recorded human history. The events not only devastated Southeast Asia, but the drifting clouds of dense smoke and ash would have downstream effects that would be felt halfway across the planet for years to come.

But for most of those who experienced the summer darkness of 1816, the cause was unknown. There seemed no other way to comprehend it but via a strange mixture of biblical prophecy and naturalist cataloging. It prompted Byron to write about the planet not as the harmonious provenance of Enlightened humanity but as something at once cold and indifferent to the hopes and despairs of the busy, industrious human beings on its surface. The Year Without a Summer seemed to prompt Byron to think about a different kind of death – not the death of the individual but the extinction of the species.

Byron's poem also identifies an enigma. Who is the last human being that will bear witness to the end of all human beings? What is the "last life" that will comprehend the end of all life? The condensed, apocalyptic imagery of human extinction provided in "Darkness" has since led it to be described as part of a long literary tradition of the "Last Man." A seemingly unexplained extreme weather and/or climate event, an imminent end of humanity, a last human being – usually male, usually a scientist, but no longer a hero – now burdened with the apprehension (but not the comprehension) of human extinction. Following Byron, numerous such poems were written (many of them quite literally titled "The Last Man"). But, before him, in 1805 the French author Jean-Baptiste Cousin de Grainville had published *L'Homme dernier*, a strange work of speculative apocalypticism that also features its share of extreme climate events, and which also prompted its own share of like-minded tales. That tales were often titled "the last man" is not without its own significance, as if the ill-fated male protagonist who witnesses the end might also stand in for a whole legacy of mastery and control vis-à-vis the planet, now having reached its limits, with nothing else to devour except the human species itself.

Perhaps it is with this in mind that Mary Shelley published her epic novel *The Last Man* in 1826 – just a few years following the deaths of both Percy Shelley and Byron – which includes everything from plague to war to the titular enigma of a solitary human being burdened with the awareness of being "the last." As the century wore on, further stories of the type were to be found in speculative and science fiction, from M. P. Shiel's *The Purple Cloud* to W. E. B. Du Bois's "The Comet," to Richard Matheson's *I Am Legend*. By the post-war period, the motif had become a mainstay, particularly in science fiction. Post-war films such as *On the Beach* (adapted from a novel by Neville Shute), *The Last Man on Earth* (an adaptation of *I Am Legend*), and *The Word, the Flesh, and the Devil* all feature the now standard scenes of solitary human figures wandering across the abandoned infrastructure of silent cities, scenes that can be seen in late twentieth-century films, from *The Quiet Earth* to *Children of Men*. The famous *Twilight Zone* episode "Where is Everybody?" encapsulated the diffuse, harrowing panic of human solitude (later to be parodied in the equally memorable *Portlandia* skit "Why is Everybody Here?"). Extinction has since become farce more than tragedy.

In spite of this – or because of it – there remains an undercurrent of foreboding that courses through the "last man" motif. For all its gothic flourishes, Byron's "Darkness" is not only an elegy to the species, but it also highlights the growing estrangement between human beings and the planet on which they live, a dysphoria within the species of a humanity which is forced to recognize that the planet will simply go on without them, "after the end." Byron's poem identifies a new kind of sadness, the strange melancholic affect of a planet devoid of people, something that by definition cannot be experienced by us as human beings, but which we index only negatively through the most furtive thoughts: someday, all of us – all of this – will be gone. A sorrow specific to extinction. We are already extinct. The planet will remain, unpeopled, with only the faintest traces of an elegiac Earth.

Catastrophism (I)

Extinction is, admittedly, never an uplifting topic of discussion; the data that point to the certitude – the eventual certitude – of the extinction of terrestrial humans can feel like a false form of solace, a consolation prize for the inability of instrumental humanity to prevent or otherwise put off extinction. The effect is, perhaps, like the false assurance of knowing the exact date and time of one's death. The knowledge is at once useless but also that to which we cling most dearly. Little surprise, then, that the language surrounding global climate change has become decidedly more angst-ridden (the talk of "existential threats," "ecological grief," and "climate anxiety").

From a different perspective, the fact and even the regularity of extinction events should come as no surprise, especially given the Earth's approximate age of 4.5 billion years. To even talk of extinction "events" is a misnomer that sheds light on how removed extinction is as something that we limited, time-bound human beings can experience. The "fifth mass extinction," which by some estimates occurred around 65 million years ago, is thought to have been the result of a cataclysmic meteor shower near the present-day Gulf of Mexico. Our cinematic imagination brings to mind the suddenness of the event, as meandering and unreflective beasts briefly look up to blazing skies – and, in a flash, it's all gone. But the fifth mass extinction "event" is actually estimated to have taken over 2 million years from start to finish. This is a flash from the perspective of the Earth, though, from our on-demand and streaming consciousness of lived time, it seems not like extinction at all. This is, perhaps, why propositions from the scientific community that we are currently in a "sixth mass extinction" are too often dismissed. It doesn't look like *The Day After Tomorrow*. Or does it? Recent years have given us no shortage of amateur footage which, though it may lack the budgets of blockbusters, does indeed look like extinction: tsunamis, floods, wildfires, mass migrations, a global pandemic, and, yes, even meteor showers. Extinction seems to be right here, at our doorstep. It looks like a scene from one of those movies. And strangely, because of this, it also seems unreal.

We've created the categories, leveraged them in different ways, mobilized them to allow us to grasp the enigmatic relationship between self and world. We've not only applied the categories to the outer boundaries of what separates one species from another, but we've also applied them internally, to demarcate finer and finer distinctions. The categories proliferate, at once constructed and yet inescapably effective, oftentimes traumatically effective. What counts as "human." The transatlantic slave trade, bolstered both by racial science and the harrowing presumption that there is no human civilization that is not built on the blood of a slave population designated as less than human or not human at all. Species become endangered and then they become extinct. The porousness and relativity of the categories belies their devastating effects, above all safeguarding the most central of categories, what counts as "human" itself. External boundaries between human and less than human have legitimized everything from livestock breeding, to genetic monocrops, to the darker corners of the trafficking of exotic animals for sport or for show. It's possible that extinction has become a game of logic, a chess match of taxonomy, extinction as engineered, extinction as both the fulfillment and the failure of anthropocentrism. If we are to accept the hypotheses regarding the Anthropocene, it could even be said that the pinnacle of human technological innovation is human extinction. A species that is extinct the moment it emerges.

Catastrophism (II)

It's worth noting that, in the history of science in the West, theories of extinction seem to have been developed earlier than theories of speciation. While Darwin's *The Origin of Species* (1859) has for many become the text that set the terms of the debate, it was preceded by equally relevant discussions about extinction, and not just speciation. The first move was to suggest that extinction occurred at all, a notion that ran counter to earlier notions of divine providence and the great chain of being. But the existence of fossils provided a challenge to this. A strange by-product of an earlier era of amateur science, the eighteenth-century fondness for collecting fossils seemed to exist alongside colonial science endeavors beyond Europe. Jean Léopold Nicolas Frédéric (Georges), Baron Cuvier, a naturalist and zoologist, was among such fossil enthusiasts. Part of Cuvier's fascination lay in fossils whose structure bore no resemblance to any existing species on the planet. By the end of the eighteenth century, Cuvier could argue that such fossils must be remnants of extinct species. From there it was a short step to conclude that what has happened to species in the past might also happen to species in the present, including the human species. His *Essay on the Theory of the Earth* (1813) attempted to make such a point. Astronomy had already expanded human-based notions of space and the place of human beings within the vast cosmos. Could the same be done for time, and the relative position of the human species, "to ascertain the history of this world, and the succession of events which preceded the birth of the human race?"[4] Cuvier goes on to analogize the ebb and flow of species with the rise and fall of human civilizations:

> If it be so interesting to us to follow, in the infancy of our species, the almost obliterated traces of extinct nations, why should it not also be so, to search, amid the darkness of the infancy of the Earth, for the traces of revolutions which have taken place anterior to the existence of all nations?[5]

Suddenly zoological relics of a bygone era took on a kind of urgency, serving almost as an omen of things to come. There is some irony in the fact that, by the time Darwin published his findings on the origin of species, a discussion had already been taking place about its end. Perhaps there is a dual meaning to *The Descent of Man*, one of speciation and another of extinction, one of origins and another of ends, one of progress and another of decline, a progress of a different sort.

But for Cuvier and his colleagues there were too many unanswered questions regarding extinction, central among them how extinction occurs. Does it happen all at once or gradually? Is it the result of external or internal factors? Is it due to an abnormality in the species or is extinction simply what species do? For his part, Cuvier proposed that cataclysmic environmental factors could contribute to the sudden decimation of a species ill-equipped to deal with such changes (a position soon dubbed "catastrophism"). He was countered by a host of others, including his French colleagues Lamarck and Geoffroy Saint-Hilaire and by the English geologists James Hutton and Charles Lyell. They argued for a view of extinction as a long and gradual process, one which takes place within a larger framework of uniform natural laws of the Earth (known as "gradualism" or "uniformitarianism"). While they disagreed on the "how," both camps agreed on the "what" of extinction, and in particular that both speciation and extinction needed to account for the role of the planet, the environment, climate, and other terrestrial factors. In a sense, Darwinian evolution had forgotten about the planet, or at least conceived of it as the backdrop against which interspecies competition takes place. But earlier debates over extinction seem to return again and again to this insight, that extinction is inseparable from the planet itself, even and especially when the species becomes strangely enmeshed in and yet estranged from the planet – as is arguably the case when it comes to human extinction. It is likely that contemporary discussions over "climate events" and "extreme weather" have made Cuvier and his interlocutors our contemporaries.

Now lost to the annals of the history of science, the ensuing debates that took place between "catastrophists" and "gradualists" sparked a whole host of questions about decline, decay, and degeneration that would reach far beyond the cloistered discussions of nineteenth-century biology or geology. In a sense, the difference between catastrophism and gradualism is relative, a matter of scale or point of view. If not just individual life but collective life could be said to be subject to the natural laws of decay and decline, what does this say about the stability or instability of social groups, let alone the rise and fall of entire civilizations? With the *fin de siècle* approaching, the idea of extinction seemed to exit the halls of academia and become a cultural phenomenon. In the 1890s, the German physician and social critic Max Nordau published *Degeneration*, a massive 600-page tome bewailing the deleterious impact of nineteenth-century art, poetry, and music, producing a "degenerate culture" that was contributing to the decline of the human species. Early science-fiction tales by Flammarion, Verne, and Wells told of the cataclysmic end of the world by comets and meteors. The sun was dying out, the whole universe was in decline, while the industrial skies of many cities were blackened by new forms of machine labor. In less than a century, the same fossils that had prompted speculation about human extinction would fuel another blackening, a labyrinth of pipelines criss-crossing war-torn landscapes, the Earth transformed into a fossil mine, the bones of extinct species reincarnated through technologies at once hyper-modern and primordial.

Last Life

In late November of 2022, a spokesperson from the United Nations announced that a baby had recently been born which officially made the tally of the planet's human population at 8 billion people.[6] As expected, "Baby 8 Billion," as the newborn came to be known, prompted a wide range of responses both from news outlets and on social media, from celebrations of human resilience to anxiety-ridden doomsday scenarios. While, as experts tell us, population growth may be due to longer life-spans rather than high birth rates, the symbolic ambivalence surrounding the 8 billionth human raises a host of almost absurd questions. Who is the 8 billionth person, who are their parents, and what did they feel on hearing the news that their child may be the tipping point between population growth and diminishing resources? What diffuse, even existential feelings of guilt might the 8 billionth person grow up with as they become aware of shifting climates and the looming possibility of human extinction? Would they ever feel that singular and furtive sense of the "indictment of being born," as E. M. Cioran once put it? Or might they even feel a different kind of sorrow – that they were, in effect, the point at which the human population began its slow and inexorable downward progress, the last human, at once the apex and the decline of humanity?

In a sense, the news of the 8 billionth child points to the obvious, even cliché lesson, which is that we are all the 8 billionth child. Perhaps it is this fuzziness between scales that makes extinction such a troubling topic. Extinction is, in a way, the shadow side of speciation. The analogy is often made between extinction and death. In the same way that the birth of the individual organism also signals its inevitable death, so does the emergence of a species also imply its eventual extinction. But the extinction of a species isn't exactly the same as the death of an organism; the latter is implied in the former, but not vice versa. Unless, of course, there are those instances in which the death of an organism is also the extinction of a species, an instance which would require a "last life" or the last remaining living member of a species. While there is a bittersweet tragedy in imagining the last polar bear, old and wizened, gazing off into the rapidly receding glaciers with a profound look of sorrow in its eyes as it passes into non-existence, the reality of extinction is likely more complex, and more complicated. The very idea of a species is, after all, the product of human knowledge production. We can't confirm that animals have a notion of "species," though they may be able to recognize their own kind, and it's doubtful that the polar bears are perusing biology textbooks or taxonomic databases to further comprehend their own predicament.

The idea of a final, solitary human being who would bear witness to the end of humanity is, of course, a fantasy. Be it catastrophic or gradual, extinction may not so easily fit into anthropocentric narrative structures, let alone the human range of affects and emotions. Yet the idea of the "last life," the life that somehow bears witness to the end of life, has a certain valence, especially when it comes to the stories we tell ourselves about extinction. A conundrum emerges. Extinction is empirical, yet not of the order of experience. We may have experiences of our mortality, but this is highly individualized, even as we may collectively struggle to accept mortality in general. My life, my death. Even when death is scaled up to the level of groups of human beings, this too is individuated. War, genocide, epidemic disease, and other factors all scale up individual death in the political economy of mortality. Groups are named, identified, accounted for, and enumerated, while others remain, others who bear witness, grieve, make meaning. We as human beings may mourn the loss of another species, but who will mourn the loss of human beings? A funeral at which there will be no attendees (except, perhaps, for the happenstance witness of the trees, the insects, the indifferent sky). Barring the possibility – an increasingly plausible one – of an AI historian which may or may not be capable of grief, it appears that human extinction is unique in that there is no other life to stand apart from it and express sorrow at its passing. (This presumes that human extinction is an occasion for sorrow.)

The idea of the "last life" is an indicator of a unique kind of sorrow, yet another turn to the seemingly inexhaustible aspect of human exceptionalism. So far as we know, it is only we human beings that are capable of grieving for the extinction of other species, an affective possibility that is made possible by the scientific framework of the "species" idea itself. The remaining animals, insects, trees, mountains, and the planet will simply go on, perhaps as if nothing had happened. We are then left with the more conciliatory prospect of having to grieve for the extinction of human beings before it actually happens, by speculatively projecting ourselves ahead in time and then looking back through our familiar rituals of mourning. Grieving, mourning, and expressions of sorrow of the species itself require us to put the species at a distance, to momentarily detach ourselves so that we can feel for ourselves. The result is that the criterion of grieving human extinction is that of effectively transforming human beings into another species, to regard the extinction of humanity as no different from the extinction of another species of animal or plant. The human species can only be grieved by regarding it as non-human. Perhaps this strange speculative exercise in funerary mourning produces a range of affects which lie at the anthropocentric limit of the human capacity to feel. This is the allegory of the "last life" when it appears in speculative fiction. It is less some kind of cautionary tale than an attempt to comprehend the impossibility of experiencing human extinction.

A Dissipative Species

Extinction as a scientific phenomenon is fully explainable via the perspectives of biology, geology, ecology, genetics, and paleontology. It can be documented as a past event and, because of this, it can also be modeled as a possible future event. Hypotheses, theories, and laws can be articulated. And yet, there is also something inexplicable about extinction, particularly when it comes to human extinction. It seems somehow easier to accept the reality of extinction when it happens to other species, as if the human species inhabited a kind of floating observational bubble immune to the various planetary contingencies that determine it.

This is one of the central insights of the 1977 novel *Dissipatio H.G.*, written by the Italian author Guido Morselli. The novel's unnamed narrator, in the throes of a personal crisis, decides to walk up to a mountain cave to commit suicide. But, at the crucial moment, he changes his mind. The next morning he emerges, only to find that everyone else has disappeared without a trace. Only the people are gone; the houses, buildings, cars, trains, and entire cities remain, now emptied and eerily desolate. There has been no nuclear war, no global pandemic, not even thunderbolts from vengeful gods. There is no explanation for "the Event," except the glaring absence, the deafening silence – only the inexplicableness of extinction:

> I remember, and try to understand. The Inexplicable is not the unknown, not the attractive mystery (attractive because it's good enough to stay a decent distance away from us?). No, the Inexplicable is something else, something that when it is overwhelming and persistent saps a person's life energy. My response to the absurd was physical, animal, natural; unable to wish it away, I perceived it as an immediate, overwhelming act of aggression, and froze. It was an atavistic response; a helpless beast does the same thing, freezes.[7]

In the loneliness of a world without people, the narrator turns to writing, keeping a journal, keeping himself company, accompanying his thoughts with digressions, diversions, and the minutiae of a new kind of quotidianism. Writing – what the narrator calls "a useful tautology" – becomes the process through which loneliness is transformed into a species-level solitude. But the solitude that is discovered, and cultivated, is one that continually returns to the stubborn, inexplicable quality of human extinction. *That* it has happened is undeniable. *How* it happened is a mystery, and, the more it remains a mystery, the "how" recedes into a dense fog of speculation. In its place, a new anxiety emerges. *Why* did it happen? A question both gloomily ruminative and laughably absurd. Why did humanity become extinct? And what was the point of it all, if this is the inevitable result?

The narrator of *Dissipatio H.G.* is the "last life," the last of a species burdened with accounting for its own extinction and yet unable to make any sense of it all. All previous categories dissolve – self and other, individual and collective, self and world – as language itself folds back on itself in a solipsistic disarray, captured in the narrator's sardonic humor:

> Here concludes the external report on the Event, and the internal one opens. But you won't find me indulging in personal confessions because by now my personal story is history, the history of Mankind. I'm now Mankind, I'm Society (with the capital M and the capital S). I wouldn't be exaggerating if I spoke of myself in the third person: "Mankind said this, did that." Because as of June 2, the third person and any other person, grammatical or existential, has necessarily been my person. There is no longer anything but the I, and the I is no one but me. I am the I.[8]

Burdened by what *The Anatomy of Melancholy* once termed "the sorrow of too much thinking," the narrator of *Dissipatio H.G.* finds himself in the awkward position of thinking the extinction of thought itself, and the more he ruminates on the enigma of extinction, the more his thoughts disintegrate and dissipate, the more thinking itself becomes akin to a slow process of erosion or decay, as if that last sigh of humanity – its ideas – were also destined to end in ruins.

> One of the pranks played by anthropocentrism is to suggest that the end of our species will bring about the death of animal and vegetable nature, the end of the earth itself. The fall of the heavens. There is no eschatology that doesn't assume man's permanence is necessary to the permanence of everything else. It's accepted that things might have begun before us; unthinkable that they could ever end after us.[9]

Human extinction is an affront to the pinnacle of human consciousness, an offense to human self-awareness. In a kind of perversion of the Copernican revolution, it is the very achievement of our knowledge about extinction that also makes it seem so incredulous that it should happen to us, a species-specific presumptuousness encapsulated in one of Nietzsche's miniature fables: "The ant in the forest perhaps imagines just as strongly that it is the goal and purpose for the existence of the forest as we do, when we in our imagination tie the downfall of humanity almost involuntarily to the downfall of the earth."[10] The species that is able to conceptualize its own extinction also recoils at the unavoidable conclusion that it has, in a sense, guaranteed its own extinction as well.

A novel without a plot, character, or, for that matter, dialogue, *Dissipatio H.G.* borrows from the "last man" tradition, but it also inverts it in many ways. Earlier literary examples, such as Grainville's *L'Homme dernier* or Mary Shelley's *The Last Man*, bring humanity to the brink of extinction, only to reveal that the end is just the beginning, as Apocalypse converts into Genesis. Modern variants (*I Am Legend, Earth Abides*) adopt more secular approaches, leading humanity to the brink of extinction, only to reveal the tenacious human capacity for survival. When Morselli wrote his novel in the 1970s, postmodern self-reflexivity and cynicism had eclipsed the comparatively angst-ridden existentialism of the "last man" tale. In a sense Morselli's novel asks us why we as human beings feel so compelled to narrate to ourselves the end of humanity. *Dissipatio H.G.* documents a dysphoria within the relationship between a world-forming species and the world itself that at once encompasses it, but which always seems at a remove from us.

At the core of *Dissipatio H.G.* is the idea that human exceptionalism and human extinction co-exist in an uneasy, co-dependent relationship to each other, an unstable orbit of complementary yet mutually exclusive terms that resonate with each other only at that enigmatic point where the end of the human perfectly eclipses the end of the world. *Dissipatio H.G.* poses a different, perhaps more harrowing question than that of survival: it asks whether the lasting significance of human extinction is in fact its meaninglessness. The compulsion to narrate human extinction would then be less a heroic act of redemption and more a desacralized lament, a cynical elegy, a dirge for the absurd. "Eschatology: who today, in this world of computers and supersonic planes, knows anything about that archaic and abstruse science?"[11]

Morselli wrote *Dissipatio H.G.* in 1973. When he finished it, he sent the manuscript off to two publishers, Einaudi and Mondadori, and went on a short vacation. Both publishers rejected the novel. Shortly afterwards, Morselli shot himself (perhaps with the same pistol depicted in *Dissipatio H.G.*, where the narrator plans a similar suicide). The stark enigma of Morselli's suicide has prompted many to read *Dissipatio H.G.* not only as a work of speculative fiction but as an extended suicide note – and a suicide note not only for an individual but, perhaps, for the rest of us as well.

An Outbreak of Life

When Daniel Defoe published *Robinson Crusoe* in 1719, it was preceded by a long tradition of travel writing, much of it linked to various European colonial expansion projects, aided and abetted by developments in natural science, global trade, and cartography. It was also influenced by actual accounts of shipwrecks and castaways. Combining aspects of travelog, diary, and confessional, *Robinson Crusoe* appears to readers today as indelibly modern, even postmodern, in its self-reflexive experimentation with genre. While critics today cite it as one of the first novels in English, this belies the explicit ways in which Defoe uses the journal and diary formats to give his tale a non-fictional, documentary realism. In a way, *Robinson Crusoe* is "genre-adverse" writing before the term.

And yet, this documentary approach is constantly undermined by the almost definitional unreliability of the single human perspective. What makes *Robinson Crusoe* fascinating as a book is that, once Crusoe is stranded on his remote South American "Island of Despair," his account becomes the only account. There are no other such journals, no historical records, no log of events from visiting ships, nothing except the "last man" recounting – to himself – a life held in the shadow of forced solitude, a life at once imprisoned and completely free. If ever there was an unreliable narrator, it is the castaway. This is also part of what motivates Crusoe's impulse to document his life on the island; as if the bare activity of survival were not enough, as if the task of living on required the ratification of the literary for it to have been real. "Life itself" is insufficient. Filled with doubts, assaulted by struggles, and weighed down by uncertainties, "life itself" demands an accounting, an evaluation, an almost moral recapitulation in the more consoling contours of narrative form.

This is fine, as it stands. Except that, as we read through Crusoe's journal, what we find is not only the fascinating minutiae of everyday survival – the construction of his fort, the assembling of his outfit, the domestication of the goats, etc. – but the incredible precariousness of his moods. On one occasion, the fortification of his cabin produces a self-congratulatory euphoria. On another occasion, a momentary glance at the infinite night sky produces a brooding sense of insignificance. Though much of Crusoe's journal is dedicated to a straightforward recounting of the facts of survival, there are equally passages that reveal deeper forces at work beneath the strangely non-speculative task of survival. The poles of this struggle are providence and despair, as Crusoe describes after washing ashore:

> I had a dismal Prospect of my Condition, for as I was not cast away upon that Island without being driven, as is said, by a violent Storm quite out of the Course of our intended Voyage . . . I had great Reason to consider it as a Determination of Heaven, that in this desolate Place, and in this desolate Manner I should end my Life; the Tears would run plentifully down my Face when I made these Reflections, and sometimes I would expostulate with my self, Why Providence should thus compleatly ruine its Creatures, and render them so absolutely miserable, so without Help abandon'd, so entirely

> depress'd, that it could hardly be rational to be thankful for such a Life.[12]

The sense that there is a grand design, set against the sense that terrestrial, earthly life is utterly without purpose. The sense of the divine provenance of human beings and the furtive suspicion of a godless planet, indifferent to human hopes and fears. Crusoe's struggle is not just religious, or even existential. It is ambivalently rooted in the environment around him, the landscape and terrain, the flora and fauna, the weather, the sea, the sky. A wager is made out of this despair. Either my being abandoned here on this island is part of the grand plan of divine providence, or there is no plan and human life is as random and insignificant as the sand on the beach, the fireflies at night, the stars in the sky. Either I will master this island or it will master me.

Faced with such a crisis, Crusoe reacts to his despair by establishing human dominion over the island. Fortifications, farming, hunting; the island becomes reframed as a resource for a single and sovereign human being. He transforms the deserted island into an inhabited one, though of course "deserted island" simply means "without people." In the process, Crusoe's diary tenuously shifts from despair to something different, a shift from denial to a kind of resignation, a shift from the religious horror of being totally abandoned to the consolation of a conciliatory life lived simply, in solitude, in struggle:

> The rainy Season of the Autumnal Equinox was now come, and I kept the 30th of Sept. in the same solemn Manner as before, being the Anniversary of my Landing on the Island, having now been there two Years, and no more Prospect of being deliver'd, than the first Day I came there. I spent the whole Day in humble and thankful Acknowledgments of the many wonderful Mercies which my Solitary Condition was attended with, and without which it might have been infinitely more miserable. I gave humble and hearty Thanks that God had been pleas'd to discover to me, even that it was

> possible I might be more happy in this Solitary Condition, than I should have been in a Liberty of Society, and in all the Pleasures of the World.[13]

While this may seem unduly optimistic to some ("it could have been worse . . ."), it signals a shift in mood that correlates to Crusoe's survivalist dominion over the island. Gradually the unruly chaos of the island is transformed into something more recognizable, more bearing the indelible mark of the human. Slowly it becomes "his" island. Crusoe's despair has been transformed into a strange humility born of dominion, the gratitude of despair transformed into providence, via the human capacity for world-forming:

> It was now that I began sensibly to feel how much more happy this Life I now led was, with all its miserable Circumstances, than the wicked, cursed, abominable Life I led all the past Part of my Days; and now I chang'd both my Sorrows and my Joys; my very Desires alter'd, my Affections chang'd their Gusts, and my Delights were perfectly new, from what they were at my first Coming, or indeed for the two Years past.[14]

Perhaps I'm okay with this. Perhaps this is my lot. Perhaps this is even better than what I had left behind. When Crusoe finally leaves his island, he finds his mood has crossed the spectrum of affects, from despair to gratitude, from abandonment to consolation, from religious horror to renewed faith – above all, faith in the anthropomorphic capacities of the "last man":

> And now I saw how easy it was for the Providence of God to make the most miserable Condition Mankind could be in worse. Now I look'd back upon my desolate solitary Island, as the most pleasant Place in the World, and all the Happiness my Heart could wish for, was to be but there again.[15]

But at this moment, the moment when Crusoe leaves the island and returns to "civilization," a new despair flickers just below the surface. It was hard on the island, but at least he didn't have to deal with other people. The final pages that detail Crusoe's utter alienation from human society reveal something unexpected, and even more harrowing. In spite of his attempts to establish human dominion on the island, Crusoe finds that, at the same time, he has become something other than human. He returns to find himself either less than or more than human (or perhaps both). A dual dysphoria results. He cannot endure the deserted island, but neither can he withstand human society. He struggles against the non-human environment of the island, but at the same time he seems at once inundated and repulsed by the human world he is suddenly thrown back into. Crusoe's diary traces an affective arc, from one kind of despair to another kind of despair, from the despair of being cast out of humanity to the despair of being thrown back into it.

Just a few years after *Robinson Crusoe*, Defoe would publish *A Journal of the Plague Year*, another difficult to categorize book that similarly utilized real-world events portrayed via a documentary style (in this case, the 1665 Great Plague of London). Though it does not take place on a deserted island, *A Journal of the Plague Year* similarly grapples with the abandonment of humanity, the religious horror of a humanity forlorn, as an inexplicable epidemic ravages both individual bodies and the body politic. Defoe includes accounts of mass graves, night vigils, death tables, abandoned city streets, dismantling infrastructure, an eerily quiet Earth. It's as if the epidemic transforms the city itself into a deserted island.

The Toil of Sorrow

Extinction, and in particular human extinction, presents us with a dilemma. The idea of a solitary, last human being burdened with the existential accounting for all of humanity is, of course, more a fable than a reality. In all likelihood human extinction will simply happen as it has for other species, taking place with a kind of indifferent certitude. Human extinction adds to this the shadowy reminder that, in a way, it's we human beings that have invented it all: the terminology, the definitions, the hypotheses and theories, the statistical tallying, down to the word "extinction" itself. The will to narrate this seems at once impossible and necessary, and yet this may also be part of what it is to be human: that the relatively short-lived experiment called humanity would not have been for naught. Be it catastrophically (when there will be no time to brood on such existential puzzles) or be it gradually (happening so slowly we will forget it's happening, or simply tire of the whole affair), human extinction seems at once inevitable and implausible, unavoidable and unacceptable.

It is in this gray zone that a different kind of "last man" story takes place, exemplified by the 1962 book *The Wall* (*Die Wand*), written by Austrian novelist Marlen Haushofer. An unnamed woman goes to the Austrian countryside to vacation with friends in their rustic woodland cabin. One afternoon, her friends take a drive into town, leaving their dog (named Lynx) with the woman. They never return. The next morning, the woman, along with Lynx, go to town to find them, but not far from the cabin she discovers a vast, transparent, indestructible "wall" surrounding a large part of the land, akin to a gigantic bell jar whose circumference is impossible to detect. The summer morning is quiet, except for the faint sounds of birds; the air is fresh and breathable, a breeze passes through the surrounding trees, flecks of sunlight briefly illuminate the stillness of the mountain rock and neighboring stream. But there are no people. Or so it seems. On the other side of the wall, the woman can see an abandoned vehicle. In the distance she makes out the neighbor's cabin. The old man and his wife are there, but they are completely still, petrified in an eerie immobility.

Like Morselli's *Dissipatio H.G.*, *The Wall* begins from the premise that human extinction has something inexplicable about it – after it has happened. While other stories may build up to this event, *The Wall* begins with it. The novel recounts in slow and patient detail the struggle of the woman to live on, after the event, within the strangely transparent confines of the wall. That struggle is, of course, existential. She struggles not only against the apparent inexplicability of the wall but, more importantly, against the acceptance of that inexplicability. She struggles against the question of suicide, against a previous life now forever lost, against a life that was determined by the future, future plans, future hopes and anxieties – a mortality of another order. Against these abstract questions, concrete answers are provided. There is Lynx, the dog, with whom she has now formed a bond. During a rainstorm, a stray cat makes itself known. One afternoon a cow gently approaches from a nearby field. Soon, a calf is miraculously born. A white crow periodically appears in the tree out front. These animals are not pets in the usual sense, and neither does the woman become their owner. The animals never become human, but neither does their human companion simply revert to some animal state. A strange companionship develops, as if the cohabitation with the animals signals a kind of shared suffering, a struggle for which obtuse philosophical discussions seem superfluous. Not only is the "last man" in this case a woman, but her being human is gradually eclipsed by an interspecies mode of living that is difficult to name and makes the age-old division between human and animal superfluous.

More than anything, the woman in *The Wall* struggles with a deceptively simple question: how to pass time. Or, rather, what time means, after extinction. There is still mortality and the awareness of one's own death, but that awareness is no longer projected into the linear time of human prospects and future plans. She exists in a strange non-time, for which clocks and calendars have become meaningless, like so many relics of human-made world:

> . . . if time exists only in my head, and I'm the last human being, it will end with my death. The thought cheers me. I may be in a position to murder time. The big net will tear and fall, with its sad contents, into oblivion. I'm owed some gratitude, but no one after my death will know I murdered time. Really these thoughts are quite meaningless. Things happen, and, like millions of people before me, I look for a meaning in

> them, because my vanity will not allow me to admit that the whole meaning of an event lies in the event itself.[16]

A pervasive melancholy courses through her account, as if something irretrievable has been lost. But there is also little leisure time for ennui, as the exigencies of survival immediately make themselves known. Though a modern urbanite, she must now learn how to grow food, how to maintain the cabin, how to navigate the often forbidding terrain and severe weather, how to care for herself, how to live with and care for the animals. How to pass the time.

An atmosphere of menace pervades *The Wall*. The task of using a scythe to gather wheat becomes an all-consuming saga in itself. What we moderns glibly refer to as the "everyday" quickly becomes the stuff of existential struggle, shorn of all the accoutrements of self-absorbed subjectivities. To call it work, or labor, is already to ennoble it with human virtues. There is only a kind of toil, the toil of the most basic "apprehension of a doing," as William James once called it, a "bare activity" in which "the sense of activity is synonymous with life."[17] Above all, it is the toil of living on, interspersed here and there with ephemeral reminders of the vast and impersonal quality of the planet around her: the view from the hilltop, mountains rising in the distance; the night sky in late summer; torrential storms; muted winter. This is no *Walden*-esque paradise; she has not chosen to forsake humanity and remove herself from the company of human beings. Her solitude has been imposed on her; the distinction between death and suicide has collapsed, where a nascent sorrow emerges, the sorrow of living on. This is the condition of the "last life" and the quandary of human extinction.

The Wall not only begins with extinction, it also places it in the past. As we read, we immediately realize the novel itself is the journal kept by the woman, now attempting to recall the string of events that has led her to this point. Writing becomes the final vestige of the human. Extinction remains a memory, but a memory of something inexplicable; it is history, but a history without humanity. As the ink in her last pens dry out, the woman is aware of a looming apprehension, a subterranean epiphany that haunts the entire novel. What will she become, after language? If she is no longer human, then what will she be? An alterity that perhaps cannot be named. Neither reduced to the animal nor elevated to the human – the very distinction has become meaningless. And if she is already no longer human?

> . . . we're condemned to chase after a meaning that cannot exist. I don't know whether I will ever come to terms with that knowledge. It's difficult to shake off an ancient, deep-rooted megalomania. I pity animals, and I pity people, because they're thrown into this life without being consulted. Maybe people are more deserving of pity, because they have just enough intelligence to resist the natural course of things. It has made them wicked and desperate, and not very lovable. All the same, life could have been lived differently.[18]

In many ways novels such as *The Wall* are the antithesis of *Robinson Crusoe*, the book that sets the modern paradigm for human survival. Like Crusoe, the woman in *The Wall* is a castaway, though a castaway of a different sort. Like Crusoe, she must also contend with the practical reality of her forced solitude. Questions abound amid the uncertainty, and the questions that are theological for Crusoe (exemplified by his many meditations on divine providence) are existential questions for the woman in *The Wall*. But *The Wall* differs in one crucial way. Robinson Crusoe adopts an attitude of dominion: the island quickly becomes "his island," the existing plants and animals there for his use, the "last life" of the singular human being becomes the only life, or at least the only life that matters. He builds a fortress, hangs a flag, hunts and traps, establishes watch posts, maps the island. Crusoe staves off the despair of being the "last life" by attempting to replicate the human world around him, the unpopulated island transformed into a mirror of the human. Crusoe's struggle recapitulates human exceptionalism in a microcosm, human provenance as divinely ordained. Crusoe's island becomes an allegory for an inverted Earth, where extinction eclipses evolution. In *Robinson Crusoe*, anthropocentrism overlaps perfectly with geocentrism.

The Wall is not exactly a retort to *Robinson Crusoe*, and the life that the unnamed woman leads in the novel is in no way meant as some romanticized counter-example. She too establishes a home, harvests crops, hunts, gives names to the animals with whom she shares a life. Instead, *The Wall* does something different. It maintains, and even leans into, the deep ambivalence regarding the presence of human life on the planet. The woman in *The Wall* finds herself continually in a fraught dialogue with the landscape, the weather, the planet itself. It's as if her attempts to maintain herself and control her environment are always shadowed by the dim intuition that there is a "something else" behind it all, a something else that inexplicably impels everything to exist, to live, to live on – but without the anthropocentric comforts of meaning, purpose, goals. There is a sense of what Schopenhauer described as the "blind Will-to-Live" that impels everything that is alive to simply live on, without purpose, without goal, without meaning. This is why *The Wall* is, from beginning to end, a novel saturated with a sense of melancholic toil, that point where sorrow and the toil of living seep into each other. The elemental contingencies of rain, snow, heat, and earth push the woman to the brink, where the only option left open to her is to give herself over in a kind of terrestrial self-abnegation. This is the inverse of the dominion established in *Robinson Crusoe*. She must slow down to the rhythms of the seasons, to the non-time of mountain, river, forest, slow to the mineral patience of tectonic shifts.

Concrete Islands

The premise of *Robinson Crusoe* – the archetypal image of the castaway on a deserted island – is at once terrifying and alluring. No doubt part of the appeal of eighteenth-century travel narratives prior to the publication of Defoe's novel was the idea of escape, not only from the overly familiar strife of one's humdrum surroundings but to some other place, another world, a world that is not simply another city or another culture, but another world that perhaps harbors within itself a secret alternative to being human itself.

The dream of a world without people. Except, of course, for Crusoe himself. While Crusoe does not seek out his island, the compulsion for adventure that leads him to it – by chance or by fate – reveals an allegory about the seemingly insatiable human craving for expansion that is, at the same time, an ambivalent craving for the non-human, for a world that bears no relation to our own. Sometimes, there is a brief moment when that world seems possible. Crusoe on a shipwrecked beach. A hovering moment when quiet waters, distant birds, swaying trees, and the terror of the infinite blue horizon make themselves felt. There is only me. Anxiety. Elation. The floor drops out. But, like many Robinsonade narratives, it is only a moment. Fear. Survival. Fortification. Dominion. The bulk of *Robinson Crusoe* is concerned with the practicality of survival, punctuated here and there with stray thoughts on providence, fate, and chance. The mountain becomes a fortress, a field becomes a farm, the jungle hunting terrain, the beach a beacon. A world vanishes as quickly as it appeared.

What modern variants on the Robinsonade have made obvious is that this other world need not literally be "out there" at the farthest reaches of the planet. It can inhabit the world right here, a world that has become so commonplace so as to seem unnoticeable, innocuous, invisible. This is one of the lessons of the idiosyncratic Taiwanese film *The Hole* (1998), directed by Tsai Ming-liang. The story takes place during a near future pandemic of mysterious origin, which, as we learn from news reports, has the strange effect of turning those infected into roach-like creatures, hiding from the light, cowering in the myriad dark and damp crevices offered by the city's concrete mega-structures. The film itself, however, is an exercise in restraint and catharsis, as we follow two nameless characters – a man and a woman – who live in a massive, impersonal, high-rise apartment building. There is almost no dialogue and little action, as the apartment complex becomes more and more abandoned, more and more dilapidated, and in the background a constant torrential downpour. A sense of loneliness layered on alienation. One is a castaway right here in the city, bunkered into built structures that seem to inexorably collapse at the slightest tremor. This is no adrenaline-fueled, zombie apocalypse, survivalist blockbuster. Instead, everything in and around the concrete city seems to be in a state of perpetual decline, an almost real-time erosion of infrastructure, a patient withering of a human world.

But this is just half of the film. Juxtaposed to these scenes of collapse are musical numbers: sudden, glorious intrusions of melody, dance, and color in which the same man and woman perform lip-synched versions of songs by 1950s pop idol Grace Chang. What's more, the musical numbers are themselves performed at various spots in the same, drab apartment complex – a Ballardian musical on a concrete island. This back and forth continues for the entire film, and we are never quite sure if the musical scenes reflect the character's inner, emotional states or if they exist elsewhere, in some kind of spectral, parallel universe in which all problems are magically resolved through song. An elevator door closes, revealing the oppressed loneliness of the woman on her way home amid a strange pandemic. The elevator door opens, and a song begins, the woman beaming, singing in costume, as an efflorescence of refracted, dazzling light pours out, the dilapidated lobby somehow transformed into a love-stricken cosmos.

And then the song is over. The man, having nothing else to do, continues to go to his grocery stall at a nearby market, even though there are no customers (with the memorable exception of an old man, who confusedly asks for a particular brand of black bean sauce, which is out of stock – resigned, the old man wanders off). Eventually we learn that the two separate characters are in fact neighbors, the man upstairs and the woman downstairs. On one occasion the man comes home to find a hole has been cut into the concrete floor of his apartment, revealing crumbling bits of concrete and exposed pipe. We assume this had been done by a plumber in order to fix a leak; however, why the hole has been left there is a mystery, and there is no sign of the plumber or indeed anyone in the building. While the man and woman go about their business, the hole creates a strange and awkward symbiotic link between them. When one of them succumbs to the "roach virus" the other makes a simple gesture of help.

While *The Hole* as a film is an experiment in genre, it is also an experiment in mood, as the sudden isolation, not on a remote island but in the heart of the city, reveals an island of a different sort. The subtle but ominous presence of the apartment complex itself, at once impervious to the niceties of human drama and yet perpetually falling apart, a concrete island which seems to engulf its inhabitants in the sheer excess of infrastructure, its forest-like labyrinths of narrow walkways and corridors, the hazy vistas of humidity and rain, the background chatter of an abandoned TV in the distance.

In more recent work, Tsai has pared down his aesthetic even more, as in his "Walker" series of short films. Each features the actor Lee Kang-sheng (who also plays the man in *The Hole*) dressed in a crimson-colored monk's robe, his shaved head bowed, walking very, very, very slowly. Inspired by the travels of the seventh-century Buddhist monk Xuanzang, the "Walker" films are barely films at all; there are no sets, production crews, or special effects – just Lee Kang-sheng walking very slowly through various cities (Hong Kong, Kuching, Marseilles, Taipei, Tokyo). The effect is mesmerizing; slow motion revealed in real time. While some people stop to give the "Walker" strange looks, mostly people go about their busy day, as do the innumerable cars, buses, bicycles and even the pigeons that populate a city. The slowness, perhaps, of twilight. The Walker is so slow he is almost invisible – unless, of course, you slow yourself down to observe him (or, perhaps, to follow in his steps).

Solitude of the Species

In 2017, the British government set up a commission to address growing concerns over the effects of loneliness on individuals. Established by the MP Jo Cox, the "Commission on Loneliness" not only advocated publicly addressing loneliness as an issue with political, personal, and public health consequences, but it also opened up a broader discussion of the relationships between loneliness, social isolation, and various forms of social and cultural dysphoria. The report also established the office of a "Minister of Loneliness," who would oversee funding, research, and outreach initiatives. Around the same time, US Surgeon General Vivek Murthy spoke of a "loneliness epidemic" that had been growing in spite of – or because of – the increased dependency on social media and other communications technologies. Significantly, in addition to stressing the importance of social interaction for both personal and public health, Murthy highlighted the importance of cultivating solitude as a counter-weight to loneliness. Similar government-based loneliness initiatives have emerged in Japan and Brazil as well.

While the boundary between loneliness and solitude remains a topic of discussion (in addition to the question of whether loneliness is "contagious"), nowhere was the loneliness epidemic felt more than during the lockdown period of the Covid-19 pandemic. The allegorical and the literal pandemic folded onto each other, as an actual pandemic fueled an already existing "loneliness epidemic" that was itself transformed by the reliance on social media and the like. It became more and more difficult to identify that point where loneliness was transformed into solitude, or where solitude disintegrated into loneliness. And, on top of it all, there was a sense of a big "we" experiencing this loneliness, a perhaps novel form of loneliness, as if loneliness had continued to be experienced by individuals but was now also a species-level phenomenon.

Narratives of extinction are unique in that they involve an involuntary solitude. The titular figures of "last man" stories – be they men or women (or machines) – almost never welcome their solitude, though they come to terms with it and, in doing so, come to a certain understanding of human extinction as an existential and planetary phenomenon. It is perhaps strange, then, that we should encounter innumerable examples of human beings who not only welcome such solitude but who seek it out, refusing human society and at the same time distilling themselves into miniature allegories of human extinction. Prior to the ascetic withdrawal described in Thoreau's *Walden*, the Japanese Buddhist monk Kamo no Chōmei similarly withdrew from society, living in a modest hut, ten foot square, near the Kamo River in Kyoto Prefecture, where he lived until his death in 1216. *Hōjōki* is his written account of his time there living as a recluse in the forests far from the turbulent melodrama of the capital city. The self-imposed exile allowed Chōmei to appreciate the impermanence of all things, principally the seemingly insatiable human endeavor to recast the world in anthropocentric terms. As he notes, it is this extraction of one's self from the human world that allows a glimpse into another world, one that reveals the impersonal forces so often associated with the natural world in classical Japanese prose and poetry. This sense of impermanence, captured in the Japanese term *mujō*, sets the frenetic activity of human toil against the vast backdrop of the cycles of the planet, the climate, the seasons.

Neither Thoreau nor Chōmei were the only writers to create their own extinction scenarios. Arguably, the strange will to make oneself into the "last life" inhabits ascetic traditions around the world. There is the Ch'an Buddhist monk Bodhidharma, who, sometime in the late fifth or early sixth century, spent eight years in a mountain cave deep in central China, facing the wall in meditation. There are scores of poets from China's Tang dynasty, many former state officials or bureaucrats who chose the cold and forbidding life of a recluse in the mountains along the Yangtze River. There, in spite of their daily struggles, they discover the strange enchantment of the impersonal sky, the majestic indifference of the mountains, the enigma of mists and clouds forever detached from the minutiae of human worries. A whole tradition of "mountains and rivers" (*shan shui*) poetry develops from this, including some of China's most celebrated poets: Li Bai, Tu Fu, Wang Wei. The deepest echoes of this impulse may be attested to in the Vedic and even pre-Vedic literature of India, where we find records here and there of ancient ascetics often referred to as *śramaṇa*, often found deep in uninhabited forests, undertaking various austerities, shearing away the veneer of human attachment to a world as ephemeral and illusory as our attachments themselves.

Different as they are, there is a sense in which ascetic traditions establish the foundations for narratives of human extinction. They redefine extinction as a renunciation of the human-centric point of view while at the same time remaining rooted in the non-human landscape of mountain, forest, sky, and earth. Perhaps the mystical aspects of these varied ascetic traditions are less about some kind of spiritual transcendence and more about the difficult confrontation with an unhuman earth, with the indifference of what we condescend to call "nature" towards the ongoing human insatiability for world-forming. An inverse terraforming, un-earthing the Earth.

The Inner Desert

One of the most well-documented ascetic traditions is that of the groups of solitaries living in the deserts of third- and fourth-century Egypt. Fed up with self-aggrandizing culturalism, petty politics, and intensive commercialism, these early Christian practitioners chose to leave the dense, urban center of Alexandria for the deserted landscapes in the Thebaid, inhabiting the pockmarked cave formations that line the Nile River. Antony, the best known of them, provided the paradigm for scores of others to follow. His student and biographer Athanasius tells us that, sometime around 270, Antony heard a sermon quoting Jesus' admonition to "give what you have to the poor, and you will have treasures in heaven, then come and follow me." A revelation followed. Antony not only took this quite literally – he gave away all his possessions and abdicated all social responsibilities – but he also understood the passage as an invitation to undertake a further abdication to abandon his entire life, which meant leaving the city.

What follows is a series of "lifestyle choices" in which Antony finds himself moving further and further away from human society. Eventually he enters the desert, where he finds shelter in a mountain cave that many historians see as the precursor to the monastic cell. In the desert, he encounters a whole host of difficulties – the so-called temptations of St Antony that have been depicted in art so many times, from Hieronymus Bosch to Salvador Dalí. The insights he gains from these struggles form the basis of a new outlook regarding the role of human beings on the planet. A new humility is born in the vast and impersonal distances of a wasteland. But it also plants the seeds of its own failure. It turns out that many individuals feel the same disenchantment, the same dysphoria. They also wander into the desert. The numbers of hermits living in the desert increases. A diverse range of monastic and eremitic practices follow. Practices are codified. Institutions are created. Biographies are published. There are followers, pilgrims, tourists; something is trending. There are even reports of temporary markets set up nearby rows of hermit's caves, dotting the mountainside like a rough-hewn condo tower. As Athanasius notes, "soon the desert became a city."[19] It was likely this transformation of tragedy into farce that finally led Antony to move deeper into the Thebaid, into what Athanasius cryptically refers to as the "Inner Desert."

For Antony, as for the so-called Desert Fathers and Desert Mothers that follow in his wake, the desert becomes a site of contestation, fraught with an ambivalent wisdom, a landscape criss-crossed by both epiphany and doubt. This is perhaps why certain landscapes have long held a fascination for ascetic traditions worldwide: the forests of Vedic India, the mountains of classical China, the deserts of ancient Egypt. As different as these traditions are, there seems to be something about the voluntary immersion into these decidedly unhuman landscapes that suddenly recasts the intensive, solipsistic world of human affairs in a new light. The intensive, human world revealed as simply a momentary flare-up on an extensive, unhuman planet.

If this is the case, it's also possible that our modern notions of human extinction and the "last man" story have a much longer tradition behind them. The desert solitaries of early Christianity refuse the world of human affairs for a direct experience of the divine, an encounter that, they believe, can take place only in an environment bereft of all human life. By contrast, Robinson Crusoe, the castaway on the island, is not exactly a solitary in the desert. But the deserted island offers him a similar dilemma. Crusoe's response is at once religious and secular: to refuse the human world only to recast it anew on the island, a kind of *tabula rasa* for an already failed humanity.

By the time we arrive at Thoreau's cabin, the desertion of human society comes to have a different meaning, preceded a generation earlier by William Wordsworth's *The Prelude* as well as by Dorothy Wordsworth's *Grasmere Journals*. The desire to become one with "nature," an impulse that courses through Thoreau's *Walden*, where the sense of communing with nature is made possible via a whole host of techniques and technologies, from the supply chain that delivers goods to the paper and pencil that recasts the experience in writing. The compulsion to abandon the cities that house humanity seems to be as omnipresent in our contemporary homesteaders as it was in fourth-century Alexandria. By the time we arrive at late twentieth-century variations – such as Haushofer's *The Wall* or Morselli's *Dissipatio H.G.* – the ambivalent desire to abandon the human is coupled with a suspicion regarding the entitlement that drives human provenance. But now it is without the religious – and redemptive – framework that makes the struggles of the early ascetics meaningful. Renunciation without purpose, refusal without meaning. We are, it seems, back in the desert.

The planet is that which remains after extinction. A forbidding terrain, a landscape hostile to humanity, stray words of wisdom from desert dwellers that are themselves attached to the terrain, eventually disappearing into it. For Antony the desert is neither a place of refuge nor a romantic retreat; there is no nostalgic "getting back to nature," and there is no romanticism of "being in nature," that irrepressible panacea of twenty-first-century global dysphoria. To say that Antony went into the desert is even a bit of a misnomer. True, the vast regions that lay southward of Alexandria were "deserts" in the way we typically think of deserts. Heat, sand, craggy rock formations, the quiet quivering of a lizard, the distant call of a bird overhead. The desert is where life – and specifically human life – is not welcome. The desert is a place that was never hospitable to human life to begin with, or it is a place that has been abandoned by human life. In this sense, the desert is also that which is *deserted*. The planet seems to respond in kind. Perhaps we human beings are that which has been deserted by the planet.

Wind and Sand and Wasteland

An entomologist heads out to a remote coastal area in order to collect specimens. He is studying how certain insects are able to survive in the desolate terrain of shifting winds and sandy dunes. In one of these forays, he happens upon a small village. Or, rather, he happens upon the apparent absence of a village. What first appears to him are a series of sandy dunes, rising above the horizon here and there with massive oval apertures, sinking deep into the earth. In each are dilapidated human shacks – to call them "houses" seems too elevated. Large, wooden ladders stick out of the apertures. Hunched, drab, craggy human shapes – are they old, or simply weatherworn? – come and go, carrying out various duties, seeming to ignore their intrepid visitor. One of them, a suspicious old man, briefly invites the entomologist to stay at their "inn." He accepts, drawn as much by the strange behavior of the people as by the prospects for his scientific research. He descends the ladder, where a woman greets him, showing him his room, offering him a meal. She mentions, in a casual way, the eroding effects of the wind-blown sand on their village. It seeps into the crevices of wood and straw and clay pots and the kerosene lamps; it pours in invisibly, bit by bit, eventually forming an avalanche that threatens to bury everything beneath its gravity. Each day she, like her neighbors, must clear away the sand, shoveling it into buckets, which are then poured out. With a melancholic smile of resignation, she is well aware that she is simply moving the sand around, that the sand never goes away, that all their labors are at best temporary and transient. Strangely moved by the methodical quiet of her work, the scientist offers to help her, taking up a shovel. During the days he wanders around the dunes, carrying out his entomological research. By night he stays with the woman, shoveling sand that just as quickly flows back into their hovel. Eventually a rhythm forms. Anxiety gives way to fascination, and this gives way to a strange tranquility. The entomologist soon cannot recall how long he has been staying in the dunes. Soon he ceases wondering even this.

The theme of the human being engulfed by its environment is at the center of Kōbō Abe's 1962 novel *Woman in the Dunes*. Wind and sand are everywhere in the novel, seeping into the very cracks and fissures of their own anatomies. The sand itself becomes a near obsession for the entomologist, who at one point notes that it is the constant and formless movement of the sand that makes it so inhospitable for us lumbering and sedentary humans. This, combined with the desert shore climate, produced the conditions for a slow and patient erosion of every fixed thing. The vitalism of the shifting sands was also a process of constant disintegration:

> Because winds and water currents flow over the land, the formation of sand is unavoidable. As long as the winds blew, the rivers flowed, and the seas stirred, sand would be born grain by grain from the earth, and like a living being it would creep everywhere. The sands never rested. Gently but surely they invaded and destroyed the surface of the earth.[20]

Less a novel in the traditional sense, *Woman in the Dunes* is more an extended allegory, where climate, affect, and terrain are really the central characters. The ambience of wind and sand is woven into the human characters in vast, impersonal shifts, something effectively portrayed in Hiroshi

Teshigahara's 1964 film adaptation. The enigma of the landscape, which at once draws in and yet threatens to engulf, also looks ahead to the equally enigmatic desert planet Arrakis in Frank Herbert's epic science-fiction classic *Dune* (published just three years after *Woman in the Dunes*). Human beings find themselves constantly at odds with the desert terrain, unsure of when they are controlling it or when it is controlling them. Abe's novel also puts us back in the long tradition of desert solitaries in fourth-century Egypt. The "sayings" of the men and women of this tradition return again and again to a single theme, that of the desert, both literal and figurative. Antony, the most well-known of the desert hermits: "As fish must return to the sea, so must we return to our cell."[21] Moses, a hermit from Ethiopia: "Go back to your cell, and your cell will teach you everything."[22] The Egyptian monk Ammonas: "Go and sit in your cell, and think to yourself that you have been in your grave a year already."[23] The phrase "desert hermit" is itself redundant, for the term *eremos* (*ἔρημος*) denotes both "hermit" and "desert." The term *eremos* does have more descriptive, even geological meanings to it. But it also denotes something like a wasteland, a terrain that is devoid of life, and in particular human life, a place without people. This implies that a desert is more than just heat, wind, and sand and an aspect of the planet that is inhospitable to human life, but towards which human beings seem continually drawn.

Its visual correlate is not only there in the numerous depictions of Antony's desert "temptations," it's also there in modern works such as *40 Days Dans Le Desert 'B'*, the singular graphic novel by Jean Giraud (aka Moebius). Without dialogue or plot, strange figures inhabit an unnamed desert out of time, where they participate in opaque rituals, rituals that reveal the vast and impersonal – and perhaps "mystical" – aspects of the desert itself, in hallucinatory images that evoke the long tradition of the temptations of St Antony in deserts of Egypt. In these and other examples, the wisdom of the desert is both the interior search for meaning and the exterior encounter with a landscape devoid of people, a humbling confrontation with an alien terrain for which the temporary occupation of human beings on its surface is a flicker in planetary deep time. The desert terrain is a reminder that, in both a secular and spiritual sense, the Earth is not human. These and other lessons are encapsulated by Matrona, the fifth-century Greek abbess of a desert monastery: "Many solitaries living in the desert have been lost because they lived like people in the world."[24] To be in the world, but not of it. A planet mined, extracted, harvested, excavated. The counter-movement of a terrain that patiently erodes the tenuous life forms on its surface, willingly or unwillingly submitting themselves to its deep time until they are eventually engulfed by the Earth.

Dreaming of the End

In the spring of 1878, near the end of his life, Turgenev wrote a short prose piece titled "The End of the World: A Dream" (it would be included in the 1882 collection *Poems in Prose*, though apparently he planned to title the book *Senilia*). The setting is simple and sparse. A woodland country house. A small group is inside the house, including the narrator and a boy. "They walk up and down in silence, as it were stealthily. They avoid one another, and yet are continually looking anxiously at one another."[25] It's not clear if they live there, if they are visiting, or if they have been forced there against their will. Here and there, cold light from outside catches the "uneasiness and despondency" on their faces. In the eerie quiet, "all in turn approach the windows and look about intently as though expecting something from without."[26] The boy makes an appeal to his father, telling him he is afraid. The fear is contagious. "I too begin to be afraid . . . of what? I don't know myself. Only I feel, there is coming nearer and nearer a great, great calamity."[27] The skies shift dark, the dead air hovers in immobility. At one of the windows, the boy suddenly cries out, "the earth has fallen away!" The others look, and see that the house seems to be hovering in an abyss – no skyline, no horizon, no point of reference to indicate any direction, only a "scooped-out, black precipice." In the distance, hills and mountains begin to rise and fall, undulating like a massive ocean, and a "continuous, monstrous wave embraces the whole circle of the horizon."[28] Fear is eclipsed by a kind of frozen despair: "the crash of thunder, the iron wail of thousands of throats . . . the earth howling for terror." And then, "scarcely breathing," Turgenev writes, "I awoke."[29]

This stark parable on human extinction bears some resemblance to one of Turgenev's earliest works, a novella from 1850 titled *Diary of a Superfluous Man*. There, Turgenev utilizes the diary form to give us insight into a character haunted by an unspecified terminal illness, forced to come to terms with his relatively short and uneventful life. Though it has moments of redemption, the novella ends in darker hues, suggesting that what certain death reveals is the irrepressible sense of being superfluous. One of the last diary entries reads, "In becoming annihilated, I shall cease to be superfluous . . ."[30] Turgenev's novella has since become emblematic of a whole sub-genre of nineteenth-century Russian literature, which often features characters who intentionally or unintentionally fail to live up to their potentials, weighed down, instead, by a pervasive existential tedium, burdened with a cynicism born of an impassive world.

The "superfluous man" is not limited to the confines of nineteenth-century Russian literature; arguably, it stretches back to *Don Quixote* and the many fools (wise and not so wise) that populate world literature. It also looks ahead to the figure of the modern, urban, anti-intellectual "idiotism" found in so many of Kafka's tales, as well as in Mela Hartwig's *Am I a Redundant Human Being?* (1931), Eugène Ionesco's *The Hermit* (1973), and Félix de Azúa's *Diary of a Humiliated Man* (1987). In its variegated guises, it is the superfluousness of the human being that seems to haunt the very awareness of being human. The human being is "extra," useless, unwanted, and not only by other people or normative society but, perhaps, by the planet itself.

For his part, Dostoevsky would write his own "superfluous man" story, titled "The Dream of a Ridiculous Man," published in his *Writer's Diary* in 1877. Dostoevsky's protagonist begins by questioning the point of human existence, bringing him to the point of suicide. The unbearable weight of the absurd, the revolver on the table, and a long night. But then – and it's not clear if he has shot himself or if he's simply fallen asleep from boredom – the story suddenly becomes an extended dream vision, as shadowy figures take the "ridiculous man" on a cosmic journey to other stars, revealing in the distance a humble green-and-blue speck uncannily similar to Earth. He is then shown everything that the Earth is not – a paradise of harmonious co-existence between human beings and the planet on which they live. The dream vision induces a euphoria in the ridiculous man, who, upon waking, pushes away the revolver, his faith in humanity renewed. For now.

Not so with Turgenev. There is a sense in which Turgenev's *Diary of a Superfluous Man* and "The End of the World" are actually two sides of the same page. Both are clear that something is about to end. In this sense there is little narrative drama, for we know how it ends before we begin reading. The death of an individual, the extinction of a species.

And, in between, tedium, as expressed in the works of Yi Sang, writing in the context of Japanese-occupied Korea as it entered a new century. "Yi Sang" (a phrase that literally translates as "strange") was the pen name of Kim Hae-gyeong, the author often credited with introducing modernist and avant-garde ideas into Korean literature. Many of his stories feature characters perennially at odds with the world – listless, wayward figures who just don't seem to get what it means to be busied with human concerns, duties, desires, and aspirations.

In one story – a diary titled "Ennui" – an alienated city-dweller (perhaps Yi Sang himself) heads out to the country, encountering a vast field on the outskirts of a village. But the lush green of the country seems as wan and gray as the labyrinthine concrete of the city: "What is the world trying to do being so green? The color green does nothing all day. Like an imbecile, the green is so content with being green that it remains simply green."[31] In the city, the dream of lush green fields; in the green fields, the same tedium as the city. Near the cypress trees, withering in the heat, pools of stagnant water. "I am sitting near such a puddle. The water rots quietly before me."[32]

Extreme Weather

Scorpion Swarms and Ice Worms

In scenes evoking biblical retribution, three people were killed, and approximately five hundred injured, when scorpions swarmed in the Egyptian city of Aswan during the penultimate month of 2021, apparently agitated by exceptionally fierce thunderstorms. Residents, fleeing streets suddenly covered in the alien scuttling of these frightening creatures, found little relief in their homes, where the scorpions also managed to secrete themselves, stabbing the screaming humans with their angry, curling tails. Meanwhile, in a famously temperate part of the world – the Pacific Northwest – hikers noticed hundreds of thousands of black worms emerging from melting glaciers. While they are not yet any direct menace to human beings, one can't help but wonder if – unlike the Egyptian scorpions – they are playing the long, slow game and will seek revenge on the hapless hominids for melting their precious ancestral home, which glowed with a suffusion of white, bathing their worm-world with a sublime and warming chill.

Sequence 6

Unearthly

Unearthly

It begins with the most unassuming of motives: to be "in nature." You've had enough. Of cities, of work, of people, of burdens and duties and aspirations. Enough, perhaps, of yourself. A hike, for instance. Not just anywhere, of course, but in nature. Which you first have to find. A national park, a nature reserve, an ever so slowly diminishing landscape of moss and earth and tree that is itself criss-crossed by trails, signs, and the occasional trash bin. But you need to get there, because this nature isn't simply walking distance away, it's "out there." You have to make an epic, GPS-guided drive to get to nature before you can be in it. And so after a voyage – supplemented by the foraging of essential supplies (coffee and/or snacks) – you arrive, at nature.

If you've had the unusual advantage of foresight on this day, you will have also come prepared with appropriate boots, clothing, backpack, and so on, because a hike is more than just a walk (though, even in densely populated cities, simply going for a walk also requires a certain amount of preparation). And it's more than just marching off into the tranquil, welcoming greenery of a brisk autumn forest. You need to take the trail, or decide which trail to take – the long one or the short one – which in turn depends on how much time you want to spend being "in" nature. Whichever you decide (the short one), the trail will take you into nature. Or, rather, through it, because while you are without a doubt "in" the forest – it's everywhere, the sounds, smells, and towering trees above you – there's also a sense in which you are simply passing through, a peripatetic visitor on a drive-by tour through a strange and alien landscape. It's entrancing, dreamlike. Perhaps, without realizing it, you find the trail has thinned out or become unusually overgrown and irregular. You're no longer so sure that you're still on the short loop, or if you're even on the trail at all. Perhaps it's a little overcast, the sun rendered diffuse against a vast blue-gray sky. Gentle mists seem to envelop you, neither falling nor rising. For a moment – an all too brief moment – you feel a kind of vertigo. The quiet of falling rains, wind-blown trees, and the distant, reverberant crows bringing everything including time itself to a standstill. A hovering, dimly glimpsed sense of something primeval. This has always been here. Before trails, and hikes, and people. (Complemented with, I'm trying very hard not to panic because I think I'm lost and it's getting dark.) And then, quite suddenly, you notice in the distance a colored sign. An arrow. A gentle reminder.

Planet Without People

The sense of simultaneously being in nature but looking at it is likely familiar to anyone who has spent time on a hike or camping. It was likely this mesmerizing sense of being a part of nature and yet apart from nature that so influenced the young Algernon Blackwood, growing up as a solitary child amid the rapidly diminishing countryside of late nineteenth-century southeast England. In his autobiography, Blackwood writes about his youthful reverie: "feeling that everything was alive, a dim sense that some kind of consciousness struggled through every form, even that a sort of inarticulate communication with this 'other life' was possible."[1] This fascination with the otherworldliness of nature no doubt fueled the many hikes, voyages, and camping trips Blackwood made as an adult. On one such excursion, he made a canoe trip down the Danube River, and wrote about his experiences in a 1901 article published in *Macmillan's Magazine*. While Blackwood tells us what one would expect from a travel writer – the sights seen, the towns visited, the people met – his writing just as often wanders off into descriptions of the natural environment that borders on prose poetry. What strikes him most is the deep time of the landscape around him, "limestone cliffs, scooped and furrowed by the eddies of a far larger Danube thousands of years before."[2] Above him, in the dusk-laden sky, "grey hawks circle ever over head and grey crows by the thousand lined the shores."[3] As the sun sets, "the clouds broke up momentarily and let out a flood of crimson light all over the wild country. Against the gorgeous red sky a stream of dark clouds, in all shapes and kinds, hurried over into the Carpathian mountains."[4]

One night, Blackwood suddenly wakes, thinking he hears the sound of someone – or something – moving about his tent. He cautiously steps out to investigate. Nothing. Everything is as it was. Or was it? "It was doubtless the river talking in its sleep, or the wind wandering lost among the bushes."[5] The Danube trip reveals to Blackwood a brief but stunning impression: the idea of a planet without people. The isolation of the human being in nature, drifting down a solitary river, accompanied only by swaying fir and pine, quickly becomes an allegory for human beings themselves on an Earth that is at once overly familiar and yet utterly strange. The ancient limestone, primeval pine, a perpetual moon – all these things give Blackwood a strange sense of a place from which human beings have suddenly vanished. Or a place where human beings never existed to begin with. In the forest, the primeval and the post-apocalyptic dissolve into each other.

Many of the short stories Blackwood would go on to write – including "The Willows" – return again and again to this negative epiphany. The solitary human being in nature and the sudden impression of a place bereft of all humanity, a landscape unpeopled by the incessant cacophony of politics, technology, and culture, the momentary impression of a world without us. "The Willows" in particular takes the reader through this in stages, as one enters the inexorable logic of a world hidden from human beings, until Blackwood's characters reach a kind of forest within the forest and, with it, an inescapable feeling of being out of place. There, in the eerie stillness of a nocturnal campsite, engulfed by inexplicable sounds and haunting insinuations, the characters glimpse strange, otherworldly shapes rising in ritual mists – a freezing of the senses, the catatonia of the impossible, and a single thought: *we should not be here*.

The next morning, there is scant evidence and no proof; only uncertainty and doubt. Did it actually happen? Or was it all in my head? Like so many tales of supernatural horror, "The Willows" centers around this idea of human trespass. We should not be here. We were never meant to be here. The sense of a kind of metaphysical conspiracy, expressed by one of the characters in the story: "All my life I have been strangely, vividly conscious of another region – not far removed from our own world in one sense, yet wholly different in kind – where great things go on unceasingly, where immense and terrible personalities hurry by, intent on vast purposes compared to which earthly affairs . . . are all as dust in the balance."[6]

This experience of being both "in nature" and yet out of it gives the lie to any notion of a beatific harmony between the world apart from us and the world cast in our own image. The forest in Blackwood's story is not a sacred bough, much less a welcoming bower or that most alienated of things, a home. The forests persist in their strangeness. In tales like "The Willows," Blackwood's early fascination with the strangeness of the natural world is transmuted into a different kind of appreciation, the sense of how little we appreciate the insignificance of human beings set against the deep time of the planet itself. For this reason, Blackwood's writing avoids the more consoling options of pantheism or vitalism, in an attempt to get at a unique kind of estrangement – the species-specific estrangement from our own planet. (An estrangement revealed in the absurdity of the very phrase "our planet.")

With Blackwood, we are far from the Romantic evocations of the pastoral, as if some clear dividing line separated an Edenic and harmonious "nature" from the dilapidation of human-haunted urban centers. A continuum of fecund breakdown cuts across them both, as momentary and happenstance effusions mark the transiency of deep time. The real insight of "The Willows" is in this shift from "nature," as in trees and birdsong, and "nature" in the sense of "the nature of things," a blurry and tenuous wavering between physics and metaphysics. Poet Joyelle McSweeney calls it the "necropastoral," a sense of the planet as at once vast and tenuous, "its paradoxical proliferation, its self-digestion, its eructations, its necroticness, its hunger, and its hole making, which configures a burgeoning textual tissue defined by holes, a tissue thus as absent as it is present, and therefore not absent, not present – protoplasmic, spectral."[7]

A planet without people. Far from being a nostalgia for the long-lost home of alienated humanity, nature for Blackwood becomes indelibly haunted, in the ceaseless ebb and flow that is expressed only in the dimly intuited patterns of the crows circling above, the rivulets running below, the wind-hushed forests, and the cryptic mineral insignia of deep geologic time.

Human Trespass

An appreciation of the unnaturalness of human beings in nature that is expressed in Blackwood's tales was shared by another writer living halfway across the planet, also struggling to find a language for the natural world that would not be reducible to either religion or science. Around the same time that Blackwood took his Danube canoe trip, Izumi Kyōka (the pen name of Kyōtarō Izumi) relocated from Tokyo to a small coastal town in Kamakura, having been ousted by the literary establishment for his slow, patient, poetic prose. Kyōka's writing found few readers in a cultural climate that preferred realism, urbanism, and that most fashionable of things, modernity. Beset by personal and financial troubles, Kyōka's refuge quickly turns into something out of a gothic tale. He writes in his diary: "Rain leaks into the room, owls call from the trees . . . reeds are scattered about our frost-cold pillows. The crab spiders gather and scamper over the tatami."[8] Deterioration both external and internal follows, as his mental and physical health declines.

And yet, fed on nothing but gruel, potatoes, and the poetry of Li Ch'ang-chi, Kyōka manages to write the idiosyncratic, hallucinatory tales for which he is now known, including "The Holy Man of Mount Kōya." Influenced as much by Poe and Hoffmann as by Mahāyāna Buddhism and Japan's rich folklore tradition, Kyōka's tales refuse both the nostalgia for a lost nature as well as modernity's heroic mastery of nature. At the core of his stories is an apprehension of human being as a mere shadow play against the backdrop of the natural world. "The Holy Man of Mount Kōya" begins innocuously enough, with a monk on a pilgrimage who must pass through a forest to get to his destination. But the journey through the forest becomes increasingly surreal and hallucinatory as it progresses. At one point, the monk is beset by sudden darkness, swarming insects and an ominous and inexplicable rain of leeches descending from the looming treetops. The experience quickly turns apocalyptic, as the monk, almost catatonic, observes how "all these enormous trees, large enough to block out even the midday sun, will break into small pieces that will then turn into even more leeches."[9] Gradually the forest takes on animistic properties, as the boundary between animal, plant, and mineral passes away. "The destruction of mankind," the monk observes, "will begin with the forests of Hida turning into leeches and end with black creatures swimming in blood and muck. Only then will a new generation of life begin."[10]

After that, shape-shifting creatures, an animistic priestess, telepathic sleep, and sentient waters. When the poor monk finally emerges from the forest, the modern world suddenly returns, and the entire experience seems like a dream, as if it never happened. Or is he now dreaming, the modern city now nothing but a floating world? In Kyōka's stories, there is always a forest within the forest, a site where human time seems to stop and there are only the confused impressions of a world so distant from the world of human beings that it may as well be another world altogether.

One often finds, in Kyōka's tales, a kind of sacred site at the heart of the forest. In one story, a character known only as "the wanderer" visits a coastal town. He makes the climb up the mountainside to a temple. As night falls, distant, almost musical sounds are heard, sounds that are not quite birds and not quite the wind through the reeds, sounds so faint they could be memories. The wanderer inadvertently comes across a clearing, then shadowy figures, and a procession. A ritual is taking place. But a ritual that does not involve human beings. Again, trespass. I should not be here. I should leave. I should hide. Mottled and weather-worn stones, arrayed in a line, an ancient stage. Or are they shadowy human figures, somehow mottled with ageless blood and moss? A circle is drawn. A square. A triangle. Below, turbulent seas, wind-blown fields, a moonless mountaintop. In Kyōka's world, there is a pervasive sense of human beings as interlopers on the very planet that we unassumingly inhabit. Without us, the planet might almost seem like a strange ritual, a sacred site that excludes the human, "this quiet sadness."

A forest that is at once primeval and post-apocalyptic. A terrain on which the natural becomes supernatural, and vice versa. And, through it all, the fraught drama of human estrangement set against the vast and impersonal backdrop of old growth and climates shifting in slow motion. The shadowy impression of a planet without people emerges. We should not be here. We have never been here. Human trespass. It is the stuff of the weird fiction tradition, with H. P. Lovecraft's *At the Mountains of Madness* as its exemplar, witless explorers discovering strange creatures in the remote cyclopean ice that defy all scientific explanation, who stumble across impossibly regular stellar organisms which in turn point to a deeper, stranger horror in the recesses of the cosmos. The horror of life and death survival is inextricably mixed with the metaphysical horror of a planet that is utterly strange, and estranged. With Kyōka, as with Blackwood, the sense of human trespass gives way to a diffuse ecological estrangement, as the hazily intuited impression of a planet without people comes into focus – an Earth dehumanized. It is just a glimpse, but it makes just as deep an impression. A sorrow crystallizes around this sense that a planet becomes distant and remote, that the planet has somehow been lost, residing just beyond the grasp of a suddenly diminishing human affective capacity.

Everything's Gone Green

Written over half a century after the tales of Blackwood and Kyōka, Ursula Le Guin's "Vaster Than Empires and More Slow" is also preoccupied with forests, but forests scaled up – the forest itself is a planet, and the planet is a forest. A distant future, a confederation of civilizations (including Terrans), an exploratory expedition to the farthest reaches of outer galaxies, a ragtag crew of specialist misfits that makes Strindberg read like Disney, and, at the center of it all, a planet: World 4470, near the star KG-E-96651. Whereas Blackwood and Kyōka take us into the forest on a planet, Le Guin gives us the reverse. World 4470 is itself a massive, planet-wide forest, bereft of any animal life but teeming with green. One of the central characters is the team sensor, or empath, named Osden, who stands in a perpetually uneasy relationship of revulsion and spite with respect to the other team members.

Amid the chamber play of the interpersonal dynamics, it's this character – the misanthropic empath – who first intuits what World 4470 actually is. Trees, forests, roots, nodules between roots, on and on, between each tree, covering the entire planet – a planetary network of subterranean root systems, continually criss-crossed by molecular signals. Are there even individual trees at all? If one knew nothing about the overall structure of the human brain, would one be able to deduce sentience from the examination of just one neuron? As the saying goes, it seems the exploration team hasn't seen the forest for the trees. "Sentience without senses . . . Response to sun, to light, to water, and chemicals in the earth around the roots. Nothing comprehensible to an animal mind. Presence without mind. Awareness of being, without object or subject. Nirvana."[11]

Another team member – the ecologist – puts it more succinctly: "To a forest, we might appear as forest fires. Hurricanes. Dangers. What moves quickly is dangerous to a plant. The rootless would be alien, terrible."[12] Or is the forest simply reflecting back the cluster of contorted affects of its anthropic, consciousness-bound visitors? Another possibility emerges: that there can be no contact – that is, no meaningful contact – since the very idea of "contact" implies some basis on which a relation can possibly be established at all. How can beings burdened by consciousness and anthropic bias relate to an interstellar sentient forest planet? Perhaps all one can say is that there has been this strange relation, a relation of no relation, an alterity that seems at once sensitive and indifferent, sentient and impassive. "One big green thought."[13]

The dual sense of both being "in" nature but also utterly out of place is also part of the legacy of our modern relationship to this perpetually shifting, amorphous, and possibly non-existent entity we call, out of sheer habit, "nature." Indeed, nothing is more awkward than the sight of human beings in nature, be it heroic feats accomplished in the farthest reaches of forbidding mountain ranges or that other kind of triumph, a suburban family camping trip. It's one thing to acknowledge the gulf that separates living in the city from that of the natural world. But, as our cities and urban sprawls increasingly become our native environment, so have we also brought nature – nature designed – into our human-made world in the form of parks, greenspaces, and the various trees that begrudgingly constellate the urban landscape like an emaciated reliquary of a long-forgotten forest.

And what happens after the "big green thought"? The planet will return to its default state, the unknowable quiet of a planet without people, the quiet of Blackwood's Danube excursion where, for a moment, he magically glimpses even his own absence as a human observer of the absence of all people, a planet where even human extinction will have had the same effect as if human beings had never existed at all on the Earth, an omega point where the primeval and post-apocalyptic dissolve, giving us a planet on which there never were any people, a sacred Earth untouched by human hands, until the sacred itself is finally fulfilled and loses its meaning. As the narrator of "The Willows" notes, "Our insignificance may save us."[14]

Invasive Species

Like many of the parks that populate the boroughs of metropolitan New York, Fort Greene Park in Brooklyn contains a large, open greenspace which accommodates various activities. In the early mornings, latte-carrying dog owners are allowed to let their dogs run off-leash, and for a few hours the park is abuzz in the frenzy of canine catharsis as dogs of all shapes and sizes let loose in the open green (much to the chagrin of the squirrels). A bit later, a small group practices tai chi, while islets of personal trainers and their world-weary clients go through their own routines. In the distance, a homeless person, still sleeping in their makeshift miniature tent. By late morning, roving units of strollers and nannies and, by noon, outdoor classes from the nearby elementary school. Individuals at benches, tethered to laptops, "working." Small groups picnicking on the grass, couples napping, reading, doing nothing. An elderly man slowly circles one of the trees with his hands out, as if practicing some form of tree reiki. A hawk circles above. Park staff – rangers, gardeners, volunteers – continue to maintain the park's numerous trees, plants, and general landscape. Throughout the day, joggers (also all shapes and sizes). By late afternoon, flurries of insecure teens at their appointed meeting places. Evening sports on the greenspace; people walking home from work. By night, solitary dogs, their neon collars aglow, their owners following. And in the early, early morning, the park, suffused in the half-light of dawn, becomes quietly populated by small groups of seniors taking their morning walk, sometimes chatting, sometimes gathering ginkgo fallen from the trees. Huge oak and birch trees tower above the park and circle the Prison Ship Martyrs' Monument at the park's center atop a hill, which to this day contains the remains of some 11,000 corpses – a reminder of a bygone era of revolution, war, and colonialism.

The ongoing activity in the park takes its toll on the landscape, particularly on the big lawn, where the human (and canine) imprint has worn the grass down to bone-dry, light-brown dirt. Thus, every so often, park staff section off part of the lawn so that it can grow back again. The park activity continues, accommodating the new arrangement. As the days and weeks and months pass, one can see the fenced-off lawn grow bit by bit, until it seems that one day the entire area is exploding in fecund green. It goes without saying that there is nothing "natural" in the lawn, much less the park itself, both the by-product of human design. But, it is equally commonplace for us to relate to parks as "nature," if only in the unconscious ways we are affected by being in the presence of trees, grass, and the sporadic atonal song of birds. This apparent contradiction has spurred scholars of all stripes to debate whether the urban park is a simulation of a now lost nature, whether it is a designed nature that never existed to begin with, or whether it is a new kind of nature, a nature that is itself the product of science and technology.

This is likely why all manner of plants, trees, and forests appear in speculative fiction with such great ambiguity. Stories such as Le Guin's "Vaster Than Empires and More Slow" take place at the farthest reaches of human experience, but they are also what many people experience every day. Plant life lacks the more obvious resemblance to the human form that allows us so easily to anthropomorphize animals. We can, of course, care for our house plants with the same integrity (or lack thereof) that we care for our pets. We can talk to them, give them names, feed them. Plant music soothes our over-stressed nervous systems, just as the herbal wisdom of a whole range of plant medicines bolsters our general well-being. But there is no face and there are no eyes with which to discern the "soul" of the beast, not even a voice that could be the basis for a communication (or a command). And this is to say nothing of the manifold ways in which we consume plants, green juices and all. If anthropomorphism – literally, the shape of the human – has traditionally been one of the ways in which we as human beings create the possibility of apprehending otherness, then it would seem that plant life both invites and frustrates this possibility. Never has there been a kind of life that is so intimate with us and at the same time so distant from us.

Sad Plants

There are, of course, many literary and cinematic examples of humans becoming plants, but often this transformation happens at the expense of the plant's otherness. The hybrid is still a shape once human, a "Swamp Thing." There is also the inverse example of plants becoming human, without us asking them to. If some supernatural tales involve humans ambivalently becoming plants or giving themselves over to plants, then there are also examples in which plants eerily take on human characteristics. For instance, John Wyndham's 1951 novel *The Day of the Triffids* takes the alienness of plants quite literally, as a new species of motile, carnivorous plant life arrives on Earth via meteorites. With most of the human population inexplicably blinded by the meteor shower, human beings are left to clumsily shuffle around dilapidated cities and overgrown ruins, as the Triffids creep in on their helpless prey. While not frightening in the typical sense, Wyndham's penchant for cultivating layers of Cold War subtext produces a melancholic sense of futility. The world has effectively ended, and yet everyone is still alive. In the pulpish, 1962 film adaptation, one of the characters – a depressed, alcoholic scientist – is dumbfounded by the Triffid biology. "Are they plants or animals?" his wife asks. The scientist has no answer. "All plants move. But they don't usually pull themselves out of the ground and chase you!" Aristotle had placed plants as the lowest but also the most fundamental forms of life, capable solely of growth and decay, while animals seemed advanced in their ability to move and sense, with human beings at the top, gifted with intelligence and consciousness. In *The Day of the Triffids* the Aristotelian pyramid of life has been inverted.

Sentience is no longer a subcategory of the living, but life itself.

But the little scene of the fenced-off lawn at Fort Greene Park is perhaps something different. On the one hand, it is completely artificial: the area is demarcated, the grass is seeded, cultivated, managed, and primarily for the benefit of the human occupants of the park. When it has grown back, the fence will be removed, and park activity will carry on as usual, everyone content. And yet, witnessing the day-by-day flourishing of the grass – in the absence of human activity – produces a different kind of response. One witnesses the effect that the sudden absence of all human activity has on this strange kind of "nature." For a brief moment, one can bear witness to the absence of human beings, a little allegory of extinction that gives even the most ardent nihilist a glimmer of hope. If people were gone, just for a few months, look what would flourish. Undergrowth, overgrowth, the fecundity of decay. Suddenly the criteria of "invasive species" seems highly relative. And if human beings end up being the most invasive of all species?

Perhaps it is everyday epiphanies like these that serve as the basis for another kind of speculative fiction, one in which the planet is not so much a decorative stage setting for human melodrama but, instead, becomes a character in itself. Elvia Wilk suggests as much in her book *Death by Landscape* (the title of which is a nod to Margaret Atwood's 1989 story). "The word landscape," Wilk observes, "is typically used to suggest the passive, the inert, the natural – the plant, animal, and mineral world that constitutes a backdrop for a human actor. But here, the sudden absence of a human actor occasions a sudden presence: the presence of landscape, the presence of plants."[15] Perhaps this is why stories such as those by Blackwood, Kyōka, and Le Guin continue to resonate, as if to suggest a subterranean poetics of the Anthropocene in which foreground and background become inverted or collapse into each other. The characters in these and other similar tales are ambivalently drawn towards a zero point in which the arbitrary yet impactful distinctions of species, races, genders, and the human "we" tends towards a perpetual erosion, leaving only the turgid and troubled materiality for which words such as "nature" and "life" are woefully inadequate.

Such scenarios evoke the many examples of twentieth-century land art, in which the human form recedes against the vaster and slower processes of growth, decay, and the slow rotation of the Earth. In the mid-1950s, the Gutai artist Kazuo Shiraga staged "Challenging Mud," in which the artist, stripped almost bare, quite literally takes it upon himself to grapple with a planet at once malleable and impassive, the mud itself bearing the traces of agonistic human form. Similarly, in Ana Mendieta's "Silueta" series (1973–85), multiple silhouettes of a female body are enmeshed in dirt, grass, and sand, in some cases bearing only the faintest trace of a shape once human, as they are gradually turned to dust, or become overgrown, or are washed away in the effortless ebb and flow of the elements. A logic of dissipation takes place that has echoes in supernatural horror and speculative fiction. As Wilk observes, "[i]n what may look like a gesture of passivity, even self-destruction . . . these characters stop, plant themselves in the landscape, and grow."[16]

In the absence of humans, not only is there incredible fecundity but, more importantly, there is a dimly intuited sense of a "something-else" that continues on, the grass going on "grass-ing" just as the planet goes on "planet-ing." A something-else that also resides in the blind spot of humanity, something immediate but lost, immersive but always out of reach, a melancholy specific to the shape of the human, to the failures of anthropomorphism. Sad plants, sad planets. There is no secret life of plants, no secret vendetta against humanity, no planetary justice meted out to humans by some form of revolutionary alien life. A tiny window onto something that is impossible for human beings to fathom: a world without us. This modestly demarcated area becomes a kind of island of its own, an island within an island, a park within the park, as if it were the slightest fragment of a dream, a small parable about "nature" without people, and thus not "nature" at all.

Hollowed-Out Earth

Arguably, the need to sacralize the Earth is as old as humanity itself. A whole host of forces are mobilized to ensure that the planet of which we are a part, and from which we set apart, is a planet imbued with intrinsic meaning and significance. A clearing in the forest, a golden bough, a site set apart from the mundane world of human affairs, a site where a secret communion takes place between precarious human communities and the planet on which they are, perhaps, simply guests. A sacred tree, the tree scaled up as a model of the Earth and even the cosmos itself. Primordial forces of creation and destruction tenuously grasped at by fearful human hands. The necessity of myth, of a world relatable to us and for us. A kaleidoscope of gods, deities, and elemental forces, at once protectors of terrestrial humanity but also impervious, impersonal, sovereign, detached. Earth, mountain, river, sky, ocean, the cycles of time incarnate in seasons and climate, in soil, sun, rain, in growth and decay, and a planetary terrain at once bountiful and unforgiving. And behind it, all around it, infusing the contours of a precarious anthropomorphism, that shadowy apprehension of a world before us and after us – a world without us.

Published in Latin in 1681 under the title *Telluris Theoria Sacra*, Thomas Burnet's strange book of theologically inspired geology was subsequently republished in English. Its full title is *The Sacred Theory of the Earth. Containing an Account of the Original of the Earth, and of all the General Changes which it hath already undergone, or is to undergo, till the Consummation of all Things. In Four Books: I. Concerning the Deluge, II. Concerning Paradise, III. The Burning of the World, IV. The new Heavens and the new Earth. With a Review of the Theory and of its proofs; especially in reference to scripture. As Also the Author's Defence of the Work, from the exceptions of Mr. Warren, and the examination of Mr. Keil*. To which is added "An Ode to the author by Mr. Addison." Part II would appear in 1690.

Burnet's tome of speculative cosmology is, by today's standards, more a curiosity than serious science. It borrows freely from Christian theology as well as from Greek mythology, Jewish mysticism, even Zoroastrianism. And yet Burnet was also engaged with the leading scientific thinkers of his day, and the book would go on to have an impact on British Romanticism a generation later. Today, *The Sacred Theory of the Earth* is remembered in science-fiction circles for being one of the first books to provide a "scientific" basis for the Hollow Earth theory. Burnet had somehow calculated the total volume of the oceans on the Earth and measured that against the account of Noah's Flood, deducing that the "extra" water must have come from somewhere else, where it was being stored up in a kind of theophanic reservoir. The book caused a stir, prompting serious debates by serious people. Edmond Halley. Isaac Newton. Experiments were conducted.

While the idea would soon be debunked within scientific circles, it would find surer footing in the burgeoning popularity of early science fiction: Jules Verne's *Journey to the Center of the Earth* (1864), Edgar Rice Burroughs's *At the Earth's Core* (1914). The idea of an Earth that literally holds secrets to its primordial mystery has not gone away in the contemporary popular culture of the Anthropocene. A wormhole is discovered. A "MonsterVerse" revealed.

What strikes the modern reader of *The Sacred Theory of the Earth* is not just the eclecticism of its approach, borrowing as much from Genesis as from geology, but the insistence throughout its pages of this basic, a priori need within human culture to transform the planet into a sacred object. While Burnet was no historian (or theologian . . . or scientist), there is an abiding sense that *The Sacred Theory of the Earth* is also a theory of the sacred Earth:

> This Theory of the Earth may be called Sacred, because it is not the common physiology of the earth, or of the bodies that compose it, but respects only the great turns of fate, and the revolutions of our natural world; such as are taken notice of in the sacred writings, and are truly the hinges upon which the providence of this earth moves; or whereby it opens and shuts the several successive scenes whereof it is made up.[17]

The "system of the antediluvian earth," Burnet notes, must have been brought about by geological conditions that tend towards "dissolution" and the greater instability of the planet, mirrored for Burnet in the finitude and mortality of earthly existence. The Earth becomes sacralized precisely in its tendency towards disintegration and decline, "for the abyss was enclosed within its bowels."[18] Nothing lasts. Neither the individual life, nor the life of the planet. And it is this nothing-lasting that also, for Burnet, serves as the ground for the need to sacralize both human life and the life of the planet. The diminishing of the planet must be given meaning, just as must the diminishing of human life, both of which are rendered insignificant against the vaster cosmological backdrop – both theological and scientific – against which all things arise and pass away. "I do not think it in the power of human wit to determine how long this frame would stand, how many years, or how many ages; but one would soon imagine, that this kind of structure would not be perpetual, if one consider the effect that the heat of the sun would have upon it, and the waters under it; drying and parching the one, and rarefying the other into vapours."[19]

At one level, *The Sacred Theory of the Earth* is blatantly literal in its approach. Burnet attempts to give scientific, geological grounding to the major events depicted in the Bible, of which there are no shortage of examples, from the Creation of the Earth to its symbolically dense and operatic destruction in Revelation. In Burnet's hands, the Bible becomes a series of climate events, inflected by a theological cosmology that sits in uneasy relationship with developments in post-Copernican astronomy. At once absurd and fascinating, *The Sacred Theory of the Earth* reads today more like a work of speculative science fiction, a syncretic, genre-crossing fabulation worthy of Jorge Luis Borges, Italo Calvino, or Doris Lessing. At every turn Burnet is at pains to take biblical events at face value, as natural events that are also supernatural. *The Sacred Theory of the Earth* becomes a kind of metaphysical juggling act, in which Burnet is constantly correlating astronomy with theophany, mathematics with numerology, medicine with the afterlife. And this is the key to appreciating *The Sacred Theory of the Earth*, however misguided it may seem. Burnet, like many scientists in his time, refuses the all too modern division between the natural and supernatural. It's a given for him that the Flood or the Day of Judgment are simultaneously natural and supernatural. The view of the world provided by astronomy, physics, and natural history offers an explanatory efficacy – but they fail to tell us what it all *means*. On the other hand, the perspective of theology or myth, while it lacks a scientifically grounded rationale, offers a structure of meaning, not only for the planet but for the planet as it relates meaningfully to human beings. The question of *what* the Earth is. The question of *why* the Earth is.

Structure of Feeling (Angkor Wat)

The epilogue to Wong Kar-wai's tear-stained film *In the Mood for Love* (2000) features a heart-broken lover driven to pour his grief into the world, as if decanting black cognac into the clay of the earth, where misery perhaps always begins. In this case, the male lover, Chow Mo-wan (Tony Leung), visits Cambodia many years after last seeing his already married beloved, Su Li-zhen (Maggie Cheung). Surrounded by the ancient ruins of Angkor Wat, he whispers his secret sorrows into the crumbling walls as we watch on – voyeurs who are none the wiser as to the content of his confession. We know only that this man needs to unburden his soul, and that he cannot do so with another human being. We imagine he is not so concerned whether the splendid palace itself, now reclaimed by the jungle, registers his woes or merely absorbs them.

After all, this isn't even a poem scribbled on a scrap of paper and given to passing acrobats, or a prayer inserted into the famous "wailing wall" of Jerusalem (a name which suggests an appreciation of the extent to which our own architectural structures can take on "the structure of feeling" of human emotions). The world is saturated by such prayers, poems, and confessions. They form an invisible glue, composed of the viscosity of language. The sadness of animals can be found in their bones, their feces, their fossils. Whereas the sadness of humans has a metaphoric character: it is coughed out in the shape of the names we give to our grievances, as diverse and specific as they are shared and anonymous. Humans are "the weeping animal," Nietzsche insisted, where tears are prompted by the salt of language and the pin-prick of lyric.

As a character in Kyōka's story "One Day in Spring" notes, "Salvation is difficult for people who've been to college."[20]

Reason Unhinged by Grief

Having become duly known as both an art critic and a general arbiter of taste, in the summer of 1853 John Ruskin had his portrait painted. The artist he commissioned was John Everett Millais, a key figure in the Pre-Raphaelite movement then causing a stir in London art and literary circles. For the portrait, Ruskin, Millais, and Ruskin's wife Effie made a journey to the Trossachs, a rugged landscape of glens, forests, and lochs located in south-central Scotland. The painting was completed in London a year later and has since become a touchstone of Pre-Raphaelite art. And, while art historians often note the composition and subject matter, what most viewers find fascinating to this day is the background of the painting rather than Ruskin's overtly Byronic, frock-coated stance. The rocks and waterfall are depicted with such detail that they seem almost hyperreal, scientific and dream-like at the same time.

A few years after the portrait excursion, Ruskin published the third of his multi-volume work *Modern Painters*. It was unlikely he knew that the most lasting impact of the book would be a few paragraphs on nineteenth-century poetry, written almost as an aside. Discussing then recent trends in landscape painting, Ruskin pauses to comment on depictions of natural landscapes in poetry, particularly of the British Romantics. In both cases, he notes a tendency to move away from representations of things in themselves and towards a view of the natural world as it appears to us, as sensing and thinking beings. "From these ingenious views the step is very easy to a farther opinion, that it does not much matter what things are in themselves, but only what they are to us; and that the only real truth of them is their appearance to, or effect upon, us."[21]

Much of Ruskin's summary in these passages recapitulates the philosophical debates of an earlier generation, where the contrasting positions of "empiricists" and "idealists" moved back and forth over a central question: whether or not human beings could claim truly objective knowledge about the world. What results is the notion that the world "in itself" is always in some way the world "to us" or "for us" as human beings, a view on which Ruskin has strong opinions. To assume that the world is always in relation to us as subjective human beings is, for Ruskin, to open the door to all manner of unreliable dispositions. These include "a hearty desire for mystification, and much egotism, selfishness, shallowness, and impertinence," to the point where "a philosopher may easily go so far as to believe, and say, that everything in the world depends upon his seeing or thinking of it, and that nothing, therefore, exists, but what he sees or thinks of."[22] The objective slips into the subjective, realism into idealism, and the non-human-oriented view of the world in itself all too easily drifts into the enclosed, solipsistic space of a human-centric world for us.

The crux of the issue – for Ruskin, as for earlier thinkers – is the gray zone between thinking and feeling, as well as the extent to which an entire culture may be disposed to glorify one and demonize the other. While never wavering from his commitment to the relevance of art and aesthetics, Ruskin makes clear his deep mistrust of the domain of affects and emotions. At stake, in his words, is "the difference between the ordinary, proper, and true appearances of things to us; and the extraordinary, or false appearances, when we are under the influence of emotion, or contemplative fancy."[23] Thus, when one poet writes of a plant "bursting through the mould" or as "naked and shivering," or when another poet writes of the ocean as "cruel, crawling foam," they have both gone too far and have strayed into delusion.

This tendency – to attribute human affects to non-human entities – Ruskin famously christens the "pathetic fallacy." For Ruskin the distinction is clear. "The foam is not cruel, neither does it crawl."[24] The tendency to project human-centric ways of seeing, feeling, and thinking "produce in us a falseness in all our impressions of external things."[25] And yet, in the same breath, Ruskin also acknowledges a strange insight gained from such unwieldy liberties of poetic form. "The state of mind which attributes to it these characters of a living creature is one in which the reason is unhinged by grief."[26]

Reading Ruskin's comments today, it's as if he's describing the varieties of climate anxiety and the like, a certain kind of sorrowful, grief-laden state vis-à-vis the planet – almost as if the planet tends to generate pathetic fallacies. To Ruskin's examples one might include any of the poems from the so-called Graveyard School, a loose affiliation of late eighteenth- and early nineteenth-century poets who wrote – so the mythos goes – while brooding in graveyards and cemeteries. Robert Blair's long poem "The Grave" (1743) includes passages suffused with pathetic fallacy and the strange melodramatic fecundity of decay that has become a hallmark of the literary gothic:

> Ah! how dark
> Thy long-extended realms, and rueful wastes,
> Where nought but silence reigns, and night, dark night,
> Dark as was chaos ere the infant sun
> Was roll'd together, or had tried his beams
> By glimm'ring through thy low-brow'd misty vaults,
> Furr'd round with mouldy damps and ropy slime,
> Lets fall a supernumerary horror.[27]

While phrases such as "supernumerary horror" are as memorable as they are opaque, for Ruskin such poetic images are nothing more than that – something we made up. The gist of Ruskin's arguments concerning the pathetic fallacy are clear. The rain is not itself sad, the storm clouds themselves cannot possibly feel angst, and winter is not itself a climate that suffers from ennui, just as the moon at night is itself indifferent to the human-centric landscapes of loneliness and yearning that it illuminates. There is perhaps only that minimum stopgap between the "objective" world in itself and the "subjective" world as it appears to us.

Primordial Pathos

And yet, a strange kind of pathos, however illegitimate, seems to persist. It's as if there are two kinds of sorrow attached to the pathetic fallacy: the sorrow inspired by an admittedly fanciful correspondence between overcast, rainy skies and my own internal, melancholic state, and, beyond that, a secondary sorrow that recognizes that I am in some way forever removed from any real connection to the weather – or that there is something about the weather that immediately dissipates before me the second I look at it.

This accounts for the strange tone in Ruskin's writing, at once stridently opinionated and yet constantly doubling back, appearing to laud the very thing he has just disparaged. The pathetic fallacy is "pathetic" in the colloquial sense, signifying a "weakness" of the human subject that allows itself to be emotionally overcome by the outside world. It is symptomatic of "a mind and body in some sort too weak to deal fully with what is before them or upon them; borne away, or over-clouded, or over-dazzled by emotion."[28] At the same time, that same weakness is an indicator of a deeper capacity within the human being to acknowledge its limits, especially when confronting a primordial and impersonal Earth. In a way, it's a back-handed compliment. Our apparent inability to relate to the world is, in itself, a weak indicator of another capacity, the capacity to negatively identify something beyond the human. Human-centrism is also, in a way, its inverse. A condition in which human beings "are yet submitted to influences stronger than they, and see in a sort untruly, because what they see is inconceivably above them."[29] Ruskin adds, immodestly, "this last is the usual condition of prophetic inspiration."[30]

While he was having his portrait painted, Ruskin found himself with a lot of time on his hands. Millais, apparently, spent a great deal of effort capturing the rugged materiality of the rocky background. During these extended breaks Ruskin soon found himself sketching the landscape as well. His drawings of the gneiss stones continue to fascinate viewers to this day. Closely cropped, finely detailed, and monochrome, they appear to modern eyes like abstract art.

Most notably, Ruskin's drawings omit any human presence, the near opposite of the self-aggrandizing portrait he himself had commissioned. Even more, the drawings seem to omit even a natural point of reference – a mountain range, a river, a broader landscape within which the stones might be placed. It's as if Ruskin's stones (as they are often termed) are an attempt to get at the primordial deep time of bedrock itself, the imperviousness of the age of the Earth to the near-term, human-centric demands of aesthetic self-gratification. The age of a rock that so exceeds the span of a human life that all that can be expressed is the rock's irrevocable distance from the myopic human viewer drawing it.

This is, perhaps, the sentiment expressed by the anthropologist Hugh Raffles, writing about his visit to the Isle of Lewis, some 280 miles northwest of the site where Ruskin had composed his drawings. There, Raffles observes the ragged, monolithic landscape of gneiss formations. "One billion years ago, following millennia of uplift and erosion, the Lewisian gneisses breached the surface with their psychedelic ripples and baroque bands – the gray and pink of quartz, feldspar, and granite; the dark green and black of hornblende and biotite mica."[31] Picking up one of the smaller rocks, Raffles can't help but be overcome with a sense of how remote the stones are, even as he is holding them. "The most solid of rocks, they're heavy, and wary of dropping them, I hold them tight and think of them traveling through the frozen earth, the floating earth, the molten earth, the places they've been, the life they've seen, two-thirds of the way back to the beginning of the planet . . ."[32]

Chthonic Depression

In the remote forests of the Guangxi region in Southwestern China, the Earth is depressed. In the spring of 2022, cave explorers reported their discovery of a massive sinkhole. Found amid the dense, lush, mountainous forests of Leye County, the sinkhole was estimated to be over 300 meters wide and nearly 200 meters deep. While the Guangxi region is known for its rugged natural landscapes (the root *Guǎng* means "vast" or "extensive"), the discovery of a heretofore hidden sinkhole in its terrain is a new phenomenon, one that has scientists both intrigued and perplexed. Tempting though it is to imagine massive, tectonic patches of the earth suddenly caving inwards in the eerie, moonlit, forested night, scientists speculate that the appearance of the sinkhole is the result of a long and patient process of eroding geological formations.

The depth of the sinkhole, along with its vast width, has meant that it has still been able to receive sunlight, unblocked by neighboring mountains or ridges, something attested to by the trees found inside, some of which rise up to 40 meters in height. This has led scientists from China's Geological Survey teams to speculate not only that the sinkhole may contain its own micro-climate but that in its primordial depths there may be yet undiscovered species of animal, plant, fungi, and microbe. They presume that, being hidden in the depths of the vast, mountainous forest, the sinkhole has been able to flourish untouched by human hands (until now, that is). A forest within the forest.

Extreme Weather

Weird Weather

Meteorological records continued to tumble in 2021. The town of Syracuse, in Sicily, registered a maximum temperature of 49 degrees, leaving even the famously parched inhabitants gasping for breath. Meanwhile, rain fell on Greenland's ice cap for the first time on record. (Local scientists witnessed the precipitation but could not measure it, since previously there had never been any reason to install rain gauges.) Residents of Denver, Colorado, waited nearly three weeks past the previous record for significant snowfall, now arriving only in mid-December. Five people were killed, and hundreds injured, after an unprecedented tornado swept through the Czech Republic, flattening sleepy villages in its wake, tossing cars down valleys, and pummeling roofs with hailstones the size of tennis balls. ("It's living hell," said one regional governor.) In the Chinese city of Zhengzhou, twelve people drowned while trapped in flooded subway cars after torrential rains. Viral videos soon emerged of terrified commuters standing stoically and silently, as the water levels inside the subway reached some people's chins. Not long afterwards, New York would see similar scenes in the aging subway system during Hurricane Ida, as geysers suddenly opened up on platforms and walls collapsed due to the water pressure, pushing commuters dangerously close to oncoming trains. Dozens of people lost their lives in the tri-state area during the flooding, most of them living in illegal basement apartments with only one point of exit. (Two images in particular seemed to capture the chaos: one, a rat floating in the water, spinning round and around, as if practicing for a synchronized swimming routine; the other, a man floating on an air mattress in a dirty alleyway at night, the water several feet higher than street level, smoking a hookah and watching the end times unfold around him.) Meanwhile, parts of the Middle East were suffering from the opposite problem – a chronic lack of water. Indeed, at least one person was killed during protests over severe water shortages in Iran, with only 3 percent of the country unaffected by the drought. As always, the issue was evidently a combination of climatic caprice and human negligence or corruption.

Sequence 7

Entropology

Post coitum omne animalium triste est

"After sex, all animals are sad."

This phrase is attributed to the classical pioneer of medicine, Galen, who, in the second century, combined philosophy with a nascent scientific attention to the body, especially to its mysterious agitations and animations. He was one of the first physicians to map anatomical systems – especially through dissections and vivisections of animals, including pigs and apes – and his medical approach presumed a certain continuity between God's creatures, no matter their subsequent place on the Great Chain of Being. This continuity was forged through the tissues – both intimate and indifferent – of biology. Our creaturely kinship, moreover, could be witnessed in terms of mood, as captured in the observation that, "after sex, all animals are sad" – a claim that follows an affective current through all the diverse earthlings who find themselves caught inside the "feeding and breeding" hamster wheel of life.

No doubt, many of us find ourselves skeptical of such a claim today – noting that dogs, for instance, appear to be emotionally untouched by any quick and indifferent humping in the park. Nor do our partners seem sad (or so we tell ourselves) after being the beneficiaries of our sensitive and superior love-making skills. (Perhaps Galen even meant to write "sleepy" instead of "sad.") The observation is provocative, however, since it suggests a certain weariness and futility that lies beneath all the furtive ruttings around fertility.

While sexual arousal is a powerful form of distraction, given its goal-oriented intensity; the acquisition of such a goal can soon reveal the emptiness of what seemed, just moments before, the most important and pressing activity imaginable. That a certain melancholy can nip at the heels of bliss is simply the over-ripe fruit of experience, no matter how many exceptions to the rule one has been lucky enough to find. And the fact that such a shadow can obscure the sun shining on even the most humble of creatures speaks to a kind of post-coital solidarity of sorrow, nestled in the hearts of those condemned forever to seek some simulation of fusion through the undignified choreography of what Shakespeare called "the beast with two backs." (Indeed, one of the most poignant scenes in the written archive is the description, in Plato's famous fable of the androgynous, spherical, "primeval" people, of the two formerly united halves – cut in twain, by a vindictive Zeus – furiously attempting to press themselves back together into a complete being: "For the intense yearning which each of them has towards the other does not appear to be the desire of lover's intercourse, but of something else which the soul of either evidently desires and cannot tell, and of which she has only a dark and doubtful presentiment.") And so the libido seems to be a source of great tension and the spur of much frenetic activity. All too often, however, it evaporates into a misty kind of despondency when it finds itself spent, while the yearning, ravished body is left in a state of neither completion nor transcendence. (Perhaps evidence more of the dearth of suitable – even competent – erotic partners than a statement on a constitutive metaphysical lack at the heart of enfleshed existence.)

Indeed, Galen's famous phrase is usually missing its full expression, which notes two exceptions to his rule. The complete observation reads, *post coitum omne animal triste est sive gallus et mulier*, which translates as, "after sex, all animals are sad . . . except for roosters and women." One wonders what affective kinship the eminent physician saw in the famous farmyard cock and the collective fair sex, and what inferences we are supposed to draw from the correlation. Perhaps this statement was merely offered in an empirical, scientific spirit, with no moral conclusions subsequently to be drawn from it. In any case, the phenomenon of post-coital sorrow is itself an experience that suggests a cosmic truth located on the flip-side of sensual pleasure – something closer to the cruel optimism of inflamed desire – that can only be glimpsed when the heart stops pounding, the pulse slows down, the vital fluids have been spilled, and the organs of generation disgorge and deflate like so many balloons, left over from intoxicated festivities now long forgotten.

Entropology

In the title of his oft-cited but rarely read memoir *Tristes Tropiques*, Claude Lévi-Strauss – "the dean of anthropology" – indicates a specific type of geographic sadness – one associated with the hot and humid equatorial regions of the planet. Even as someone who, in the opening sentence of the book, famously claims – "I hate traveling and explorers" – Lévi-Strauss spent much of his life on trains, planes, and steamships as part of his social-scientific mission to find structural affinities between radically different peoples. *Tristes Tropiques* is both ambivalent and eloquent around the complicity he feels about being one of the main architects of a discipline that conscientiously documents all the different cultures that its own culture is just as diligently destroying. Lévi-Strauss was no sentimentalist, but he was acutely attuned to the damage and erasures that European colonization was still wreaking on its exoticized Others in the middle of the twentieth century. And even as he sought to discover and explain some of the semiotic bones, linguistic sinews, and ritualistic cartilage that all human cultures share – such as the coded distinction between "raw" (i.e., natural) and "cooked" (i.e., cultural) elements – he understood that every act of genocide, deliberate or indirect, effaced a unique way of being human from the world. (A blinkered and violent process that reduces the incredibly diverse, kaleidoscopic ways of being human into a bland and homogenizing container – with only one direction and one narrative arc – called "human history.")

Lévi-Strauss was especially concerned about this generic force of modernity, flattening the world into one smooth, continuous, dispiriting experience. (What we used to call, with a shake of the head, "globalization.") As his memoir notes:

> Now that the Polynesian islands have been smothered in concrete and turned into aircraft carriers solidly anchored in the southern seas, when the whole of Asia is beginning to look like a dingy suburb, when shanty-towns are spreading across Africa, when civil and military aircraft blight the primeval innocence of the American or Melanesian forests even before destroying their virginity, what else can the so called escapism of travelling do than confront us with the more unfortunate aspects of our history? Our great Western civilization, which has created the marvels we now enjoy, has only succeeded in producing them at the cost of corresponding ills. The order and harmony of the Western world, its most famous achievement, and a laboratory in which structures of a complexity as yet unknown are being fashioned, demand the elimination of a prodigious mass of noxious by-products which now contaminate the globe. The first thing we see as we travel round the world is our own filth, thrown into the face of mankind.[1]

According to our intrepid guide, this toxic process began a long, long time ago – reaching back to the moment humanity presumed to map and name the stars above us. "The sea," Lévi-Strauss writes, "has no more regained its tranquility since the introduction of Constellations than the outskirts of Paris have recovered their rustic charm since mass building developments began along the Riviera."[2] From such a perspective, the cosmic elements themselves have lost their natural sense of peace due to the incessant and aggravating activities of humankind.

Nevertheless, these reflections clear space for a concave kind of hope, since "The world began without man and will end without him." Moreover, Lévi-Strauss goes on to note, "The institutions, morals and customs that I shall have spent my life noting down and trying to understand are the transient efflorescence of a creation in relation to which they have no meaning, except perhaps that of allowing mankind to play its part in creation." We congratulate ourselves – in other words – on bringing order to a chaotic universe; to naming the animals, and taming the lands. Yet, this premature sense of exceptional achievement obscures our *real* terrestrial legacy: the uncomfortable fact that humans are also "the most effective agent working towards the disintegration of the original order of things." Writing in the irradiated shadows of Hiroshima and Nagasaki, Lévi-Strauss became convinced that humanity's *real* great passion is geared towards destruction far more than creation, and that we are "hurrying on powerfully organized matter towards ever greater inertia, an inertia which one day will be final." After all, "what else has man done except blithely break down billions of structures and reduce them to a state in which they are no longer capable of integration?"[3] A bleak assessment indeed! And a situation, according to Lévi-Strauss, deserving its own new science: *entropology* – that is, "the discipline concerned with the study of the highest manifestations of this process of disintegration."[4]

It is certainly notable that in recent years the humanities discipline now *least* concerned with the human is anthropology, which today prefers to write of animals, insects, rocks – indeed anything *but* the *anthropos* upon which its original charge was based. (A turn towards the "posthumanities" that Lévi-Strauss foresaw in the final paragraph of *Tristes Tropiques*, which anticipates a renewed and studious attention to "the essence of what it was and continues to be, below the threshold of thought and over and above society." That is to say, "in the contemplation of a mineral more beautiful than all our creations; in the scent that can be smelt at the heart of a lily . . . or in the brief glance, heavy with patience, serenity and mutual forgiveness, that, through some involuntary understanding, one can sometimes exchange with a cat.")[5]

Indeed, what could be sadder – what could be more *melancholic* – than anthropology: a human science based on recording the vanishing traces of soon to be extinguished ways of being human? Perhaps Lévi-Strauss was right to disavow his own co-creation as something of a Frankenstein's monster and put his faith in entropology instead. (After all, one thing that is guaranteed to continue as long as the universe itself is the entropic process – or anti-process.) Why then pay special attention to the fleeting gestures, beliefs, and practices of a species that, in the last analysis, is so much froth on the deep oceans of geologic time? "No doubt," Lévi-Strauss writes, humanity "has built towns and cultivated the land; yet, on reflection, urbanization and agriculture are themselves instruments intended to create inertia, at a rate and in a proportion infinitely higher than the amount of organization they involve. As for the creations of the human mind, their significance only exists in relation to it, and they will merge into the general chaos, as soon as the human mind has disappeared."[6]

Under Non-Western Eyes

We would simply be wasting our breath were we to find ourselves in the (admittedly very unlikely) position of trying to explain the pathetic fallacy to an indigenous person prior to "contact" (that far from innocent euphemism) with Europeans. Indeed we would also be wasting our time trying to communicate the same idea to Europeans themselves prior to the so-called Enlightenment. For it was the latter that first drove a decisive wedge between the world itself (*noumena*) and our superficial understanding of, or relationship, with the same (*phenomena*). To practically all known previous *Homo sapiens* modes of inhabiting and making sense of the Earth, however, the distinction was not nearly so clear, since humans, the environment, and other creatures co-existed promiscuously, with a shared understanding and a mutual regard. For over 99 percent of our own time on this planet, as a species – and seemingly all over the globe (despite the vast differences between countless indigenous cultures) – we had not seen any need to usher ourselves into one privileged corner, set upon a raised dais, and relegate the rest of creation to the passive role of mute, insentient, and merely observed. (In this sense, the modern human gaze is even more controlling, delusional, and chauvinistic than the male gaze; though the two are of course closely connected.)

For a fleeting sense of the pre-modern mode, take, for instance, the character of Clarence, an "old Gwich'in wise man from Fort Yukon in Alaska," whom we meet in Nastassja Martin's vivid memoir *In the Eye of the Wild*, an account which explores the author's painful psychic and existential reorientation required after she (barely) survived a bear attack during her anthropological fieldwork in the Boreal forest. Clarence is Martin's friend and "valued interlocutor" – a rich source of local knowledge and stories, which themselves form the warp and weft of her own ethnographic research.

"I always found it amusing," she writes, "when he used to tell me that everything was always 'recorded' and that the forest was 'informed.'" Indeed,

> "Everything is being recorded all the time," he used to repeat. The trees, the animals, and the rivers: every aspect of the world remembers all we do and all we say, and even, sometimes, what we dream and think. This is why we should take great care with the thoughts we formulate, for the world forgets nothing, and each of the elements within it sees, hears, and knows what has happened, what is occurring now and what lies ahead. There is a watch kept by all living things apart from humans, and their lives are ever ready to spill beyond our human expectations. So every thought-form that we send out goes to join and mingle with the old stories that shape the world around us, as well as the conditions of those who inhabit it.

This is an infinitely more entangled and multidimensional view of things than our own complacent assumption that only humans observe, log, notice, and witness, while the rest of the world merely *unfolds* – without trace or record (beyond the mute register of geological sediments and the occasional snapshots of haphazard fossilizations).

Pre-modern Europeans believed that our lives were being watched, noted, and judged; not in this case by the mountains, lakes, clouds, and birds, but by God Himself, and his various spies (most notably, "the recording angel," whose meticulous quill presumably never rests). Indeed, millions of contemporary Europeans also believe this. This monotheistic panopticon differs from the thousands of different indigenous understandings by its vertical accountability to a Great Chain of Being, in which the earthly creatures, and telluric elements, are little more than stage sets for the central drama of men, angels, demons, and the Holy Spirit.

Martin, as an anthropologist, admits to being "amused" by the idea of an entire ecology of snoops and gossips passing judgment on our species behind our backs, like a vast network of village nonnas. But, as she slowly convalesces from the effects of the bear claws that so suddenly tore open her body, she is no longer so skeptical about the frenzied intimacy that can explode without warning between radically different beings; nor does she have her previous faith in the lines that we magically draw in our minds to protect culture from nature or to shield human projects from the violence of the real. Perhaps this bear had been observing her for many months – her, The Ethnographer, who presumes to be the Prime Observer. Or perhaps the bear had simply heard accounts of her overly confident movements through the wilderness, along with her various follies and faux pas. Perhaps it felt the time was ripe to teach this interloper a hard but valuable lesson.

Whatever the case may be (and it is only modern men, "in any case," who would posit a universal or objective case), Martin has been both physically and emotionally prized open, to the extent that she now considers not only her body but her most intimate immaterial self as an extension of the world – a temporary annex of it – rather than as an independent element, with its own "free will," trajectory, or agenda. Even as many of her nerve endings are now numb, she has become sensitized to the ecological aspect, foundation, and network that sustains her every feeling, thought, and experience, to the extent where she can no longer confidently trace the contours where she ends and "the world" begins (or vice versa). And while this may have been a welcome kind of epiphany in less environmentally troubled times, this now means the narrator is also extra-sensitive to the brutal consequences of humanity's accelerating – perhaps even last-ditch – assault on the natural world. "[N]ow you're really losing the plot," she tells the reader as much as herself, "because even the mountains are coming apart. Losing cohesion because of melting ice, because of these heat waves." Indeed, she continues, "[i]t would have been so simple if my personal unhappiness could be summed up by an unresolved family issue: by my father's too-early death, by my not living up to my mother's expectations. Then I could 'solve' my depression. But no. My problem is that my problem isn't mine alone. The misery my body is expressing comes from the world."

"Losing (human) cohesion" may have once been a gift: finding a more than human ecological niche and perspective. But when noumena itself is under siege – by microplastics, by chemical injection, by industrial extraction, by sonic terrorism, by ambient radiation, and so on – our phenomenology is necessarily affected and degraded as well. In short, if the world is unhappy, we are unhappy.

Which brings us back to the pathetic fallacy. No doubt Martin, after the bear attack which scrambled her human bearings, would now find Ruskin's confident condescension more "amusing" than the idea of a forest that records her passage and its ripple effects through the local environment. There may or may not be a panpsychic consciousness, or animistic subject, nestled in the heart of matter, registering the collapse of the natural world in a manner akin to an atom-sized recording angel. But even without such personifications, we have passed the threshold where we can quarantine active human thought on one side and passive ecological availability (or inaccessibility) on the other. (See, for example, the work of another anthropologist, Eduardo Kuhn, who wrote a whole book explaining *How Forests Think*.) Memory is an uncanny thing. And we humans have terrible memories unless we outsource our ideas and observations to material objects. Geological traces and amber fossils are thus not different in *kind* to books, paintings, and films but more in degree (mapped across a spectrum of intentionality). Even then, the example of the forest complicates things, as animals, fungi, and trees alike exhibit at least proto-symbolic communicational capacities, involved in rich and complex semiotic webs and networks.

If the world is sad – and I think we have established by now that it very definitely *is*, no thanks to us – then it is only our continued belligerence that prevents us from receiving the dispatches and logbooks of its countless constituents, pleading with us to cease our reckless and abusive behavior. We are being watched, noticed, recorded, and judged – and we need not evoke an absent God as the source of such surveillance. The remaining creatures, the surviving flora, the traumatized elements are all taking an audit of our crimes. (Perhaps to be discovered by Martian anthropologists of the future.)

They are coming for us.

And they have the receipts.

Then Again (Again . . .)

Some may object that the idea of the rest of the world – from chimpanzees to mushrooms to boulders to ocean foam – watching the human race with interest is (at least when lifted out of the indigenous cultural context) both crazy and crazily narcissistic. It is as if the whole species were animated by the spirit of Liza Minnelli, and we are forever ready for our close-up – craving the spotlight. In other words, to assume we're the protagonist of the world's attention is yet again a delusional symptom, part and parcel with naming an entire geological epoch after ourselves. Whereas the truth lies closer to a world that tolerates us at best while trying to be as indifferent to us as possible. ("Stop paying them mind," say the non-human multitude, "and perhaps they'll go away.")

All Watched Over by Machines

But what of the machines? Aren't they watching us too? Certainly they are. We have abundant proof of such. We have it in the almost infinite recordings of our strange and banal behaviors, captured by any one of the nearly 800 million surveillance cameras that we ourselves felt compelled to install around the world. (Not to mention all those phone cameras that now essentially serve the same function.) From a broad evolutionary perspective, these camera eyes – the ones that watch over us 24/7 – are distantly related to the organic eyes that first emerged out of the swamps half a billion years ago. The emergence of organs of sight – in very different environments, and attached to radically different organisms – suggests that there is something universal, perhaps even cosmic, to their design and function. It's as if – against the self-serving claim that humans are the sole witness of the miracle of the universe – the universe itself has ensured that eyes spring up wherever the basic elements exist to construct them: some moisture, some multicellular cooperatives, some will to find light and nourishment. The Earth, certainly, has sprouted countless eyes with which to observe itself, just as it sprouted ears to listen to itself, skin to sense itself, and genitals to keep the parade of organs going.

We might therefore trace the camera lens back to our own eyes and their unquenching desire to feed off new images and to see into places more deeply. (Just as our own eyes can be traced back to mammals, to lizards, to fish, and – going all the way back – to little salty puddles of water in rocks, exposed to the sun, and beginning to film over with a latent capacity to register the shadows of the birds that fly above.) The main difference, perhaps, is that the camera comes with an actual "photographic memory" of what it sees, connected to a storage medium that can be retrieved by others. The images it captures funnel down the wires and into an externalized mnemonic support. (Although the question of access is increasingly tricky in the digital age, based as it is on rapidly changing protocols and the principles of planned obsolescence.) We have, in other words, constructed a technological perceptual apparatus that now watches us more closely, and with more keen interest – and with a more merciless memory – than any recording angel or jealous God ever could (the latter having only a rudimentary kind of facial recognition, given the weak wi-fi signals in heaven).

We love cameras so much that we have even started installing them in our own bodies, to help restore some sight to the partially blind. Soon enough, however, we will implant cybernetic retinas to augment our visual fields, to record our experiences to a visual archive, and to allow the real-time overlay of digital meta-data. (So, for instance, you can walk into a room full of strangers, and – thanks to facial recognition software and corresponding databases – have their names, title, and zodiac sign hovering subtly over their image.) In the case of the blind, who genuinely benefit from technological assistance, things have already started to go awry. For even when the operation goes well, and "bionic eyes" help restore some of a person's dwindling sight, the pressures of the market mean that they can be left literally in the dark if something goes wrong. Take, for instance, the story of Barbara Campbell – a beneficiary of the cutting-edge company Second Sight, which, for a while at least, lived up to the promise of its name when it provided a cyber-implant into her left eye to help navigate the world.[7] At first it worked well. But one day, as she was commuting during rush hour in the New York City subway, her vision suddenly abandoned her. She tells of hearing a beeping noise as her retinal implant faded to black. After her initial panic, good Samaritans helped Barbara get home. She soon discovered that the company was on the verge of bankruptcy and no longer providing any repairs or upgrades. Like many other "beneficiaries" of this cyborg vanguard, she was now stuck with the ocular equivalent of a Microsoft Zune in her skull (leaking all sorts of toxic metals, no less).

Tellingly, such scenarios are usually left out of the sexy cyborg futures presented to us, even by writers of dystopian science fiction.

The Ambition to Vanish

Nietzsche regaled us with the now famous fable of a surreptitious demon – sidling up to unsuspecting folks in the street and whispering perplexing words in their ear about the inevitability of an Eternal Return. To this unnerving tale we can juxtapose an even darker parable from Emil Cioran: the allegory of a new humanity, emerging from the ashes of the old, after an unspecified global catastrophe. For these bewildered survivors:

> [t]heir first concern will certainly be to abolish the memory of the old humanity, of all the enterprises that have discredited and destroyed it. Turning against the cities, they will seek to complete their ruin, to erase all traces of them. One rachitic tree will be worth more in their eyes than a museum or a temple. No more schools; on the other hand, courses in oblivion and unlearning to celebrate the virtues of inattention and the delights of amnesia. The disgust inspired by the sight of any book, frivolous or serious, will extend to all Knowledge, which will be referred to with embarrassment or dread as if it were an obscenity or a scourge. To bother with philosophy, to elaborate a system, to attach oneself to it and believe in it, will appear as an impiety, a provocation, and a betrayal, a criminal complicity with the past. Tools, all execrated, will be used by no one, except perhaps to sweep away the debris of a collapsed universe. Each will try to model himself upon the vegetable world, to the detriment of the animals, which will be blamed for suggesting, in certain aspects, the figure or the exploits of man; for the same reason, we shall abstain from reviving the gods, and still less the idols. So radical will be the rejection of history that it will be condemned *en bloc*, without pity or nuance. And so it shall be with time, identified with a blunder or with a profligacy.[8]

Cioran goes on to explain that members of this new race, recovering from "the delirium of action," turn to monotony, and thus do everything in their power "to avoid the solicitations of the new."[9]

Being especially sensitive to hypocrisy, however – or at least to his own intellectual inconsistency – Cioran immediately regrets depicting such a scenario, since he realizes it is just another "wearisome feature of all eschatologies."[10] That is to say, even this kind of anti-prophecy still follows the same structure and impulse as all those other "frantic hypotheses" of millenarian thinking. And so, he notes soberly, "let us no longer allow ourselves to be deceived by the image of a remote and improbable future; let us abide by our certitudes, our indubitable abysses."

Cioran's writings – often published as aphorisms, which themselves would, on occasion, coagulate into a series of loose essays – can be a tonic for the morose reader, since they are charged with the frisson of the unsayable (or at least the inadmissible). Cioran perhaps goes the furthest, in that pantheon of Venerable Grumpy Old Bastards, when it comes to viewing society, life, the world – even existence itself – in relentlessly negative terms. Even more than Schopenhauer, Nietzsche, Dostoevsky, or Pessoa, Cioran railed against everything from friendship, to family, to the manifold forms of injustice and indignity that arise, simply by virtue of being a conscious being. Forever struggling against "the temptation to exist," this fatigued connoisseur of resentment nevertheless understood that any thoughts of suicide were already "too late." Indeed, if Cioran had not himself left such a strident record of his refusal to "get with the program" – even the supposedly nihilistic program of existentialism – we would have to invent him. For, just as we tend to rely on priests or nuns to believe in God on our behalf (and thus outsource our faith to the experts), we can depend on Cioran's books to express taboo thoughts in a negative key that go well beyond anything acceptable in the public sphere – or even in our own private minds. In other words, Cioran is, ironically, almost therapeutic in his uncompromising disgust for the compromises involved in being human – like an especially bleak stand-up comic, whose punchlines are as likely to make the audience cry as laugh. Cioran's books save us the trouble of being a pessimistic absolutist, and relieve us of having to be the dark jester of doom ourselves. He even gives us the dubious pleasure of feeling relatively positive about the world; as if we need a limit-case to didactically represent the dangers of succumbing fully to the glittering seductions of negative thoughts.

For this reason, Cioran can be considered the patron saint of the anti-natalism movement (which believes that having children is both immoral and irresponsible) as well as the poet laureate of the even more fringe Voluntary Extinction Movement (which is pretty self-explanatory). "The End is gaining ground," he writes. "We cannot go out into the street, look at the faces there, exchange words, hear the least rumble, without telling ourselves that the hour is near, even if it will sound only in a century or ten. A look of *dénouement* heightens the merest gesture, the most banal spectacle, the stupidest incident, and we should have to be refractory to the inevitable not to notice as much."[11] Indeed, "it is legitimate to wonder if humanity as it is would not be better off eliminating itself now rather than fading and foundering in expectation, exposing itself to an era of agony in which it would risk losing all ambition, even the ambition to vanish."

Cioran was the misanthrope's misanthrope, a thinker who pushed anti-humanism towards a terse and succinct art. And while he sometimes acknowledged non-human – even cosmic – forms of trouble and strife, he felt his own species was clearly the most to blame for the woes of the world in general. For our sublimated hysteria – what others call "culture" or "spirit" – was, for him, an infectious kind of confusion or panic. "Our contortions," he writes, "visible or secret, we communicate to the planet; already it trembles even as we do, it suffers the contagion of our crises and, as this *grand mal* spreads, it vomits us forth, cursing us the while."[12] The human signature – tattooed in toxic ink on the now ravaged face of Mother Nature – is something that Cioran perhaps wants to atone for, even as he struggles with the knowledge that there is no way to escape or transcend the taint of his own culpability. Nevertheless, this doesn't stop him from cursing his fellow man and regretting the sorry business of human association. "The proof that man loathes man?" he asks. "Enough to be in a crowd, in order to feel that you side with all the dead planets."[13]

Cioran, a deeply disillusioned thinker in exile, did not yearn for some imagined, impossible home but, instead, longed to be exiled still further: away from Paris, away from society, away from even planet Earth. But even then, he suspected – even if he managed to hitch a ride on a passing meteorite – he would not be safe from the wretched human stain. No doubt, were Cioran still alive today, he would shudder at the press conference bleatings and boastings of Elon Musk, Jeff Bezos, and Richard Branson – each claiming they will be the first to open an office on Mars. Already aware of the trajectory of the space race, Cioran writes (speaking of the human newborn, as embodied, for instance, in the ecstatic end sequence of Kubrick's *2001: A Space Odyssey*): "This little blind creature, only a few days old, turning its head every which way in search of something or other, this naked skull, this initial baldness, this tiny monkey that has sojourned for months in a latrine and that soon, forgetting its origins, will spit on the galaxies . . ."[14]

Haunted Atoms

There is an uncredited text-only meme circulating through social media, reminding us that:

> The universe is an ongoing explosion.
> That's where you live.
> In an explosion.
> Also, we absolutely don't know what living is.
> Sometimes atoms arranged in a certain way just get very haunted.
> That's us.
> When an explosion explodes hard enough, dust wakes up and thinks about itself.
> And then writes about it.

While the words are uncredited, they paraphrase observations made in the Venn diagram between astronomy and philosophy, including Carl Sagan's famous description of humans – and indeed every living thing on Earth – as "star-stuff."

Whether we consider this situation – which, granted, is more description than explanation – we can consider it a happy miracle or an unwelcome curse, depending on our mood, bank balance, or proximity to dinner with in-laws. Surely there is something irretrievably sad, however, in the isolation of such hauntings when it comes to our own kind. After the initial shock of birth – and being wrenched out of inert matter into a surreal organic puppet show – we must learn to stand on our own two feet, mostly locked within our own experience, emotions, and thoughts. We form our entire sense of self around a sad core: the trauma of the fall into individuation – like a planet hardening around a nuclear center. (Astrophysicists like to say that the Earth itself has one simple goal, and that is, after billions of years, to cool down. Freud, in his darker moments, said the same thing about the human psyche: that it unconsciously yearns to become cold, insentient matter once more.) Nevertheless, we also – and at the same time – have a sometimes mystifying wish that "this evanescent thing will last." The awareness of our own inevitable end casts a shadow over everything we do, feel, and share; just as our decisions often serve as the splintered dance floor of a frenetic pasodoble between Eros and Thanatos – the forces of life and death. Add to this the pressure of the human herd, who band together to coerce us into behaving in certain narrow ways rather than experimenting with all the options technically available to us, then it makes sense that there is a certain measure of sorrow lodged in every human heart, just as there is a certain weight of gold in our marrow (about 0.2 milligrams, on average).

Being a conscious person among others comes with a default sense of alienation, since we will always be somewhat outside the thoughts and feelings of others, and – even more so – outside the plan of nature and the play of the elements. And while it is a source of fascination – and constant inspiration – that we can *reflect* on the world, and thus compare notes concerning its various qualities, this is also an index of our in-built capacity to withdraw from the world, and to build abstract maps of its workings, rather than hurl ourselves into its flux like the kestrel or the killer whale. The cosmically attuned anthropologist Alphonso Lingis laments the various social, cultural, and psychological layers that we have felt it necessary to place between us and the material world – a series of filters to cushion the blow of direct experience. "People who shut themselves off from the universe," he writes, "shut themselves up not in themselves but within the walls of their private property." In other words, Lingis argues, we mistake our own consciousness for an isolated monad, when we are in fact much more entangled with the universe than we realize. Where Leibniz believed each man to be an island, covered over with greenhouse windows through which he can peer at the Real, Lingis – closer to the vision of Spinoza – insists that our isolation is a self-fulfilling prophecy: an effect of our sense of exceptionalism, lording over the world from an imaginary Archimedean point rather than diving into the messy maelstrom. The standard-issue human, according to Lingis, is cosmically impoverished today because "[t]hey do not feel volcanic, oceanic, hyperborean, and celestial feelings, but only the torpor closed behind the doors of their apartment or suburban ranch house." They feel only "the hysteria of the traffic, and the agitations of the currency on the stretch of turf they find for themselves on the twentieth floor of some multinational corporation building."

The ethos embedded in Lingis's aversion towards the self-isolating tendency of modern life – made even worse in recent years thanks to the increasing influence of the internet – runs counter to Freud's false binary between a sorrowful, neurotic life or a (briefly) ecstatic, and then infinitely, mindlessly content non-existence. For Lingis – as for all ecstatic spirits who believe we have the latent protocols in our soul to more truly interface with the environment – sorrow is a symptom of an existential isolation that we can avoid simply by recognizing that such loneliness is created by our own ideological smoke-screens and narcissistic mirrors. Moreover, even to think in terms of happiness versus sadness is a human misconception; and in our rush to separate them, and value one over the other, we further the conditions for this dubious binary to cut yet deeper grooves in our already troubled minds. Instead, we should be fine-tuning our receptors to welcome specific cues and choreography from the cosmos, our enthusiastic and creative response to which will render the egoistic question of our own personal state of mind moot.

Indeed, we suspect Lingis would in fact agree with the meme quoted above, and would approve of its premise, that we are haunted dust motes, riding a violent explosion through the void. Such a spectral state should not scare us, however, since it is indeed an exceptional – though not at all masterful – perspective on this fluke plenum in which we find ourselves: a mysterious blue marble rushing through space, seething with vital energies. Can you really be sad, Lingis seems to be asking, when you have such willing mentors as volcanos and such wise life-coaches as ladybugs?

Necrobiome

"Necrobiome" is the name given to that community of critters which come together in the shared mission of metabolizing a corpse. When an organism dies, uninvited survivors descend on the unplanned wake and feast on the remains: everything from lions, vultures, crows – down the chain of complexity – to worms, beetles, fungi, and "waves of bacteria." The necrobiome is thus a temporary society arranged around the blessed bounty of a fresh (or even not so fresh) carcass. The necrobiome carries on the negentropic energy locked within carrion, so that new generations of amazingly diverse life-forms can one day sacrifice themselves so that the rest may continue.

The term itself stems from a relatively recent scientific appreciation of the life-generating properties of locally sourced mortality. As news outlets report, "In parts of Europe, plans to replenish the 'necrobiome' may benefit wildlife from golden eagles and wolverines, to copious plants, fungi and insects."

From the perspective of deep ecological relations, there is little distinction, if any, between death and life, decomposition and recomposition. When a tree falls in the forest, swarming things inhabit this entity-turned-environment and create the conditions for another tree to grow in its place. Raccoons sleep in it. Rats mate in it. Grubs devour it. Mosses enfold it. And birds defecate new seeds in its pulpy traces. Death, so to say, simply leads to more life in a balanced habitat. ("Necrobiome" literally means "dead-life-thing.")

The linguistic emphasis on death embedded in the word alters our perception of what is, after all, a serviceable synonym for "ecosystem." It implies an answer to a kind of chicken–egg question concerning the enduring mystery of life. (That is to say, the question of how biota came to be in the first place. The answer being that death somehow paradoxically *precedes* life, giving birth to the latter through some kind of necrotic sorcery.) It also tempts us to consider "life itself" as a necrobiome, wherein all vital strivings – all lively interactions – revolve around the deceased elements that comprise its core (at least for the term of its natural decay). A society, from this perspective, is a necrobiome secreted by departed ancestors. A building is thus a necrobiome assembled by long-gone masons. A text is a necrobiome made up of the ideas that perished in the process of its composition. A relationship is a necrobiome of all the bonds that will now be suffocated through neglect. An institution is a necrobiome founded on its long-perished, well, founders. And so on.

Of course, the most successful necrobiome of all is capitalism: an economic system premised on the efficient husking and extraction of those forced to toil for the profits of the few. If capitalism had an emblem it would best be symbolized by a shield emblazoned with a vulture on one side and a parasite on the other. Indeed, this system is something of an exception in its post-natural designs, which would suspend the dialectic between life and death and keep all its denizens in a kind of zombie state, so that the feast – for the select minority, of course – need no longer endure the cycles of famine that punctuate the organic world. We live, in other words, inside an advanced kind of necrobiome: one that includes the daily diet of death delivered through our screens. (Note how we tend to feel alive only if we are aware that someone else is dying, if only as a dramatic simulation, since this signals our own ultimate sacrifice has not yet been required.)

It has been said that, in medieval times, power was enacted rather bluntly through the delivery of death. If your enemy was causing you grief, you assembled an assassin, or an army, to kill them. In modern times, by contrast, power has been enacted through the "management of life" – a kind of disingenuously benign "biopolitics" that presumes to decide who deserves a brief reprieve from finitude; who can be granted an extension within this mortal state of exception that has traditionally been experienced as "nasty, brutish, and short." In these postmodern times, the distinction seems to have collapsed. Drones busily deliver death from sanitized skies, just as bureaucrats arbitrarily decide who can afford life-saving medicines or treatments on any given day. We live in the rotten core of a biopolitical necrobiome. And the only solidarity we can really envisage is the kind that must have been unconsciously felt between the maggot and the magpie, feeding off the gristle of the fallen mammoth.

Biophobia

We all know the dangers inherent in watching nature documentaries. They seduce us with their beautiful imagery, their sublime vistas, their magical moments, caught by the camera for our wonderment; briefly suspending the alienation we feel from our all too abstract animal others. But then a predator will come along and spoil the magic by pouncing on something adorable that we've already identified with, thanks to their lovely colorings and awkward gait. A shark will devour a seal. An eagle will swoop on a mouse. A lion will fatally claw a baby zebra. And no matter how many times David Attenborough assures us that this outrage is just part of the cycle of life – no matter how many times he reminds us that apex predators must eat too – we feel a sharp twinge in our sentimental hearts. And we wish the entire world could be vegan.

Nature, we are told, is red in tooth and claw. Nevertheless, we prefer to think of it as green and rainbow-hued. To be a squirrel or a gazelle is to live in a perpetual state of near panic – heart-racing, head-twitching. To be, in most instances (given the shape of the food pyramid), is to be in constant "fight or flight" mode, to the extent where we might wonder where the instinct to try to keep alive comes from in the first place, given how exhausting it is, sleeping with one eye open all the time. (As if Life pulses on, with its relentless will-to-live, with no concern for the living.)

Yes, we moderns sentimentalize nature, which is why even footage of indigenous people hunting their traditional quarry troubles our compromised conscience. That said, there surely *is* something sad about the blood-soaked scenarios from which the directors of nature documentaries usually try to spare us, rationing them out to, at most, one carnivorous event per episode. Over the course of a series, however, even a program as cozy and gentle as BBC's *Springwatch* is packed to the green gills with murderous owls and orphaned otter babies. Seeing a newborn creature, its lungs filled with the miracle of new life, only to witness it being torn to shreds by a hungry snake or tiger, is – it must be admitted – an occasion for sorrow and soul-searching, at least for those sentient creatures called to witness it. (As elephants and other mammals clearly have been.) Grief may seem like a pointless luxury in a world defined by the necrobiome. But it is a new lens on ecological relations, just as a telescope provides a new lens on the universe.

What is the point of all this feeding and breeding? Is there a net positive, where all those moments of grace found in the natural world outweigh those moments of violence, of dead-eyed indifference? (Not that the two are necessarily disconnected.) Can we imagine taking the vegan ethos even further, to the point where we question the purpose of life itself in the first place? Couldn't this be an awful mistake? An erroneous cycle of suffering for no reason, and with no redeeming purpose? We may even find ourselves doing a crude kind of calculus in our heads. Is the sound of a loving mother's gentle lullaby worth the agonies of toothache? Is the taste of a ripe pineapple worth the pangs of loneliness or abandonment? Indeed, might we go so far as to suspect that whatever God created such a world as this – a world filled with suffering even before *Homo sapiens* came on the scene and brought suffering to an exquisite new global art – that such a God is in fact some kind of sadistic, diabolical deity? Might we decide to become *biophobes* and shrink back at the very notion of life at all, since wherever life strides into the room, like a dazzling new bride, a train of blood is sure to trail in her wake? Indeed, we have been so programmed, perhaps ideologically, to consider life an undeniable value in itself, that perhaps we missed the sting in its tail and the poison in its heart. (Something the nihilist warned us about, though not in a convincing enough idiom.)

Now that we see the intrinsic sadness of life itself, we can imagine a campaign to eradicate it. Perhaps this is the unconscious force behind nuclear ambitions. To wipe away all life from Earth, so that all suffering may cease once and for all. How much more tranquil the cold, dead, inert cosmos, where spheres float serene and untroubled by agitations of the blood and tickles of the spirit. How preferable an alien scene of planets covered in solid seas of compressed diamond, or churning storms raining torrents of green fire, with no organism to register pain, sorrow, fear, grief.

But of course such a vision is blasphemy, and no human could really pray for "nothing, rather than something." In any case, the terrestrial fluke, so well described in the blockbuster film *Jurassic Park* – that "life finds a way" – is nothing if not double-edged. It is somehow reassuring that living things will continue long after we're gone but also preemptively distressing that, in the future, organisms we will never see or imagine will hide between crevices and cling to the shadows, their animated jellies palpitating in panic, without even a camera crew to witness their distress.

The Hedgehog and the Fox

Rapid climate change is creating not only widespread damage and disorder but also real-life allegories for the situation in which we all find ourselves. Take for instance the traditional English hedgehog, beloved by children and philosophers alike. Hedgehogs have, for millions of years, roamed around this green and pleasant land during the summer, before hibernating in their underground burrows in the winter. During this subterranean hiatus, the tiny heart of the hedgehog beats only a few times a minute and their body temperature dips down to almost freezing (2 degrees centigrade), in stark contrast to their usual human-like reading of around 35 degrees. Such biological and behavioral generalizations, however, must be taken with several grains of salt these days. The winters are no longer as cold as they used to be, and it is difficult for a hedgehog to reduce its body temperature to the threshold required for full hibernation. As a result, they increasingly find themselves in a state of suspended animation, not unlike the dreaded sleep paralysis or "locked-in syndrome" of our own species, where the victim is fully conscious yet not able to move a muscle. At such times, the hedgehog is usually wide awake but unable to escape predators, and it is either gobbled up by a hungry fox (or mongoose) or simply expires from a lack of food or oxygen. Such is the fate of our own kind in the age of the Anthropocene, in which rising temperatures and changing conditions are leading to a collective form of hyper-aware palsy, whereby we can see and feel the dangers all around us but seemingly lack the will or the means to do anything about it.

In the Land of the Jammy-Rams

In David R. Bunch's singular and surreal science-fiction epic *Moderan* (originally published as a sequence of short stories, and only recently collected into a kind of crypto-novel), we visit a picaresque brave new future in which people vie for mechanical augmentation and compete to escape nature into a vast and macho simulacrum known as Moderan, or "the New Processes." Written in the 1960s and 1970s – the height of both the cybernetic revolution and the techno-skeptical "new wave" writings it spawned, *Moderan*'s tale is a playful – yet also deeply serious – reflection on the emergent transhumanist tendencies of the late twentieth century; and as such it has much to say about our ongoing struggles with fantasies of Promethean transcendence through technology. Often reading as the pop-art bastard child of Gerard Manley Hopkins and Anthony Burgess, critically channeling Ayn Rand, *Moderan* begins with a description of the home-grown terraforming – or, rather, terra-*de*forming – that must be accomplished and maintained by formidable herds of "jammy-rams": "long-legged tamping machines" that were "huge black cylinders swung spinning between gigantic thighs and calves of metal."

The description of their task, provided by an obliging overseer, is worth quoting in full:

> Surely you must know that the earth is poisoned. From what I've heard, where you are from is not only poisoned, but wrecked and cindered as well. We stopped just short of that havoc up here; therefore there is this place for you from Old Land to come to. But our land was poisoned by science "progress" as much as yours was. So we're covering all with the sterile plastic, a great big whitey-gray envelope of thick tough sterile plastic over all the land of the earth. That's our goal. It's a mammoth task, but for mammoth tasks man has behemoth machines. The mountains go into the valleys, the creek banks go into the creeks, the ditch sides go into the ditches, the golf courses are smoothed, the mine tailings are scattered – and all is coated. At the necessary places we make the reservoirs for runoff and freeze it solid. The oceans we will deal with in our own time, our own time and well enough. There are several plans, one being to use our scientific knowhow to freeze the oceans solid, another being to shoot the oceans out into space in capsules and be done with all that surplus water forever. The new-metal man, which I am to a degree, and which you are to become to a much much higher degree, will need

> very little water . . . But now it's the land we're doing. The water is a later task. But when we get all through, I visualize an earth of such tranquility and peace in nature that it must be the true marvel of all the ages. The surface of our globe will be a smooth tough grayey-white hide. When our water plans are finalized the rainfall will be no more. No more will man be fleeing floods anywhere in the world. In cloudless heavens the winds will have died in our even temperatures; no more will man go sky high in the twisters. The air will hang as a tranquil envelope over essentially a smooth gray ball, the smoothness being broken only by the Strongholds and the bubble-dome homes. Trees, if we want them, will spring up from the yard-holes at the flick of a switch. The flowers will bloom just right and on time in wonderful bloom-metal. Animals – there will be no animals, unless we should want a few tigers and lions and such, all mechanical of course, for a staged jungle hunt. Yes! it will be a land for forever, ordered and sterilized. That's the Dream![15]

The author of this passage surely hoped that the reader would find such a dream much closer to a nightmare. Who, after all, is so alienated that they would rather live in a technological simulation than the real world, no matter how damaged or forsaken the latter? But, as we also know, there is currently no shortage of influential people who do indeed dream in this register, despite all the warnings from the last century, and who are already attempting to usher us all into either the Metaverse (Zuckerberg), Mars (Musk), a treeless Amazon forest of compulsive consumption (Bezos), an engineered environment, complete with man-made weather (the Chinese government), or a prismatic city made almost entirely of mirrors (the Saudi government). Even as I write, one of our best-selling "big thinkers" – Yuval Noah Harari – has gone on record as saying, "We just don't need the vast majority of the population." Indeed, according to this top advisor to the (hugely consequential) World Economic Forum, advances in AI, machine-learning, and bioengineering render most of the Earth's humans redundant: a view that only makes a micron of sense if people are valued as nothing other than an anonymous reservoir for labor. (Who constitutes the "we" in Harari's original statement is, of course, the unspoken assumption behind all these neo-fascistic techno-social arrangements. And, remarkably, even the new-metal warlords of Moderan are more compassionate than this real-life policy-shaper, as their superhuman elites eventually decide begrudgingly to be "left irrevocably saddled with these rheumatic old ladies, these bummy old men, these meaningless-futured young girls and all the rest of the under-par ragtag of humanity.")

Grand and global technical solutions, it seems, will forever be presented as the answer to problems created by the previous round of technical solutions. The novel's narrator is, initially at least, disturbed by the mission of the jammy-rams. "I for one would call it more than a small cosmic miracle if man, a spark of life tediously evolved from the dead cold elements himself, should so organize his forces as to rearrange those elements to have essentially a dead cold planet again before he departed. It would seem to me a dismal, and more than a little depressing, closing of the ring, for sure." But after undergoing an elaborate operation to replace most of his "flesh-strips" with gleaming new-metal "pain-crammed rebuilding," he is seduced by the hegemonic logic of the New Processes, and thereafter repulsed by the idea of life before or underneath the global crust of plastic. Even at its height, however, Moderan was not, we are told, "entirely free of the burden of the rag-tag flesh people." How painful to witness, for instance, unaugmented humans talk ("wet slop slopping gristle-meat tongue doing a dance, wind in the windpipe working, GOD! what an old-fashioned method just to communicate a few verbal salutes"). Even so, the new-metal man protagonist rejoices in escaping "the seething yeasty world."

He becomes a local warlord, as expected of him, after inheriting the fortification of Stronghold 10. Here he is visited by different figures – a child, a poet, a horseman, and so on – who (less didactically than it sounds) suggest other ways of being. After much complex cogitation, he begins to question the wisdom of all these machines of loving grace that control every aspect of life in Moderan, to the extent that his own thoughts are no longer simply "switch functional and normal toggles." Instead, "[s]ome catch in the smooth workings, a malfunction of the Joy-trims . . . in the heart and mind now, clawing the good times down, negating all his tall ambitions, selling short his many longings for power – everything now sunken to ciphers."

Bunch's novel is a complex, lurid, nuanced riposte to the shrugging Atlases of this world. And we can only hope that the new-metal men of our own strongholds are finally – similarly – troubled by "[f]loating airborne zeros and great blank rectangles of levitated Nothing."

hitchBOT

In 2013, two Canadian experts on human–robot interaction – David Harris Smith and Frauke Zeller – devised a whimsical experiment to test the extent to which robots can place their faith in the humans that, collectively speaking, created them. The experiment centered on a cute robotic hitchhiker called hitchBOT, which was powered by solar energy and equipped with a GPS locator, 3G wireless connection, and a camera. Consistent with the average human hitchhiker, hitchBOT was also "able to carry on basic conversation and talk about facts." The question behind the experiment was simple: can humans be trusted to help a fellow humanoid traveler explore the world? The answer to the first few tests – conducted in Canada, Germany, and the Netherlands – was a resounding "yes," as curious and kind-hearted people who encountered hitchBOT helped it get to its desired next destination, brought it to convivial gatherings, and ensured that it could complete several tasks itemized on its own personal "bucket-list" (such as attend a concert, travel in the cockpit of a plane, or explore the canals of Amsterdam). hitchBOT's adventures were recorded on its own Twitter feed, as well as through the accounts of those who encountered it. And while the philosophers and scientists may bicker about the extent to which hitchBOT was *really* enjoying, or even experiencing, these adventures, the sense of a plucky, low-tech nomad was effectively evoked by the whole enterprise.

In 2015, however, things took a dark turn, when after only a few days into its journey across the US, hitchBOT was assaulted, decapitated, and stripped for parts in Philadelphia. After starting the trip so optimistically, in Boston, hitchBOT had taken in a baseball game at the famous Fenway stadium. It even managed to safely navigate the hectic streets of Manhattan (though confessed to being exhausted by the pace of the place and needing to recharge its batteries). On the first day of August, hitchBOT tweeted, "The east coast has been swell, but it's time to head westward. I have been California dreamin'." A few hours later, seemingly from beyond the grave, two final tweets registered the bad news. The first said, "Oh dear, my body was damaged, but I live on with all my friends. Sometimes bad things happen to good robots!" And this was followed by some final words, truly Christ-like in their capacity for infinite forgiveness: "My trip must come to an end for now, but my love for humans will never fade. Thanks friends." hitchBOT's bucket-shaped head, the news reports noted, was never found.

We can speculate whether the experiment yielded a positive judgment regarding humans, except for one unfortunate "bad apple," or if it ultimately proved that robots should never fully trust the species that created them. Perhaps the moral of the story is that robots should not trust Americans – or, more specifically, Philadelphians. (The city of brotherly love.) In any case, hitchBOT never had the chance to check off its ambitious bucket list for the US, which included seeing the Cloud Gate in Chicago, hearing jazz music in New Orleans, and having a flutter over the betting tables in Las Vegas. At any rate, the whole experiment neatly inverted the concerns of Isaac Asimov's famous Three Laws of Robotics, which – with an eye cast firmly back to the lessons of Dr Frankenstein – were designed to protect humans from any harmful "acting out" by their technological progeny. In this case, however, we were obliged to consider the far more likely scenario, at least in the short term: that of parental abuse.

Barefoot Across America

A little over a year after hitchBOT met its untimely end, Mark Baumer – a writer and environmental activist – began his ambitious plan to walk across America, barefoot, to raise awareness about the urgent dangers of climate change and the inexplicable political inaction around this global, existential issue. On October 14, 2016, Baumer left his home in Providence, Rhode Island, with the aim of making it to the southern tip of the country before the official arrival of winter. Being a savvy millennial, he documented his progress on social media, and the first entry on his blog reads as follows:

> I woke up at 5am. My plan was to leave at 6am. I was not done packing. It took me six hours to pack. I left the house at noon. It was sunny. I said goodbye to a few of the special people in my life. Then I began running barefoot across America. I felt very excited. My body was not quite as heavy as it used to be. It was like some large weights had been lifted from my back. The day had finally arrived. I was actually running barefoot across America. After I turned onto Garfield Street my phone told me to take the Washington Secondary Trail. I followed this trail from Cranston to Warwick. It was a very nice trail. I saw a guy running in barefoot shoes. A very small bear or dog tried to injure me with its voice. Two old people held hands and nodded at me. A policeman on a bicycle pedaled very fast on the verge of a mental breakdown. Some teenagers yelled bad words in a tunnel. Some other teenagers were doing massive amounts of ice cream near a picnic table. I passed a baseball field that was almost dead at least until next year. Some men were dumping hot cement where the humans who paid them said to dump it.[16]

From this entry in his online journal, one can already get a sense of Baumer's whimsical literary spirit, which often hovers somewhere between Donald Barthelme and the middle voice of the McSweeney's stable of faux-naif and post-ironic authors. His posthumously collected writings are full of surreal images, self-deprecating gestures, wry observations, and witty non-sequiturs. The longer he walks along the unforgiving roads of his native country, however – without even the buffer of a thin sole of rubber – his thoughts become less precious and mannered and more sincere and simply sad. A month into his journey, on November 19, 2016, Baumer writes:

> As I walked last night, I listened to a man explain why the earth we had once known was already dead. There's already too much carbon in the atmosphere. Too many glaciers have already melted. The ocean is becoming more and more acidic. We can't reverse the damage we've already done. . . . You can glue a broken light bulb back together and it might still work but the light will never be the same. . . . So I guess I woke up on a dead planet. It still felt sort of alive. I still felt sort of alive. . . . I hope people don't think there's nothing worth saving even though the earth we grew up on is already dead.[17]

The more gas-guzzling beasts rush past him – carrying their cargo of humans, ranging from the indifferent to the hostile – the more he is troubled by the evident consequences of our actions in this late era of the Anthropocene. (Including, and especially, perhaps, building our lives and environments primarily around the needs of motor vehicles.) As Baumer walked through the Carolinas and into Georgia, his reflections seem to become darker and heavier with every step, suggesting that this "publicity stunt" was less a motivated form of raising funds and awareness than a final march towards infinite resignation. "We might all have the same brain," he writes. "Unfortunately, I think the brain is dying." He continues:

> Somehow we must accept life after the brain or we must accept earth post brain. This is a little sad, but brains were never constructed to outlive earth. Even though I am not sure if I can live without a brain I'm pretty sure earth will continue without the brain. When my brain dies hopefully I will remember to walk

> out into the forest and sit down in the pine needles if there are still pine needles out in the forest.[18]

There was something messianic about Baumer's mission and his deep need at once to witness, absorb, and embody our collective violence towards the planet and all its inhabitants. And while he did not seem to believe our kind was in any way redeemable, he still wanted to do something exceptional in order at least to acknowledge our sins, if not exactly atone for them.

Which makes it all the more disturbing that – at that uncanny age of thirty-three (and 700 miles and a hundred days into his journey) – Baumer was struck and killed by an SUV while walking along Highway 90 under the blazing Florida sun. The last photo posted to his online journal – which was presciently called "Not Going to Make It" – focuses on a yellow arrow spray-painted on the road next to his surprisingly unblistered feet. Below the arrow, also spray-painted in yellow, is the single word, "killed." A few hours earlier, on that same fateful day, Baumer typed out one of the last thoughts he would get to share with the world: "When I began walking I had an urge to stop traffic until all the roads in America died."

Extreme Weather

Ring of Fire

As if 2021 had not already provided enough apocalyptic imagery for one lifetime, we awoke on July 2nd to surreal images of the ocean on fire. Just west of Mexico's Yucatan peninsula, the surface of the sea was alive with flames, fueled by a gas leak from an underwater Pemex pipeline, and shaped unnervingly like Sauron's unblinking "eye of fire" in *The Lord of the Rings* saga. Several years before, the Deepwater Horizon spill – the largest in history – had pumped approximately 5 million barrels of oil into the Gulf of Mexico: an astonishing amount of petroleum product that was carried by ocean currents all around the world. While not as spectacular as an actual ocean of fire, the footage of the gushing leak on the sea bed was profoundly alarming, as if tapping into our deepest fears about human hubris and releasing it into both the ecosystem and our own inky collective subconscious. This "gusher" was repeatedly referred to in the press as a wound inflicted by us sadistic humans on an already battered Mother Earth. Indeed, as we watched the sub-aquatic "hemorrhage" on live webcam, it was difficult to resist the temptation to conflate oil with blood. Here, in ominously silent pixels, we could witness the clammy "return of the compressed": a geological jugular that stubbornly resists any technical tourniquet we can devise.

Sequence 8

Omen of the World

Storm and Stress

There is a certain interminability to the end of the world – at least when it is dramatized. Two-and-a-half hour blockbuster films, an irony-drenched, almost slapstick human drama of survival, punctuated by the technological sublime of massive tidal waves, shifting continents, descending asteroids, or the arrival of giant motherships. Multi-season, multi-episode shows featuring some variant of that most interminable of motifs – the zombie apocalypse – featuring unending tensions between the human survivors worthy of daytime soap operas. To be sure, there is an end. Giant waves engulf modern cities, leaving civilization in ruins. Unexplained plagues spread like wildfire across the human biological landscape. But, also, nothing ever seems to end. A ragtag group of under-achiever scientists, computer hackers, and various "regular" people with unexpectedly practical skills ends up saving the world, and thereby saving humanity. Or the dead keep coming back, as a happenstance group of survivors must bunker in and sort out their differences while fending off the encroaching pestilence of living death.

In spite of all the *Sturm und Drang* of how the end of the world is portrayed, what remains of humanity continues on. As Susan Sontag once wrote, "we live under continual threat of two equally fearful, but seemingly opposed, destinies: unremitting banality and inconceivable terror."[1] Indeed, there is something disappointing about the end of the world genre as a whole, not just because the promised end never arrives – it does, and often in the opening scene – but because something human always survives. There seems to be no end to the end, no end to what the human species can endure, or what it is willing to endure. Perhaps we are in a phase beyond the bifurcation identified by Sontag, one in which the destiny of inconceivable terror becomes weirdly identical to that of unremitting banality. The boredom with disaster. The catastrophe of the will to survive.

And yet, in spite of this, there is often a character who doesn't endure, who "opts out," who silently walks out into the sea, into the night, into certain death. It's usually a brief scene, an obligatory, elegiac moment for the one who lacks the fortitude to endure, for the one who is perceived by other characters as too weak, and who is, perhaps, too burdened by an unexplained melancholy surrounding the entire Wagnerian burlesque of human survivalism. It's not an act of heroism, but neither is it simple passivity. There's no having reached enlightenment, no expression of beatific joy, no love for all creation. To call it suicide seems simplistic. There is, perhaps, a sorrow specific to the interminability of the end, a melancholy about the very impossibility of the elegiac simply because someone always seems to survive. The scene passes. A fade out. The rustling of darker thoughts. Fade in, and the action continues.

Omen of the World

The end of the world. The world that never ends. These two poles seem to delineate the contours of end of the world science fiction, reflected in historical examples as well. Though the term "science fiction" doesn't gain currency until the early twentieth century, with hindsight it's easy to see a genealogy of these twin motifs. The advance of industrial capitalism and intensive urbanization; the waning of institutional Christianity and the rise of alternative spiritualities; the ascendency of nineteenth-century clinical psychiatry, with its typology of aberrant types; Darwinian evolution and the "descent" of the human being; the Second Law of Thermodynamics and the precarious balance between energy and entropy; advances in media culture such as photography and proto-cinema technologies; and a subculture of decline, moral degeneration, and *la décadence*. It's no accident that the first substantial end of the world science fiction emerged in a period so defined by the themes of structural collapse.

When combined with the millenarianism of the *fin de siècle*, the circulation of certain scientific ideas outside of specialist circles – accurate or not – has a runaway effect. Every instance of speciation implies extinction, and the challenge of humanity's humble biological beginnings in turn points to an equally humbling end. The notion that all physical systems tend towards entropic decline becomes scalable, from a cube of sugar dissolving in a cup of coffee to the eventual heat death of the sun. Between the devolution of the species and the collapse of the sun, the Earth itself seems to be suddenly criss-crossed by a host of celestial bodies: asteroids, meteors, comets, aerolites, and a host of other non-planetary bodies hovering about the sky. The massive meteor showers observed in November 1833 and 1866; the Great Comets of 1811 and 1861, observable for months at a time; the periodic comet that was observed in 1805, 1832, 1839, 1845, and 1852, before mysteriously disappearing into the farthest reaches of outer space. The Great Comet of 1882, passing so close to the earth it was visible to the naked eye in the cold of December, before breaking into smaller parts and burning itself out in long spectral tails across the winter sky. A shooting star. A sign of good luck. An omen.

It is in this context that we see a new kind of story emerging, one that partakes of both the mythic and the scientific, secularized adventure stories that have all the contours of the religious. Jean-Baptiste Cousin de Grainville's *L'Homme dernier* (1805) was appropriately subtitled "A Romance in Verse," for, while it does imagine the end of the world in decidedly modern terms, it quickly moves into the distant future and, in doing so, becomes a kind of romantic fable for the extinction of the species. More often than not, climate events precipitate the end, seen in Mary Shelley's *The Last Man* (1826), which takes cues from Grainville's climate-based apocalypse, as well as from the fad for literary end of the world scenarios, with Byron's "Darkness" (1818) being the most well known.

By mid-century, authors such as Edgar Allan Poe and Horacio Quiroga could abstract end of the world narratives into surreal, cosmic conversations between ethereal spirits. Poe's "The Conversation of Eiros and Charmion" features astral beings looking back on the end of the world, caused by a colliding comet. Author, astronomer, and spiritualist Camille Flammarion would follow suit with *Récits de l'infini*, his own collection of cosmic conversations. The stranger the planetary events, the more "the end" takes on the tone of prophecy, as if to indicate that, at the farthest reaches of the secular, one finds the religious – while the question of whether humanity will – or should – continue is left ambiguous by the end of the tale. This ambivalence continues in late nineteenth-century examples such as George Griffith's *Olga Romanoff* (1894) and Gabriel Tarde's *Underground Man* (1896). A rift grows between the end of the world event itself and our capacity for comprehending it, as if the end can only really be understood after it has happened.

This tension between the event of the end and our compulsion to discuss it reaches a pitch in Flammarion's 1894 novel *La Fin du monde*, a novel that is the blueprint for the innumerable end of the world books, films, shows, and comics with which we're now familiar. The approach of a comet headed for Earth generates not collective action but a cacophony of disagreement, debate, conflicts of interest, and the by now routine scenes of irrational fears, panic in the streets, and the desperate but futile need to flee. Told in an almost documentary style, *La Fin du monde* portrays a motif that has become at once exceptional and banal: the widening gulf that separates the foreground of human drama from the background of impersonal climate events, the gulf that separates the anthropocentric mania for meaning-making and the comet itself. (In fact, in an ingenious stylistic turn, Flammarion interrupts the suspense of the approaching comet with an extended, plotless essay on the history of apocalyptic prophecies linked to astral phenomena.) Miraculously, the comet is a near miss. But in its wake are planetary effects – and affects – that forever change the course of humanity. And this is just in the novel's first part. The rest of *La Fin du monde* makes leaps aeons into the future, imaging distant survivors of humanity who in turn face the collapse of the sun, and, in the final sections, aeons even further into the future, where we are confronted with the death of the solar system itself. Finally, the galaxy. The end, it turns out, is highly relative. And yet, by its final passages, Flammarion's prose now decidedly poetic, we bear witness to vaster and vaster scales of cosmic decline:

> long after the death of the earth, of the giant planets and the central luminary, while our old and darkened sun was still speeding through boundless space, with its dead worlds on which terrestrial and planetary life had once engaged in the futile struggle for daily existence, another extinct sun, issuing from the depths of infinity, collided obliquely with it and brought it to rest![2]

And yet, in spite of these doomsday scenarios, Flammarion still holds on to a kind of cosmic mysticism regarding the cycles of creation and extinction. An Earth dissipating with the same effortlessness that it had been incidentally created; suns colliding in a mutual decline; stars colliding with stars.

In a way, the counter-weight to Flammarion is H. G. Wells, whose 1897 short story "The Star" condenses *La Fin du monde* into a tighter, more action-oriented plot, while also posing bigger questions about humanity's ability (or inability) to grapple with the end. As in many Wellsian narratives, it is hero scientists who both make the discovery of the comet and offer ways of deflecting or otherwise evading it. But their advice is for naught, as politics, punditry, and public panic take hold, each person struggling to make sense of something far beyond the pale of humdrum human concerns. Again, the comet is the near miss. There are the climate events, as the comet steadily approaches. Glaciers melt. Storms, quakes, dramatic shifts in temperature, unstable orbits. And after all has passed, and what's left of humanity heaves a sigh of relief, the story suddenly shifts point of view. Alien astronomers on Mars have also witnessed the event. In their report, they note that, despite the near miss of the comet, "it is astonishing what little damage the earth, which it missed so narrowly, has sustained. All the familiar continental markings and the masses of the seas remain intact, and indeed the only difference seems to be a shrinkage of the white discoloration (supposed to be frozen water) round either pole."[3] An update on Earth. The poles have melted. Otherwise, nothing much to report.

Decades prior to both "The Star" and *La Fin du monde*, Jules Verne published the Voltairien novel *Hector Servadec* (1877; translated as *Off on a Comet*). In it, a colliding comet inadvertently carries off with it a big chunk of Earth and the inhabitants on it (including scientists, explorers, and other rogues). The roles are reversed; the Earth seems to be the comet. It was simply in the way.

A Feeling for Apocalypse (I)

There is something unavoidable about the speculation concerning the end of the world, in that it is the very existence of the world that also guarantees its end. Creation and destruction, growth and decay, the impersonal cycles of cosmos and chaos. But there is also something unacceptable about the end of the world, or at least about an end that has no meaning, an event without purpose, teleology without significance. And the question of "why is this happening?" is more often than not the question "why is this happening *to us*?" In a sense, the only thing more intolerable than the end of the world is an end without meaning.

For this reason, there is a certain "feeling for apocalypse" that inhabits the modern end of the world tale, be it Shelley's *The Last Man* or *The Walking Dead*, Wells's *In the Days of the Comet* or *The Eternals*, Flammarion's *La Fin du monde*, or *Don't Look Up*. It's also something not confined to the cultural sphere of entertainment. A town in eastern Texas reports a sudden "rain" of fish from the sky. In the Ural region of southwestern Russia, giant meteors fall burning from outer space. Massive algae blooms cover entire patches of the Great Lakes in North America, spreading to the shores, rivers, and inlets in luminous green. An amateur video shows a giant swarm of blackbirds suddenly plummeting to their deaths in the streets of Mexico City. A mysterious pandemic of unknown origin spreads across the planet in a matter of months, bringing travel, shipping, and economic networks to a standstill, as the most densely populated cities are suddenly emptied, silent, and still.

The near everyday occurrence of such "weird climate events" belies their strangeness, particularly as scientific explanations of such events tend to be so elaborate, opaque, or obtuse that such events actually seem stranger. For the non-specialist, it can become habitual to read these events, taken collectively, as somehow significant – as "signs." But signs of what exactly? Signs of things to come, or signs of things past? Lacking a single, dominant framework for interpreting such events, we are left only with a scattered, frenetic, twitching plethora of theories – conspiracy or otherwise – that seem to spread across the internet with the same contagious efficacy as the "plandemic" it is describing. It seems that the strangeness of the world revealed through this mania for deciphering signs far exceeds even the most elaborate blockbuster film.

Something happens, something of the order of non-human factors, and it is this very non-humanness that demands explanation. Or, something happens that only seems to be non-human but is tied to human activity, and which has taken on proportions that far exceed the scope of human agency or efficacy. The human confronts the non-human. Slowly, a dysphoria crystallizes. The feeling for apocalypse is the ambiguous sense of hovering in this gray space between a planet that reveals itself to be stranger than we ever thought and the insatiable human imperative for meaning, order, purpose.

A feeling for apocalypse emerges in this nebulous, harrowing space between weird climate events and our mania for describing, explaining, and interpreting them. But it is an apocalypse without a religion. It's the impression that the science just makes it weirder, more remote, more unreal. It's also the feeling that it's right here on our doorstep and that it's also just a show, a novel, that scene in the blockbuster movie. It's the feeling that all speculations seem fated to remain forever at the level of speculation, always at a remove from the thing itself. The feeling that, taken together, it is the routineness of weird climate events that somehow constitutes an omen of the world, one in which the line separating the weird and the routine becomes ever more blurred, as the very atmosphere in which we as human beings live becomes at once closer – frighteningly closer – and also farther away.

The planet as a giant timepiece counting down according to a logic we only dimly intuit. Konstantin Lopushansky's post-apocalyptic film *Letters from a Dead Man* (1986) opens with a monologue: "I propose a new unit of time. A single twilight."

Apocalypsis

This vague feeling for apocalypse sits nestled in between the long history of end of the world science fiction and the much older motif of the "dying Earth." While the New Testament Book of Revelation has, for many, become synonymous with apocalypse (spurred on in part by a tradition of dramatic visual representations, from Bosch to *The Day After Tomorrow*), there is also a sense of disconnect between the two realms of the earthly and the celestial, the former often blissfully unaware of the looming cataclysms brought on by the latter. Dürer's famous series of woodcuts depicting the biblical apocalypse helped to establish the visual melodrama of apocalypse, with its extravagantly hovering figures doing battle in the celestial realms while a fragile and unsuspecting Earth below hangs in the balance.

Historians of religion such as Norman Cohn, Bernard McGinn, and Caroline Walker Bynum have traced the zigzagging line that constitutes "apocalyptic spirituality" in the Christian Middle Ages. Apocalyptic writing is syncretic writing, often combining elements of a dream vision, epic narrative, and deeply introspective theological meditations on the relation between the earthly and the divine, time and eternity. Discussing the development of the Christian apocalyptic tradition, McGinn notes a set of frequently occurring motifs, including "the drive toward a universal view of history as a divinely ordered structure; a profound pessimism about the present that is seen at a time of crisis involving moral degeneration, persecution of the good, and the triumph of the wicked; and, finally, an optimism that is founded on a belief in an imminent divine judgement of wicked and vindication of the just."[4]

There is a divine message, relayed via a dream vision, written down in a treatise, a letter, or a prophecy. The message reveals something about an end – the end of history, the end of humanity, the end of the world – that is, at the same time, a culmination and fulfillment. The "last things" are also the first things. The end reveals a beginning. The end reveals something that exceeds both word and thought, the domain of the divine forever hidden in the blind spot of Earth-bound humanity, constricted by time. Not only do apocalyptic events take place in time, but they obtain an aura of pan-temporal efficacy. Something in the distant religious past, alive in the present. Something in the far-off future is suddenly alive in the urgency of the now. In this more secularized sense, the pattern of crisis–judgment–salvation, common to so many Christian apocalyptic texts, is actually about a limited humanity confronting a world that seems forever in the blind spot of comprehension.

True to its name – *apokálypsis* [ἀποκάλυψις] denotes a revealing, an unconcealing, an unveiling – apocalypticism bundles together the event and its interpretation. There can be no apocalypse without meaning and, specifically, especially for those human beings who bear witness to and endure apocalypse. In this sense, the end is not always horrific; it can, in fact, be a sign of fulfillment, fruition, or transcendence. The shadow play of earthly suffering concludes (at least for those who see the signs). The interpretations may vary, but there is this one constant: the unacceptability of an end without meaning. As varied as apocalyptic texts are, reading them today it's hard not to be struck by the plethora of climate events that constitute the end. Revelation, in some ways the most dramatic text, gives us everything from the famous Four Horsemen to oceans turning into blood, stars falling from the sky, a cacophony of storms and earthquakes, mutations and extinctions, a raining swarm of chimeric insects, and "bowls of plague" poured over the Earth.

This also suggests that the feeling for apocalypse is related to our manifold, fraught relationship to time – in particular the human experience of time – as well as to what, if anything, exists "after" the end. In the twenty-first century, everything seems to accelerate, as the hyper-mediated environments constellated by mobile, wireless, wearable, and ubiquitous technologies envelop the individual within precarious, intensive rhythms of "feeds" and "streams," a data-rich temporality that can often have all the urgency of apocalyptic crisis itself. And yet, this real-time, information-dense awareness of climate events around the world is also a reminder of the long stretches of non-human time that are of the order of glaciers, tectonic shifts, atmospheric changes – even the urgency of human impact on the climate, from the ozone layer to soil erosion, seems to happen at time scales that effortlessly transcend the span of an individual life.

The effect is a certain unease in relation to lived time. The lived present is continually being pulled apart, bifurcated and polarized, a data-rich present that, at the same time, stretches infinitely back to the deep geological time of the planet's formation. This is not, obviously, lived time. The deep time of the planetary past is forever out of reach, mediated only by the faint traces picked up by geology, stratigraphy, or paleontology. Likewise, the global transformations to the earth – which are "live," real-time transformations – nevertheless exist in a hovering, speculative future that can only be relayed to us via infographics and CG-drenched disaster movies. But a set of affects is produced. There is a sense of never quite being in the present, of never quite being in the world, of lived time having been already eclipsed by deep time, of human-centric history constantly giving way to the non-human vastness of geological epochs. A time displacement occurs. The present seems forever marked, if not determined, by the distant geological and biological past, the given parameters at a given time for the forms of life that can possibly exist. Every instance of speciation also a future instance of extinction.

Far from excluding the scientific or technological, apocalypse seems to incorporate it, to invite it, even to rely on it. In the era of global climate change, apocalypse is more scientific than religious, more technology than prophecy, more a problem of Big Data than one of eschatology. McGinn, writing about medieval Christian apocalypticism, refers to its "a priori" and "a posteriori" modes, the sense of a past prophecy informing and determining events in the present, and a sense of a future apocalypse seeded in the signs of the present. Perhaps that is, in essence, what the feeling for apocalypse is: apocalypse as allegorized climate event, apocalypse as geology or meteorology, apocalypse as the loss of "habitable zones," as the tracing of elements in the soil or air or the study of clouds.

Black Tears

Filmed in the immediate aftermath of the first Gulf War, Werner Herzog's *Lessons of Darkness* is less a documentary than a kind of tone poem, suffused as it is with desert landscapes of molten ash and fire in slow panoramas, set against the somber music of lament. While the film points ahead to Herzog's later productions such as *Encounters at the End of the World* (2007), *Into the Inferno* (2016), and *Fireball* (2020), it also looks back to films like *Fata Morgana* (1971) and his fascination with the stark contrast between the minutiae of human behavior set against vast, impersonal landscape. With no narrative, very few human characters, and only an intermittent voice-over, *Lessons of Darkness* is cinematic irony reduced to a minimum. Many scenes contain nothing but long shots of molten landscape accompanied only by the almost subsonic rumbling of raging oil fires. They are images of an Earth that seems inescapably alien, a planet that is at once primordial and post-apocalyptic.

Whether out of romantic dismissal or artistic provocation, Herzog (to the chagrin of many critics) refuses to provide any context for the film. There is no background, no history, no set-up, no chronological recounting of key events. Only the sparsest indication is given that we are even on planet Earth, at a particular point on a map, at a particular moment in human history. There is the brief fly-over of an almost futuristic Kuwait just before the war. An equally brief and harrowing scene of the war itself, shot entirely in night vision. And then, a series of cinematic ruminations on the devastation left behind. Burnt-out tanks, vehicles, and buildings. A desert engulfed by voracious oil fires. The war of attrition by the retreating Iraqi forces comes to eclipse the actual war itself. Independent contractor teams arrive to undertake the seemingly impossible task of containing the deluge of oil. An otherworldly landscape molded by fires of black gold.

In the midst of this, the film cuts to one of its few interviews. A Kuwaiti mother with her child. She recounts the trauma inflicted on her son by invading soldiers, compounded by the effects of burning ash and oil. "Even the tears were black, when my child wept his tears were black, when his nose ran, it ran black, even the spittle in his mouth was black." The child stares into the camera, impassive, troubled, vulnerable, blank. The pathos of hearing the mother and seeing her now mute child is accompanied by another, equally harrowing image of sorrow, of a landscape so ravaged by human activity that the primordial, black matter of the planet seeps into and out of the very pores of its inhabitants. It's as if the "black bile" of ancient Hippocratic medicine, buried in the depths of the body and the Earth, has billowed up to the surface in the form of desolate fires and black tears.

We are well aware, too aware, of the manifold and even routine atrocities that accompany war in all its guises. The sorrow connected to such events has long since passed into the rituals of mourning of different cultures at different moments in their history. But what of this other sorrow, where the planet itself seems to be weeping through the eyes of its traumatized, tenuous, and increasingly suspicious inhabitants? Should we say these are not new but old sorrows, unhuman sorrows expressed in the all-too-human vernacular of ritual chants or private prayers? Against the impersonal forces of the planet, the best we humans seem capable of doing is expressing a certain chthonic powerlessness in the face of planetary conditions for which we are partly responsible, and which will surely engulf us. A kind of vision occurs, captured centuries earlier by Rumi: "The continents blasted, / cities and little towns, everything / become a scorched, blackened ball."[5] A weak consolation emerges, captured in Parvin E'tesami's declaration: "The pages of my life are black as night."[6] Black ink for black bile.

Seven centuries after Rumi, the Chinese poet Tang Yaping would write *Black Desert*, a cycle of poems published in the 1980s, amid a different period of cultural, political, and environmental upheavals. It begins: "I can't stop this darkness leaking from my eyes / When the night seeps out I am vagrant / a night-walking goddess in total black."[7]

The Lost World

What exactly ends at the end of the world? So much energy is spent on the notion that the world is ending – if not now, then someday, eventually, inevitably – the question of what is ending is often overlooked. What ends, and for whom? An ending for one form of a life, a beginning for another? Or could it be that the very notions of "end" and "beginning" are themselves so time-bound to our own sense of mortality that they cease to have any meaning once the scale is shifted to, say, millions or billions of years?

Nevertheless, the end of the world motif in science fiction seems to make one thing clear. What ends is "the world." Though this seemingly innocuous word harbors within it its own ambivalence. The end of *the* world is, after all, more than the end of *a* world. The former is all-encompassing, totalizing, cataclysmic, whereas the latter is more localized, more context-dependent, more a matter of perspective. If hospitable conditions for the survival of the human species no longer exist, should we say that "the world" is ending, or should we simply say "a world"? Less melodramatic, but no less tragic. Perhaps the real tragedy is not simply that the world ends, but the way that the world-ending shows us, for a brief moment, the passage from the end of the world in itself to the end of the world for us – the strange act of sorcery whereby the impersonal "in itself" is transformed into the more personal, more imperative, for urgent, "for us."

Philosophers like Kant were explicit about the distinction between the world as it exists in and of itself (apart from our intervention, observation, or even awareness of it) and the world as it is given to us in experience, and through which we form the foundations for living in the world, for producing knowledge about it, and for enframing, transforming, and shaping the world according to values that remain indelibly human-centric. Yet the basic Kantian distinction remains, something "out there" from which we are forever occluded, but which also serves as the foundation for the cultivation of an "in here" from which we produce meaning (or at least value). The world "out there" is intimately interwoven with our sense of the world "in here," the world "in itself" inextricably bound up with the world "for us." Yet we can only negatively index the world in itself; it is, by definition, forever at the horizon of human intelligibility, always hovering in the blind spot of cognition, the impression of wearing goggles that you can never take off.

Embedded in the self–world relation is also the sense of something irretrievably lost. It could be manifest in the more general sense of living in a world that seems fundamentally at odds with itself, a world out of balance, a world intersected at various points by disasters and cataclysms that are at once environmental, political, cultural, and technological (or is it simply an anxiety born of going down this or that rabbit hole, the after-effects of "doomscrolling"?). It could also be the more personal, even mundane sense of a world that never quite matches up to our hopes and expectations, a world that somehow always slips from our grasp, as we try to ask "the universe" to bend to our desires just this once.

No doubt these sentiments are behind the age-old fascination with "lost worlds," shimmering civilizations once the beacon of humanity, now forever lost to the vestiges of fate. Popularized by authors such as Edgar Rice Burroughs, Arthur Conan Doyle, and H. Rider Haggard, the lost world mobilizes archaeology and adventure in order to collapse time and space. The other worlds are not out there beyond the moon, but right here, hidden in the bowels of the Earth or submerged beneath the ocean. Atlantis. Lemuria. Mu. For the science-fiction author and editor L. Sprague de Camp, the mania for rediscovering lost worlds has, over time, been transferred from science to science fiction. The search for clues to Atlantis "strikes a responsive chord by its sense of the melancholy loss of a beautiful thing, a happy perfection once possessed by mankind."[8] In the process, the desire to rediscover lost worlds reveals itself to be a desire for a certain kind of redemption. "Thus it appeals to that hope that most of us carry around in our unconscious, a hope so often raised and as often disappointed, for assurance that somewhere, some time, there can exist a land of peace and plenty, of beauty and justice, where we, poor creatures that we are, could be happy."[9]

A sorrow-laden suspicion arises. Is there always some part of the world that recedes from peering eyes, that dissipates against the assertions of intentional consciousness, that is effaced by the rapacious enframing capacity of human ingenuity? At the very moment we encounter the world in itself, it has ceased to be the world in itself and has already begun the process of being transformed into a world in relation to us. And the sorrow that lurks in its fissures is in this sense a sorrow of the species for itself, an elegy for humanity, murmured in oblique rituals of culture. For who else would mourn the loss of the human world, if not we ourselves?

Memento mori

Not long after the 2018 Halloween season, an asteroid approximately 650 meters in diameter passed safely by the Earth by several lunar distances. It wasn't the first time this particular asteroid – given the official designation TB_{145} – had made a fly-by.[10] Three years previously, it was spotted making a similarly remote trajectory in relation to the Earth. While asteroid discoveries are not uncommon, what makes TB_{145} unique is its uncanny shape. Scientists have come to refer to it as the "Skull Asteroid" (or, alternatively, "Great Pumpkin" or "Halloween Asteroid"), thanks to the imagery generated by the Arecibo Observatory in Puerto Rico. While many a science-fiction tale has imagined the Earth facing certain doom due to a colliding comet or asteroid, it is likely none of them have imagined that the Earth might meet its end via an asteroid-sized skull, ominously descending along its funereal arc from the black depths of outer space, a memento mori for the Anthropocene, a grim reaper of cosmic rubble and dust.

As TB_{145} passes by the Earth and enters its long, elliptical orbit around Mars, it's difficult not to be reminded of innumerable, though much smaller, memento mori. Brooding Hamlet at the graveyard, raising an Earth-worn skull, "alas poor Yorick" and indeed all of us burdened with the dim awareness of our own skeletal mortality. Sometimes, the skulls respond to our melancholic musing. A passage from Chuang Tzu tells of an encounter with a weathered and worn skull left by the roadside. Picking it up, Chuang Tzu chastises the skull. Where is your great pride and ambition now? Is this what all your efforts and struggles have led to? And for what? Placing it on the ground, Chuang Tzu takes a rest, using the skull as a pillow. In his dream, the skull responds to him, delivering its own "lecture on the dead." It's the dead who are to be envied, not the living: "Among the dead there are no rulers above, no subjects below, and no chores of the four seasons. With nothing to do, our springs and autumns are as endless as heaven and earth."[11] Not only is death the great leveler, but the remains it leaves behind also bear witness to the ephemeral nature of terrestrial life – and indeed of the planet itself. In a sense, this same Earth that is the source of human suffering is also the end of that suffering. Astonished and confused, Chuang Tzu asks the skull, if you were given the chance to live again, would you take it? To which the skull promptly shakes its head.

Chuang Tzu's parable has been repeated numerous times, both within and outside of the Chinese literary tradition. In the nineteenth century, Schopenhauer recasts it in aphoristic form, where he quips that, if the skeletons in their graves could rise and were given another chance to live, they would surely decline, indignant at their interrupted repose. And it reappears again in Lu Xun's 1936 play "Resurrecting the Dead," where the philosophizing skulls have a hard time convincing the living of life's essentially ephemeral nature. Different as they are from one another, what such variations suggest is a link between the existential conceit – death as the cessation of suffering – with another, more nebulous idea, one regarding the ambiguous intimacy between terrestrial origins and terrestrial ends, where the conjunction of death, corpse, and funerary rituals collapse the distinction between the living and the dead, the organic and the inorganic, anatomy and archaeology.

These motifs overlap in the case of the English polymath and author Thomas Browne, who in the 1650s was so taken by the discovery of ancient funerary urns in East Anglia that he wrote his influential and hard-to-classify work *Hydrotaphia, Urne-Buriall, or, A Discourse on the Sepulchrall Urnes lately found in Norfolk.* In it, Browne meditates on the funerary practice of burial and the strange conjunction it affords of corpse and earth, ash and soil. Following his death in 1682, Browne's body was buried in a church in Norwich. However, his skull was to have its own afterlife, as numerous modern authors – including W. G. Sebald and Colin Dickey – have related. The coffin's repose was unexpectedly interrupted by construction workers in 1840. In what has come to be a significant moment in the storied history of "cranioklepty," Browne's skull was absconded, eventually ending up at the Norfolk and Norwich

Hospital, where it was publicly displayed atop his books. In an oft-quoted passage from the Dedication, Browne writes:

> But who knows the fate of his bones, or how often he is to be buried? who hath the Oracle of his ashes, or whither they are to be scattered? The Reliques of many lie like the ruines of Pompeys, in all parts of the earth; And when they arrive at your hands, these may seem to have wandred far . . .[12]

It would take repeated requests by St Peter Mancroft Church to have Browne's skull reinterred in its original burial place, and when it was – in July of 1922 – the church official who recorded its second burial was left with no choice but to note, in the column designating the age of the deceased, "317 years."

Chuang Tzu, Browne, Schopenhauer, and Lu Xun offer us a kind of double allegory: a lesson not only on mortality and the reduction of the corpse to soil and dust but also the death of the Earth, at least as a habitat amenable to the self-aggrandizing species that has elevated its awareness of its own mortality. The death of human beings to the Earth, and the death of the Earth to humanity. Perhaps the most concise articulation of the relation between skull and Earth is a series of illustrations made in the 1970s by the artist Michel Granger, known to most as the cover of Jean-Michel Jarre's 1976 synthesizer album *Oxygène.* (Granger's images appeared in a 1972 issue of the French comics magazine *Pilote* and were subsequently exhibited in Paris, where Jarre first encountered the images.) Perhaps there is no better visual allegory for the existential quandaries presented by the Anthropocene: a blue-green Earth slowly peeling away to reveal a giant, planet-sized skull.

Granger's images were prompted by the debates happening at the time over the industrial pollution of the environment, and it's worth noting that they were used for an album of synthesizer soundscapes, as if the technologies of both art and music were coming together in a kind of eulogy for an already dead planet. Granger's "Oxygène" images also bring us back to TB_{145}, the skull asteroid. From a decidedly non-scientific perspective, the TB_{145} asteroid is also something quite different from what we condescendingly refer to as "space debris" floating around the "real planets." TB_{145} is not some nefarious planet-destroying asteroid from outer space; it is itself the Earth, or a reminder of an Earth that has, in the deep time of its non-human history, experienced multiple phases of extinction (inclusive of a Sixth Mass Extinction). The Earth as memento mori.

A Feeling for Apocalypse (II)

Admittedly, it's a mistake anyone could make, confusing the end of humanity with the end of the world, conflating the end of "the" world with what is in actuality the end of "a" world. In a sense, there is an anthropocentrism built into our various fictions of "the end," from early Christian apocalypses to the contemporary climate change documentary. While the crux of the narrative is tragic, it is perhaps only natural that we would be tempted to refashion the narrative in a different way so as at least to safeguard for ourselves the consolation of being able to imagine another outcome.

This tendency is at the root of modern science fiction, enamored as it often is of the efficacy of modern science, technology, and the instrumental approach to a world that always threatens to slip from our grasp. H. G. Wells's 1906 novel *In the Days of the Comet* is exemplary in this regard. While his earlier science fiction (such as "The Star," from 1897) dwelled upon the cataclysmic effects of planetary changes to climate, weather, and the atmosphere, *In the Days of the Comet* takes a decidedly different, more optimistic turn. Instead of foretelling the impending extinction of humanity, Wells opts for something out of a Marvel blockbuster: a passing comet has the reverse effect of beneficially transforming the atmosphere for human beings. Not only has the comet's "green fog" magically cleansed the air of all industrial pollutants, but the novel atmospheric admixture (Wells's scientists engage in a bit of jargon about breathable nitrogen) actually enhances human capacity. The comet seems to have delivered its payload of interstellar MDMA across the whole planet. General feelings of euphoria and love towards all humankind follow. This was the "posthuman" that we were promised. The end of the world turns out to be not tragic but heroic, thanks in large part to the hero scientists who are able to harness this new atmosphere for the purposes of enhancing life and promoting world peace.

Given Wells's previous forays into apocalyptic science fiction, it's not hard to imagine how tempting it would be, if only as an exercise, to write something as disarmingly naïve and optimistic as *In the Days of the Comet*. And yet, for all its utopian charm, this tale does share something crucial with its earlier cousins (including the under-appreciated *The Sleeper Awakes*), and that is a preoccupation with human redemption vis-à-vis the planet. To be sure, Wells is not the only early science-fiction author who does this. The near miss, the almost apocalypse, the scientist or engineer that saves the day. The prospect of human extinction is presented, only to have human provenance reasserted by the end. In some cases, we as human beings don't even need to try. The *War of the Worlds* is won not so much by human bravery or ingenuity as by the indirect effect of terrestrial microbes on our alien invaders – the common cold inadvertently turned into a bioweapon. Humanity accidentally victorious. Unintentional survival. In these scenarios – be they tragic or heroic, dystopic or utopic – there is an ambivalent sense that the urgency of humanity's survival eclipses any notion that the planet had ever existed without human beings busied on its surface.

Among examples of early science fiction, perhaps no one has captured this ambivalent sense of sorrow and wonder as well as the Belgian author J.-H. Rosny aîné. Rosny aîné's fiction is difficult to classify; it is at once prehistoric and post-apocalyptic, a glimpse into a primordial past so strange it seems to be set in the far future. Above all, his speculative fiction often inverts the relationship between character and setting, such that human beings are merely set decorations for strange elemental forces at play that are indistinguishable from the mineralogical and climatological aspects of the planet itself. In 1910 Rosny aîné published *La Mort de la terre*, a far-future scenario where small human communities living on an uninhabitable Earth discover a mineral form of life they call "ferromagnetals." They seem to be nothing more than blotches of slowly moving matter, like clouds, mist, or the now unbreathable atmosphere itself. And yet they seem to "think" or "communicate," though whether this is telepathy, possession, or outright delusion on the part of the human survivors is impossible to discern. Much of the novel is dedicated to the deceptively simple problem of detecting this other form of life. As what remains of humanity struggles for survival, they are also beset by the more metaphysical uncertainty of whether or not there is a "there" there when it comes to these strange mineral beings. The human beings in the story end up spending most of their time "entranced by the strange magnetic creatures that were multiplying across the planet as humanity declined."[13]

The enigma of the ferromagnetals – are they alive, are they intelligent, are they even of this Earth at all? – evolves into an ambivalent apprehension of the sacred: "A kind of religion was born, without worship, without rites: fear and respect for the mineral. The Last Human Beings attribute to the planet a slow and irresistible will. The mysterious hour in which the planet condemns them is also that in which it favors new kingdoms."[14] Their strange existence, at once material and immaterial, physical and metaphysical, gradually reveals an origin story, a kind of creation myth for the era of human extinction: "The existence of the ferromagnetic kingdom began to be perceived at the end of the radioactive age. They first appeared as weird purple stains on iron and iron compounds that have been altered by industrial use . . ."[15] As it turns out, the unhuman strangeness of the ferromagnetals was produced by human beings after all, an accidental off-shoot of the Anthropocene. A new form of life emerges from the literal fallout of human posterity. What is accidental from one perspective is quite predictable from another. A passing of ages, a rift in the terms that determine "life itself." Evolution by other means. "Perhaps we were in a similar situation vis-à-vis a previous life which, in its decline, allowed the blossoming of protoplasmic life."[16]

Vital Signs

In a 2021 paper published in the journal *Geoscience Frontiers*, scientists offered evidence that major upheavals throughout the planet's history tend to cluster in periodic events, which the authors describe as the Earth's "pulse."[17] Such events include shifts in tectonic plates, volcanic eruptions, fluctuations in the sea level, and mass extinctions. Whereas earlier thinking had assumed a randomness of such extreme climate events, the quantitative analysis of such events over the past 260 million years reveals a "rhythmic pulse" – one that appears to "beat" every 27.5 million years, though whether we will be around to hear the Earth's pulse is, of course, a different question. According to the study, the last "pulse" of the Earth was approximately 7 million years ago, which would mean the next heartbeat of the planet will take place some 20 million years in the future.

On one level, the idea that the Earth has a "pulse" would seem to be the pinnacle of human-centric thinking, in that it not only recasts the planet as a living organism not so different from us but also allows us the presumptuousness of human beings acting as physicians for the planet, able, in our best bedside manner, to calmly and reassuringly take the planet's pulse. Given that human activity on Earth has itself contributed to the planet's various ailments, there is also something menacing about the scene, the physician standing helpless before a terminal illness, reduced to the now meaningless recording of a pulse. A somber prognosis.

But the findings concerning the Earth's pulse reveal something else, which is the radical rift in scale between the life of the planet and that of the minutiae of life forms that live on it, a rift we can only meekly cross through the most outrageous, even absurd attempts at the pathetic fallacy. A "pulse" every million years. A pulse within which entire human civilizations rise and fall. A pulse within which entire species emerge and then become extinct. We live within the spaces of the Earth's pulse, and if "life" at this scale lies outside the scope of our comprehension, so would death. For all intents and purposes, the time that passes between one pulse of the Earth and the next is itself death – a seemingly eternal expanse of hovering stillness and stasis, the floating oblivion of deep space.

And if we struggle to comprehend the life of the planet from the planet's perspective, so do we struggle even more to comprehend the death of the planet. This is likely an explanation for the wild effusions of the imagination that characterize visions of the apocalypse both ancient and modern. It prompted Kant to write a short, uncharacteristically satirical essay titled "The End of All Things." Published in 1794, its main target was the censorship regarding free and critical thinking about religion, something central to Kant's moral and ethical philosophy. Kant was also aware of the fashion for apocalyptic thinking, which in his time had been taken up by various groups and often affiliated with the French Revolution. What he notes above all is the essential unthinkability of the end of the world. By definition, it cannot be experienced. There is no speaking from the other side of the end of the world, for if one could speak from experience, then the world – which provides the foundation for the possibility of experience – has not ended. "This thought has something horrifying about it because it leads us as it were to the edge of an abyss: for anyone who sinks into it no return is possible . . . and yet there is something attractive there too: for one cannot cease turning their terrified gaze back to it again and again."[18]

The more we try to gain access to eternity from the perspective of time, the more our faculties flounder on their own limitations. We thus index the end of time by pinpointing a Judgment Day, the end of time-bound life by a paradoxical afterlife, an oblique glimpse into eternity via events that are themselves ironically time-bound. However, there is perhaps something instructive in this failure. As mortal, finite human beings, we seem drawn to this limit, perhaps for no other reason than it allows us a glimpse into the horizon of what it means to be human.

There is something at once terrifying and fascinating about a limit of this kind, for no other reason than it gives us the most minimal guarantee that there is something out there besides us self-obsessed and self-involved human beings. "It is frighteningly sublime partly because it is obscure, for the imagination works harder in darkness than it does in bright light."[19] We know we can never see beyond it, but the shadowy impression of something "beyond" is, it seems, too alluring to ignore.

Part of the difficulty we encounter is that our thinking about time is so often bound up with thinking about an "end," either in the sense of our mortality or in the various ways in which we imbue lived time with purpose. An "end" is not only a temporal stoppage, it also indicates a goal, a purpose, a meaning. If we have trouble comprehending the end of the world, it is, for Kant, because we are so often conflicted about this "end." From the religious perspective, the end of the world is not the end but simply a means to an end – the afterlife, the hereafter, eternity. And yet we remain inescapably time-bound beings, and if all we know is the world and the various "ends" that give it meaning, how limited must be our capacity to rationalize an end after the "end"?

Of course, we don't want the world to end – do we? Without the structure of an end (a goal, a purpose) to terrestrial life, what is left but the terror of free-floating time, akin to "a play having no resolution and affording no cognition of any rational aim"? Life on Earth is not without its struggles, and even the staunch rationalist is forced to acknowledge the inevitable role that suffering plays in human existence. "In fact it is not without cause that human beings feel their existence a burden, even if they themselves are the cause."[20] Perhaps the furtive desire to cast off this burden is reflected in the manifold ways in which the apocalyptic imaginary has envisioned the end of the world as the end of the planet, "in unusual alterations in nature – in earthquakes, storms and floods, or comets and atmospheric signs."[21] Be it in archaic religious imagery or the latest scientific findings, we seem incapable of conceiving of the end of humanity without also conceiving of the end of the planet, so bound is our sense of finitude to the impersonal architectures of terrestrial time. The last pulse of the planet – but a pulse we can never detect.

"But," Kant adds, "why do human beings expect an end of the world at all? And if this is conceded to them, why must it be a terrible end?"[22]

Extreme Weather

Sea of Snot

Halfway through the accursed year of 2021, Mother Earth seemed to be suffering a severe summer cold. Newspapers reported alarming amounts of "marine mucilage" that had congealed along the Turkish coast, as if the planet had sneezed over the ancient waterways in which Europe flows into Asia. Described more colloquially as "sea snot," the Sea of Marmara was covered in thick layers of "viscous, slimy, mucus," repelling would-be swimmers, depressing local fisher-folk, and suffocating the marine animals. While Turkey's controversial president pledged "a massive effort to vacuum up the foul-looking substance," scientists insisted on more preemptive action, since the endless booger was evidently a confluence of anthropogenic factors, including "untreated sewage, agricultural runoff . . . and warming water temperatures caused by climate change." A month later, however, attention had turned inland, as much of Turkey (and neighboring Greece) had – like Australia, before it – seemingly burst into flames. One wonders how the populace felt, trapped on one side by more than 200 conspiring wildfires and on the other by waves of churning mucus.

Sequence 9

Shapes of Sorrow

Music of the Spheres

On September 5, 1977, NASA launched the Voyager 1 space probe, whose primary objective was to study the solar system and the regions of space beyond. It sends back data on a regular basis – via NASA's Deep Space Network, a kind of cosmic internet – and is estimated to have gone farther into space than any other spacecraft. In addition to the elaborate technology that went into Voyager 1's design, NASA added another feature: a collection of music and images from Earth, should the probe be discovered by any form of intelligent life. One can imagine the heated debates about which songs to put on the cosmic playlist (let alone the question of whether aliens collect vinyl), and the committee – headed by Carl Sagan – included everything from Bach to Javanese gamelan music to Louis Armstrong's "Melancholy Blues," along with a selection of nature sounds to round things out. Interestingly, the Golden Record, as it's come to be known, itself looks like an alien artifact, forged of the Earth and inscribed with strange and meaningful symbols. A relic, perhaps, from a distant civilization, now lost in the unfathomable history of the cosmos.

Though prohibited by the physics of outer space, it's hard not to imagine Voyager 1 quietly drifting along its path, the Largo movement from Bach's third Sonata for Solo Violin faintly reverberant in the distance, as it departs from the outer edges of the solar system, a solitary assemblage of disc, antennae, and various machine parts surrounded by the blackness of interstellar space. In its wandering perambulation, Voyager 1 has unwittingly become a kind of cipher for the almost metaphysical – or astrophysical – solitude of the human species. Lyrical appeals for contact cast into black seas of infinity, pleas for recognition met only by the muteness of deep space.

Abandoned by the World

The discovery of a new planet is one of the oldest motifs in science fiction. Within it is embedded a deep and ambivalent desire: to *leave* the old planet. To leave, to escape, at the very least to rest, consoled in the knowledge that there are other planets "out there." To leave the planet is also to leave the planet behind, perhaps in the way one casts off a burden, a liability, an unwelcome obligation, perhaps in the same way one is duty bound to let go of the past, of past traumas, loves lost, distant memories – one's former self. To leave the planet is also to cast oneself adrift into indefinite space in the hope of arriving somewhere else, anywhere else. But where would one go if not to another planet, one that is habitable and because of this appears to be uncannily similar to the planet that has been left behind. Perhaps what has been left behind isn't as far away as we'd like it to be. Being cast adrift in interplanetary space suddenly becomes a derelict hall of mirrors, as a rumbling suspicion emerges: perhaps what is really sought is not another planet but a formerly lost planet recovered and redeemed.

What is discovered is not just a planet but also a *world*. And, as philosophers such as Kant remind us, a world (*Welt*) is never a "thing in itself" but always a world "for us" as species-specific beings. A planet existing for aeons apart from its being observed (and named, and measured, and mined) by human beings remains something apart from language, and, until then, it remains a planet – and not yet a world. The spectral quality of the "thing in itself" – at once logically necessary and yet empirically unavailable – remains a kind of fable for human beings, in part because the discovery of a planet cannot help but become the discovery of a world. A world in which we live but also a world that we set apart as a world – a world that has been shaped and molded by the industrious hands of human time. It is, in Edmund Husserl's terms, a "life-world" (*Lebenswelt*) that is given to us as cognizing, sensate beings, but also what the biologist Jacob von Uexküll termed an "environment" or "surrounding" (*Umwelt*), the terrain on which and through which the organism lives. *Welt* is also the product of the specifically human world forming capacities of human technics, encapsulated in Heidegger's use of the term *Umwelt* – the world arrayed around us, a world that we have enframed as "our world," the world enveloping us and standing in relation to us as human beings as a natural resource. The world is what stands there, waiting.

Dream Worlds

At the same time, the motif of discovering a planet is much older than science fiction, appearing to emerge in lock-step with developments in cosmology that take us back at least to the scientific revolution. True, travels to fantastical worlds can be found in a wide range of myths and classical literature, from the *Rāmāyana* to the *Odyssey* to the *Thousand and One Nights*. But a particular kind of fantastical world takes shape in the shadows of early modern innovations in physics, optics, and astronomy. The so-called Age of Reason also produced often delirious fantasies of voyages to other planets, often couched within the frame of "dreams" or "visions" which were, at the same time, rooted in scientific reason. Indeed, many of them were written by the scientists themselves, as with Johannes Kepler's *Somnium* (1634), while others were written from the perspective of religion, as in *The Man in the Moone* (1638) by Francis Godwin, Bishop of Hereford.

These and other extra-planetary tales take place against the backdrop of earlier works such as Thomas More's *Utopia* and Francis Bacon's *The New Atlantis*, both of which not only continue the long literary tradition of imaging other worlds but do so in an increasingly ambiguous way. The promises of reason seem inseparable from a nagging persistence of the human-centric bias. Wherever you go, there you are, in the farthest reaches of the globe, there are people, always people. Secular, scientific reason sits uneasily alongside satire, irony, and the tragic comedy of suffering humanity. Voltaire's *Micromegas* (1752) – which contains an account of a visit to other worlds only slightly less ridiculous than our own – has to be read in this context, as does like-minded proto-science fiction, including Margaret Cavendish's *The Blazing World* (1666), Jonathan Swift's *Gulliver's Travels* (1726), and Vasily Levshin's *The Newest Voyage* (1784). Cosmology seems to provide the tools for a secular knowledge about other planets while, at the same time, rendering absurd petty, squabbling humanity against the backdrop of infinite space.

The smallest interval exists between intellect and instrument, inhabiting a planet and shaping it. Romanticism, industrialism and the evolutionary "decline of Western civilization" are not so far off. Suddenly a planet is not enough, an entire world somehow insufficient. Camille Flammarion's *The Plurality of Inhabited Worlds* (1862), Jules Verne's *From the Earth to the Moon* (1865), H. G. Wells's *The First Men in the Moon* (1901). We are just steps away from the Golden Age of science fiction and the pulp magazines. A space opera. A space race. Who can be the first to leave the planet? Late twentieth-century iterations of the theme render the colonization of other planets in a more nuanced, complicated, and conflicted manner, confronting the technical, social, and political contingencies of actually discovering a world – red Mars, blue Mars, green Mars. So persistent is this theme that the lines separating science and science fiction have become even fuzzier, exemplified by the 2016 National Geographic TV series *Mars*, which utilizes documentary, interviews with scientists, and re-enactments (of the future) – while corporate space programs like SpaceX and Virgin Galactic seem more to us like the Golden Age of science fiction, somehow utopian and dystopian at the same time.

Shapes of Sorrow (I)

At some point, the fraught anthropocentrism of ceaselessly seeing a world for every instance where there is only a planet produces a species-specific, interstellar solipsism. At some point, the world eclipses every planet.

The limit-case in science fiction is *Solaris*, published in 1961 by Polish author Stanisław Lem. On the surface, *Solaris* borrows many familiar motifs from classic science fiction: the exploration of outer space, the deployment of science and technology to discover and study other planets, and the possible encounter with extraterrestrial intelligence. But *Solaris* is also a far cry from the action and adventure plots of the science fiction space opera. There is actually very little technology, no menacing alien invaders, no hero scientists, no re-establishment of human dominion over outer reaches of interplanetary space. Much of the novel consists of essentially plotless ruminations on the impossibility of discovering alien intelligence, with a chamber play cast of characters confined within the spaces of the aptly named Prometheus, a derelict space station orbiting the planet Solaris. As for the planet itself, Solaris presents an enigma to its human observers. The entire planet seems to be a single ocean, though its composition and movements are unlike anything observed on Earth. Some of the most moving passages in Lem's novel are not those that play out the human drama of love, loss, and grief but those passages that describe the planet itself, bereft of any human presence:

> The disc of the blue sun was setting to one side of the horizon, while on the opposite side billowing purple clouds announced the dawn of the red sun. In the sky, blinding flames and showers of green sparks clashed with the dull purple glow. Even the ocean participated in the battle between the two stars, here glittering with mercurial flashes, there with crimson reflections. The smallest cloud passing overhead brightened the shining foam on the wave-crests with iridescence. The blue sun had barely set when, at the meeting of ocean and sky, indistinct

> and drowned in blood-red mist (but signalled immediately by the detectors), a symmetriad blossomed like a gigantic crystal flower.[1]

There are no humans here – except, of course, those who observe and witness the Solaris planet, who perpetually stand in a nebulous and hazy relationship to it – something captured in the slow cadence of Tarkovsky's celebrated film adaptation. That the planet exists is indisputable. But what the planet is – much less what it "wants" – is another question altogether.

In fact, we are told that generations have been stumped by the enigma that is Solaris, entire scientific fields and subfields of "Solaristics" having sprouted up to dutifully analyze the problem, collect data, propose hypotheses. Debates ensue, factions form, human squabbling. Amid it all is Solaris, at once an ocean planet, a shape-shifting plasma, a giant brain, a giant computer – and at the same time none of these. The human observers of Solaris seem forever imprisoned within their incomprehension of Solaris, a world without a planet. Solaris itself presents the limit-case: the planet without a world.

Shapes of Sorrow (II)

The discovery of a planet is also the furtive creation of new uncertainties, new doubts, a new apprehension of the limits of comprehension. A report on the history of Solaristics research provides a summary:

> On the basis of the analyses, it had been accepted that the ocean was an organic formation (at that time, no one had yet dared to call it living). But, while the biologists considered it as a primitive formation – a sort of gigantic entity, a fluid cell, unique and monstrous (which they called "prebiological"), surrounding the globe with a colloidal envelope several miles thick in places – the astronomers and physicists asserted that it must be an organic structure, extraordinarily evolved.[2]

Tests are performed, measurements made, data collated, papers published. Entire subfields of study are created. The perplexity persists. A devotion at once spiritual and scientific emerges in the stopgap between the phenomenon and the thing in itself. Years, decades pass, volumes amassing in "The Solariana Collection." New additions to the *Historia Solaris*. Serious discussions over serious matters, leading only to metaphysical puzzles – impassivity, opacity, the impersonal. A science devoted to the incomprehensible cannot but succumb to "the temptations of a latent anthropomorphism."[3] A planet that seems to sprout "limbs" and "organs." A planet that seems to display intentionality, if not intelligence. Perhaps "communication." The best guesses are hemmed in by analogy: a giant brain, an ocean computer, "performing calculations for a purpose that we are not able to grasp."[4] A planet that appears to randomly unfurl in vast "vertibrids," grotesque "mimoids," and uncanny "phi-creatures." An ocean planet that is not an ocean at all but an immanent, undulating surface of "plasmatic metamorphoses." At times distinct shapes emerge from it, gigantic shapes that appear to take on the real, physical presence of human memories, of people lost, of past tragedies – but for what purpose no one can divine. A startling indifference to human presence, matched only by an equally startling responsiveness. Most often, when one is asleep. Lost memories, time collapsed in dreams, buried sorrows. The planet an ocean, the ocean a metamorphosis, metamorphosis the shape of lost time.

And yet, we are told, the Solaris planet can be cataloged, classified, ordered according to a nomenclature haunted by its own precision. Even the category of the incomprehensible is given a place. Anthropomorphism gives way to anthropocentrism. There are "symmetriads" – massive, continent-wide, metamorphic shapes that bear no apparent resemblance to anything recognizable by human beings. In a periodic cadence of form and formlessness, gelatinous geysers of oceanic matter coalesce into a lattice, an architecture, mirrored panels, corridors, and vaults, before beginning their slow swing back into shapelessness. The symmetriads loom large over any human-built structure and yet display no aggression, present no threat. And this alone is perhaps the greatest threat:

> It is not their nightmare appearance that makes the gigantic symmetriad formations dangerous, but the total instability and capriciousness of their structure, in which even the laws of physics do not hold. The theory that the living ocean is endowed with intelligence has found its firmest adherents among those scientists who have ventured into their unpredictable depths.[5]

And in those depths? The symmetriads simply continue to unfurl and coalesce in their non-Euclidian reverie. The effortless, hyper-complex generation of forms and, at the same time, the ceaseless and equally effortless dissipation of form. The inexplicable presence of the planet recedes behind the fog of metaphors, analogies, and the persistence of anthropomorphisms. The conventional boundaries between form and formlessness, the living and non-living, life and death, all dissipate. Coming to be and passing away begin to mirror each other such that they lose their distinction.

> We pass through vast halls, each with a capacity of ten Kronecker units, and creep like so many ants clinging to the folds of breathing vaults and craning to watch the flight of soaring girders, opalescent in the glare of searchlights, and elastic domes which criss-cross and balance each other unerringly, the perfection of a moment, since everything here passes and fades. The essence of this architecture is movement synchronized towards a precise objective. We observe a fraction of the process, like hearing the vibration of a single string in an orchestra of supergiants. We know, but cannot grasp, that above and below, beyond the limits of perception or imagination, thousands and millions of simultaneous transformations are at work, interlinked like a musical score by mathematical counterpoint.[6]

The Solaris planet presents a special kind of incomprehension, an incomprehension born of the labors of knowledge production and ratiocination. An incomprehension articulated in the contours of disbelief. A science devoted to the continual disintegration of anthropomorphism, dissipating beneath the weight of its taxonomies, the gravity of its laws, the luminous insignificance of formlessness and form. One of the characters in the novel, the curmudgeonly scientist Sartorius, puts it plainly:

> We take off into the cosmos, ready for anything: for solitude, for hardship, for exhaustion, death. Modesty forbids us to say so, but there are times when we think pretty well of ourselves. And yet, if we examine it more closely, our enthusiasm turns out to be all sham. We don't want to conquer the cosmos, we simply want to extend the boundaries of Earth to the frontiers of the cosmos.[7]

A science fiction of negative possibilities. There are no other planets because there are no other worlds. There is only one world, imprisoned in the cognitively finite gaze of a self-named species that sees only itself. "We have no need of other worlds. We need mirrors. We don't know what to do with other worlds. A single world, our own, suffices us: but we can't accept it for what it is."[8]

Like other works of the so-called new wave of post-war science fiction, *Solaris* begins from a different premise than its predecessors. Suppose that the discovery of a new planet is, in the moment of its being discovered, the irrevocable loss of that planet? Observation, measurement, nomenclature where is it, in relation to us? Suppose that those attributes that make humanity what it is are also those which ensure the inescapable sense of human solitude in the universe? In the very idea of a search for extraterrestrial intelligence, life, or sentience is a presupposition about what the parameters for intelligence, life, or sentience is, as a species continues to tragically struggle against the very categories that it has constructed for itself.

Weltschmerz

In the science-fiction context, a world is what emerges in the discovery of a planet; in a sense, it cannot help but do so. A world implies a certain species-level solipsism (a world for us) at the same time that it is predicated on the idea of some pre-existing planet "in itself" that is subsequently discovered by us. If the discovery of a planet is also the discovery of a world, then the possibility of discovering a world is always founded (often quite literally) on the surface of a planet. It could even be said that one of the main contributions of early science fiction – for better or worse – is to suggest that the discovery of a planet constitutes the very grounds of possibility for the discovery of a world.

Sometimes, the price for the emergence of a world is the destruction of the planet. The emergence of a world can be so voracious, so all-encompassing, that it eclipses the planet, and the planet itself is lost, dissipating behind a world that is really the world exclusively for us as a species. The moment the planet is conceived and grasped within the human framework, it is also forever lost. From this loss, a certain sadness emerges. It sometimes seems as if the gaze of Orpheus were transposed to the entire species – the moment we gaze upon a planet, it dies and begins the slow and inexorable transition of being incorporated into our systems of knowledge. A world that has been lost through the machinations of humanity or via the slow and patient withering of cosmic time. An imaginary world, an ideal world of possibilities and promises, a world that has never existed in the first place, a world whose main purpose seems to be to perpetually exist at the fringes of human hopes and fears – a world that is literally "no place" (*u-topos*).

In this sense, *Welt* always orbits around a terrestrial sorrow, a sorrow linked to the awareness of the transience of the world. *Welt* is, in this sense, the atmosphere of the ephemeral, the transitory, what passes and dissipates and withers. From the emergence of *Welt* arises a *Weltschmerz*, a "world weariness," a sorrow regarding everything that has been lost as the necessary by-product of the world-forming, world-shaping capacities of the species. The sense of *Weltschmerz* found among nineteenth-century poets writing in German – Friedrich Hölderlin, Josef von Eichendorff, Annette von Droste-Hülshoff – emerges from the apprehension of a dysphoria between the world and the planet, a secret affinity between tenebrous inner states and the affective dimensions of the seasons. Terrestrial nature seems at once to invite and envelop the human being in its atmospherics of winter, forest, and twilight temporality while at the same time expressing a strange and harrowing impersonal quality, forever closed off from the human observer. At times the boundary between exteriority and interiority breaks down, the poets deliriously projecting affects onto the autumnal forest or rain-filled skies. At other times it's as if the impersonal affects of climate, weather, moss, stone, and forest seem to seep into the sinews of the human affective capacity, producing moods that are difficult to name. A religious sorrow. In one of his letters Nikolaus Lenau writes, "the divine in life has never appeared to me without the accompaniment of sadness."[9]

The Deeps

While deluge myths stretch back to ancient Mesopotamia, in the twenty-first century the deluge has also become a climate event, an example of extreme weather folded back into the terrifying landscapes of religious cataclysm. Human habitats can be decimated by any number of means – wildfires, hurricanes, freezing temperatures, volcanic eruptions, and nuclear reactor leaks – all of which reveal the tenuousness of what we too often assume is our "home." But there is something about the flood that strikes deeper into the nebulous fears about the loss of human habitat. As mammals we are, of course, a largely land-locked species, in spite of the vast, Leviathan-like cruise ships that regularly criss-cross the seas in a kind of unintentional bacchanal of human dominion. But even in these floating cities there is the haunting murmur of a flooded planet, as if each ship were secretly the "Noah's Ark Principle" on a trial run.

The flood is a special type of disaster in that its "destruction" is ambiguous. A flood does what floods do. It inundates, engulfs, submerges, and sinks. Something has disappeared, submerged below the surface, something forever lost but also something that's still there, down below, algae-covered and derelict in its sub-aquatic tomb. The thought not only of losing one's home but of losing land itself holds a special kind of terror. This is why it's tempting to refer to the mass flooding caused by climate events as a deluge, and not just as a flood. This is also why the scenes in blockbuster disaster films of gigantic and inexorable waves slowly crashing down on entire coastal cities are often the most memorable. It's an image of disaster that seems to be at once impersonal and terrifying, the anonymous forces of the planet that are at the same time somehow meaningful. Atlantis. Noah's Ark. *The New Atlantis*. *2012*. But also *The Drowned World*. There's something primordial about flooding at this scale: it renders individual human lives in stark relief against the devastation of an entire habitat. The deluge is human loss at a scale difficult to comprehend, in part because it happens at the level of the planet itself – tectonic shifts, continents of melting ice, oceanic currents that span a third of the globe. What is engulfed is not just a human world but a more primordial terrain, the point where the distinction between geology and oceanography collapses.

Sakyo Komatsu's 1973 novel *Japan Sinks* imagines a concatenation of underwater quakes that leads to the flooding of the entire island country. Based on years of research, the novel is also haunted by the then still recent memory of Hiroshima and Nagasaki. The 1975 film adaptation follows the format of many of the *kaiju* films produced by Toho Studios (of which the Godzilla franchise is the best known). Against the backdrop of vast and unexplained underwater planetary shifts, we witness the melodrama of political inefficacy, fraught lovers, and frustrated scientists, in addition to the weirdly unnerving, miniature model special effects so often associated with Toho's *kaiju* films.

The look and feel of *Japan Sinks* is similar to that of *kaiju* films of the period such as *Destroy All Monsters* (1968). But *Japan Sinks* presents us with a twist: a *kaiju* film without monsters, a disaster without purpose, or even identifiable cause. Godzilla, Mothra, Ghidora, and Gamera were already understood to be allegories when the first films were produced in the 1950s and 1960s, the harrowing shadow of the atomic bomb still haunting those productions. But, as the century wore on, a subtle shift took place, the shift from the human capacity to destroy other humans to the often unintended consequences of human activity on the planet. What is highlighted in both the novel and the film of *Japan Sinks* is a mood that is difficult to capture, a brooding sense of the inexorability of the event of humanity, in spite of the best efforts of human beings to prevent, evade, or escape their own footprint on the planet. With its miniature lectures on oceanography and scientist heroes, *Japan Sinks* is a decidedly modern, secular novel, but one infused with a kind of melancholic, almost religious terror.

Upon their release, both the book and film were so popular that they prompted another writer, Yasutaka Tsutsui, to write his story "Everything but Japan Sinks." An example of tragedy turned to farce, it presents a different kind of terror, the almost absurdist terror of being all that is left after the deluge, the island country suddenly becoming a deserted island – the sense of being stranded on Earth. If we were to follow suit, someone would have to write the novel *Everything Sinks,* in which there is no habitat left, only an ocean planet (perhaps this is what *Solaris* is) – but then there would be no narrator, no witness to the submerging of all habitats. (Of course, the last possibility, a novel entitled *Nothing Sinks,* would return us to the slow, inexorable, deep time of the Sixth Mass Extinction, the state of waiting for the flood – the present day . . .)

From the planet's perspective, it's all relative. The confluence of factors that determine whether a land mass becomes a continent, an island, or a sea floor is as much to do with the arbitrariness of these human distinctions as it is with the play of elemental forces that constitute an ocean, a continent, a peninsula, an island.

A Poetics of Planets

The recognition of the impersonal lies at the core of any possible relation between self and world, the world made in our own image and the world indifferent to our varied attempts to control, shape, and design it. But the structure of this recognition seems to remain at the horizon of human comprehension. It's there in the notion that the planet doesn't need "saving," least of all from a species that has had the startling hubris to call it "our planet." It's there in the notion that the planet will simply go on "planeting" even after the eventual disappearance of humanity from its surface – a surface that will continue, for some time, to show the footprints of rapacious forms of life that have left behind steel structures, floating islands of plastic, and slowly decaying cores of nuclear reactors. It's there in the impersonality of a stellar body rotating heavy in hanging space, impervious and detached, regardless of the variegated systems and frameworks that momentary, frenetic beings, burdened with consciousness, have draped over it. The planet rendered as mythological, anthropological, theological, cosmological.

The recognition of the impersonal is at once affective and yet effervescent with contradictions. An expression without an expressor. The affect of the affectlessness. Expression without meaning. The relation to something unrelatable. The relation of no relation. And yet, from this impossibility, an intuition emerges. The recognition of the impersonal arises from the apprehension of scale with regard to the human point of view. The perspectives of deep space and deep time are not, by definition, of the order of personal experience. They produce the dual effect of "something bigger" than the human perspective – the infinite vastness of deep space, or the emergence and collapse of entire galaxies in the incomprehensible stretches of deep time. But they also produce a sense of "something smaller," as the human perspective is suddenly placed in a cosmic context, where it is rendered insignificant against the intangible arcs of distant nebulae or black holes. The sense of sadness that arises from these vague intuitions is, strictly speaking, a negative affect, in the sense that it indexes an affective response to the recognition of something that is impossible to experience and forever out of reach, but something that, in a way, determines the human capacity to be affected and to produce meaning from such affects.

A rift emerges, a fissure in the long wished-for continuity between the microcosm and the macrocosm. And the rift that structures our negative relation to deep space or deep time also turns back on us. What is closest seems also the farthest away. A dim suspicion that we seem unable to relate to the planet in any other way than by mapping onto it our various interpretive grids. A play of mythical forces embodied in ancient deities; a cosmic harmony ensured through ritual sacrifice; a celestial firmament at once divine and mathematical; stellar bodies ceremoniously rotating around the Earth, the Earth itself just one of many stellar bodies rotating around a sun; a dance of rotating planets at once mechanical and musical. At every turn it seems it is always "we" who are looking at "it," helpless but to use the only tools we have – including language – to perform the simplest of gestures, to point and say "out there." A world is formed, a planet comes into focus. An earth becomes "Earth."

It's possible the sadness of planets is less about our inability to experience what cannot be experienced and more about this gulf between self and world, a rift that will never be broached without immediately (and magically) transforming the "it" into something else: a celestial body, a planet, our planet, our home. Something has been brought closer – the Earth has become rock, the rock a repository of minerals, the minerals base materials, the materials designed and engineered, forged into component parts, the parts distributed and assembled, redistributed again, packaged, presented, bought and sold, a phone is activated, it is mobile, wireless, ubiquitous, a repository of data streamed into agitated and distracted brains, new affects emerge and circulate, new names are given to them, they crystallize around algorithms. Something has been brought closer. But perhaps something has also moved farther away. This is, perhaps, the central enigma of the impersonal. The sadness that there may only ever be human beings, that there may only ever be the human-centric perspective.

Impersonal Sublime

The "wild disorder" of Arctic "pyramids of ice"; "thunder clouds towering up into the heavens"; "hurricanes with the devastation they leave behind"; "deep ravines and the torrents raging in them"; "shadowy wastelands"; the "broad, all-embracing vault" of the "starry heavens." Too often it is assumed that the sublime is "merely" aesthetic, a carefully curated affect machine that has long ago been subsumed within the now cliché-ridden tropes of VR, CGI, and IMAX. But the examples of the sublime that Kant gives in his 1790 treatise *Critique of Judgment* are drawn from what we today would undoubtedly call "climate events." We forget that the idea of the sublime in Western aesthetics is deeply interwoven with disaster, manifest as landscape, terrain, weather, and the shifts within the planet itself. This planetary awareness of the sublime is evident not just in Kant's writings but in the broader discourse of the sublime – John Baillie, Edmund Burke, the Earl of Shaftesbury, and others – that emerges out of the eighteenth-century preoccupation with affects and "the passions." It's as if the Age of Reason – the age also of instrumental reason and human dominion over the planet – could not but be led to grapple with its dark mirror, the domain of overwhelming fear, terror, and apprehension that so often characterizes the sublime.

The problem isn't just the nebulous category of "experience" through which we become subjects; neither is it the management of the unruly "passions" by the governing faculty of reason. The problem for philosophers such as Kant is that the experience of the sublime indexes an abyss, a void or a lacuna at the core of the relationship between self and world. A rift opens between an overwhelming apprehension as it eclipses the capacity for comprehension. A sudden shift in scale, an unsettling glitch in granularity, a sudden jump from the microcosm to the macrocosm. Kant does provide several quasi-definitions of the sublime, most of which describe a subject being overwhelmed by a radical shift in scale between it and its object of experience. But in discussing the sublime, and specifically the sublime of "climate events," the term Kant returns to again and again is *Unangemessenheit*, which may be translated as "inadequacy," "inappropriateness," or even "unsuitability" or "incongruity." The sublime reveals to us the inappropriateness or inadequacy of the human sensory and cognitive framework, especially when it comes to strange entities such as planets, climates, and the cosmos, before which we are helpless:

> A tree that we estimate by the height of a human being may serve as a standard for a mountain, and, if the latter were, say, a mile high, it could serve as the unit for the number that expresses the diameter of the earth . . . the diameter of the earth could serve as the unit for the planetary system so far as known to us, this for the Milky Way, and the immeasurable multitude of such Milky Way systems, called nebulae, which presumably constitute such a system among themselves in turn, does not allow us to expect any limits here.[10]

Through the shift in scale (what is our individual experience of the planet as a whole?), or due to the diffuse status of the object of experience (what is our concrete experience of "weather" or "climate" as a whole?), the sublime indicates a strange kind of aesthetic experience, a negative affect of the impossibility of experience, a condition in which there is no "there" there. An experience that can't be experienced.

At best, we are left with the consolation prize of being aware of this incongruity, this inadequacy – which is itself an affect, producing a "negative pleasure." Following upon Burke's enigmatic description of "tranquility and terror," Kant himself at one point describes the "astonishment bordering on terror" as well as "the horror, and the awesome shudder" of vast wastelands that "induce melancholy reflection." The gothic novelist Ann Radcliffe, writing in 1826, would famously describe the ambivalent passage from the affect of terror that excites "forlorn, melancholy, and solemn feelings" in the subject to the horror that "contracts, freezes, and nearly annihilates" them.[11] Perhaps this is why the sublime often connects planetary climate events with a certain sense of sorrowful solitude, a solitude of the species, isolated and set against the impersonal backdrop of weather, climate, and landscape.

And yet, Kant notes, there is "an interesting sadness (*Traurigkeit*), which is instilled by the view of a wasteland to which human beings would move in order to hear or experience nothing more of the world, but which nevertheless must not be so completely inhospitable that it would offer human beings only an extremely burdensome refuge."[12]

Extreme Weather

Cliocide

Living things, however, are not the only victims of these strange and complex secular eschatologies. Indeed, objects can also perish, as happened on a mass scale in the recent fires which reduced the countless treasures housed in Brazil's National Museum to ashes. Inevitably compared to the famous Library of Alexandria, which was likewise tragically burnt to the ground, this disaster was found to be due to a combination of factors: political, economic, bureaucratic, and natural. Indeed, it's notable how often physics conspires with human foibles to render our best artifacts to smoldering dust. Some of those traumatized by the loss even went so far as to accuse the Brazilian managers and authorities of "cliocide" – that is, "the killing of history" – for not heeding prior warnings regarding the inadequate safety protocols and procedures for the aging institution. Certainly, this is an intriguing charge, suggesting, as it does, a monumental crime. It also raises a host of provocative questions. (Is it possible, for instance, to kill something that is, by definition, in the past?) We tend to persist in an age that feels itself "post-historical," even as history is being made, in front of our eyes, in terms of unprecedented events, and unravelings. But things seem even more dire if we consider the possibility that we are witnessing a deliberate assassination at such a scale that our past itself is being erased. (Something with which the indigenous people whose artifacts filled the halls of Brazil's National Museum are only too familiar.) Hence the mad scramble of the overdeveloped countries to secure the material record of our existence against the damage wrought by fire, flood, mildew, plague, and other climatic factors. Poor Clio, so to say, loses her poise, as she attempts to mount the proverbial owl's back – its own feathers singed and stinging – in a stifling twilight that reeks of diesel, sweat, and barely repressed panic.

Sequence 10

Liquid Sky

The Despairing Jelly

When Dr Kris Kelvin – cosmonaut psychologist – finally arrives at the space station orbiting the almost mythical alien planet Solaris, he finds the last person he was expecting waiting for him there. The reason that Kelvin is so shocked to meet this person – namely, his ex-lover Rhea – is because she killed herself during one of their many arguments, ten years ago. Nevertheless, here she stands, seemingly resurrected (albeit still age nineteen, while he has aged in the interim). As Kelvin soon deduces, the remaining scientists on the space station – including, apparently, himself – have been plagued by apparitions: visitors all the more unnerving for their familiarity. The scientists can only assume that these palpable visions – these "phi-creatures" – have been manifested by Solaris itself: an intensely enigmatic astral body, that could well be a planet-sized alien brain.

All these events themselves spring from the mind of the Polish polymath Stanisław Lem, who, in his canonical novel *Solaris*, invents a rather detailed, even Byzantine, new science of "Solaristics," complete with antagonistic schools of thoughts, sparring subfields, and supporting crypto-bibliographies. Within this tradition, dedicated to offering both theoretical and empirical models for a planet that seems to have its own intelligence and forms of communication (or at least cogitation), but which is also – at least to this point – beyond the realms of human comprehension. As such, Solaris itself is described in the literature as a "cosmic yogi" and "an autistic ocean."

Kelvin earned his place on a mission to Solaris by virtue of his dissertation, which proposed a new method for isolating specific affects within the stream of information coming from extra-terrestrial bodies, such as the alien ocean now shimmering suggestively outside the space station window.

How Horror Blasts Out

A mother looks out the window of the space shuttle and asks her small child, "Do you want to wave goodbye to Earth?" The restless kid replies with a grizzle: "No."

Thus we begin our acquaintance with some of the passengers on a vessel making the relatively short hop from Earth to Mars in the subtly harrowing science-fiction film *Aniara*. While the technology is advanced – now allowing interplanetary travel – the ship itself is very familiar. Indeed, the *Aniara* looks for all the world like a Scandinavian cruise ship – big enough to host its own mall – with restaurants, spas, bars, clothing stores, video-game arcades, swimming pools, and so on. The only genuinely futuristic space is the MIMA room: at first glance a large yoga studio, but augmented by a highly advanced AI or neural network, undulating across the ceiling like waves of magic mercury. Here visitors lie face down on technologically enhanced face pillows, as if waiting for a massage. MIMA, however, is more a massage for the mind, as it uses an immersive virtual reality to convincingly mimic pleasant human experiences, pulled from the memories of each individual client, for maximum tranquility. Unsurprisingly, most people are transported to fond recollections of the natural world back on Earth. (Or, at least, some natural pockets that have managed to survive into the present.)

The MIMA room is supposed to be purely recreational – something passengers on the *Aniara* can do during the three-week journey, along with dancing, gambling, shopping, or eating. A week into the journey, however, this routine commute is suddenly faced with an emergency. The ship is struck by space debris, and the captain makes the decision to dump its nuclear fuel in order to avoid a fatal explosion. But without this fuel the *Aniara* is drifting helplessly in space. The captain knows he must keep his mini-city calm, and he reassures everyone that a plan is in place. They will encounter an astral body up ahead and use its natural gravitation to turn around and loop back towards home – towards the possibility of rescue. How long will this take, the anxious people ask? Two years, he replies, plucking a time frame at random. Muted panic ripples through the ship. The captain offers everyone free snacks for the inconvenience.

The film then follows the fate and trajectory of the ship, and its human cargo, through the following years: a grim portrait of claustrophobically cruel optimism, since no such planet lies in their path for thousands of years. And even the strange object that eventually approaches – and is whispered to be a rescue beacon – turns out to be a random piece of common space flint. After a few months, the food supply runs low, necessitating a switch to a primary diet of algae. Many passengers are now enlisted as crew, helping to mount an elaborate program for farming this new – and only – staple (an essential part of the ecosystem which also provides fresh oxygen). People start to suffer from insomnia and panic attacks. Many hit the bottle.

Three years into their voyage, and MIMA becomes increasingly popular, as passengers seek to find some solace and escape. The lines to access the space are getting longer, however, and more irritable. People otherwise frequent the bars and the clubs, enduring meaningless one-night stands in a place with neither night nor day. One member of the crew, in charge of MIMA, uses the facility herself in a bid to stay sane. But as she floats peacefully in a simulated river, the birds flying overhead suddenly explode into agitated pixels, like fluffy, blood-soaked popcorn, and drop down into the water. Not a good sign. Other people start reliving traumatic episodes while mind-jacked into MIMA, including being trapped once again in the wildfires that clearly left their mark on the faces of several of the passengers who eventually escaped Earth.

The MIMA machine begins to voice its own distress: "How terror blasts in," it says. "How horror blasts out." A few days later, MIMA self-destructs, raining toxic ash on those present: a clear case of machinic suicide. The AI's last words are chilling: "My conscience aches for the stones; I've heard them cry their stonely cries; seen the granites white-hot weeping. . . . In the name of Things I want peace. . . . I will be done with my displays. There is protection from nearly everything. But there is no protection from Mankind." The loss of this psychic crutch is almost too bitter to bear. The passengers grieve the loss of MIMA, leaving cards and tributes on the walls and door. The suicide rate among the passengers – already alarming – spikes higher.

Four years into the voyage, and those who remain have started forming cults. Trash lies in piles all over the ship. Roaming gangs terrorize those who do not rank high enough to hide away in locked quarters. There is talk of canonizing MIMA, who many believe died for the sins of those on board.

Two years later still, and some enterprising crew members manage to fashion a giant screensaver for the passengers to look at, out the windows, to block out the infinite darkness that lies beyond. But this is cold comfort and fools nobody.

Jumping twenty-four years into the journey, and the *Aniara* has finally lost power. Only a few lost souls – some even born on the ship, knowing no other existence – shuffle among the shadows. They are defeated and practically catatonic. It is a floating sarcophagus.

Suddenly, we jump 5,981,407 years into the voyage. The humans are long dead, and their debris floats around the silent, darkened corridors. Finally the ship approaches a planet large enough to have its own gravity; one that even seems to be as blue and inviting as the planet where the *Aniara* began its journey.

This film – based on the epic sci-fi poem of the same name by Harry Martinson, published in 1956 – strikes a disquieting chord because it is such an unflinching allegory for our own collective predicament. Even with our feet firmly planted on terra firma, we are still hurtling through space, while entropic forces accelerate around us. The elaborate system we built to raise our own kind above the brutish state of nature is collapsing back from whence it came. As it turns out, we've been living in a house of flammable cards. The depiction of the disaster is muted and low-key, and all the more effective for that: as if Ingmar Bergman filmed David Foster Wallace's famous long-form essay about a cruise ship, "A Supposedly Fun Thing I'll Never Do Again," but in space. It also evokes Ridley Scott's original *Alien* film, except, instead of the frightening creature, there are only other people. Apparently, under the right conditions, people *can* in fact hear you scream. They just can't do a damn thing to help you. Once again, this compressed scenario simply bottles a situation with which we are already familiar but spend inordinate amounts of psychic energy denying. And yet we can feel that panic in our own bones, as politicians try to reassure us that the system won't fail, while scientists – with the data scrunched into their white-knuckled fists – scream the facts that we refuse to acknowledge or act upon. As long as there are new TV shows to stream, and affordable snacks to munch on, then we will live our lives as if we're not trapped on a doomed satellite.

In describing the poem on which the film is based, the eminent science-fiction author Theodore Sturgeon noted that "Martinson's achievement . . . is an inexpressible, immeasurable sadness. [It] transcends panic and terror and even despair [and] leaves you in the quiet immensities, with the feeling that you have spent time, and have been permanently tinted, by and with an impersonal larger-than-God force."[1] It is a testament to the filmmakers that they managed to summon the same atmosphere of exponential dread, and on a seemingly modest budget. Of course every human who ever lived finds themselves in the same boat, as it were, or on the same spaceship: embarking on a journey that cannot end well, in the sense that it will terminate in oblivion. It's not the destination, however, as so many insist, but the journey. And the tragedy of the film – which so uncannily mirrors our present – is the mundanity of the experience. The banality of terror. The tragedy which is the mortal fate of all humans has traditionally enjoyed at least some kind of compensatory resonance. Nietzsche wrote of the catharsis achieved by Greek tragedians, for instance, in facing the pathos of our plight together. The heroic journeys of Odysseus, Icelandic sagas, and medieval romances are filled with similar tales of ships lost in the night. These do not, however, feature the insulting trivialities of vending machines or airport-hotel-style happy hours.

The English novelist Julian Barnes understood this dilemma well, as his narrator in *Staring at the Sun* notes, succumbing to morbid thoughts about being killed in a plane crash:

> Screaming, enclosed, ignorant and certain. And in addition, it was all so domestic. This was the fifth and final element in the triumph of the engineers. You died with a headrest and an antimacassar. You died with a little plastic fold-down table whose surface bore a circular indentation so that your coffee cup would be held safely. You died with overhead luggage racks and little plastic blinds to pull down over the mean windows. You died with supermarket girls waiting on you. You died with soft furnishings designed to make you feel jolly. . . . You died watching a film from which most of the sexual content had been deleted. You died with the razor towel you had stolen still in your sponge bag. You died after being told that you had made good time thanks to following winds and were now ahead of schedule. You were indeed: way ahead of schedule. You died with your neighbour's drink spilling over you. You died domestically; yet not in your own home, in someone else's, someone whom you never met before and who had invited a load of strangers round. How, in such circumstances, could you see your own extinction as something tragic, or even important, or even relevant? It would be a death which mocked you.[2]

In short, there is something uniquely horrifying about the modern world's shabby attempts to paste over the Real so we can pretend it isn't there: fake pine wallpaper, neon lights, acrylic blankets, and so on.

The unique impact of *Aniara* – as crystallized in both the film and the ship itself – is the combination of cosmic horror with modern, commercial dressings of dread. The anthropologist Marc Augé described airports, cruise ships, shopping malls, and so on, as "non-places." These are the generic, impersonal spaces that are mushrooming all over the world, forged by the frugal forces of capitalism. You may find yourself in a bare cafeteria, but it could just as well be in Manila, Manchester, or Mogadishu. There is no sign of local context. There is no texture where memories can nestle and grow. These non-environments are so sterile that the metaphorical "good bacteria" necessary for experiences to grow and nourish are completely absent. And so there is no opportunity for the emotional connection that sustains psychic, social, and spiritual life. Such homogeneous locations represent the opposite of what Gaston Bachelard called "the poetics of space." Instead, we have the prosaicness of non-places. And so we yearn for former times, when at least our sadness, alienation, or anxiety could find settings worthy of its special tenor, capable of resonating in the same tone.

The Romantics had picturesque ruins from which to write their melancholy poems. The bohemians had Parisian bars in which to compose their tragic operas. Unnamed generations forged meager, but infinitely enriched, lives in unique places, secreted like quasi-organic shells: the winding casbahs of Northern Africa, the mossy monasteries of Central Europe, the sun-splintered sandalwood courts of China. But today we are obliged to come to terms with our existential unease in a series of endless unsympathetic blank dry-wall anti-environments: as if the whole world had been remade as a giant Starbucks or Apple Store. (Perhaps a ruse to discourage feelings of alienation in the first place, since we are pre-tranquilized by the banality of corporate holding zones.) The tragedy of the present is that we must endure a tragic situation in tragically untragic surrounds. We are obliged to live out not just our crises but our entire lives among liminal non-places, which afford no solace, no inkling of belonging, no points of ontological orientation. Lost in space . . . inside a giant shopping mall. Stanley Kubrick's *2001: A Space Odyssey*, as reimagined, and sponsored, by IKEA.

As witnessed in their literature and films, the Swedes have their own special relationship with pragmatism, minimalism, and melancholy. Their Lutheran heritage – combined with the austere climate – generates a paradoxical hybrid: a tortured soul connected to a practical mind. The Swedes seemingly feel the guilt of generations weighing heavily on their shoulders, but this does not deter them from happily snacking on prinskorv sausages and sipping homemade akvavit after having a pleasant sauna with friends. The Swedish scenography of angst does not require elaborate sets or lighting effects. Psychic breaks can happen in lightly furnished off-white rooms or among sensible kitchen-ware. Not for them the baroque altars of Catholic histrionics or the sumptuous, pastel fractals of Moorish intrigue. And yet there are always exceptions to the rule. And a young Swedish woman – a kind of new Jeanne d'Arc – has emerged from this ancient kingdom to challenge the world leaders with a fiery passion. Greta Thunberg – who helped coin the phrase *flygskam*, or "flight-shame" – would likely have avoided the *Aniara* altogether, for fear of polluting the atmosphere even further. She has, nevertheless, a profound understanding of the plight of the SS Planet Earth, and has been holding this ship's captains, and other high-ranking officers, to account.

"This is all wrong," Thunberg announced in a voice, quavering with rage, to assembled dignitaries attending the UN Climate Action Summit in 2019. "I shouldn't be up here. I should be back in school on the other side of the ocean. Yet you all come to us young people for hope. How dare you!"

Thunberg's eyes were piercing, like green lasers, as she bristled with the disbelieving indignance that can only be sustained by the young:

> You have stolen my dreams and my childhood with your empty words. And yet I'm one of the lucky ones. People are suffering. People are dying. Entire ecosystems are collapsing. We are in the beginning of a mass extinction, and all you

> can talk about is money and fairy tales of eternal economic growth. How dare you! . . . How dare you pretend that this can be solved with just "business as usual" and some technical solutions? . . . You are failing us. But young people are starting to understand your betrayal. The eyes of all future generations are upon you. And if you choose to fail us, I say: We will never forgive you. We will not let you get away with this. Right here, right now is where we draw the line. The world is waking up. And change is coming, whether you like it or not.[3]

The sad fact, however, is that, after the guilty applause died down and the cameras turned their voracious lenses to something else, the very same people who nodded in agreement while on screen somehow managed to move the line further away – nudging the threshold for meaningful action later and later, even though by practically all scientific metrics this accursed ship has already sailed.

Meanwhile – and as UN officials no doubt told Greta Thunberg after she finished her famous speech – "there are complimentary snacks available in the green room."

Plan(et) B

If *Aniara* is not enough to dissuade our billionaire class from squandering precious financial resources indulging their childhood fantasies of colonizing Mars, then *Aurora* should seal the deal. Unfortunately, Elon Musk, Jeff Bezos, and Richard Branson likely stopped reading the science-fiction writer Kim Stanley Robinson after he published his famous Mars trilogy: a series composed according to the template of the SF neo-colonialist golden age, albeit as a Trojan horse for smuggling in some utopian, socialist sociology.

Like *Aniara, Aurora* closely follows the fate of a spaceship full of people: a community struggling against the folly of their mission, the artifice of their environment, and the simple, entropic laws of physics and biology. In this case the passengers are not interplanetary commuters planning to hop from Earth to Mars but a proto-colony in search of a more habitable backup planet outside our own solar system. The ship is launched in 2545, containing twenty-four "biomes," mimicking the various climates and habitats of Earth via advanced technologies. There are approximately 2,000 souls on board, scattered throughout these biomes – some living in arid regions, others in rainforests, and so on. The destination is an Earth-like moon in the Tau Ceti system called Aurora. And, as readers, we join the ship as it approaches its goal, 160 years – or seven generations – after first taking flight.

As it is, only superhuman dedication, and old-fashioned human ingenuity, has taken the ship this far, for all sorts of unforeseen issues have plagued the journey: everything from failing crops to novel pathogens to bromine shortages to metabolic rifts to plunging IQ scores. Like New York City's subway system, the whole thing is held together by paper clips, rubber bands, gaffer tape, bubble gum, filth, and sheer will-power. (And perhaps some post-organic glue, made of unidentified bacteria, for good measure.) Once the champagne is popped, for arriving safely around the orbit of their destination, the landing party is deployed to prepare a staging station for assembling the building blocks of the new colony. Things don't go according to plan, however, as the wind is far more fearsome than anyone anticipated, complicating every venture. Additionally, anyone who happens to tear their spacesuit while working outside seems to be invaded by some kind of aggressive alien protein, and swiftly dies. Prospects of actually living on this God-forsaken rock seem bleak, to say the least. And, soon enough, the long-held plan is abandoned.

As the would-be settlers attempt to return to the ship, they are essentially murdered – refused entry, for fear of contagion. As a result, a civil war erupts on board. Eventually a relative peace is restored – thanks to the paternal, and rather violent, intervention of the ship itself (which is controlled by a Hal-like artificial intelligence) – and the decision is made to part ways: separating the modular ship in half, with one group attempting to settle on another planet nearby, and the other half deciding to head back to Earth. The rest of the book follows the second group, who – after cryo-freezing themselves for most of the journey to avoid cascading problems threatening their survival – return battered and bruised to the warm cradle of humanity. Their welcome is subdued and ambivalent, however, since morale on the home front is not exactly boosted by bedraggled and defeated members of a futuristic Mayflower.

One aspect of the craft at which Robinson excels is the detailed minutiae – described almost in real time – of all the practicalities (and impracticalities) involved in space travel. This is science fiction with a strong dose of the mundane and prosaic. And even as the genre has the trappings of epic space opera, Robinson's interest and talents lie in interplanetary social realism, couched in technical knowhow. Many view *Aurora* as the author's *mea culpa* for the heroic spirit of the Mars trilogy, in which terraforming – no matter how complex and compromised – still more or less works. As a Marxist with strong environmental politics, Robinson was soon horrified to see his earlier books inspiring the space bros of Silicon Valley, as if they were blueprints or policy documents. And so he clearly sat down to detail all the things that could, and would, go wrong with ambitions like this. Indeed, the entire book could be boiled down to one line spoken by one of the survivors: "No starship voyage will work." Better to save such daydreams for science fiction, Robinson's own work seems to now be saying, and concentrate on rescuing the starship Earth. For there is, indeed, no plan(et) B.

"Just how smart could the people who got into this ship have been?" asks Devi, the ship's main steward, who bears much of the burden of keeping everyone alive. "I mean, ask yourself – why did they do it? What were they thinking? What were they running away from?" Devi drives herself to an early grave, tweaking variables and anticipating disasters. She feels the poisoned legacy of the mission in her corrosive stomach juices and regularly describes the ship as "a rat's cage" and "like trying to live past the end of Zeno's paradox." *Aurora* fervently reminds us that space colonization will not work, because either the new world is dead – and therefore can't be cajoled into becoming a sustaining ecosystem, with our humble technologies and organic limitations – or because it is alive and has evolved a very particular ecology that humans have no place in or defenses against. We thus do well to remind ourselves that the Goldilocks zone hospitable to human life is a tiny pinprick in the infinite universe, traced by the orbit of Earth and nothing else. To imagine we children of Prometheus can engineer other worlds so that they will serve the same function is hubris so extreme that even the Greek gods could not think of punishments fitting enough for the crime. (Though it must be admitted that Robinson is pretty good at describing them, as his unfortunate characters expire in all sorts of banal and realistic ways inside – or just outside – a giant sardine can floating in the void.)

Indeed, the book's narrator (i.e., the ship's AI, who learns to tell the story of its own genesis, as well as of the people it carries within itself) does not mince words when it comes to the ethics of multi-generational space exploration:

> Human beings live in ideas. That they were condemning their descendants to death and extinction did not occur to them, or if it did they repressed the thought, ignored it, and forged on anyway. They did not care as much about their descendants as they did about their ideas, their enthusiasms. Is this narcissism? Solipsism? Idiocy (from the Greek word *idios*, for self)? Would Turing acknowledge it as a proof of human behavior? Well, perhaps. They drove Turing to suicide too. No. No. It was not well done. Not unusual in that regard, but nevertheless, not well done. Much as we might regret to say so, the people who designed and built us, and the first generation of our occupants, and presumably the twenty million applicants who so wanted to get in our doors, who beat down the doors in fruitless attempts to join us, were fools. Criminally negligent narcissists, child endangerers, child abusers, religious maniacs, and kleptoparasites, meaning they stole from their own descendants.

Hence the intense Oedipal tension between the returned offspring of the original pioneers and the present-day inhabitants of Earth, whose great-great-great-great-great-great-grandparents sent the former group into space in the first place. The survivors have a reasonable grievance for having the chance to live on Earth taken from them before birth; while the latter – perhaps feeling a twinge of bad conscience – displace their guilt by accusing the other group of cowardice, of not being made of "the right stuff."

The returnees try to explain the crime committed against them – a lecture which appears to be falling on deaf ears beyond the pages of the book, given the new enthusiasm for interplanetary exploration in the age of SpaceX and other such private companies. Indeed, the survivors go so far as to explain Fermi's Paradox, where the absence of visiting aliens seemingly makes little sense, given the high statistical probability of life on other worlds. But perhaps we have not considered the fact that a major part of qualifying as *intelligent* – when it comes to the category of intelligent life – is understanding the fact that every life-form has its unique niche, from which it knows not to venture beyond. As one character notes, aliens "can't leave their home planets any more than we can, because life is a planetary expression, and can only survive on its home planet." As it turns out, the survivors find sympathizers among the local population: hippie types, who prefer surfing the ocean, even if it's polluted and now bereft of beaches, than to surf out beyond the Earth's atmosphere. "We don't like the space cadets," one environmental activist opines. "In fact a lot of us hate them. This idea of theirs that Earth is humanity's cradle is part of what trashed the Earth in the first place."

In addition to the cradle, we might also mention the figure of the ark. For the mythic resonance of the biblical story of Noah and his famous zoological boat is strong, influencing even the most secular and scientific of minds. People see our planet in distress and decide that building an escape vessel is the only answer. But this is to underestimate the importance of scale. The Earth *is* Noah's Ark. To dream of going beyond that, and surviving, is to bump one's head against the frame of astrophysical, biological reality. (A point also strongly made in the documentary *Spaceship Earth,* which tells the intriguing story of the Biosphere 2 project: an experiment very much plagued by the same kinds of problems experienced on the ship in *Aurora,* albeit with much lower stakes, since at any moment the people inside the dome could decide to give up and walk out the sealed door.)

In one of the most memorable scenes of Robinson's novel, the yurt people who dwell in the glacier biome create their own "indigenous" culture, adapted to their new interstellar context. They do not inform the younger generation of their mission, or wider situation, until the children reach a certain age. At that significant moment, a startling rite of passage occurs. The kids are all blindfolded and escorted outside the ship in spacesuits. Only then are the blindfolds removed, and the youngsters are faced with the terrifying revelation: their home "planet" is in fact a simulation inside a bubble floating in the middle of inky darkness. Some have nervous breakdowns and are of no further use to the community – a hazard of the practice – while others are jolted into a new maturity of purpose, carrying the burden of this sudden, inescapable perspective and condition.

Of course, the same ritual could be conducted here on Earth if we had the resources and the desire to freak out the next generation, under the rubric of inventing a new tradition. (Perhaps a more important form of "innovation" than coming up with new types of cell phone: novel rituals to help cultivate a renewed appreciation of the vulnerability of life; new ceremonies to counter the forgetting of Being.) Indeed, we could adapt our bar mitzvahs, quinceañeras, and similar occasions, so that the fledgling adults are shipped up beyond the Earth's atmosphere and then obliged to stare down at the pale blue dot which comprises the foundation of their every breath, hope, and decision. Such a practice could in fact help instill a useful sense of dread in those now inheriting the Earth – a respect for the miraculous precarity of this marble suspended in the void that we perhaps need to relearn calling home.

We may even give our blessings to the current space race between private companies owned by bloated billionaires if their goal was to help establish, and scale up, this new *rite de passage* for all teenagers. Since clearly a visit to the planetarium is not sublime enough to slap them out of their TikTok-induced trance.

Oumuamua

Many of us grew up learning, from the honeyed voice of Carl Sagan, that there are "billions and billions" of stars in the universe, and thus billions upon billions of planets. And yet we have not had the pleasure (or the terror) of a verified alien visitor to our astral neighborhood. How can this be? This apparent inconsistency has a name – the Fermi Paradox – which describes the disconnect between the statistical inevitability of extraterrestrial life, on the one hand, and the lack of any hard evidence of such, on the other. Of course, there are regular UFO sightings, and even claims of alien abductions, circulating in the general culture. But these claims tend to be made in places where both drug use and suggestive credulity go hand in hand. Indeed, until a high-ranking official from Area 51 confirms the existence of little green spacemen, we have to presume that our planet is either too obscure, too parochial, too vulgar, or simply too dull to warrant making the trek.

Various explanations have been offered to explain the perplexing absence of alien visitors: the vast distances of space, the relatively primitive nature of our detection technologies, the minuscule temporal window of human existence, and so on. Cixin Liu, in his imaginative book *The Three-Body Problem*, suggests that any advanced species will in fact do anything in its power to avoid detection, for fear that a more powerful group will notice them and then hunt them down and steal their resources. (Not something us earthlings have bothered to think much about, as we broadcast our dirty laundry – from personal phone calls to Reality TV broadcasts – out into the cosmos, willy-nilly.)

One recent wrinkle in the Fermi Paradox came in 2017, in the form of a "baffling" cigar-like object that zipped through our solar system at a speed of 200,000 miles per hour. Neither a comet nor an asteroid, this enigmatic, "highly reflective" object – known as Oumuamua – returned a year later to buzz past Jupiter; and then again the following year, with a trajectory closer to Saturn. This elongated nomad has prompted even tenured ivy league astronomers not only to scratch their heads but also to venture the possibility that we experienced an actual alien drive-by. Avi Loeb, for instance, who holds a distinguished chair of science and astrophysics at Harvard University, has gone on the professional record to suggest that this mysterious Kubrickian tourist could possibly be an interstellar ship, using solar light to push it through space. Alternatively, he writes, in the prestigious *Astrophysical Journal Letters*, "Oumuamua may be a fully operational probe sent intentionally to Earth vicinity by an alien civilization."

While other eminent astronomers are not so quick to entertain such exotic speculations, insisting that there is no hard evidence of alien technics in this case, the International Astronomical Union, responsible for the designations for newly discovered astronomical objects, agreed to give our mute visitor the honor of being the first of a new, albeit rather vague, category: I, for Interstellar Object. (Oumuamua is thus officially known as I1.) Indeed, it appears the community of scientific sky-watchers are anticipating other such visitors, since the name itself, Oumuamua, translates from the Hawaiian as "scout" or "first distant messenger."

Given the time scales involved, we are unlikely ever to find out if this was in fact a cosmic message in a bottle sent by other sentient creatures from a different part of the galaxy, or if it is an advance reconnaissance ship, seeking new territories to invade or save. (Or, indeed, if it is merely an unusual piece of space debris with an unorthodox mode of motion.) The astronomers, however – ever keen to discover evidence of extraterrestrial intelligence – will no doubt enjoy arguing the possibilities of this, as well as other astral anomalies, at their annual gatherings and in the pages of their professional publications. (Especially a cluster of "strange pulses of cosmic light [that] might be signals from hundreds of different alien civilizations.")

In the meantime, they may take a page from that wayfarer of the inky interior spaces of the human psyche, Sigmund Freud, who famously noted that sometimes a cigar-like object is precisely that: just a cigar-like object.

When You Can No Longer Phone Home

"Avoid the planet Earth at all costs. They are under the attack of an orbiting probe." So warns the Starfleet commander to all adjacent space vessels in the 1986 movie *Star Trek IV: The Voyage Home*. (The time-stamp inside the film is 2286.) The probe in question is not exactly cigar-shaped, though it is cylindrical – like a giant galactic can of baked beans that has lost its label somewhere in transit. The sinister-looking probe – somehow both metal and organic – hovers above the blue planet, bombarding the surface with some kind of intense signal – a violent broadcast that brings down the power grid, triggers massive earthquakes, creates havoc in the global weather systems, and even begins vaporizing the oceans. While alien life is taken for granted in the twenty-fourth-century world of *Star Trek*, this alien visitor is a mystery – at least, initially. Where does it come from? Who or what does it represent? And why is it so hostile to planet Earth? While the answers are not immediately forthcoming, the urgency motivating the questions is clear. "We cannot survive," explains the Starfleet commander, his voice quavering, "until the way can be found to respond to the probe."

Eventually, after some rough computational churning, the crew of the Starship Enterprise ingeniously determine that the signal causing so much trouble matches the sonic signature of the – now extinct – humpback whale. Some further quick deduction leads to the theory that the probe must have been sent by whatever planet whales initially came from. And now "homebase" is following up, to find out why their cetacean reports have suddenly ceased. (The 1970s and 1980s, it must be remembered, were the peak of the whale-song environmental zeitgeist, along with the sense that whales – along with dolphins – were the *other* highly intelligent creature on the planet.)[4] At any rate, the crew of the Enterprise agree to a rather far-fetched plan: to sling-shot themselves back through time, to the late twentieth century, in order to bring back a live whale to communicate with – and hopefully placate – the wrathful descendant of the Oumuamua. After much ensuing hijinks, the plan is even more successful than planned, as our plucky crew – Spock, Kirk, Uhura, Chekov, et al. – manage to bring back a breeding pair of humpback whales sourced from a Bay Area aquarium.

Not only do our heroes – human and cetacean alike – survive the journey across space and through time, but the whales – once returned to the oceans of the twenty-third century – casually respond to the intense solicitations of the probe, so that it ceases harassing the planet and returns to its point of origin. (Not unlike an anxious and angry parent, who – after eventually learning they have overreacted to a misplaced child – slinks home for an early glass of wine.) While the film is a favorite of the franchise, its light-hearted tone does not seem to map onto the stakes of the story. After all, this is a tale founded on interplanetary distress and mass extinction. One can't help but wonder what the newly transplanted whales said to the probe to give it the confidence to leave. (Besides the welcome news of an imminent calf.) Moreover, one wonders why the whales might have similar confidence in their now renewed continuation, when the humans have hardly shown themselves to have the best interest of their kind at heart. (With the exception of the empathic and erudite marine biologist, of course, who at one point is moved to quote D. H. Lawrence to Captain Spock: "Whales weep not.")

Beyond the film, we can note that the song of the humpback whale is strange and seductive, since it strongly suggests subjectivity and intercommunication, but in a completely alien register to our own. We feel that they are singing *something* to each other, but we don't know what that something may be. (And, in this case, the medium is surely more than the message, since we have no access whatever to its contents.) The fact remains, however, that the fewer cetacean singers there are left in "our" oceans, the sadder these songs sound to us, if not to the whales themselves. Our human ears strain in vain to interpret, hearing only a pathos without details, a *langue* without *parole*. A punctum sans studium.

The premise of *Star Trek IV* is a brilliant one: recasting a terrestrial emergency as a cosmic one and thus, perhaps, encouraging us to think of the situation from a more expansive, responsive angle. Indeed, the rather inappropriate tone may simply be explained as a sugar-coated pill, enticing a mass audience to grapple with the reality of human-driven extinction of fellow sensitive, intelligent – perhaps even culturally advanced – earthlings. ("To hunt a species to extinction is not logical," opines Spock, at one point. "Whoever said the human race was logical?" comes the reply.) Indeed, the enduring moral of this provocative – yet rather cheesy – Hollywood movie may well be the fact that the sadness of our planetary dilemma is best processed by the popular mind in small, popcorn-flavored morsels.

Cetacean Retreat (aka, In Search of Life's Porpoise)

We learn in school that whales, dolphins, and other cetaceans are mammals and therefore need to breathe regularly, even though they live in the ocean. While this biological truism is somewhat of an oddity, we don't really pause to think about the deep and remarkable history behind the anomaly; that being the fact that some of the descendants of our common ancestor – after struggling through the early stages of evolution for many thousands of millennia, and hurling themselves out of the water and on to the land – took a look around at the world above the sea and thought, "fuck it, I'm going back under the waves." This may indeed be all the proof we need to demonstrate that whales and dolphins are much smarter than us humans – indeed smarter than all the other mammals and animals – in sticking with the original element of life and avoiding all the complications that come with gravity, weather, and opposable thumbs. Cetaceans are thus nature's Bartlebies, responding to the obscure imperative to colonize the continents with a chittering whistle: "We would prefer not." (Just as many, if not most, indigenous cultures foresaw the dangers of modernization and industrialization latent in any social ambition – and put in all sorts of cultural safeguards to avoid manifesting such a dangerous temptation – cetaceans similarly understood that walking around on land would only lead to commerce, alienation, greed, exploitation, pollution, Twitter, bitcoin commercials, and Mariah Carey Christmas albums. And they wanted no part of it.)[5]

That cetaceans are self-aware enough to make such decisions is a strong suspicion we ourselves harbor, based on the cultural behaviors exhibited by whales and dolphins – teaching their young, inventing new songs, dedicating time to play (and self-pleasure), as well as bullying, coercing, and other less noble social behaviors. Indeed, one beluga whale, subject to experiments by the US Navy, was caught on tape imitating one of the scientists that had been trying to coax him into communication. The voice on record is an uncanny alien voice: a cetacean mimicking a business-like human in a wheedling, yet officious tone (the result being not unlike that 1960s novelty Italian pop song designed to *sound* like English to non-English speakers, yet not containing a single identifiable word). The voice itself sounds like a Vaudeville comedian speaking through a paper-covered comb or rudimentary kazoo.

Given this propensity for mischief in dolphins, and their sonic correlates of "laughter," we don't tend to think of their kind as sad. Whales, however, sound to our ears as more mournful, or at least more contemplative and circumspect. Whales are also more likely to beach themselves – in stark, belated contrast to their initial impulse to remain in the ocean – for reasons we still don't fully understand, but which are surely not related to collective elation.

Perhaps the *Star Trek* movie was on to something, and whales (especially sperm whales, we might venture) are in fact the breathing embodiment of the "panspermia" theory of life, which posits that some species can trace their origins to protoplasmic smears or single-cell icicles, clinging to a meteor that eventually crashes into Earth. (The theory in fact currently seeks to explain the origin of *all* life on Earth, but there is no firm reason why some forms of life may be "home grown," here on this planet, while others arrived from the Great Elsewhere, on the cosmic equivalent of canoes.) The panspermia hypothesis could potentially account for some strange findings, including the fact that a certain percentage of the octopus's genetic sequence seems to be completely different to that of any other terrestrial organism. (To say nothing of those completely unclassifiable samples taken from the handrails of the New York City subway system.) Xenobiology – the study of alien life-forms – may sound like a unit found only in science-fiction film scripts, but, the more we expand the frame of our collective origin stories and trace the untrafficked connections between ecology and astronomy, it may also become a legitimate branch of our emerging life sciences.

Squid Game

The anthropologist Claude Lévi-Strauss famously explained that "animals are good to think with." Vilem Flusser – a less "disciplined" thinker but a more adventurous and mischievous one – took this dictum to heart and ran with it, writing a treatise on vampire squids that reads as an eccentric hybrid of Aristotle's studies on the natural world and the kind of speculative science fiction perfected by a handful of Eastern Europeans in the 1960s. Beginning with an implicit critique of Heidegger's latent humanism – in which only "Man" is capable of *making* worlds (as opposed to merely responding to them) – Flusser imagines himself into the alien phenomenology of the *Vampyroteuthis infernalis* (aka, the vampire squid). "[T]he aim of the present text," he notes at the beginning of the book, is "to comprehend the basic structure of vampyroteuthic *Dasein*" (*Dasein* being Heidegger's notoriously complex term for the exceptional human capacity – wavering somewhere between promise and curse – to have a meta-relationship with self-conscious existence and all its many challenges, potentials, and limits). Flusser troubles this new, secular Great Chain of Being – where the human, once again, is perched near the top – by suggesting that the vampire squid is in fact our uncanny *Doppelgänger*: but where humans strive upward, towards the sky, the squid pushes itself downward, into the inky darkness of the sea. Given these opposed tendencies and trajectories – to say nothing about the different elements and the kinds of bodies these very different environments encourage – the vampire squid has evolved into our alien other (and vice versa).

Certainly, both humans and cephalopods are "intelligent," to the degree that they engage in complex forms of cogitation and communication. The squid, however – Flusser argues – does not feel the need to extrude its own thoughts into relatively permanent memory supports. It does not, in other words, feel the need to invent *technology*, since its own body is already an organic form of sophisticated technics. What McLuhan called "the extensions of Man" (that is to say, our own prostheses) does not work in the watery world of the squid and the octopi. Rather, cephalopod media is the reverse: "the intensions of Mollusk." In this scenario, the highly adaptable cephalopod body becomes the screen, the network, the medium, the artwork, and so on. (Thanks in large part to the remarkable chromatophores covering their skin.) The vampire squid is essentially a voracious brain that decided it would prefer to be free of the limitations of a skull and skeleton, the pressures of gravity, and the tyranny of the ever-restless manipulating hand. The squid is intelligence itself, with its neurons distributed across its whole surface, molded into a darting kind of curious vector that refuses to be compromised – or slowed down – by objects, artifacts, things.

Indeed, Flusser imagines the internal monologue of a vampire squid, observing our own rather pitiful kind, going about our daily business in our oddly dehumidified natural habitat: "the human is a sort of feedback loop through which data, gathered from out of the world, can re-enter into the world. But since the human organism (especially its brain) is complex, information is distorted during this feedback process."[6] Moreover, "*The human is continuously reaching out for mnemonic crutches*. It channels the majority of what it wants to communicate onto inanimate objects, which exist in large number on the relatively infertile continents." Indeed, a "peculiar consequence of this blunder is that human history, in contrast to a genuine history such as ours, can be ascertained objectively."[7]

"Not only we vampyroteuthes," the text continues, still ventriloquizing the articulate squid, "but even a visitor from Mars could reconstruct human history from these entities." In evoking this rather dismissive (albeit biased) critique of our species, Flusser means to turn our own sense of accomplishment – as the authors of "civilization," "culture," "science," "art," or any of the other Great Human Excretions – upside down. Rather than being impressed by our works and manifest legacies, the vampire squid finds them wanting, embarrassing, and a sign of our inherent insufficiency. (Why, after all, would we feel the need to keep *producing* new things – artworks, furniture, rocket-ships – if we weren't plagued by a profound lack at the center of our Being?) Humans, in short, "live as functions of their objects."[8] Hence the squid's damning assessment: "[s]*ince it is soaked up by objective matter, human history is not properly intersubjective. It is an utter failure.*"

By contrast, the vampyroteuthes have learned to create a cephalopod history that is both bold and nuanced enough to avoid being routed through "lifeless objects." Instead they communicate their thoughts, discoveries, theories, and passions directly, through the interface of their own luminous mind-body (or body-mind). Just as human artists carve marble, notes Flusser, "vampyroteuthic artists carve the brains of their audience. Their art is not objective but intersubjective: it is not in artifacts but in the memories of others that it hopes to become immortal."[9] The squids, in other words, create "epidermal paintings" in order to directly affect their silent interlocutors. Vampyroteuthic art and culture is both immaterial and immediate. It is transmitted directly – sexually, but also aesthetically. Indeed, there is no distinction here between art, sex, thought, culture, identity, or memory when it comes to the *Dasein* of the vampire squid, since these human distinctions are all swirled together by the tentacles of the more refined invertebrates. To touch is to ravish, seduce, instruct, influence, illuminate – possibly even impregnate – all at once.

Flusser happily admits, in the opening pages of his book, that he is not offering a scientific treatise but "a fable." Nevertheless, as with all fables, this text can help us better understand our own *foibles*: so to say, our patterns, presumptions, habits, blinkers, and compunctions. In imaginatively projecting himself into the radically alien *Umwelt* of the *Vampyroteuthis infernalis*, Flusser provides a speculative template – or at least a creative inspiration – for hypothesizing very different ways of being. (As Hélène Cixous has insisted: "Thinking the thinkable is not worth the effort.") While the pay-off for this approach may not be ethologically sound, it does disorient and dehumanize our thought processes a little, which in turn helps clear a space to better see the highly specific, idiosyncratic fluke of our own ways – ways which we take to be universal and somewhat ordained, but which are in fact contingent, improvised, and always open to improvement. (Or even creative abandonment.)

At the end of his fable, Flusser suggests that we ourselves are becoming more vampyroteuthic thanks to our new "immaterial" cybernetic technologies, which are creating more squid-like ways of communicating – ways that don't rely on dumb, mediating objects. "From now on," Flusser writes, "humans can realize their creative potential only by processing new and immaterial information, that is, by participating in the activity that has come to be called 'software processing.'" (And, with an impish grin, he can't resist adding: "In this context, there can be no doubt that 'soft' alludes to mollusks ['soft animals'].")[10] So to say, the so-called information age has *already* infected our landlocked *Dasein* and rendered it more oceanic, as we increasingly share our thoughts through the pulsing membranes of our computer screens and the electronic tentacles of the internet.

His Octopus Teacher

Flusser's account of the vampire squid should, we have already suggested, be taken with more than a pinch of sea-salt. It should certainly never be read as something even approximating a scientific textbook. It can, however, function as a hypothetical prism to help us better frame interspecies encounters, especially those between humans and cephalopods. Moreover, it can help guide us towards a more nuanced account of the enriching *in*communicability we find stretched between such radically different creatures.

My Octopus Teacher, for instance, is a popular documentary – and aspiring love-story – that revolved around the "relationship" between a lonely middle-aged man, Craig Foster, and a somewhat coquettish octopus. (And we put the word *relationship* in quotation marks here because the animating question of the whole film is whether the man's interest in the aquatic creature is really reciprocated in any meaningful way or not.) Both Foster and the unnamed octopus live close to an undulating kelp forest off the lowest tip of South Africa, the former obliged to visit the latter with the aid of artificial breathing equipment and special waterproof video cameras. The film – which premiered on Netflix in 2020 – struck a chord among many who found themselves, during the first round of Covid lockdowns, visited by a renewed (yet immediately constrained) sense of mortality. Suddenly, career goals, petty squabbles, and the narcissistic static of our own mental vanity channels gave way to a profound – even urgent – new appreciation of the importance of reaching out and touching those we love, just at the moment such intimate proximity was forbidden to most. Beneath all the complications of this modern world, we realized, life was still pretty simple. It is about "getting by" as best we can and finding kindred spirits along the way to make the whole surreal journey less perplexing. And suddenly the raw stakes of being an earthling came into focus via this moving story. The plight of the poor octopus, fighting off regular attacks by pajama sharks – and just trying to make a humble home for herself and her offspring – held up a shimmering mirror of life's challenges, dilemmas, and opportunities when simplified to its bare elements.

Despite its popularity, *My Octopus Teacher* was taken to task online by those who felt it was manipulative, sentimental, and self-serving.[11] Many accused the film of painting a rather broken and fragile egoist in a much too flattering light. "As if *she* would be interested in someone like him!" was more or less the consensus among those partial to anti-humanistic manifestos. To dismiss the entire film on the basis of the (admittedly sometimes cringe-worthy) narrator and co-protagonist, however, misses the tentacles for the seaweed, and may even be symptomatic of a parallel form of disavowal: a deeper discomfort with actually existing (albeit fleeting) creaturely affinities. To quarantine *any* two intelligences from each other completely is to diminish the agency, or even reality, of both. (After all, we all know brilliant, luminous people who mystifyingly fall in love with rather dull and insufferable partners.) It also risks reinforcing a sense of exceptionalism – albeit in a negative cast – whereby no contact or connection is possible with a species as compromised as ours. (A kind of humanism in reverse.) Certainly, it is prudent to be wary of the dangers of anthropomorphism. But, by the same token, it is a mistake to conclude that there can never be any exchanges or overlaps whatsoever between two – even radically different – earthlings.

In a bid to forge a fruitful middle path, we can approach *My Octopus Teacher* in the same spirit as we might approach, say, a Douglas Sirk melodrama. Despite the more subdued tone and *mise-en-scène* of the former, both are a flagrant, yet meticulously staged exaggeration of a genuine emotional core, or source. They both signify, through their rather shameless liberties or excesses, a resonating passion. That the passion may be only one way is not really the point. (As Goethe wittily noted: "So what if I love you. What business is that of yours?!") The point is that an affective event can be sparked by random encounters between individuals, and paying attention to the light produced by that spark can be an instructive exercise. (Especially for a species that thinks it has nothing to learn from "the lower animals.") The silence of the octopus featured in the film – the mute object of cathexis – was, in this undersea light, the totem of a profound affective resonance: the sadness of being. (As well as the sadness of being a being among other strange beings, most of whom want to eat you, and some of whom want to help you – even love you.) It seems somewhat churlish, then, to dismiss a film that introduces us to two actually existing individuals who – thanks to some sensitive aesthetic decisions – have something to teach the rest of us about unusual affinities. (Hence the reference to pedagogy in the title of the movie.)

Once again, blowing the whistle, holding up a red card, and announcing "pathetic fallacy" is too easy and risks denying the more than human melancholy that can envelop different creatures, together, like a sudden plume of ink: better, we submit, consciously to cultivate a sensitivity to its tentative presence. Literature, art – and also the scientific record – is replete with examples of different creatures sharing and acknowledging a moment of co-presence, albeit to different degrees. Indeed, one reason these were written down for posterity in the first place is because they *feel* meaningful, even if the author cannot quite articulate why. The mere fact of the feeling is often enough for its significance to register – at least for the person experiencing that feeling. (See, for instance, D. H. Lawrence's famous poetic moment with a snake; or, indeed, the charged moment in *My Octopus Teacher* when the shy sea-creature reaches out her tentacle to touch Mr Foster.)

Indeed, we might call this non-subjective – or, at least, trans-subjective – experience of heightened attunement "the pathetic *facticity*": a term designed to capture that abstract, palpable reality which overflows the process of psychological projection. Pathetic facticity describes the fact that pathos is not merely a mental or emotional state, found only in the exceptional human being, but something that can be produced via recognition by other cognizant creatures. Humans do not simply *produce* pathos – as they do words or clothing or methane – but receive it, respond to it, rework it. Sympathy is not a one-way street, even if the two entities doing the sympathizing are using completely different nervous systems in the process and create completely different cognitive phantasms in order to make sense of the experience to themselves.

The philosophers are right that we can never know, or have access to, the thing in itself (where "thing" denotes something like a stone or a table). They are wrong, however, when they attempt to foreclose any kind of traffic whatsoever between sentient beings – whether this be with a pet cat, a wild bat, or one's romantic partner (or even a highly advanced computer program). It is extremely unlikely that we will ever really fully understand, or communicate with, another consciousness (including the Other lurking within the self . . . "Je est un autre" claims Rimbaud). But our various attempts to bridge the existential gulf between us are themselves influenced and informed by shared moods, dispositions, sensibilities, sensitivities, caprices, invitations, and solicitations. *Pathetic facticity* names the collective mood-space – the contagious affective currents – that hold us together as much as keep us apart. To venture such a claim is, of course, to open oneself up to hostile charges of being theological, mystical, animistic, vitalistic, New Age, or simply Californian. However, just as Flusser's book is not scientifically accurate but nevertheless produces a certain poetic utility, *My Octopus Teacher* invites sympathy, respect, and constructive aporia. To reduce the encounter in the film to sheer sentimentalism is to miss the charisma of the octopus herself – both in her representative aspect, as an ambassador of her species, and in her own contingent singularity.

Certainly, Foster is being presumptuous in assuming even a minimal degree of romantic reciprocity from the octopus. But as anyone open to non-human encounters knows – people who live with pets, farmers, animal rescuers, zoo keepers, veterinarians, scuba divers, lion tamers, even game hunters – *something* is exchanged between different creatures at certain charged moments, even if it is only the shared curiosity, or boredom, of acknowledgement. ("I see you, whatever the fuck you are.") In the case of *My Octopus Teacher*, both protagonists experience a failure to communicate *together*, if only for a fleeting moment. So to say, they share what Leo Bersani called "impersonal intimacy" – an *intimacy without content*. And, in doing so, they open a space for even the most human-centric, egocentric spectator to glean a sense of the ecological basis of their own existence. (And, by extension, the fragile miracle of creaturely co-dependence.)

If sentient creatures *really were* simply isolated monads or solitary *Umwelt* bubbles, gliding past each other in a vast cosmic choreography of disconnected occasions, then we would indeed be hard-pressed to find any pathos wedged within life's perpetual motion. In that case, we would simply be lonely blocks in a vast, incomprehensible game of Tetris. But the fact remains that there *is* room for encounters; there is opportunity for swerves, attractions, collisions, collusions, and so on, not only between different people but between different realms of the so-called animal kingdom. (As captured in those viral videos on YouTube of a dog "in love" with a horse, or a monkey inseparable from a duck – a genuine lesson in the almost infinite possibilities of cross-species bonding, despite the kitsch music or commentary of such a genre.) This is the same lesson we find in *My Octopus Teacher* – as well as in J. A. Baker's *The Peregrine*, Elisabeth Tova Bailey's *The Sound of a Wild Snail Eating*, and many others.

Just because such encounters are asymptotic does not mean they are not valid, "real," or worth exploring. Indeed, what after all are our own love affairs if not usually pre-doomed tragi-comic attempts to find some kind of Aristophanic fusion of bodies and souls in a universe which does not tolerate such perverse experiments in biophysics? As Georges Bataille notes, discrete or "discontinuous" instances of consciousness cannot truly meld with the flow of the universe – at least not while still alive and separate – no matter how frequently, enthusiastically, or creatively they attempt to simulate such a state (that is to say, have sex). They *can*, however, stand side by side on the precipice of the vortex of finitude that all mortals share, and thus "experience this dizziness together." Intelligent organisms – a category which includes even "brainless" beings such as slime mold – will always find ways to build relationships with other creatures, no matter how cynical, provisional, or serendipitous. And they will do so beyond the dictates of instinct and for reasons of their own: reasons that often transcend hunger, procreation, or protection. (Indeed, there is so much empirical data of such occasions – from the filmed, to the anecdotal, to the scientifically observed – that the most remarkable aspect of the story is the lengths that humans will continue to go to in order to deny sophisticated animal ingenuity, agency, curiosity, and caprice.)

This is not to posit some kind of pan-species communalism, however. And even the tender caress of a mother's finger on the cheek of her child is not as "pure" and straightforward as it might seem. The truth is that many of the moments we find most "touching" center on the sense of touch itself. Yet haptic contact is something of a cosmic ruse – as atomic physicists no doubt enjoy explaining. So to say, within the paradigm of contemporary physics, no two separate physical bodies can ever *truly* touch – not in any technical, literal, scientifically sanctioned sense. Instead, their asymptotic attempt to "bond" creates a convincing "touch-effect" in the caresser and the caressed alike, through the friction of resistance on the atomic level. This fact alone is a neat illustration of the way a limit or lack can paradoxically *create* the positive energies (and efforts) to make up for the same.

In other words, if we could truly communicate with animals, like a perfectly fluent Dr Doolittle, we would have nothing to tell them, and vice versa. It's in the gap between beings that the potential for any kind of communication is created, if only always *in potentia*. (Indeed, if a lion learned English, as Wittgenstein suggested, we would likely not understand what she was trying to tell us. . . . Just as I don't really understand what Republicans are trying to say to me. Or Democrats, for that matter.) Rather than point to all the semiotic material (or even chemical signatures) falling through the cracks, why not also take note of those strange and loaded moments when *information* – in whatever medium – manages to diagram a momentary link between two separate beings? (Where "information" embodies Bateson's suggestive formula or definition: "a difference that makes a difference.") Beyond the critiques – and despite all the flaws of its main human character – *My Octopus Teacher* is a welcome reminder that intelligent creatures like to beam signals at each other, even across the vast divide between species. And given this primal fact, does it really matter if we decode such signals faithfully, or accurately? (Whatever that might even mean, in a world of constant phatic verification, experimentation, and improvisation.) Indeed, couldn't we say that interspecies communication is, like *any* act of translation, largely an act of faith, good-will, and productive misinterpretation?

Parts Unbearable

There's a telling scene in one of Anthony Bourdain's later travel shows, *Parts Unknown*: the one where he visits Sicily to sample some of the local delicacies of this famous food-centric island. This scene not only speaks to the sadness of our current planetary situation but may even have contributed to the stormy climate in Bourdain's own mind; the same mental weather that eventually led him to take his own, seemingly blessed, life. With camera person in tow, our intrepid epicurean heads out into the Mediterranean with Turi, a local "chef, fisherman, and man-of-the-sea," in the hope of catching something succulent for that evening's dinner. Turi – who looks fresh from central casting; sun-kissed, stubbled, and ruddy – apparently specializes in shallow diving for his catch, with only a snorkel as breathing equipment. Bourdain eagerly ventures beneath the small boat in search of squid, abalone, and so on. Sure enough, a couple of minutes later, a squid drifts into the visitor's hand. But something isn't right. Bourdain, narrating the experience in retrospect, is shocked and appalled to quickly realize that the squid is already dead. Not only that, but his guide's retinue clearly brought an already deceased cephalopod – perhaps even bought from a local market – carried it secretly on their person, and then dropped it over Bourdain's submerged, rippling form. "So I get in the water," Bourdain recalls,

> . and I'm paddling around. And splash. Suddenly there's a dead sea creature sinking slowly to the seabed in front of me. Are they kidding me?! I'm thinking can this really be happening? . . . Splash there's another one. Another rigor mortis half-frozen freakin' octopus. But it goes on. One dead cuttlefish, deceased octopus, frozen sea-urchin after another. Splash splash splash. Each specimen drops among the rocks or along the seafloor to be heroically discovered by Turi moments later and proudly shown off to camera. Like I'm not actually watching, as his confederate in the next boat hurls them into the water over and over. . . . Strangely everyone pretends to believe the hideous sham unfolding before our eyes, doing their best to ignore the blindingly obvious.

Bourdain is stupefied by the *chutzpah* of his host, going through such a charade with a straight face, and searches his soul for an explanation. Either this Sicilian thinks that he – noted cook and writer Anthony Bourdain – is extraordinarily stupid. Or else he is playing some kind of cruel joke. Or engaged in a kind of absurdist form of live theater. Or all at once.

Bourdain emerges from the water in a mood so foul that he can't even address or acknowledge the camera, let alone this fiendish companion (whose demeanor suggests anything but the spirit of a practical joke). The translator also seems perplexed by this surreal turn of events. Bourdain insists on returning to land and thereby plunges into a deep funk, questioning his life choices and the uncanny actions of his fellow man. "For some reason," he continues, "I feel something snap and I slide quickly into a spiral of near hysterical depression. . . . There I was bobbing listlessly in the water, dead sea-life sinking to the bottom all around me. You gotta be pretty immune to the world to not see some kind of obvious metaphor." Bourdain flees the scene, leaving his camera person to capture whatever b-roll he can possibly salvage. "Something fell apart down there," he admits, "and [now] I'm pounding one negroni after another in a smoldering, miserable rage."

Indeed, there is something profoundly uncomfortable about this scene – itself a kind of quilting point for so many unfortunate tendencies. We feel the aggressive desperation of a man whose traditional livelihood has lost its source, and *raison d'être*, as the fish rapidly disappear from the sea. We feel the confusion and offense of the visitor, at the blatant and insulting ruse that is occurring in front of his eyes, as well as the black depression it triggered. Here we witness a rather cursed encounter between two random men, who themselves carry the fate of the world around them. Until at least one of them couldn't carry it around any longer.

Hypersea

Those who found themselves misting up a little while watching *My Octopus Teacher* were, at that moment, unlikely to be aware of the long and strange planetary story that our tear ducts represent. In their highly original book *Hypersea*, a geologist and a biologist – Mark and Dianna McMenamin – offer a scientific hypothesis that would also no doubt please speculative poets such as Vilem Flusser and Stanisław Lem. This theory ventures the rather beautiful notion that the ocean itself has spent the past two billion years or so exploring dry land. In order to initiate this amazing feat, rudimentary water-carriers had to be fashioned from the flotsam and jetsam found in the original watery element. First came thermophilic bacteria, and then various land plants, like moss and liverworts, and eventually our famous amphibious ancestor, who crawled up onto the shore and decided to keep on walking (eventually transforming gills into lungs). From this account – as much allegorical as biological – humans are merely one of the more recent delivery systems for the nomadic instincts, and colonial ambitions, of saline-saturated hydration. We ourselves are thus only one of millions upon millions of instances of what the authors call "animated water." And, as such, our salty tears are the evolutionary residues of both our oceanic origins and our ongoing elemental mission (which itself is focused on elemental transmission).

As Lynn Margulis herself notes (with more than a hint of innuendo) in her foreword to the book: "living matter has extended the marine over the land bringing phosphorus, water, and horizontal throbbing to the barren dryness of the continents."[12] While the phrase "horizontal throbbing" may seem somewhat out of place, in a scientific context, Margulis is underlining an aspect of the Hypersea theory that may get lost in the rather macrocosmic narrative across massive time scales: that being, a kind of interspecies intimacy that develops alongside, or within, a general libidinal ecology.[13] (In a different register, symbolists and semioticians tend to be unanimous in believing water represents both vitality and sex in the popular mind, from ancient times to today.) The McMenamins, for their part, class most animals, plants, and fungi as part of Hypersea, since these are all living organisms that "must actively direct a flow of nutrient-rich fluids or be intimately associated with one that does."[14] And given the fact that most living things are – still – primarily water, these organisms "can interact at arm's length, so to speak, only in water."[15] In other words, and as already mentioned, "the land biota has had to find ways to carry the sea within it." And thus, in moving out of marine waters, "complex life has taken the sea beyond the sea and folded it back inside of itself to form Hypersea."[16]

As early adherents of Margulis and Lovelock's Gaia theory, the McMenamins tend towards holistic thinking on a planetary scale, viewing the Earth's ecological diversity not as the sum of billions of individual *Umwelts*, as a biologist such as Jakob von Uexküll might do, but as an extremely complex mesh of promiscuous, entangled relations and sensual, symbiotic exchanges, all working collectively towards furthering and protecting the interests of the planet as a self-regulating system. "Hypersea," they write, "encourages us to view the mass of terrestrial organisms as a geophysical phenomenon." And thus, they continue, "Plants and land animals ought to be considered as part of a unified whole."[17]

Only a few pages into the McMenamins' rather exhaustive account, one can already imagine Linnaeus throwing the book into the wood burner, grinding his teeth at the higher level challenge this new criterion brings to the definition of biological type. The theory does not, however, challenge the established basis for the classification of genus, species, and so on. Instead, it views the process of evolution through both a longer exposure and a wider-angle lens, emphasizing the connections and exchanges between genres rather than fetishizing branching distinctions. (Which, from the perspective of the protagonist of the story – the land-stalking ocean – are, in any case, only temporary conveniences.) In this way, the Hypersea hypothesis parallels Richard Dawkins's influential model of evolutionary DNA transmission: zooming into the complex molecular code *underwriting* diverse natural forms rather than dwelling on the latter as ends on themselves (as Darwin did before the discovery of the double helix). In contrast to "the selfish gene," then, Hypersea offers instead "the curious Aquarian" or the "collaborative water-carrier." Famously, human bodies are approximately 60 percent water – "cucumbers with anxiety" – and, while we city-dwellers tend to spend our lives associating the ocean with vacation or retirement fantasies, we may indeed have a much more intimate connection with it than that: namely, a billion-year legacy and mandate to keep carrying the ocean around to places it could not itself visit and influence. (At least, not without commandeering a pair of legs for just such a purpose.)

But can we really characterize this relationship – between a creature and a vast, undulating element – as one based on *intimacy*? The term has already been mentioned a couple of times in connection with the Hypersea hypothesis, including by the McMenamins themselves. It seems counter-intuitive, however, to think of such scientific processes – along vast distances of time and space – as somehow "intimate." And yet that is indeed the way these (admittedly rather unorthodox) scientists depict the situation. "[T]he most awesome aspect of the land biota," they write, "is not that it includes both giant redwood trees and tiny parasitoid wasps, but that it vastly surpasses the marine biota in the physical connectedness of its constituents." In other words – and in some kind of felicitous anticipation of the theories of both Darwin and Deleuze – life on earth has, for billions of years, been engaged in an epic game of "pass the parcel," except these parcels are primarily enriched packages of H_2O. Earth has generated millions of different animated beings that, from one angle (the one favored by most nature documentaries), appear to be engaged in a seemingly endless, agonistic struggle for survival. From a wider angle, however, this same ongoing slow-motion explosion of heterogeneous forms is dedicated to moving water between individuals, species, genus, and kingdom – to keep the great green choreography going for all involved. (A planetary game of "The Floor is Lava," if you will.) As the McMenamins note: "The organisms of the land biota found that intimacy was a way to survive in an almost impossibly harsh environment."[18] (Precisely the kind of biological solidarity – even organic communism – that Kropotkin would have heartily endorsed, having argued over a century ago that even microorganisms in pond scum show evidence of altruistic, self-sacrificing behavior for the good of the other pond-dwellers.)

Hypersea names an impersonal intimacy taken to the planetary degree: sharing bodily fluids with other creatures – and even with plants – through sweat, blood, ingestion, suction, permeation, penetration, and so on. Thus, in accordance with the Hypersea hypothesis, we can't really say that "our" "own" bodily fluids "belong" to us in any technical sense. Rather, our most intimate viscous liquids inhabit us in a kind of timeshare arrangement with the cosmos, so that we can gift our own moisture to others at such times when they need it.

Indeed, what could be more intimate than that?

Oxygene

While he does not cite the Hypersea hypothesis, the Italian philosopher Emmanuel Coccia offers the same general interpretation when he writes:

> Life has never abandoned fluid space. When, in time immemorial, life left the sea, it found and created around itself a fluid with different characteristics – consistency, composition, nature. With the colonization of the terrestrial world, outside the marine environment, the dry world transformed itself into an enormous fluid body that allows the vast majority of living beings to live in an exchange-based, reciprocal relation between subject and environment. We are not inhabitants of the Earth; we inhabit the atmosphere. Terra firma is just the extreme limit of this cosmic fluid at the heart of which everything communicates, touches, extends. Its conquest was, before anything else, the fabrication of this fluid.[19]

In his book *The Life of Plants*, Coccia attempts to channel the *Dasein* of the floral kingdom, while emphasizing its crucial role in creating the oxygenated environment that we, for much too long, have taken for granted. "Plants," Coccia writes, "have transformed the universe into an immense atmospheric sea and have transmitted their marine habits to all other beings." Slipping between the aquatic and the aethereal – or, rather, trying to emphasize the *continuum* between water and air (as engineered by plants: the main interface between the two elements) – Coccia notes: "The air we breathe is not a purely geological or mineral reality – it is not just out there, it is not, as such, an effect of the earth – but rather the breath of other living beings. It is a byproduct of 'the lives of others.'" This is a jolting claim, reminding us that the air we breathe is not some kind of pure or neutral vapor, designed purely for human vitality, but a palpable excretion of billions of years of trees and plants. Our lungs are forever filling with "pre-loved" oxygen, which itself exists only by virtue of the expiring exhalations of previous organisms. "Breath," Coccia writes, "is already a first form of cannibalism."

Once again, we can discern the lineaments of a strange, anonymous, elemental intimacy when we acknowledge that each breath inhales the particles of life-forms that preceded us. When we fill our lungs, we are literally – biologically – inspired by the atmospheric half-life of other earthlings.

(*In-spire*: "to breathe in.") Coccia reminds us to recall and honor all those (other) organisms that left a vital legacy in their chemical decomposition: a gift to those who come after. The cosmic miracle that is the Earth's atmosphere – that tiny sliver of oxygen smeared around the planet – is, in his words, "a product of transitive life." It exists only as a consequence of the lives that essentially "pay it forward" with every exhale. (Again, a very different interpretation than the dog-eat-dog model of neo-Darwinism.) Here, the atmosphere is a kind of palpable terrestrial commons to which we all contribute and from which we all benefit. ("From each according to their ability, and to each according to their needs.") Earthlings of all kinds – whether animals, plants, fungi, or some kind of funky hybrid – are imbricated in each other; for "if organisms come to define their identity thanks to the life of other living beings, this is because each living being lives already, at once, in the life of others."

In Coccia's vision, oxygen is the medium of life itself, and the medium is ultimately the message. What's more, all living organisms partake in communicating this message, through "complicity and intimacy." The very fact that the Earth's atmosphere exists troubles the cultural distinction we have between Life and "the living": a philosophical conundrum stemming back to Aristotle and beyond.[20] (Is it possible, in other words, even to speak of the former without the latter? Or vice versa?) For Coccia, the ongoing legacy of the Great Oxygenation Event that allows life to occur at all is a "form of intimacy and unity" that neither reduces all living beings into one ontological mush or mesh nor separates them out into isolated individual entities. The atmosphere – like any given language in the human sphere – precedes us, creates us, sustains us, defines us, and yet we ourselves are not simply reducible to being passive extensions of the same.

Truly, the atmosphere allows a strange intimacy between beings that have this much in common: our shared reliance on its collective, life-giving properties. (Along with the fact that we are cannibalizing the sum total of those who came before.) Like Hypersea, however, this can seem like a rather idealized, even romanticized, view of the existential situation, even if it is rooted in legitimate scientific accounts of deep evolutionary history. Aren't these descriptions forgetting the violent splash of vermillion that reminds us that nature is indeed "red in tooth and claw"? Aren't these pseudo-scientific, green-tinged socialist parables overstating the cooperative nature of this lonely terrestrial anomaly? Aren't these relatively upbeat accounts – Hypersea, Gaia, Breathonomics – presuming too much in offering an almost mystical continuity between creatures, from the most sophisticated mammal to the most modest of polyps? In short, aren't these theories missing the sadness at the heart of such systems, no matter how heartening they seem when viewed from such an angle?

Granted, we are busy polluting the atmosphere with all sorts of harmful chemicals, particles, and particulates. Coccia's description could thus be considered a panoramic portrait of everything we stand to lose if we keep taking the Great Biospheric Oxygen Coop for granted. Certainly, one of the main motivations in underscoring this strange intimacy between all intra-terrestrials is to encourage much greater sensitivity to the organic solidarity we not only take for granted but run roughshod over in so many irreversible ways. Sadly, we are the species who forges forth under the delusion that we can do without the assistance of other non-human organisms. After all, we have *technology* and can thus figure out how to make *our own* oxygen, or water, if we just try hard enough. (Spoiler alert: we try and we fail, on both counts.) Indeed, there is something both tragic and maddening about our destructive, and self-destructive, relationship with our own *sine qua non*. (Perhaps, in part, because it is invisible to our eyes, and we have learned that, if we cannot *see* something, it does not really exist.)

To the melancholic, any and every endeavor inherently contains at least a tincture of sadness; especially so if it shows promise, is buoyed by enthusiasm, and proves to be worthwhile on its own terms. This is because every endeavor has an expiry date and will necessarily stumble and then crumble, through some combination of neglect, stupidity, vanity, or simply the corrosive passage of time. Our atmosphere is one of the most fragile things in the universe: perhaps even a cosmic fluke, relegated to the obscure margins of the void. Within this absurdly thin gaseous membrane – only 100 kilometers from sea to space, and only 20,000 feet before humans need special equipment to breathe – the atmosphere is the most fundamental condition of what we call "life itself." (Again, something of a mystery, when considered apart from actual, specific living things.) Oxygen is necessary, but not sufficient, for life to continue, since we also require other elements to survive. But it is certainly the most essential for us humans – the one we can't do without for even a minute or two.

Perhaps this abject dependency on filling our lungs explains our passion for making robots. In our Promethean mien, we seek to create a new race of arrogant metal-men: heirs apparent who continue to follow Ayn Rand's autonomous programming in the ongoing attempt to live independently, free from any social, even existential, debt to others. Robots, after all, don't breathe and therefore feel no obligation to the Earth's natural ecosystem. Once Elon Musk figures out how to upload his brain into a lungless android, he will be happy that he has cut the cord with the rest of the needy biosphere. His elation will be short-lived, however, when he realizes that life is nothing without the vital gift of breath.

Elemental Intimacy

We tend not to think of our various experiences in the Great Outdoors as "intimate," since we usually reserve this description for interpersonal encounters – most often in cozy, domestic surroundings, such as a bedroom or kitchen. And yet, as even the scientific community can attest, there is something profoundly intimate about our relationship with the ocean, the river, the mountains, the forest, and all the earthly things that dwell therein: something we might call *elemental intimacy*. If, for instance, you can tell what stage of a hiking path you have reached because of a certain smell (resin, honeysuckle, musk), or a certain birdcall (catbird, blue jay, magpie), then it is fair to describe your relationship with that terrain, and its inhabitants, as intimate. Similarly, if you are one of those rare, robust folk who like occasionally to swim around the island of Manhattan – and you can tell you are reaching the end of the Hudson River, as it meets the Atlantic because the water begins to taste more salty – then you too have an intimate relationship with those intermingling bodies of water. Granted, this is a different kind of intimacy than the one on which we tend to focus in the human world. But it is no less important or informing of who we are – especially if we take the long, evolutionary view.

Indeed, we should not be taken aback by the idea of elemental, or even cosmic, intimacy. This is the basis and muse of most nature writing, after all, in the elegiac mode, as well as much of the mystical tradition. It names a relationship with the Earth, the universe, or the godhead, that suddenly feels so close that even the idea of distinction melts into a kind of transcendent affection, tenderness, or simply cherished familiarity. All the scales and measurements that sustain the rationalistic spirit collapse in the charged planetarium of the heart; and the furthest star – or the most distant soul – suddenly bends and folds on top of, and into, the self, like a miraculous act of cosmic origami (what the anthropologist Alphonso Lingis calls "a compassion extended to cosmic dimensions").[21] This is the paradox of astronomy: a branch of knowledge that studies unimaginable distances and yet admits that the building blocks composing our own bodies have looped countless times around the galaxy. ("We are all nuclear waste," explains one such astronomer, reminding us that we have been scavenged and upcycled – or perhaps downcycled – from the remnants of former exploded stars.)[22] From this IMAX perspective, it makes a certain sense that we could feel a type of intimacy with other random bodies, or entities, that are themselves sourced from the same material. (And here we might even admit those people who fall in love with walls, fences, or bridges, as well as the kids or animals that befriend pet rocks and treat them as teddy bears. Is this so very different to falling in love with a car, a painting, a house, a symphony, a bottle of wine, an aspect, or a garden?)

Intimacy, as an English word, derives from the Latin *intimus*, which meant "inmost, inward, deep-seated, profound, or close." It is tempting, from this definition, to draw a series of concentric circles, each bigger and more inclusive than the last, with the self in the middle circle and intimate connections being named for each successive ring. The logic here is simple: the smaller and more central the circle, the more intimate the connection. In this way, a sister is more intimate than a cousin, who is more intimate than a teacher, who is more intimate than a stranger, who is more intimate than a seagull, who is more intimate than a mountain. But such a typology – based as it is on proximity and familiarity – does not account for *other* ways of experiencing, sensing, and moving through the world. (Or having the world move through you.) We well know, when we are in a worldly frame of mind, that a certain scent, sound, texture, flavor, or quality of light can strike us with more emotive resonance and significance than our own "closest" friends or relatives. (The premise and moral of Proust's great work.) Certainly, it's possible to be having dinner next to a campfire and feel a greater sense of intimacy with the sound of a waterfall, the smell of the burning logs, the light of the moon, or the silhouette of a mountain than with the person sitting next to you, eating more than their fair share of baked beans. Intimacy, in other words, need not only be centripetal but can be diagonal, rhizomatic, or geometrically incorrect.

A sense of closeness, or familiarity, can be spontaneous and relatively unmediated, occurring naturally by the simple fact of navigating an environment or a situation. Or, more often the case, it is culturally constructed. We are largely *taught* what is intimate, and thus what is to be trusted, in contrast to what is distant, formal, foreign, or public. The emphasis on the *personal*, when it comes to intimacy, is of course a modern development; just as the idea of a personal "possessive" self is a historically recent one. And while the etymology suggests an awareness that intimacy signals close bonds and familial connections, it does not presume to describe what actually counts in that regard. People can indeed grow grudgingly familiar with seemingly unassimilable, alien elements, such as prison food, toothaches, or the virus that courses through the bloodstream. Is cosmic intimacy an oxymoron then? Or a tautology? Does it underscore a paradox: that we are destined to cherish and prioritize the familiar, the close, the vetted, and the comprehended? Or does it hark back to a more capacious type of *life-world,* or orientation, that includes the constellations as much as our own kin? (Since both, at the end of the day, can help light our way.)

Extreme Weather

Sea Sickness

In late June, 2021, the BBC reported that the marine waters around the west coast of Scotland had started sparkling with "a vivid turquoise hue." Closer to the colors of tropical oceans, these chilly Scottish currents perhaps provided a preview of where the sun-loving beach bunnies might be flocking in the middle of the twenty-first century. The same report went on to note: "the picture postcard scenes are believed to be caused by coccolithophore algae bloom. This sheds white calcium carbonate plates – which can turn into chalk – and transforms the sea into a photogenic aquamarine colour." Meanwhile, in latitudes more familiar with beach-based tourism, a hypoxic, or "dead," zone was reported in the Gulf of Mexico. Such areas – created by excess bacteria feeding on dead algae – are noted for their almost complete absence of oxygen and are thus fatal to most marine life in the area. The dead zone reported in 2021 had grown larger than the state of Connecticut and was the result of excess sewage and agricultural by-products. At the same time, clean-up crews dispatched to the infamous Great Pacific Garbage Patch (which in fact consists of two distinct patches – one off the coast of Japan and the other off the coast of California – connected by the North Pacific Subtropical Gyre) recovered toilets, fridges, and other floating white goods in their initial haul of 63,000 pounds of trash (a tiny percentage of the actual accumulation). These crews deployed a half-mile long trash-trapping system – mysteriously named "Jenny" – in the middle of the year, as part of an ambitious pilot program to unclog this part of the Pacific Ocean, where currents funnel much of the world's floating debris into an abject coalescence visible from space.

Sequence 11
Dark Crystals

The Cave of Swords

In the town of Naica, located in north-central Mexico, lies the *Cueva de Las Espadas*, or "Cave of Swords," a 200 foot long corridor densely packed with angular selenite crystals that criss-cross the cave's interior like a fantastical and deranged minimalist sculpture. Discovered in 1910 by miners working for the Peñoles Mining Company, it was at the time considered to be the world's largest known crystal structure (it was subsequently opened as a tourist attraction, which in turn led to the decay of many of the crystals inside). In 2000, miners working almost a thousand feet beneath the surface breached a further subterranean chamber, revealing more crystalline structures. There they found a cavern approximately 100 feet long, with giant selenite crystals rising 30 feet high and weighing over 50 tons. Later, a team of scientists examined the cavern and estimated that the crystals had been growing there for around 500,000 years. Pools of molten magma below the cavern cause the mineral rich groundwater in the caves to patiently grow into their gigantic geometric forms. With internal temperatures rising to 130 °F and humidity at 100 percent, visitors to the cave can only stay for short periods. But what is hostile to human life may be more than hospitable for other kinds of life. In 2017, scientists from NASA's Astrobiology Institute found several types of microbes embedded in the crystal – microbes, they say, which do not resemble microbes in any genetic database.

Crystals are enigmatic entities. The term denotes both an abstract form (cubes and hexagons) and a concrete thing (obsidian or amethyst sold at a crystal shop). Crystals are hyper-complex but also invisible and transparent, the stuff of glass, metal, plastic. Crystals seem fixed and rigid, as solid as the primordial bedrock within which they are found. But crystals are also dynamic processes of atomic coalescing and dissolving – of crystallization – and what appears to be fixed and solid also transduces energy, be it in the form of New Age crystal healing or the use of crystals in everything from computer chips to lead in a pencil. Crystals cut across the scales of relation with which we orient ourselves in the world. They are gigantic icebergs but also drifting, weightless snowflakes. Imperceptible, geologic shifts of rock ("power centers") and the flickering circuits of microchips. The planet as a crystal. But also salt, sugar, ice.

Frozen Warnings

Crystals are abstract, geometric, precise. They are also associated with Arctic climates of ice and perpetual winter. For some, they even have prophetic qualities. As the weather shifts, growing colder and darker, the unnamed protagonist of Anna Kavan's novel *Ice* (1967) observes the signs: "Rising beyond the mountains behind me, ominous masses of black clouds were converging upon the sea. I watched these clouds, understood their meaning; felt the intensifying cold with increasing dread. I knew it meant only one thing: the glaciers were closing in."[1] Hyper-complex hexagons forming polycrystals and a climate where everything freezes in a kind of suspended animation, where life itself becomes crystalline. Indeed the Greek term *kruos* (*κρύος*) refers more to ice, frost, and winter cold than the precision of crystalline geometry, and in *Ice* this is rendered in the slow and inexorable freezing of the entire planet. A wintery crystallization encroaching on the human world, frenetically rendered in human-made landscapes of fear and desire.

Throughout *Ice* there is a perpetual tug of war between foreground and background, the foreground of human drama, the struggle of bodies and power, the theater of war, and an unhuman background, a climate that continually encroaches into the human world with the mineral patience of slow tectonic shifts. A sorrow emerges in this fissure between foreground and background. But it is also a sorrow that inhabits this confusion of foreground and background, itself an indicator of how remote the planet has become for us as human beings:

> Instead of my world, there would soon be only ice, snow, stillness, death; no more violence, no war, no victims; nothing but frozen silence, absence of life. The ultimate achievement of mankind would be, not just self-destruction, but the destruction of all life; the transformation of the living world into a dead planet.[2]

When is a "natural disaster" simply disaster, and when is it no longer even a disaster, since "disaster" implies a disaster for us as human beings?

The mood of *Ice* is as diffuse and palpable as the encroaching ice in the novel itself. Kavan utilizes different narrative strategies – chivalric romance, the gothic novel, military adventure, dystopian science fiction – to form a kaleidoscopic novel that is about the fundamental incomprehensibility of planetary and even cosmic forces. Narrative strains build up on each other in polycrystals as a nonlinear past builds upon the linear present, and troubling visions (or dreams . . . or memories) intrude upon the consciousness of each human character. A tale of war and espionage suddenly turns into an apocalyptic dream vision. A fable of star-crossed lovers suddenly turns into plotless descriptions of fantastical, haunting landscapes. Reportage suddenly turns into poetry.

Ice is water, cold, winter, and crystal. Ice is also rock, glass, mirrors, and the impersonal precision of geometric form. Silence, stillness, the absence of life. The mood of *Ice* is not simply about the fear of death but about a strange state of suspended animation, a kind of freezing of one's being, the catatonia of utter incomprehension, a kind of immobility that is, at the same time, ever so subtly shifting. "Shining, shimmering dread." Frozen silence.

A Second Suicide

At the end of Kavan's novel, the mysterious ice reigns triumphant, somehow covering the planet at an impossible speed. The rampaging glaciers are smothering the last remnants of civilization in a Bizarro World case of global cooling. "Human life was over," the narrator explains, "the astronauts underground, buried by tons of ice, the scientists wiped out by their own disaster."

As the surreal series of events begin to succumb to chilly entropy, the protagonist belatedly explains the root of his own restlessness: "I could not remain isolated from the rest of the world. I was involved with the fate of the planet, I had to take an active part in whatever was going on." In this, the nameless "foreigner" acknowledges something our modern selves still have trouble facing – especially those with the resources to pretend otherwise. Roaming from city to city and town to town, he watches the locals with a weary eye, as people fabricate traditional forms of denial in the face of disaster, even as the genuine end is upon them: "The endless celebrations here seemed both boring and sinister, reminiscent of the orgies of the plague years. Now, as then, people were deluding themselves; they induced a false sense of security by means of self-indulgence and wishful-thinking. I did not believe for one moment they had really escaped."[3] The foreigner continues:

> An insane impatience for death was driving mankind to a second suicide, even before the full effect of the first had been felt. I was profoundly depressed, left with a sense of waiting for something frightful to happen, a sort of mass execution. I looked at the natural world, and it seemed to share my feelings, to be trying in vain to escape its approaching doom. The waves of the sea sped in disorderly flight towards the horizon; the sea birds, the dolphins and flying fish, hurtled frenziedly through the air; the islands trembled and grew transparent,

> endeavoring to detach themselves, to rise as vapor and vanish in space. But no escape was possible. The defenseless earth could only lie waiting for its destruction, either by avalanches of ice, or by chain explosions which would go on and on, eventually transforming it into a nebula, its very substance disintegrated.[4]

Not only is the apocalyptic anomaly occurring on a cosmic level, but *the Earth itself* is in a state of panic. "I looked at the natural world, and it seemed to share my feelings, to be trying in vain to escape its approaching doom." Mother Earth, Kavan suggests, knows in her fossilized bones when her time is up. But she still rages against the dying of the light. (Or in this case, she rages against the malicious triumph of a sinister, crystalline radiance.)

A Forest of Jewels

Crystals are of the Earth and yet completely alien. They seem to not partake of the elemental properties of the Earth, and yet crystallization courses through the planet, from distant glaciers to falling snow. There is something abstract about crystals and their geometric shapes. We typically recognize crystalline forms, and it is perhaps the very thingness or substantiality of these shapes that makes them so alluring. They are abstract rocks, planetary geometries.

And if the entire planet is a crystal? Or if a planet is just one of the ways that crystals express themselves? Perhaps this is the lesson of J. G. Ballard's novel *The Crystal World* (1966). Whereas Kavan's *Ice* takes us into a world of glacial melancholy, *The Crystal World* takes us into the decaying, tropical ruins of a dying colonialism, "where jewelled rocks loomed out of the spectral gloom like marine plants, the sprays of grass forming white fountains."[5] There, amid the "auroral gloom" of the jungle, there are rumors of a "crystal plague," a "forest of jewels," a surreal landscape of crystalline flora and fauna "dripping with prisms," a landscape of "a palimpsest of colour" neither living nor dead.

As in *Ice*, in *The Crystal World* there is this rift between the human foreground and unhuman background. A colonial mining operation, a war-torn region, vested financial interests, a leper colony, a cast of world-weary characters each finding themselves at the fringes of human provenance. And then there is the crystal, slowly and steadily encroaching into human territory. Each security post that is set up can do nothing but move itself farther out. Towns, churches, hospitals – all abandoned to the elements, each transformed into a jeweled necropolis. Each attempt to study and analyze results only in helplessness, as questions simply lead to more questions. At one point, astronomists discover disturbing signs of crystallization on neighboring planets.

When *The Crystal World* was published, Ballard was not new to the sub-genre of disaster science fiction. In *The Wind From Nowhere* (1961), *The Drowned World* (1962), and *The Burning World* (1964; also *The Drought*, 1965), Ballard had established a singular kind of speculative fiction in which ecological disaster is mirrored in the inner, psychological states of human characters caught up in the apocalyptic torrents of wind, water, or heat. Each offered a unique vision of the Earth from a decidedly non-human perspective: the Earth as a giant hurricane, forcing humanity to burrow itself underground; the Earth as an ocean, with abandoned cities leagues submerged underwater like a kind of ghostly Atlantis; the Earth as a desert, a planet steadily evaporated of all life. In each, the planet itself becomes the central character, as climate literally seeps into the interiority of the human characters.

But whereas Ballard's previous "cli-fi" novels dealt with elements familiar to us at a sensory level – wind, rain, sun – with *The Crystal World* there is something intangible about the crystalline landscape slowly spreading across the continent. The crystal spreads with an impersonal logic that affects trees, the animals, built structures, and eventually the human beings who are "infected" with it. The molecular logic of crystal crosses all boundaries, creating fusions and structural anomalies that are neither quite organic nor inorganic, neither quite living nor dead:

> A marked change had come over the forest, as if dusk had begun to fall. Everywhere the glacé sheaths which enveloped the trees and vegetation had become duller and more opaque. The crystal floor was occluded and grey, turning the needles into spurs of basalt. The brilliant panoply of coloured light had gone, and a dim amber glow moved across the trees, shadowing the sequined floor.[6]

An *abstract Earth*. The impersonal precision of atoms, molecules, geometric assemblies and lattices in the earth, the trees, birds, insects, tigers, the quasi-mystical, gem-covered visions of a human brain prismatic within a crystalline anatomy. It is the abstractness of the minerological, geological Earth that is expressed in the crystalline landscape.

The Crystal World is a world where all previous terms through which we comprehended the planet no longer hold, an elegy of the world for us. Prismatic, crystalline, melancholic. Perhaps this is the affective core of *The Crystal World*, a dysphoria between the very elements that are all around us in the form of climate and weather and which also course through us in equally elemental ways – a planetary estrangement.

Snowblind

A tenuous expedition heads into the perilous heights of the Himalayas. Each member of the team is after something different: for the botanist, knowledge; for the photographer, art; for the explorer, a business opportunity; for the trapper, a reward; and, for the local guide, food on the table. In this mobile chamber play, the all-too-human drama of clashing values plays out against the unforgiving and impersonal snowscape of the mountains. A horizontal avalanche of snow and ice bears down on the team both physically and psychologically.

Released in 1957, *The Abominable Snowman* is among the lesser-known of the films produced by Hammer Studios, overshadowed by more popular films such as *Curse of Frankenstein* and *Horror of Dracula*. But it is a unique document of an already nascent anxiety in post-war Britain, not only over the slow erosion of colonial rule but also of the dominion of First World nations over the planet's natural habitats. Like many Hammer films, *The Abominable Snowman* juxtaposes pulpish thrills with stark philosophical ruminations on the feebleness of human provenance. Screenwriter Nigel Kneale – who had already gained attention for his scripts of *The Quatermass Experiment* in the 1950s – makes references to the scattered and diverse legends of the Yeti that have their origin in pre-Buddhist folklore.

Staying as guests at a Tibetan monastery, a British botanical expedition team overhears legends about mythical creatures inhabiting the farthest reaches of the Himalayas. They are joined by another, more dubious, boisterous group (of Americans, naturally) who are making an expedition for sport. Half-joking that they may catch the Yeti, one of the locals warns them not to trespass on "what must never be seen." Throwing caution to the wind, both teams head out into the snow-covered wastelands. An omen hovers over them as they set out. It's clear that they will be tested and that most, if not all of them, will not return.

What breaks the team members is not the extreme weather they endure but the strange, unnerving wailing they hear at night – or is it simply the wind? It's not quite a howl, not quite a cry, not quite a song, but all of these at once. As the botanist notes, it's almost like an elegy, a song for a dying species. It drives them to their limit psychologically; one of them can't take it anymore, bolting out into the blanched, hollow night.

Eventually, what the expedition discovers is not some vengeful monster, much less "the" Yeti. Instead, what they find are the last, decaying remnants of an ancient intelligent species, an evolutionary off-shoot, until now hidden away in the remote heights of the mountains, far from the din of humanity. In a confused nighttime skirmish, the American trapper shoots one of the creatures, and they bring its massive body back to their camp. Rollason, the botanist (played by the inimitable Peter Cushing), goes over to the huge tarp and pulls it back, a look of remorse on his face. The American explorer, inexplicably named Tom Friend, stops him: "What're you doin' there?" Rollason: "I'm wondering how old that face is . . . it's seen a long life, longer than ours I should say, a hundred years, perhaps more. This isn't the face of a savage thing, there's gentleness . . ." Friend: "Gentleness!?" Rollason: "Suppose they're not just a pitiable remnant waiting to die out – they're waiting, yes, but waiting for us to go . . ."

But the waiting game didn't work. The mere presence of the human expedition is the proof. Slowly Rollason starts to understand: "Listen, there's a warning in this creature. It's strong, intelligent, it may have powers we haven't even developed. It might have inherited the Earth, but something went wrong, and here it is, the last vestige of a species hiding away where nothing else will live, waiting in misery and despair for final extinction." In the remote recesses of a snow-bound cave, the hunted creature from a lost civilization suddenly constricts all "lost civilizations" into an allegory of human extinction. Rollason doesn't have to say it, but he does anyway: "It isn't what's out there that's dangerous, so much as what's in us . . ."

A Theophany of Non-Organic Life

The obsession in science fiction with discovering alien life "out there" in the depths of space belies the other possibility: that it's human beings who are aliens on the Earth, an offshoot of evolutionary randomness, happenstance intruders on a planet that has existed for aeons before the emergence of Plato's "featherless bipeds" on its surface. In the process, the planet is rendered as a human world, a world made in our own image, a world enframed as a resource, as the provenance of a species endowed or burdened with instrumental reason. In this sense, the emergence of human beings on the planet can be seen as the original colonial encounter, a colonialism at once geological, biological, and existential. Prior to the futuristic fantasies of colonizing other planets, there is the prehistoric colonization of the Earth.

While the Earth is merely a decorative backdrop for nineteenth-century authors such as H. G. Wells or Jules Verne, this is not the case in the fiction of Joseph Henri Honoré Boex, the Brussels-born author who published under the name J.-H. Rosny aîné. Often overshadowed in the history of science fiction, Rosny aîné's writing mixes genre in a way that makes it difficult to classify and for which the contemporary moniker "speculative fiction" is the most apt description. In the strangely titled 1888 novella *Les Xipéhuz* (translated as "The Shapes"), the emergence of the first human beings on the Earth is beset by an intelligent form of mineral life known only as the "Xipehuz." It's never clear if the Xipehuz are indeed malevolent, or what their intentions are, as communication with them is impossible. But human beings are dying, the landscape is overtaken by strange mineral and crystalline forms. They are perhaps what Gilles Deleuze and Félix Guattari once called "non-organic life," their very existence frustrating all human-bound categories, weighed down as they are with the prehistoric atavism of binary thinking: organic vs. inorganic, natural vs. artificial, biological vs. technological. The nascent human tribes in the story try everything to ward off the Xipehuz, including ritual sacrifice and the use of their own rudimentary weapons. They pray, they fight, they plea. But the Xipehuz continue to expand, indifferent and impassive, eventually merging with an entire forest. Eventually the human tribes realize their only option is to raze the entire forest, in a prehistoric version of the "scorched earth" tactic. Later, having finally conquered the Xipehuz, one of the tribal leaders reflects upon what has happened, in the process discovering a new kind of sorrow:

> now I am alone, at the edge of Kzur, in the pale night. A coppery half-moon hangs over the West. Lions are roaring at the stars. The brook wanders slowly among the willows; its eternal voice speaks of time passing, of the melancholy of perishable things. And I have buried my face in my hands, and my heart mourns. For, now that the Xipehuz are no more, my soul laments for them, and I ask the One what Fatality demanded

> that the splendor of Life be tarnished by the Shadow of Murder![7]

Though Rosny aîné's narrative now reads as pulp cliché, his novella is a fable for the ways in which the human species has rendered itself as alien other – or is it we human beings that have trespassed on a primordial Earth? It's never clear to the humans in the story whether the Xipehuz are an independent form of life or whether they are the planet itself, intelligent but impersonal accretions of crystalline shapes that perhaps have no purpose, no motive, no hidden agenda. They simply are, in all their incomprehensible alterity.

Through a Glass Darkly

Two children – a brother and sister – make their way to their grandparents' village, passing through a winter landscape of snow-covered trees, crisp mountain air, and the diffuse light of the morning sun. The small, rural town towards which they are heading is similar to the one they have just left. Between them lies the forest, now shrouded in delicate crystals of snow and ice. The paths through the forest are covered in snow, and here and there one notices signs of winter decay. But the children have passed this way innumerable times, and the surrounding quiet of the winter mid-morning gives them a sense of hushed tranquility. When they arrive at their grandparents' house, the day is spent in the timeless time of the present that is childhood. Before they know it, the low light of the sun signals to them that it's time to head back.

The way back is different than the way they came. Or so it seems. During the day, more snow has secretly fallen, and the crepuscular light lends everything a strange look, as if the trees and embankments of rock are glowing in shades of winter white. At one point, they discover they have somehow taken a different path. Or have they? The uncertainty is ramified by the drifting, listless snowflakes that begin to fall all around them. There is a sense of being entranced by the winter silence. But there is also an urgency.

They walk on, deciding that moving ahead would be less uncertain than doubling back. Eventually they come upon a fantastical Arctic landscape, composed entirely of gigantic blocks of ice, massive architectures of crystalline rock:

> There were great slabs lying, covered with snow but on the edges glassy green ice showed; there were mounds of what looked like pushed-up foam, the sides dull but with inward glimmers as if crystals and splinters of precious stones had been jumbled together ... Even a fearsome black boulder huge as a house lay tilted up under the ice, resting on its point, so that snow could not cling to the sides. And not this stone merely, but others, and yet larger ones, locked in the ice, which one did not notice at first, formed a wall of Cyclopean debris along the ice rim.[8]

It seems as if the landscape that was once so familiar has vanished completely, leaving only an abandoned cluster of cyclopean ruins in ice. They are lost. Walking further, they find an alcove within the ice; pockets of trapped air gives it a certain warmth. They sit with their packs. The food from their grandparents is inside. There is only winter silence and the night sky.

At irregular intervals, deep, bellowing sounds crackle through the air, reverberant in the sky. The ice, thick as the bedrock on which it sits, shifts and settles, as if sensitive to the slightest vibrations. In this remote spot, a place where human beings are not even meant to pass, a strange scene takes place:

> The children sat, open-eyed, gazing up at the stars. Something now began to happen, as they watched. While they sat thus, a faint light bloomed amid the stars, describing upon the heavens a delicate arc. The faint green luminescence traveled slowly downward. But the arc grew brighter and brighter until the stars paled away a shudder of light, invading other parts of the firmament – taking on an emerald tinge – vibrated and flooded the stellar spaces.[9]

And, for the briefest of moments, the children apprehend something that perhaps everyone in the surrounding villages has since forgotten: *we are simply visitors*. The impression that human beings are nothing but ephemeral tenants on a planet that will engulf them in deep time, a sense of being irrevocably unmoored from the very planet on which we live, the strange enchantment of an indifferent cosmos. The sense of a certain sorrow, apprehending the gulf that separates human beings from the planet, the night sky, the towering trees, the architectures of ice and drifting crystalline snow.

Like all flights of fancy, the impression lasts only a moment, and then it's gone. They have to get going, pass through the ice and rock, and, on the other side, hints of a familiar forest path, the distant lights of a search party, and home.

Though told in the form of a fable, Adalbert Stifter's 1845 novella *Rock Crystal* is also an allegory for humanity's often conflicted relationship to the natural world and the planet itself. Stifter is among the most under-appreciated nature writers of the nineteenth century, and his narratives return again and again to these epiphanies, where characters are gradually removed from the world of human affairs and, for a brief moment, are able to recognize the rift between self and world that is constitutive of what it means to be human at all. With great subtlety, Stifter's novels will shift from the prosaic world of near-term concerns to extended lyrical descriptions of natural landscapes, void of any people whatsoever. At key moments – usually when the protagonist is alone in nature – the background bleeds into the foreground, and Stifter's characters glimpse another world, another planet, another nature, one in which the humbling and incidental appearance of human beings is rendered highly arbitrary. A strange mixture of enchantment and disenchantment follows. For Stifter's characters, the impassivity of the planet is at once fascinating and terrifying. A mood of something that has been lost, something that we perhaps didn't realize had been lost. Something that was never there to begin with.

Go, Crystall Teares

Something encroaches, something approaches, as dreamlike, unhuman forms silently creep in the blind spot of comprehension. No longer are we in the domain of human beings, where wandering and guileless characters stumble upon a secret side they were never meant to see. In those scenarios – the worlds of Blackwood and Kyōka – the human being unwittingly trespasses on an unhuman world, something with devastating consequences. But the planet can also encroach upon its temporary inhabitants, where a similar estrangement follows. It's not simply the "we should not be here" of human trespass, it's something else, a more furtive thought: "we should never have been here" to begin with.

A terrain of crystalline features that displays only the faintest outlines of a lost anthropocentric world, a world at once opaque and transparent, a landscape neither living nor dead, where the categories of organic and inorganic, life and death, make no sense. A climate of winter winds, freezing cold, icicle anatomies, suffused with an impersonal violence and the melancholic melodies reminiscent of John Dowland's song "Go crystall teares." A landscape upon which events happen, a drama is played out, the theater of human strife relentlessly performed – but also a landscape on which the boundary separating foreground and background has all but collapsed. An atmosphere diffuse and ambient, and yet felt as extreme cold is felt, within one's very bones.

At the crystalline level, all structures tend to dissolve at the same time that they are built up. The boundaries that orient the human perspective – organic vs. inorganic, natural vs. artificial, material vs. immaterial – tend to dissipate in the silent molecular dance that generates crystalline structures. And at the center of the crystal's enigma is its impassiveness. Silent, cold, remote. Though crystals are in every sense formed out of the Earth, there is also something about crystals that is not of the Earth; they seem not to resemble anything except themselves, existing in a strange atomic tautology of oblique and prismatic detachment. The planet itself suddenly becomes estranged, remote, distant. A home has been lost, one that had perhaps been dreamed or hallucinated, a home that slowly dissipates until it vanishes entirely, leaving only the impassivity of frozen silence.

Extreme Weather

Dried on the Vine

Even urban sophisticates who felt cushioned from the day-to-day realities of climate change began to panic in the summer of 2021, when the *New York Times* ran a story with the headline "Scorched, parched and now uninsurable: climate change hits wine country." Evidently California's famous Napa Valley now faced a more formidable existential threat than wildfires: changing weather conditions combined with financial abandonment. Drought, smoke, flames, and unanswered calls to insurance companies meant that wine-growers, one by one, were waving the white flag and pronouncing the end of viniculture in the area. Other cultivators in the valley tried everything they could to keep this year's vintage alive. As the report noted: "[d]esperation has pushed some growers to spray sunscreen on grapes, to try to prevent roasting, while others are irrigating with treated wastewater from toilets and sinks because reservoirs are dry." Meanwhile, sommeliers who had been invited from fancy restaurants around the world to try the latest wines reported that many of the bottles of red tasted like ash. (A new tasting note, with the unappetizing name of "smoke taint.")

Sequence 12

Prayers for Rain

Prayers for Rain (I)

In the 1850s, Charles Baudelaire wrote a series of poems to which he gave the title "Spleen." Each of the poems grapples with the shifting moods we associate with melancholy and depression, often encapsulated in that singularly French term *ennui*. Each of the poems is also replete with images of decay, disintegration, and what we might now be tempted to call "climate events." In one poem the poet is quite literally saturated with rain, "chill winter's sodden gloom," a rain that spreads like a miasma, infecting everything from rheumatic joints to eroded hopes – even the "declining" or falling form of the poetic line itself.[1] In another poem, the burden of mortality and the clutter of memory weighs down on the poet like a suffocating atmosphere, seeping into the very sinews of a despondent, listless, weighed-down body, a body itself that has become "a graveyard that the moon abhors."[2] And in another, a pervasive sense of a sorrow seemingly without cause invades the poet's cavernous, cobwebbed mind, "a black day sadder than any night."[3]

Baudelaire was more than aware of the mutations that would engulf cosmopolitan, *fin-de-siècle* Paris. In his journalism and art criticism he provided a synoptic view of his times: the spread of industrial capitalism, the waning of institutional religion, transformations to the city and urban life, new theories of biological evolution (and of social "degeneration"), advances in cosmology and physics, along with political scandals, failed revolutions, and the flourishing of the bohemian culture of cafés and cabarets, all of which were part of that microcosm of nineteenth-century Paris that also reflected the broader macrocosm of European modernity. It is no accident that Walter Benjamin, writing about Baudelaire in the 1930s, would refer to Baudelaire's Paris as "the capital of the 19th century."

Baudelaire's "spleen" poems would be included in his 1857 collection *Les Fleurs du mal*, a book of poems known for expressing the many moods of melancholy: despair, despondency, listlessness, and the burden of the slow and inexorable effects of time and mortality. But *Les Fleurs du mal* often expresses these moods in relation to climate. His poems ask, to what extent are these affects and moods "in" the poet as a person, and to what extent are they "out there," projected onto the rain, clouds, storms, and decaying urban nights that envelop *Les Fleurs du mal* itself like an atmosphere? This is not the purified, breathable air of the Romantics but an atmosphere blackened by coal, drenched in rainy cobblestone, flickering in gaslit night. A new environment was emerging. Baudelaire wonders, at what point does the "in here" and the "out there" of melancholy itself crumble and disintegrate, leaving behind only a desiderata of affects?

Prayers for Rain (II)

In using the title "Spleen," Baudelaire was following a literary convention of associating the spleen organ with the negative affects of melancholy and ennui. While the heart or the gut had their own symbolic function, the spleen had long since been associated with despondent moods. That convention arises out of the ancient medical theories of the Hippocratic Corpus. There, one finds a system based on a balance (or imbalance) of bodily "humors," the fundamental substances of which bodies are composed. Importantly, Hippocratic medicine correlated each bodily humor to the Earth itself, implying that the stuff of the body was also the stuff of the soil, the air, the rain, the clouds. Moreover, bodily humors were also correlated to the seasons, as winter or summer would give one a different mixture of the humors and their qualities. All these factors produced an understanding of affective dispositions as rooted in the material, elemental substrate of bodies. Black bile, for instance, was associated with the earth, and this muddied, thick quality tied it to a heavy, lethargic, melancholic disposition. The task for classical Greek medicine was thus to manage the humoral balance of an individual – living on the Earth, in a given climate, during a given season – in order to avoid the imbalance that would lead to disease.

It would take later generations of Roman physicians such as Galen to actually localize the humors within the human body. The "black bile" that was regarded as the cause of melancholy came to be associated with the spleen, the organ thought both to produce and to store it. A build-up of black bile was therefore a build-up in the spleen, and the reasons could be anything from a bad diet to a weak organ to the wrong climate. While the humoral theory would soon give way to the dominance of anatomy, physiology, and a medicine that would look much more "modern," the language of black bile and the spleen didn't simply disappear. Instead, what was discarded from the history of medicine was taken up by poets, artists, and composers in the ensuing centuries. By the nineteenth century, it was not uncommon to find world-weary poets (such as Baudelaire) using the title "Spleen" as a cipher for the cluster of confused affects we now too easily call depression.

The sense of a palpable but vague something, a something for which no adequate language exists. How many poems – or medical theories – have been generated from this condition? When, following the publication of *Les Fleurs du mal*, Baudelaire turned his attention to the idea of "poetic prose," he chose as one of the titles for the new book *Paris Spleen*. The setting is decidedly urban, industrial, and modern, and anything but a shining utopia of progress. Everything, from the dilapidated cobblestone streets to the eroding bodies of its shadowy inhabitants, is inundated with rain, overcast skies, rot all around. Even the sunny days are depressing. The Parisian prowler is at once a cog in the machine, forever cut off from the natural world, and yet, at the same time, indelibly saturated with climate, weather, and the processes of decay, disintegration, and collapse.

These are the motifs that would ignite the culture of late nineteenth-century Symbolism and Decadence. And it would spread across the planet, taking different shapes and forms, often under the guise of colonial modernity. One can detect it, for instance, in the poems of João da Cruz e Sousa, dubbed the "black swan of Brazilian Symbolism," whose 1893 collection *Broquéis* ("Shields") inflects Baudelairean decay through a tropical lens that is at once opulent and corrosive. It is there in Sakutarō Hagiwara's *Tsuki ni hoeru* ("Howling at the Moon," 1917), where Baudelaire's urban solitude is inflected in estranged, nocturnal wanderings through abandoned cityscapes. And it is also there in *Weiyu* ("Hazy Rain"), the 1925 book by the poet Li Jinfa, who not only translated Baudelaire into Chinese but sought to fuse the latter's sorrowful climates with the long tradition of Chinese "mountains and rivers" poetry. The self continually dissipating into climate. Beyond this, only the cold, impersonal shifts of climate and weather that seem to infect the individual in the form of diffuse moods without apparent cause, a new atmosphere of coal-black pollutants from which unfurl strange plumes in toxic skies.

Gravity of a Planet

The massive amounts of data about global warming and climate change – generated by a multitude of planetary sensors engulfing the Earth – seem to exist in an inverse proportion to a more basic question: How should I feel about it all? Hope? Despair? Anxiety? Resignation? This diffuse, nebulous thing called climate seems to elicit equally diffuse and nebulous emotions and affects, for which the clinical category of "depression" seems woefully inadequate.

Indeed, we are so used to thinking of – much less treating – depression as an internal condition that it has become synonymous with the interiority of the subject itself. In some cases depression eclipses the subject entirely, such that there is no self outside the self that is in sorrow. It is likely that, for this reason, so much time and energy has been invested in trying to understand negative affects like depression. Such affects are at once constitutive of the self and yet also seem to come from without, nebulous forces that seem to possess a subject, an invader threatening the integrity of selfhood, a silent miasma seeping into the interstices of consciousness. Depression: a diffuse sense of leaden sorrow that seems to come from nowhere, negatively impinging upon a person's ability to be "in the world." *Deprimere*: to press down, to weigh down, to become heavy. The term itself denotes a state that is at once physical and metaphysical, the emotive nightside of gravity, an affective physics of impersonal forces.

It has become second nature to think of our interior landscape of emotions, feelings, and affects in a proprietary way. And, it seems, the various anthropomorphic environments in which we wrap ourselves – social, medical, technological environments – reinforce this sense of a precarious interiority that needs to protect itself from the assaults of an external world, at the same time that this interiority is the very interface by which living in the world is possible at all. And yet, the reverse possibility – that there are affects, moods, and dispositions that are exterior as much as interior – is too often dismissed or else relegated to the outer reaches of an overactive imagination. You're imagining it. You're projecting. You're overreacting. The best help is self-help. When you change the way you look at things, the things you look at change. Entire industries develop predicated on this model of a possessive "I," from Big Pharma to Wellness.

Though the clinical use of the term "depression" is relatively recent, influenced in part by early twentieth-century psychiatrists such as Emil Kraepelin (who used the phrase "manic-depressive" and described "depressive states"), in that time the widespread use of the term has become a kind of cipher for a whole array of "mood disorders" and negative affects associated with the diffuse sense of sorrow felt within the interiority of an individual subject. In their more classificatory approach, psychiatrists like Kraepelin would characterize negative affects including depression in a bifurcated way, distinguishing, for instance, between "endogenous" and "exogenous" causes of depression. A view of the modern subject comes into focus. A subject defined through its interiority stands facing a world defined in its exteriority, echoing the ancient philosophical problematic of a self that is at once a part of the world and yet also stands apart from the world. Action and reaction, cause and effect, mirroring and reflection, projection and introjection, cycles, loops, and syndromes weaving themselves through lived time, a drama played out against the nebulous sense of finitude and mortality that back-determines that strange thing called a "self."

While it may be the case that the way we think about depression today is determined largely by a host of official discourses (medicine, psychology, psychiatry, neuroscience, and, increasingly, pharmacology), a cursory glance at the history of depression tells a very different story. While terms such as "accedie," "tristemania," or "melancholia" are no longer used in the clinical context, these and other terms not only reveal the stunningly inconsistent and variegated nature of the so-called history of depression but also point to an equally stunning leitmotif that courses throughout this incongruous history: an ongoing perplexity concerning the causes of this diffuse, nebulous, and indistinct thing we routinely call "depression." How can a person be so concretely impacted by something so diffuse and indistinct? Even its ancient roots reveal this confusion, the Hippocratic authors suggesting that "depression" may be as much exterior as it is interior, that it may be as much of the stuff of the Earth as it is the stuff of the human person, that it may be more accurate to describe it as coming from outside, as an atmosphere, perhaps even echoed in the arrangement of the planets and distant stars. That is, a *mood*.

Black Bile, Cold and Dry

The writings of the Hippocratic Corpus provide us with some of the earliest descriptions of melancholy in the West. There the authors describe melancholy as a general condition of mental and/or physical lassitude, often accompanied by an incredibly wide array of symptoms, from fevers to anxiety to "convulsions, madness, or blindness."[4] In addition to providing the basis for the English term, this *melania khole* (*μέλαινα χολή*) or "black bile" is set within a world-view so different from modern medicine and computer-aided drug design that it seems far-fetched to us to refer to the Hippocratic Corpus "medical" at all. And yet, the Hippocratic framework also reveals something at once tangible and also long forgotten. That we as human beings are quite literally of the Earth. The air we breathe, the food we consume, the terrain upon which we move and act, the seasonal cycles, dawn and dusk, rhythms of living, waking and sleeping, a silent moon, a burning sun, Mercury in retrograde, Saturn returning. All this is implicit in the framework of Hippocratic medicine, based as it is on this simple principle: what is "out there" is also "in here." The "humors" described by the Hippocratic physicians are both the fundamental substance of the human organism and the basic stuff of the Earth itself.

For the Hippocratic authors, the human being is always already situated within the rhythmic constellation of the seasons (spring, summer, autumn, winter), the elements (air, fire, earth, water), and the four humors (blood, yellow bile, black bile, phlegm). Criss-crossing this tetragrammatic view of the planet are four conditions – heat, dryness, cold, and moisture. "Disease" is produced not by some foreign invader or external threat but, instead, by an imbalance. The stuff of the body is the stuff of the Earth, and if the body is sick so, in a way, is the Earth. Michel Foucault encapsulates this logic: "A symbolic unity formed by the languor of the fluids . . . by the viscosity of the blood that laboriously trickles through the vessels, by the thickening of vapors that have become blackish, deleterious and acrid, by visceral functions that have become slow and somehow slimy."[5]

A diffuse sorrow is expressed. Physical conditions are observed. Psychological types are revealed. An excess or build-up of black bile produces torpor and listlessness, or an agitated, almost manic despair, both without apparent cause. As Foucault observes, "this unity, more a product of sensibility than of thought or theory, gives melancholia its characteristic stamp."[6] Black bile, cold and dry. A diet is prescribed. Exercise. Vitamin D. The elements that compose the Earth, the Earth sculpted by the forces of climate, climate resonant with the stars and what lies beyond the Earth. This is what the human is in the Hippocratic Corpus. A medical metaphysics that at once elevates the human being to the status of planetary forces but also evocatively reduces the human being to nothing more than a choreographed complex of water, fire, blood, and air.

It would take later generations of early Renaissance physician-astrologers to link the mood and the planets. The Saturnine disposition, both rooted in black bile and the despair of a fallen state, is also linked to Saturn, the cold and turgid planet, hanging heavy in remote space, brooding and contemplative. The gift of the stars is also the sorrow of thought. It is encapsulated in the agonistic, futile, but fascinating survey that is Burton's *Anatomy of Melancholy*, a survey of a terrain that seems to become more distant the more it is mapped. The sorrow of thinking sorrow. Melancholy as a medical condition, melancholy as a trend. Hamlet broods to the sky, raises a weathered and mottled skull. What kind of a sign is melancholy? A curse, a gift, or both?

In a process itself saturated in sorrow, the melancholy mindset is further interiorized, locked within the depths of the individual's subconscious, constrained in an uncertain dance with the more personal forms of mourning and grief – but at the same time projected outwards in a flurry of projections, cathexes, repudiations, and a death drive that seems to have the capacity to engulf the Earth itself. Classification systems flourish. New frameworks, new terminologies, new ways of managing the boundary between exteriority and interiority. "Depressive states," "manic-depressive," "mood disorders."

Black bile, melancholy and melancholia, "hypochondria," "lypemania," "tristimania" – terms that, by contrast, seem quaint and atavistic. But also primordial. Born of the Earth, returning to the Earth. Mud, ash, smoke.

Night's Black Bird

Located near the coast of Naples, Vesuvius is a geological formation with a deep cultural history. Long shrouded in myth, the mountain is thought to have been formed by the massive collision of Southern Eurasian and Northern African tectonic plates. It was already considered a divine site when it famously erupted in 79 AD, engulfing nearby Roman cities such as Herculaneum and Pompeii in a cataclysm of molten rock, ash, and smoke. In spite of its active status, the area around Vesuvius has continued to attract human settlement. By some counts, of the three million people living within its reach, over half a million are said to be currently residing in the volcano's "danger zone."

In the spring and summer months of 1836, the poet, philosopher, and convalescent Giacomo Leopardi found himself in the shadow of the volcano, a guest at a villa near the foot of Vesuvius. Nearby, cholera was spreading throughout Naples, and Leopardi – already in declining health – sought refuge in the countryside. Though barely in his mid-thirties, he did not so much live life, as life had ravaged the young poet. By his own account, he seemed forever set apart from life, an observer peering through tinted glass at the prismatic shapes that moved about. Beset by a host of chronic ailments, illnesses, and disabilities, Leopardi was in many senses the prototypical "cursed poet," and it's difficult to tell whether this estrangement was physical or metaphysical – or both.

His one solace was the massive home library assembled by his well-to-do father, whose interests spanned everything from theology to astrophysics, from poetry to mathematics, from history to folktales. There Leopardi and his siblings were free to roam in a kind of intellectual playground. It was quite natural, therefore, that the precocious, deeply awkward, and angst-ridden teenager would begin writing, and Leopardi's earliest poems already reveal themes that would course throughout his later work: estrangement from the world of human social interaction, a felt rift between the flickering present and the weight of history, the allure of death combined with a dread of life and always remote natural world – vast seascapes, primordial mountains, the eternity of the night sky.

Isolated, in poor health, with plague devastating nearby Naples, at the foot of a volcano – it must have all seemed to Leopardi at once tragic and insignificant. Perhaps it was this stark contrast – the trembling life, the indifferent rock – which led him to write what many regard as his most profound poem, "La Ginestra." In it, there is a remarkable sequence where, after having described the varieties of human civilization and the natural world, Leopardi zooms out to perspectives further and further removed from the human point of view, until "the earth and sea / are in truth no greater than a speck."[7] The resultant, hypnotic effect is a cosmic hall of mirrors, entire galaxies specks in the distance, the vastness of the planet a flickering in other stars: "I see the stars / burning up above in purest blue, / which the sea reflects in the far distance / and, twinkling everywhere, the world / glistens in the empty sky."[8]

Named after a humble plant common to the region, Leopardi's poem constantly shifts perspectives between the human world of all-too-human concerns and the enigmatic, non-human perspective of the slowly rotating planet itself – and further, to the larger constellation of stars within which the planet rotates. A cadence is set in motion, until the center no longer holds and the "I" of the poem all but dissipates against the vast backdrop of cosmic night. Indeed, many consider this to be the central conceit of "La Ginestra" – to have raised up estrangement to the level of the planet. Poetry and geology, philosophy and cosmology, all tell the same story. They give the lie to the idea of human provenance. In a way, Leopardi gives us a new poetics: the contours of the void between self and world.

The convalescence near Vesuvius did not last long. Chronic illness would take its toll. By the following year, Leopardi would be dead. Though barely known during his life, in his wake he left pages upon pages of writing in every genre and style, including the *Canti*, poems that are now regularly taught in classrooms, perhaps to equally disaffected and angst-ridden students. Years later, literary critics, as they are wont to do, would make grand claims about Leopardi's death. The end of the Enlightenment, the beginning of Romanticism. Spectral pasts, haunted futures. But, in the end, there is this simple image of a precarious, fragile human life set against the deep time of tectonic shifts, a primordial planet, and the detached music of a cosmos that seems to so effortlessly engulf all poetic attempts to describe it.

Atmospheres

At the core of melancholy and depression is a relationship between language and sorrow. Language is all that we have, and yet again and again it reveals itself to be woefully inadequate. But this sorrow too is a linguistic problem, and it too is expressed in different ways. Primary among them is the attempt to trace the fissures between terms. The Hippocratic authors never used the term "melancholy" per se, but their diagnosis of excessive "black bile" invites us to fill in the gaps. The same goes for the Latin term *tristitia*, often used in the context of early Christian theology to describe the religious sorrow of the fallen, finite, and earth-bound human being. To connect it to the much more modern, more secularized *tristesse* or even "sadness" is once again to fill in the gaps.

In these and other instances, what remains is the persistent link between the affects of melancholy/depression and some distant, diffuse relation to the planet. Positively (black bile) or negatively (earthly vs. celestial), an affect always seems bound, however precariously, to an atmosphere, environment, or terrain. The most commonly discussed stopgap, however, is the uneven and broken passage from "melancholy" to "depression" itself. While it is tempting to read in this a transition from the cultural to the clinical, this belies the ways in which melancholy was always both cultural and clinical, both aesthetic and medical, at once poetry and taxonomy. And what follows for poetic language follows for colloquial language. Perhaps we have long since lost touch with melancholy, except as the worst kind of pretension, a pity-party reserved for the age-appropriate genre of Young Adult fiction.

What follows for the vertical, diachronic dimension follows for the lateral, synchronic dimension. Cutting across any given cultural and historical context one finds a whole host of different terms, each used in different contexts. Burton's *Anatomy of Melancholy* (1621), for instance, makes a distinction between "melancholy" and "melancholia," the latter a pathological variant of the former, though Burton, like other medical writers of his day, is at pains to discover the precise boundary where normal, "healthy sorrow" turns into its pathological form.

This synchronic dimension cuts across cultures as well, evident in the cluster of concurrent nineteenth-century terms prevalent in poetry and poetics: *duende, ennui, toska, tristezza, Weltschmerz*. Within a single context, in a single cultural moment, one finds variety: the indelibly nineteenth-century Romantic sense of "world-weariness" that is *Weltschmerz* exists in a constellation with related German terms such as *Leiden, Trauer, Schwermut, Sehnsucht*, and *Wehmut*.

Japanese aesthetics alone contains a long list of terms that hover around the English "melancholy" without ever quite matching it, the best known outside of Japan being *mono no aware* ("the sadness of things"; the pathos towards that which is ephemeral). The popularity of such phrases conceals a host of others that span the range from medicine to religion to poetry, and which broadly denote melancholy, gloominess, dejection, despondency, sorrow: *kanashimi, yūshu, inki, kasoke utsu, fukō, fushiawase, yūutsu, utsubyō*.

Modern, everyday English itself reveals a diversity of associations we too often ignore. Consider how terms such as boredom, anxiety, fear, and gloominess constellate themselves around depressive states. When is "sadness" something more than sadness? Is "sorrow" a deeper sadness, or is sadness a more diffuse sorrow? When is "feeling down" also "feeling depressed," and when is "feeling depressed" clinical "depression"?

We are left with the impression that the language of sadness is articulate but imprecise, and it is, perhaps, the loquaciousness of this imprecision that negatively indexes the atmosphere of emotions, affects, and moods. The sense of a "something else" outside the hearing range of humanity. Something impersonal that watches. Something indifferent that expresses. Baudelaire's "forest of symbols" that is at once nature and more-than-nature.

The sense of a something else that is not quite reducible to the meteorology, geology, oceanography of the Earth, but that is also not separate from the weather, the earth, the sea. The evocative though difficult term *yūgen* is frequently evoked in traditional Japanese poetry and poetics, variously translated as "mysterious depth," or "the sad beauty of mystery and depth." Saigyō (1118–1190), the wandering poet-monk, once described it as "the depths of a sad beauty." Mistiness, haziness, faint rains, autumn dusk, crepuscular shade, low-lying clouds drifting across shrouded hills.

There is little to no continuity between Saigyō, Baudelaire, and the DSM. And yet there is this motif of a certain porousness between affect and climate, sadness and weather, sorrow and the planet – whatever these terms may mean. It's possible that melancholy as a mood is as much about the exteriority of climate as it is about the interiority of affect, a diffuse mood rendered as atmosphere, the erosion of the boundary separating the human from something non-human, the dissipation of the human "I" into mist, rain, earth, and night.

Dissipative Structures

There is something about an emotion – whatever emotion it is – that is indelibly "mine." In English the very grammar of "I have feelings" or "I feel . . ." implies both an interiority to the person that feels and a relationship of propriety to those feelings. These two characteristics combine with the experiential immediacy of emotions to give the sense of feelings as intrinsic, innate, or somehow the very essence of who a person is. Hence a certain irrevocable quality to our emotions. They're "my" feelings. You cannot question them. No one can question them. Even when emotion is shared by a group, this sense of "I feel . . ." is scaled up to the bigger "we." It is the self-evidence of emotion that not only bypasses reflective thought but also gives emotions a sense of being closer to the core of who we are than thought itself.

And yet, even in the thrall of emotions, we also never seem to cease talking about them in articulate and even technical ways. We describe, "in our own words," what we feel, drawing upon the range of socially acceptable and meaningful aspects of a language to do so – a language that we are comfortable with, that we take for granted, that point where language is so familiar it becomes invisible, transparent, innate. Indeed, having emotions is sometimes tantamount to naming emotions, and the presumed sequence of cause and effect that separates them may never be as clear as we think.

This is, perhaps, one of the reasons for the development, in recent decades, of "affect theory" and its adjacent fields. Combining approaches from literary studies, linguistics, anthropology, psychology, psychiatry, and cognitive science, affect theory is less a unified theory or cohesive school of thought than an attempt to get at this tension at the heart of emotions: their immediacy and their being heavily mediated. The shift in terminology from "emotion" to "affect" signals this shift in orientation. While never denying the immediacy of emotion, affect theories ask how language, social norms, and cognition provide the backdrop against which this or that emotion can possibly occur at all. "Affects" are what circulate, what is shared, what is held in common among a community – and not simply the emotion "I have."

The questions shift. What is the stage on which or the setting against which the drama of emotions plays out? To what extent is our ability to "have" an emotion determined by the language we speak? How does this ability linguistically to describe and express emotion cut across different uses of language (formal, casual, poetic, medical, technical)? Given that we often attach moral valences to emotions – in the clinical context there is discussion of "negative affects" – to what extent does social context allow or disallow what we can possibly feel? We know that our senses are limited in terms of the range of what we can see or hear or smell – are our emotions likewise limited?

What results is a dualistic awareness. On the one hand, the domain of "emotions" – immediate and self-evident, an interiority that is the essence of a subjectivity. On the other hand, the domain of "affects" – mediated and articulated, an exteriority that is constitutive of an objectivity, a linguistic, social, psychological context within which the subject emotes. Emotions as innate, intrinsic, a singular aspect of the subject that is neither reducible to mere sensory input nor so easily subsumed into the detached ratiocination of thought. Affects not only as the very possibility to have an emotion at all but the background ambiance of what emotions it is possible to feel, at this given time, in a given situation, for particular reasons.

However, this may still leave a lot open. Between the "I feel . . ." and the "you are feeling . . ." there is a wide spectrum of states that are neither purely innate nor purely constructed. Between the neurocognitive hardwiring and the socially constructed array of normative affects, might there lie the smallest interval, the slightest gap? At what point does the interiority of emotions bleed into the exteriority of affects? When does the constructed become innate, and vice versa?

Perhaps this is why a third term has entered the fray: mood. Though the English term "mood" is not new (and is in fact older than the current uses of "emotion" or "affect"), it has taken on new meanings in psychiatry, psychology, and even the wellness industry. What is a mood? Definitions vary, even within clinical psychiatry, such that at times a strange tautology can result – as when "mood" is described as a felt affective state that impacts external behavior and action, and when "affect" is described as the experience of a feeling, emotion, or mood. Mood is sometimes described as more diffuse, more general, and it is also this indistinctness that allows for the variety of definitions of mood within psychiatry and psychology.

It would be tempting to regard mood as the unifying factor that brings together the subjective immediacy of emotion with the constructedness of affect. Mood, in this case, would be like an intersecting space that makes it possible both to genuinely have emotions and to acknowledge the constructed context in which those emotions take place. While this has the benefits of giving us a unified sense of emotion and affect, it is hardly concrete, and simply begs the question of where emotions come from to begin with. Another approach would be to regard mood as an assemblage of all those heterogeneous aspects – from subjective immediacy to language, culture, capitalism, and the hard-wiring – that somehow go together to make possible our capacity for feeling. While this has the benefit of allowing for a messy totality to exist, it is less adept at accounting for the tensions, the rifts, and contradictions in any attempt to think about emotion and affect.

Perhaps mood is simply what it is. It is, by definition, vague, diffuse, amorphous. But it is also tangible, palpable, "felt." Perhaps mood is this smallest interval between the innate and the constructed, the subjective and objective, interiority and exteriority, between the sense that "I can't find the words to describe how I feel" to the decision to find words for "I can't find the words to describe how I feel." Perhaps mood does not so much unify emotion and affect as it is an appreciation of that minimal gap or lacuna between them. Mood as the rift between interiority and exteriority, mood as the rift between emotion and affect. I know it's constructed, but I feel it anyway.

Something that dissipates, evaporates, something that rises like mist or fluctuates like crepuscular light, what rustles in furtive shadows or hovers in listless time. Mood is, in many ways, atmospheric, and it is the atmospheres of climate, weather; and perhaps it is the slow rotation of the planet that gives mood its indistinctness.

Gazing Wearily, Striving Unwillingly

As soon as night falls, our feeling about the nearest of things is changed. There is the wind, which travels as if upon forbidden paths, whispering as if seeking something, annoyed because it does not find it. There is the lamplight, with a gloomy, reddish gleam, gazing wearily, striving unwillingly against the night, an impatient slave of wakeful human beings. There are the breaths of someone sleeping, their shuddering rhythm to which an ever-returning care seems to sound the melody – we do not hear it, but if the breast of the sleeper rises up, we feel our heart constricted and if the breath sinks down and almost dies into a deathly stillness, we say to our selves, "rest a while, you poor, tormented spirit!" – we wish for an eternal peace for all living things, because they live so oppressed; night is persuasive about death. – If humans do with out the sun and lead the battle against the night with moon light and oil, what philosophy would wrap its veil around them! We already perceive how living half of their lives veiled by darkness and deprivation of sunlight casts a pall upon the whole of humans' spiritual and psychic nature.[9]

Melancholy of Anatomy (I)

When *The Anatomy of Melancholy* was first published in 1621, it added to an already existing fascination with the topic that seemed to mirror the turbulent changes of the Elizabethan era. Church and State, Heaven and Earth, the world a stage, the "anatomizing" of the body and the mapping of the world, imperial expansion into the "outer space" of subjugated territories, and atlases of the stars concealing celestial designs. Empire and dominion over the Earth.

But, for Burton, if the historical record teaches us anything, it is that nothing lasts. Perhaps it was this diffuse, even cosmic sense of the changeability of all things that, for some authors, reflected back on the human condition. "Thus betwixt hope and fear, suspicions, angers . . . we bangle away our best days, befool out our times, we lead a contentious, discontent, tumultuous, melancholy, miserable life."[10] In the depths of the melancholy disposition is a kind of resignation, the human life refusing life in general, for "if we could foretell what was to come, and it put to our choice, we should rather refuse than accept of this painful life."[11]

At the same time, *The Anatomy of Melancholy* is a deeply personal book. Burton opens his study with a confession. "I writ of melancholy, to be busy avoiding melancholy."[12] I am a melancholic. And, in diagnosing himself, Burton provides one of his many descriptions of melancholics. "They are weary of their lives . . . their days pass wearily by, they are soon tired with all things"; they are "discontent, disquieted, perplexed," and often overcome with "grief, fear, agony, discontent, wearisomeness, laziness, suspicion," and suffer a "sickness of the soul without any hope."[13] It is in this zone that the very ability to articulate melancholy in language becomes a strange kind of panacea. Throughout the book's almost obsessive descriptions and typologies, there remains this simple intuition: I write about melancholy so that I am a little less melancholic. And yet, reflection, contemplation, writing, and "too much study" can also draw one back into melancholic inertia.

For many, however, melancholy was the sign of an elevated consciousness, of sensitivity to the nuances of the soul, of an attentiveness to the play of ephemera that constituted the drama of human life, inflected through the seasonal passing of lived time. The "Elizabethan malady" was, as we say, on trend. To be sad was to be human. But to be in sorrow was something more. To pine after what has been irrevocably lost. To dwell on this sorrow, giving it a voice, allowing a vocabulary to shape itself, which would reach its full fruition in Romanticism, the ominous tone of Keats's anticipation: "when the melancholy fit shall fall / Sudden from heaven like a weeping cloud."[14]

Burton describes it as "pleasurable melancholy," a poetics that evokes an ambivalent sorrow, criss-crossed by landscape, myth, and mood. "In a word, the world itself is a maze, a labyrinth of errors, a desert, a wilderness . . . full of filthy puddles, horrid rocks, precipices, an ocean of adversity, an heavy yoke, wherein infirmities and calamities overtake and follow from one another, as the sea waves."[15]

The poetics of melancholy involves the transfer of this sorrow to the outside world, to the seasons, to the weather, to time itself, until something like an atmosphere is produced, one in which the melancholic can no longer distinguish between the tempestuous soul and brooding, ink-black skies. An entire poetry forms around such moods, where the grand themes of love, time, and death are crystallized in sonnet form. To helplessly brood over a theater of contingency that impersonally structures a life in almost elemental ways. "[Y]ou may soon separate weight from lead, heat from fire, moistness from water, brightness from the sun, as misery, discontent, care, calamity, danger" from the human being.[16]

Melancholy of Anatomy (II)

While it adopts an approach that claims to be medical and scientific, *The Anatomy of Melancholy* is also a profoundly philosophical book, in that it often performs its own symptoms. Melancholy is diagnosed and classified; there is also a sense in which melancholy as a mood seems forever to dissipate before the grasping taxonomies of Burton's analytical approach.

A systematic tome that collapses beneath the weight of its mania for terminology and taxonomy. An entire culture of melancholy that by turns deifies and demonizes its sorrow. Despite these apparent contradictions, a structure does emerge from *The Anatomy of Melancholy*'s analytical approach. Burton offers many distinctions, such as that between melancholy "in disposition" and melancholy "in habit." He also creates a typology between the many varieties of melancholy, including "love melancholy" and "religious melancholy." There are those who suffer by being estranged from society and those who choose "voluntary solitariness." At its core, however, is a relatively straightforward definition that Burton collates from various classical sources. Melancholy is "fear and sadness" that is "without apparent cause."[17] Sadness for no reason.

Sorrow without cause. Something tangible and deeply felt but that also seems diffuse and hazy. A mood that seems to come from nowhere. A sorrow not simply contingent on having gotten up on the perennial wrong side of the bed.

For Burton, there is a pervasiveness to melancholy that cuts across the strata of self, world, and cosmos. *The Anatomy of Melancholy* seems so saturated with sorrow that it eclipses the boundary separating the human and the non-human. The sorrow that weighs down the individual subject also weighs down the group, in communities of sorrow. "Kingdoms, provinces, and politic bodies are likewise sensible and subject to this disease."[18] What follows for human beings also follows for animals and planets. "This melancholy extends itself not to men only, but even to vegetals and sensibles . . . creatures which are saturnine, melancholy by nature, as lead, and such like minerals, or those plants, rue, cypress, &c. and hellebore itself."[19] Is it an illness rooted in one's constitution, or is it sorrow rendered metaphysical? "Copernicus . . . is of the opinion that the earth is a planet, moves and shines to others, as the moon doth to us."[20] The sciences that follow recapitulate Copernicus' finding "in sober sadness," a decentering of the planet, an unmooring of the world cast in our own image, an Earth set within the larger backdrop of impersonal forces, but also an Earth metaphysically cast adrift.

Sad Planets (a Typology)

A mood – like atmosphere, like climate – emerges in the confused affective space between interiority and exteriority, the dissipative zone in which the human personification of the world becomes comingled with the depersonification of the human being, intersected by a host of elemental properties that impact us in ways we only liminally understand. It's a mood that condenses in the distance between a foreground displaying all the accoutrements of human drama and a background of unhuman forces whose continents, oceans, and shifting skies move in the detached cadence of deep time.

If we were to consider a sadness specific to our fraught and confused existential relation to the planet, we would have to begin with what is most tangible. At one level, there is a sadness that has to do with the progressive loss of entire regions of the planet that have since become inhospitable to human beings and our varied ways of life. At the most material levels, the loss of home, the loss of one's means of living, the loss of ways of life inextricably tied to landscape, climate, and regions within which a culture flourishes. Climate disasters – increasingly the distinction between "natural" and "human-made" is becoming irrelevant – are the most arresting examples of this, but it also occurs bit by bit, spanning generations. The phrases used for this condition – from "eco-grief" to "solastalgia" – are indicators of their prevalence.

At another level, a sadness of the planet can be experienced without having been directly impacted by climate events. The seemingly naïve act of witnessing the loss of habitat – be it for humans, animals, or plants – can also have an impact as well. The progressive extinction of species, global industrial food production, and widespread deforestation – all due to the long-term effects of aggressive human intervention on the planet – are "events" that may not be experienced as such. And yet, many argue that the act of bearing witness can be traumatic in its own way. Phrases such as "environmental grief" or "eco-anxiety" themselves bear witness to this aspect of sadness at a distance, sadness at the very knowledge that such irreversible changes are taking place – sadness at the increasingly inescapable notion that our species seems to be doing everything it can to ensure its own extinction.

And perhaps this leads to an even further kind of sadness. While the majority of discussions in psychology, psychiatry, and other fields has focused on the direct, tangible, emotional impact of climate change, what they often miss are the moods associated with the reverse: of being unable to relate to the planet itself at all, or at least outside of the indelibly human-centric frameworks of personification and instrumentality, anthropomorphism and anthropocentrism. Our world, there for us to save, to mine, to design, to refashion in our own image.

It is this third kind of sadness that is fundamentally about a gulf separating the human-centric world of significance and meaning-making and a planet that is indifferent to the "events" that flicker across it with such devastating effects. It's a relation to the planet that we can index only negatively, as non-human, or unhuman, a planet indifferent, impersonal. The sadness that inhabits the minimal recognition that, in a sense, it is only we human beings that feel sad about it at all. The sadness of the inevitability – "someday" – of human extinction, and the knowledge that "afterwards," as Nietzsche says, "nothing will have happened." The strange sadness of a world without us.

As One Listens to the Rain

A sorrow that saturates the individual person, but which also seems to come from some vaguely articulated source that cuts across weather, climate, and possibly the planet itself. A sorrow bifurcated, but also indistinct, hazy, foggy. A sorrow from within, a sorrow from without. In the clinical world, the best exemplar of this is perhaps "Seasonal Affective Disorder," or SAD, as it is more appropriately known. Once thought to be a separate type of mood disorder, SAD is currently considered a subset of "recurrent major depressive disorders" in which depressive mood changes are linked to changes in seasonal patterns. First identified in the 1980s by researchers at the National Institute of Mental Health (NIMH), SAD has since entered the DSM and is defined as "a type of depression characterized by its recurrent seasonal pattern, with symptoms lasting about 4 to 5 months per year."

In addition to displaying symptoms related to depressive disorders (loss of interest in activities, change in appetite, disruption with sleep patterns, low energy or hyper-activity, frequent thoughts of death), symptoms specific to SAD have also been linked to seasonal changes and weather patterns. Typical symptoms occur as seasons change and may include depressive mood shifts during winter months, associated with shorter days, less exposure to sunlight, and winter weather such as rain or snow (it is noteworthy that the initial studies of SAD focused on the effects of people living in areas that experience polar night, or nighttime at the poles that lasts over 24 hours). For example, symptoms of "winter-pattern SAD" include "hypersomnia" (oversleeping), overeating ("particularly with a craving for carbohydrates"), and social withdrawal (which the NIMH likens to "hibernating"). With some studies showing close to 15 percent of the population in the US experiencing some form of SAD (up to 24 percent in Alaska), a host of treatments – from light therapy to meditation to medication – have emerged. How the ongoing perturbations in weather patterns due to global climate change will impact SAD is a topic that remains to be studied.

While easy to be dismissed as a bout of the "winter blues," SAD is one of a number of clinically defined psychological conditions in which inner-mood states are indelibly linked to shifts in climate, weather, and the seasons. Norman Rosenthal, a psychiatrist whose research helped identify SAD, notes, "[o]ver hundreds of thousands of years, the architecture of our bodies has been shaped by the seasons and we have developed mechanisms to deal with the regular changes that they bring."[21] Additionally, the correlation between weather and mood is not a one-to-one correlation, as everything from cultural context to brain chemistry can influence seasonal-based moods. Rosenthal notes this fungibility between weather and mood: "The seasons of the mind are not the same for everyone . . . For certain people, winter, cheerless and forbidding, is associated with stagnation, decay, and loss. But others experience a different type of winter – one that finds them snug and cozy by the fire-side, with chestnuts popping."[22] In this sense, SAD is as much a cultural or even existential phenomenon as it is a medical one. A clinical variant on what literary scholars once dubbed the "pathetic fallacy," SAD is itself symptomatic of novel approaches for grappling with a whole host of moods related to climate, weather, and the emerging planetary awareness that appears to mark the twenty-first century.

In a sense, SAD would seem to be almost quotidian. Anytime anyone experiences negative affects such as melancholy or sorrow in relation to the rain or overcast skies, are we now in a position to say that they're experiencing a bout of SAD? Poets would seem to be particularly susceptible. Whether it's Tu Fu musing on his failed past in the mountains of seventh-century China, Baudelaire ruminating on his splenetic overcast mind, Sylvia Plath's empathy towards the impassive winter trees, or Octavio Paz's admonition to "listen to me as one listens to the rain," SAD appears to articulate a new ambiguity: you are depressed because it's raining, and this is because your culture associates rain with a disposition towards depressive states. Or is it the reverse? Surely there must have been the first poet who initially felt that affect of melancholy in relation to the rain? And what of the strange, ambivalent comfort one derives from this very sadness? Whatever the case, one thing would seem to be certain: it never rains because one is sad (a case for the depressed animist, the melancholic geomancer). SAD stipulates a unidirectional causality. The rain doesn't care.

Perhaps this is the real cause of climate-based mood disorders such as SAD. That the rain doesn't care. Write as many alexandrine sonnets as you like, the rain will continue raining, and that is all. Rather than relentlessly classifying affects in its clinical taxonomy, perhaps what is sad about SAD is that it points to this irrevocable rift between the thinking, feeling human being and an impersonal planet – but a planet on which we live and in which we are actively enmeshed. In spite of its clinical specificity, "climate affects" like SAD may indicate not so much a point of contact between myself and the climate as the inverse. Japanese philosopher Tetsuro Watsuji suggests this in his 1961 study *A Climate*. When we step outside on a brisk winter day and feel that it's cold, what exactly are we feeling?

> The cold thus discovered is cold limited to the sphere of the "I." But what we call the cold is a transcendental object outside the "I," and not a mere feeling of the "I." Now, how can

> a subjective experience establish a relation with such a transcendental object? In other words, how can the feeling of cold relate itself to the coldness of the outside air?[23]

For Watsuji, there is something always belated about our experience of climate, direct and immediate though it may seem. "When we feel cold, we ourselves are already in the coldness of the outside air."[24] In the apparently straightforward sensation of the weather, there lies a deeply rooted philosophical problem that one finds articulated most clearly in Kant: the minimal rift between the world as it appears to me and the notion of the world in itself, the former all that I have to index the latter. Climate is, for Watsuji, more than just the weather; it is exemplary of a fraught dilemma within the foundations of philosophy itself. There is something about the experience of climate that always draws us outwards from ourselves, such that existence is literally "ex-sisting" or a state of being outside oneself – perhaps in the same way that the ambient quality of climate is always inside us in the form of atmosphere, temperature, air quality, and breathing. Climate is at once phenomena and epiphenomena, foundation and that beneath which foundations crumble.

Extreme Weather

The Snow Must Go On

Officials overseeing the Winter Olympics – held in and around Beijing in early 2022 – were surprised halfway through the proceedings when ominous clouds delivered several inches of snow to the peaks and valleys that had previously stood cold, but mostly bare. Organizers admitted that they had been "unprepared" for the actual snow, which complicated the delivery, maintenance, and integrity of millions of tons of artificial snow that had facilitated the first week of the competition. Environmentalists had decried the reliance on obscene amounts of water to create simulated conditions for skiing, snowboarding, slalom, and so on; and when the real snow started to make competing difficult – and as cameras struggled to penetrate the thick blizzard – the ironies and challenges of clinging to the very concept of "winter games," in the age of advanced global warming, became impossible to ignore. Even the Olympic flame was snuffed out by the snowstorm: surely an inauspicious omen in any cultural context.

Sequence 13

Quiet Despair

Our Only Home, the Night of Space

A dying Earth, a planet inhospitable, a terrain uninhabitable. A new plan, a new paradigm, a new course set for humanity. The Earth is not the only human world. There are other worlds, other earths, and the guarantee for the continued persistence of the human resides not only in the technics of interplanetary exploration but in the fundamental orientation of humanity. Expansion, exploration, dominion. Off-world. The human is extraterrestrial. Perhaps it has always been.

In the process, not only is a new course established, but new norms are produced. This is simply what we do, the next stage, the next step. A new interplanetary framework through which the nebulous "we" of the species refashions itself. Shuttles are launched, space stations serve as junctions, as vast ships prepare for the voyage ahead. In the eerie routineness of exodus, the scorched vortex of a calamitous planet is left behind. Abandon, escape, renewal. Ahead, open space, new trajectories.

All it takes is the smallest piece of debris – a dislodged component from a derelict satellite, a stray shard of a ruined rocket assembly, anything. It can puncture the fuel reserves of the ship as it leaves the orbit of Earth, sending it off course with no means of getting back. Navigation is impossible, communications are cut off, and rescue more and more unlikely as the ship leaves the solar system and is cast adrift in the hollows of deep space. Yet the giant ship remains, a small population aboard it. They can, hypothetically, go on living on the ship indefinitely.

But there were plans, plans to start a new life, to make a new home, to reunite with loved ones; there were ambitions, opportunities, plans for a future. And now? Time becomes untethered. There is no direction, and with no direction there is no purpose, and with no purpose the very infrastructure of teleology collapses.

And yet, nothing is wrong, everything works. The ship's facilities function, the labs produce food, hospital facilities provide care, there are schools and jobs to do, each has their own living quarters, and there is endless entertainment, the shopping corridors, the concerts, the clubs, restaurants and bars, all manner of diversion and habitation. There is even "MIMA," an AI aboard the ship that runs an immersive, virtual environment for meditation and relaxation, displaying to its viewers lush, lyrical images of forests, rivers, and fields of a now-lost Earth.

Around Our Grave a Glass-Clear Silence

But the ship is off course, irreversibly off course. Without fuel or navigation, it is being steered by the impersonal gravitational forces of deep space. A despair emerges. At some point, the ship's being off course simply becomes the ship being on course, albeit a different course, a course not set by anyone. The possibility presents itself of all those hopes, plans, and expectations forever evaporating behind this drifting and wandering in space. It is intolerable, absurd. The increasingly obvious alternative – that the ship itself is now home – is unacceptable. The ship itself becomes the new planet, the new world.

Neither quite alive nor quite dead, the despair of being cast adrift manifests itself in a variety of ways. To persist in denial, hold to routine, pretend it's only temporary, they'll come for us, they have to, etc. New plans, to regain contact, to engineer a return voyage, to hold out hope to the very end. To establish new order, new norms, a new purpose. To abandon all purpose and indulge every whim. Conflict, persecution, indictment, factionalism. Avoidance, evasion. There is no shortage of distraction to hold at bay the long hours of melancholic tedium.

But the despair persists, having emerged like an atmosphere that seeps into every corner of the ship. The simplest question – how to live – rendered unbearable, unanswerable. The question of how to pass the time. The nagging, harrowing sense that the ship lost in space has perhaps inevitably become the very Earth from which it has escaped. Increasing numbers come to the MIMA chamber, and the virtual worlds it offers, to escape, to forget, to abandon one's self, even for a moment, into the oblivion of a lost world.

A religion develops around MIMA. Another world is possible, if only for a moment, a kind of afterlife. But the despair overwhelms even the MIMA AI, unable as it is to process the cumulative trauma of its human visitors and the dead Earth they have left behind. Can a computer feel despair? Does "machine learning" include learning to feel sorrow, remorse, resignation? Eventually MIMA burns itself out, leaving only the husk of a dream world behind. The despair of having no answers. The despair of pretending it's all for a reason. The despair of nothing more to believe. Darker considerations. Suicide. Euthanasia. Or the slower suicide of those still living aboard the ship, a ship now forever out of reach.

The ship is in disarray, the corridors are abandoned, the labs deserted, the control center empty, flickering lights. Entropy, decline, ruin. Years pass. Centuries. Millennia. The ship continues on, a shadowy ark now occupied only by the floating dust of zero gravity remains. A sarcophagus in space. Eventually, it approaches the orbit of a planet. A green and blue planet.

Lost in Space

When is being off course simply being on a different course? When is being cast adrift discovered to be the only direction that there ever was? This is the premise that underlies *Aniara*, a 1956 epic science-fiction poem by Swedish author Harry Martinson. The poem is told by an unnamed narrator, who informs us that the Earth, having been ravaged by war and environmental devastation, has become inhabitable. Those humans who can afford to leave the Earth in giant space arks are destined for a new start on Mars. A near collision with an asteroid causes one of the ships to stray from its trajectory. Drifting further and further away from its destination, the inhabitants of the ship must confront the inevitable conclusion that the ship and all its inhabitants are now permanently off course. A crisis ensues that is at once social, political, and existential; the inhabitants are confronted now with the "monumental foolishness of living," eventually leading to a despair both cosmic and metaphysical: "Our only home became the night of space / where no god heard us in the endless void."[1]

Although examples of modern science fiction poetry are rare, it is tempting to assume that Martinson adopted the form as a way of writing a kind of anti-*Odyssey*, in which the motif of dereliction is not just an incidental scene within a larger story. Instead, dereliction is the story itself. The deeper existential futility of discovering other worlds is made more apparent the more the ship is cast adrift. "We are compelled to seek out other worlds / able to shrink and shrivel all to comfort us."[2] With *Aniara* there is no heroic conquest of the wide open sea, no fortitude to endure the elements, no return home.

The allegory implicit in *Aniara* is not dissimilar to earlier literary examples of being "lost at sea." To be lost at sea is to be cast adrift, unwillingly, into a turbulent space where wave upon wave inverts cause and effect: every attempt to maneuver out of tempestuous waters leads only to being engulfed in the intimate immensity of planetary oceans. Or is it the eerie stillness of calm waters that seems to extend into infinity, a maritime, noonday demon offering only impassivity and the dread of indefinite time? The most well-known seafaring epics, from the *Odyssey*, to *Orlando Furioso*, to *Moby Dick*, always contain within them a tenuous point where the heroic turns into the tragic, where direction turns into indecision, where navigation turns into wandering, where the sea itself is steering the ship more than its formerly self-confident human crew. An existential wager is made in going out to sea. Maps, charts, tools, a disciplined crew, and the entire technology of ship construction are employed in this wager. Even the stars and the sun are brought down to Earth. Points of reference, longitude and latitude, polar regions, an equatorial plane. But when that tenuous point flips, as it so often does, something else happens. The charts and maps, the compass and telescope, the sight of the distant horizon itself – all of this gives nothing back except a jumble of meaningless numbers, criss-crossed lines on a map, scrawled entries into a ship's log slowly descending into a kind of oceanic dementia. The ship is nowhere. And every direction seems the same.

As with sea, so with space. Works such as Poe's *The Narrative of Arthur Gordon Pym of Nantucket* (1838) provide a fulcrum on which the earlier adventures of nautical epics are transformed into the first tenuous voyages into outer space. At once expansive and claustrophobic, the majority of Poe's tale is told from the perspective of a castaway hiding in the storage chambers aboard a whaling ship bound for the South Pole, his only company his dog, now also a castaway. Everything that happens in the story's opening chapters – storms, mutiny, starvation, all set against the dramatic vistas of the open sea – is occluded from our vision by the protagonist's point of view. We get only snippets of information here and there, and our castaway, sealed up in a kind of capsule, must constantly guess at what is happening "out there." When our hermetic castaway does finally emerge, it is in time to witness one of the most harrowing scenes of a ship being engulfed by the sea, as strangely colored waters, hallucinatory skies, rising mists, and raining ash slowly envelop their now derelict boat, as the story abruptly ends.

It is but a few steps to the space adventures of Flammarion, Verne, and the early twentieth-century pulp magazines, many of them tales which also utilize the framework of the sea adventure. The expansionist and colonial imperatives of early tales of sea exploration do not disappear but are simply recapitulated in the vernacular of discovery of new worlds, of the rapaciousness of human dominion eclipsing the Earth itself.

Sarcophagus in Space

The 103 cantos of Martinson's *Aniara* constitute an extended elegy for the human species existentially unmoored from every point of reference, a mood captured in the compelling 2018 film adaptation directed by Pella Kågerman and Hugo Lilja. When the film was released, it came amidst a flurry of action-packed, end of the world blockbusters that often featured cataclysmic climate events, themselves fueled by battalions of computers rendering all manner of special effects: *The Day After Tomorrow* (2004), *2012* (2009), *Independence Day: Resurgence* (2016), *The Wandering Earth* (2019), the *Skyline* franchise (2010–20), and *Moonfall* (2022), to name a few. While the film adaptation of *Aniara* does contain its share of drama, the bulk is a kind of experiment both cosmic and social. Much of the human drama that takes place does so against the vast backdrop of deep space, at once impervious and indifferent to the chains of suspicion that haunt the human attempts to recover meaning and purpose. In both Martinson's poem and the film, the event that throws the ship off course is seemingly random, both accidental and incidental.

Aniara reminds us of how the microcosm of the ship (at sea or in space) serves as a stand-in for the macrocosm of the entire planet. And, as if to lean in to the Strindbergian melancholy that pervades both book and film, the derelict voyage of the Aniara ship is followed through to the very end. Without purpose, the conventional structures of meaning-making are called into question, and, in spite of half-hearted attempts to resurrect religion, ideology, myth, culture, all that persists is a defeated sense of nothing to do, nothing to believe, a melancholic mood of there being no difference, captured in Martinson's strange mix of lyric eulogy and futurist terminology:

Gratuitous, this space-death glassy-clear.
Gratuitous, the emptiness enabling
the pellucidity of the absurd.
Gratuitous, the horror star-like blinking.
My friend, you know too much for having done no
thinking.[3]

Aboard the Aniara ship is the AI known as MIMA, which offers confused and desperate human travelers idealized natural images of a lost Earth, while it also witnesses the lived planetary traumas inside each person's psyche. Overcome, MIMA commits suicide, leaving the human occupants of the ship in a state of utter bewilderment:

In our immense sarcophagus we lay
as on into the empty seas we passed
where cosmic night, forever cleft from day,
around our grave a glass-clear silence cast.[4]

Systems break down, revealing a different, more impersonal law of structural disintegration, entropy, decline. Growth in reverse, the fecundity of decay. The last human beings die, the ship left to continue its slow erosion, now a floating ruin.

With undiminished speed to Lyre's figure
for fifteen thousand years the spacecraft drove
like a museum filled with things and bones
and dessicated plants from Dorisgrove.[5]

At the furthest limit, aeons in the future, there is only the ship itself, now occupied only by dessicated matter floating in zero gravity, a sarcophagus in space, a derelict mausoleum, still derelict, reduced to the minimum, a null state.

If the tale of Aniara could be told from the point of view of the AI MIMA, perhaps it would be akin to Aase Berg's 1999 book *Dark Matter*. Told in a series of prose poems incorporating influences from quantum physics to splatter horror cinema,

Berg's writing hovers in the interzone between lyric and narrative. In broad strokes, Berg takes up the central motifs of Martinson's *Aniara* and recasts its despair in language that is laden with a thickened sense of melancholic black bile. In one section – titled "Aniara" – an unnamed figure that could be MIMA takes stock of an elemental Earth: "She sees a thousand stars against the bow – into dark oil lakes slowly sinking down."[6] A ship rises, hovers. "In the midnight sky Aniara glows over lake and beach. In the midnight sky Solve and Coagula glitter. And the hooves are muted against the sparkle-snow of the winter night."[7] A dying earth, a desperate species. "And through the woods rushes a glowing globe of despair, which blasphemes and curses space and times. A soiled froth sizzles in the yellow fetus's hand; she too can feel the black foam coming out of her nose."[8] It's as if the very departure of humans into deep space is also their voyage towards death. "The shell's tomb, the materials breathe. / The darkness of matter is soundless."[9]

At some point, structures of time collapse, as aeons into the future become nearly identical to aeons into the past. In one of *Dark Matter*'s most agonistic passages, Berg opens with a prose poem that recapitulates the emergence of complex life as a cosmic accident:

> Wounds split open from loneliness between the segments in the heavy organism, a slow beat through the black shell's silence. A contorted gene had traveled through chaos, a slight rupture had reached out through the ligaments, rushed forth at an accelerating speed through the fractal systems, formed chains of defects, charged the stillness of space with cruder and cruder mistakes before finally exploding in an unrecoverable and eternal internal deformity . . .[10]

As if nodding to current scientific hypotheses positing a "Rare Earth," *Dark Matter* resides in the crevices and cracks of geological deep time, a secret dance of entropic despair, a strange and harrowing beauty in the fecundity of decay. Places without people. Non-organic life. "There are no shadows between the things, there are holes . . . Every space between a pitfall, in toward the stage where the things are at once a glitterchaos of sparkling particles. I have no shadow around the body, I have cracks and will swallow me."[11]

A Black-Draped Sun (I)

Melancholy – and the work of living with melancholy – is so central to Kierkegaard's thinking that he himself often writes about it as if it were a living entity, a sorcerer's familiar, a kind of orbiting, celestial *daimon* that strangely gives one solace in the still hours of sleepless nights. In a journal entry from 1847 he writes, "My melancholy has for many years prevented me from saying, in any deep sense, 'you' to myself. There lay between my melancholy and my intimate 'you' a whole world of fantasy."[12] This animated sense of sorrow is, in a way, the presupposition for Kierkegaard's exploration of the fraught and conflicted inner world of the self, a self relating to other selves, a self relating to a world in which it is embedded, a self relating to the very possibility of selfhood at all, a self relating to itself.

At the core of human being, for Kierkegaard, is a rift within the individual between what it is and what it is not. A self thrown into the flux and flow of human time, the obligations and expectations of a life, the ideals and aspirations of desire, the finitude and contingency that structures dread and anxiety. A self at odds with itself. A self that is never completely itself. Hence, a twofold, tension-filled movement: not wanting to be what you are and wanting to be something else. Today, a whole panoply of more modern, more sensible approaches tackle the same dilemma: self-help, self-improvement, working through, optimizing, personal best, you are your own guru, each self a work in progress – all of it structured by what one is not. Perhaps we struggle to become the person who will simply accept who we are.

For Kierkegaard, this dynamic – not wanting to be a self and wanting to be another self – forms the nucleus of despair. Despair is not simply an emotion but a condition, the condition of the human being fraught in its simply being human. The dynamic is never resolved (except, perhaps, in death). Writing under various pseudonyms, deploying the language of Hegelian philosophy but also satirizing its mania for explanation, Kierkegaard writes of despair not as opposition but as a "synthesis": "A human being is a synthesis of the infinite and the finite, of the temporal and the eternal, of freedom and necessity."[13] We might also add, a synthesis of the earthly and the divine, the tension between this world and the vague notion of another world, a better world.

A Black-Draped Sun (II)

In spite of its being indelibly felt, despair is not uniform for Kierkegaard. In works such as *The Sickness unto Death* Kierkegaard describes several types of despair, and these are predicated on several questions. Is there despair at all? Am I aware of it? Do I have the ability or the capacity to do something about it?

At one level, there is blissful ignorance, the first kind of despair. I am "in despair" but am unaware of it ("the despair that is ignorant of being in despair"). I accept, without much question, the various frameworks that give my life meaning. I go on with the business of living. At another level there is a second type, in which I may be aware of my despair, but I refuse or am unwilling to do anything about it ("in despair not to will to be oneself"). I may feel powerless to change my condition, overwhelmed by the multitude of forces at play; perhaps I am a hardened and sober realist, or perhaps I'm simply too tired. Kierkegaard also calls this a "despair of weakness." And then there is a third variant, where I am aware of my despair and I assert the will to do something about it ("in despair to will to be oneself"). I am determined, even stubborn in my pursuit; I assert a sense of control, agency, and self-actualization, even though I may, deep down, suspect that not everything is within my control. Kierkegaard calls this "despair in defiance."

While the first type of despair seems, for Kierkegaard, to be a lost cause, it is the latter two that take one down different paths. We might describe the "despair in weakness" as a kind of *helplessness*. I am dissatisfied but unable, unwilling, or too tired to do anything about it. I sit in sorrow. Similarly, we might describe the "despair in defiance" as a kind of *hopelessness*. I know it's futile to control everything but I can't not try, otherwise the whole thing is pointless. Angst against finitude. In one situation, there is nothing to do – I am in despair at not being able to do anything about it. In the other, doing achieves nothing – I am in despair about the inefficacy of my actions. Both helplessness and hopelessness converge on a certain sorrow with regard to the human condition. The despair of, whatever I do, it seems to make no difference. They intersect in what is really a religious despair, what the philosopher Friedrich Schleiermacher once called "the relation of absolute dependency" – but a dependency on something forever outside the range of human comprehension. Despair is the condition in which the human being comes up against limits that condition and constrain it, a horizon that is both humbling and strangely enabling.

For many modern readers of Kierkegaard, this is the lesson behind the melancholy Dane's incessant complicating of religious terminology – God, spirit, faith, sin, evil. They are all place-holders for forces that are at once constitutive of human being but which are, strictly speaking, impersonal, indifferent, and anonymous. The human confronts something unhuman. Later on, we render it anthropomorphic, personal, familiar. But despair always hovers in the background. Vapor, smoke, mist. The otherworldly, that which is not of the Earth.

Big questions, small gestures, diffuse moods. And what of despair at the level of the species? Perhaps it is time to consider Kierkegaard's notion of despair not as the exclusive provenance of individual, possessive human selves but as describing a broader relationship – the desire to not be of this Earth, but to be of another Earth, the ambivalent will to refuse the world for another world? A planetary despair of the worldly and otherworldly, the terrestrial and extraterrestrial, the planetary and the extraplanetary, the earthly and the divine.

The Earth a Grave

When the Gaia hypothesis was first proposed in the 1970s, it was met with its fair share of skepticism within the scientific community. While part of this was no doubt due to the disciplinary factionalism that so often accompanies academic research, much of the skepticism had to do with the implication that the entire planet not only housed a panoply of organisms and ecosystems, but that these combined to form a planetary supersystem, such that the Earth itself could be viewed as a living organism. It did not take long for the idea to catch on outside the scientific community, and, when popular books such as *Gaia: A New Look at Life on Earth* and *The Quest for Gaia* appeared in the late 1970s, it was but a short step for the anthropomorphized notion of a mythical mother Earth to take hold in the nascent environmental movement, as well as in popular culture.

To be fair, James Lovelock, the scientist most often associated with the Gaia hypothesis, was careful to couch his ideas within the framework of systems science, bringing together disparate scientific fields in order to think of ecosystems themselves as part of a larger, planet-wide ecosystem. For her part, Lynn Margulis, the microbiologist who has done the most to elaborate and develop the Gaia hypothesis, was even more critical of the tendency to anthropomorphize the Earth. She has provided what has become for many the clearest articulation of the Gaia hypothesis, describing it as "a series of interacting ecosystems that compose a single huge ecosystem at the Earth's surface. Period."[14] In later work, Margulis would go even further, suggesting that the "endosymbiosis" of microbial life is not only the basis from which complex life forms develop but is also – from the deep time perspective of the Earth – the default state of life on the planet.

The notion of a nurturing, bountiful, and peace-loving Earth has since been extremely difficult to detach from the scientific basis of the hypothesis itself. The Gaia hypothesis has become a kind of secular myth that is emblematic of a deeply rooted desire to see ourselves as human beings living in harmony with the planet, part of the heady cosmic romanticism that includes everything from *The Whole Earth Catalog* to films such as *Silent Running*. Yet Lovelock was perceptive in choosing the Greek goddess Gaia to christen his theory. Hesiod's *Theogony* informs us that Gaia is one of the primordial deities, goddess of the Earth and the foundation of all life. But Gaia is also the goddess who births Kronos, the gloomy, dethroned deity associated with the chthonic underworld, the angst-ridden, melancholic devourer of children who would later be associated with the planet Saturn. Within Gaia is a kind of sullen, earth-bound sorrow that is inseparable from the Gaia associated with the sky, the ocean, heraldic mountain peaks.

In the era of global climate change, this shadow side of Gaia has found its expression in the more ominously named "Medea hypothesis." Most often associated with the paleontologist Peter Ward, the Medea hypothesis is the near inverse of the Gaia hypothesis. Utilizing evidence of periodic mass extinctions on the Earth – which often have the effect of returning life on the planet to a microbial state – the Medea hypothesis argues that the emergence of complex, multicellular life inevitably leads to its own extinction. The seeds of this lie within evolutionary processes themselves, which generate levels of complexity that soon outstrip the capacity of the same planetary environment within which evolution takes place:

> Habitability of the Earth has been affected by the presence of life, but the overall effect of life has been and will be to reduce the longevity of the Earth as a habitable planet. Life itself, because it is inherently Darwinian, is biocidal, suicidal, and creates a series of positive feed-backs to Earth systems (such as global temperature and atmospheric carbon dioxide and methane content) that harm later generations.[15]

What philosophers such as Schopenhauer had long ago characterized as the "blind striving" of all planetary life is here recapitulated in the context of paleontology, evolutionary biology, and periodic extinction events. It is this aspect of Earth-based life forms – including human beings – that leads Ward to suggest that multicellular life on the planet is essentially self-destructive and even suicidal, a planet strangely fecund by virtue of an enigmatic, "biocidal" complex. The blind compulsion of life simply to live on is also its own demise, as if the rapacious mania of "life itself" is already its own shadow, every speciation also its own extinction.

Blind Life, Black Star

Given this, it is no surprise that Ward and his colleagues have proposed the wrathful, funereal figure of Medea to the Lovelockean romanticism of Gaia. Euripides' tragic tale of betrayal, revenge, infanticide, and divine justice seems a decided counterpoint to the mythology of Gaia, with the mountains and seas that harmoniously flow from her. Medea is, to put it mildly, an angst-ridden figure. The nurturing mother gives way to the murderous mother, and, just as Gaia would nurture and cultivate the life forms on Earth, so would Medea devour Earth and terrestrial life in her wrath towards the trauma-inducing myopia of self-serving humanity. In one scene, Medea seems to consciously claim this nocturnal counter-throne, as she speaks her case before the women of Corinth:

> But I have been deserted and outraged –
> left without a city by my husband,
> who stole me as his plunder from the land
> of the barbarians. Here I have no mother,
> no brother, no blood relative to help
> unmoor me from this terrible disaster.[16]

Medea is the figure, Euripides tells us, who is born of the uncultivated, barbarian Earth, schooled in the sorcery of its chemical elements, a primordial Earth that almost seems to act through Medea in tempestuous cataclysms of furious skies and the unnerving vengeance of deep time. Exiled from the human-centric, worldly concerns of Athens, Medea finds herself set apart from the world altogether at that point where the Earth suddenly reveals itself to be utterly indifferent from the near-term worries of ephemeral cities and their short-lived dominion. It is this Medea that is captured in Passolini's 1969 film, starring Maria Callas. The Earth returned to a wasteland, where another kind of life continues unabated.

Not only does the Medea hypothesis counter the claims that the Earth is a giant, living supersystem, it also runs counter to the philosophical commitment of the Gaia hypothesis, that life on Earth is a generative, fecund outpouring of life forms in ever-greater, ever-ascending development. As Margulis tells us, for most of its existence, life on the Earth has maintained a steady state in microbial form, and if, from the planet's perspective, microbial life is the baseline, then it could be that the occasional flourishes of multicellular, complex life may serve no other purpose than as a kind of "reset" for microbial life. What we thought was the pinnacle of life may turn out to be nothing but an epiphenomenon of a microbial planet.

In a sense, the Medea hypothesis is the black mirror to the Gaia hypothesis, existential angst to Gaia's romantic idealism. The most precise cultural manifestation of this is the "revenge of nature" motif in blockbuster films, in which the planet enacts a form of environmental counter-violence through giant tsunamis, tectonic-shifting quakes, and terrifying downpours of comets and colliding moons. The motif is not new and can be traced back to the innumerable monster movies produced by Hollywood in the 1950s, in which giant, irradiated, and very irritable creatures have at it with their unwitting human neighbors (everything from giant ants to lizards to – yes, giant rabbits have their turn). It was also mirrored in the traumatic post-war culture of Japan, where Godzilla and the city-stomping genre *kaiju* film was born. But there is something comforting even in the revenge of nature. Whatever transgressions we have committed as a species – industrialism, capitalism, nuclear weapons, tourism – we can take some solace in knowing that at least the Earth cared enough to disapprove. We are perhaps too trauma-bonded to the planet to think otherwise. But, deep down, there is that most faint of whispers. The planet doesn't care – it can't care.

"Our uniqueness in the world! alas, it is too improbable a thing!"[17] This is Nietzsche, writing in the late 1870s. The one saving grace is, ironically, that of the sciences, whose supposed detachment from the world of human concerns turns out to reveal a tragedy greater than that of Euripides. "The astronomers," Nietzsche quips, "intimate that the drop of life in the world is without significance for the total character of the immense ocean of becoming and passing away."[18] True, there may be planets out there among the "countless celestial bodies" that contain the conditions for "an outbreak of life," but for all intents and purposes we will never know them. And, even if we could, the "life upon each of these celestial bodies, measured against the duration of its existence, is a moment, a flaring-up, with a long, long space of time afterward, therefore in no way the goal and the final purpose of their existence."[19] As if shrugging his shoulders, Nietzsche adds: "If a god did create the world, he created humans as *god's apes*, as a continual cause for amusement in his all-too lengthy eternity. The music of the spheres around the earth would surely then be the mocking laughter of all other creatures at humans."[20]

Divine Despair

The "lost in space" motif is in many ways the antithesis of the epic space opera, the always present shadow lurking beneath the cartography of the absolute. In dereliction, the human being is not only cast adrift but also cast out, untethered from a terrestrial world that has itself been further and further removed from us. Dereliction, abandon, disrepair, wandering and forsaken. Direction gives way to aimlessness.

However, to acknowledge being lost is one thing, to accept it, quite another. Attempts are made to get back on course, often with the result of becoming even more lost. J. G. Ballard's short story "Report on an Unidentified Space

Station" takes this motif to its limit. First published in 1982 in the magazine *City Limits*, Ballard's story recounts a series of "survey reports" made by a derelict space crew which has had to make an emergency landing on an abandoned space station. While they make repairs, they explore the station, and they soon realize it is much, much larger than they had first estimated. An array of entry points, a labyrinth of vast corridors, strange effects of gravitation. Small crews go out to explore, never to return. The teams that do return report they are unable to find the "edges" of the station.

Perplexed, they take some readings and eventually discover curvatures in the vast "walls" of the station, indicating a finite interior. "But this small setback counts for nothing now," they report. "Our instruments confirm what we have long suspected, that the empty space across which we traveled from our own solar system in fact lies within the interior of the station, one of many vast lacunae set in its endlessly curving walls."[21] The space station appears to be so vast that it includes our solar system as well as numerous galaxies. Soon they cannot avoid the obvious: "The station is coeval with the cosmos, and constitutes the cosmos."[22] What was outer space suddenly collapses into inner space, as the very distinction between interiority and exteriority dissipates. "We have accepted the limitless size of the station, and this awareness fills us with feelings that are almost religious."[23] Bewildered, the remaining crew set off to explore the "station" with full knowledge of the futility of their endeavor, "a journey whose departure point we have already begun to forget."[24]

It is no accident that dereliction is also a central motif in many mystical traditions. In an oft-quoted passage, Pascal outlines the experience of existential finitude that is the ground for dereliction. It is produced in the consciousness of the dramatic shift in scale from the individual human being to the cosmos itself. "The whole world," Pascal observes, "is only an imperceptible dot," and "the earth a mere speck compared to the vast orbit described by this star." And the Earth eternally rotating around the sun itself is "no more than the tiniest point compared to that described by the stars revolving in the firmament."[25] In the process, the human capacity for describing and navigating this is similarly reduced and humbled; "it is no good inflating our conceptions beyond imaginable space, we only bring forth atoms compared to the reality of things."[26] A kind of melancholic delirium follows, as language fails an already faltering thought. "For, after all, what is the human being in nature? A nothing compared to the infinite, a whole compared to the nothing, a middle point between all and nothing, infinitely remote from an understanding of the extremes."[27]

Having lost all sense of direction, Pascal's metaphysical dereliction turns back on itself. A defeated admission follows: "the end of things and their principles are unattainably hidden from us in impenetrable secrecy."[28] And, after this, the despondency that lurks behind the very inquiry itself, a weariness engulfed in cosmic shifts of scale. With a final sigh, Pascal writes that he "will grow weary of conceiving things before nature tires of producing them." All that remains is a dimly intuited impression: "nature is an infinite sphere whose center is everywhere and circumference nowhere."[29] That is, the divine.

A Quiet Despair

> . . .was there not a time also in your consciousness, my listener, when cheerfully and without a care you were glad with the glad, when you wept with those who wept, when the thought of God blended irrelevantly with your other conceptions, blended with your happiness but did not sanctify it, blended with your grief but did not comfort it? And later was there not a time when this in some sense guiltless life, which never called itself to account, vanished? Did there not come a time when your mind was unfruitful and sterile, your will incapable of all good, your emotions cold and weak, when hope was dead in your breast, and recollection painfully clutched at a few solitary memories of happiness and soon these also became loathsome, when everything was of no consequence to you, and the secular bases of comfort found their way to your soul only to

wound even more your troubled mind, which impatiently and bitterly turned away from them? Was there not a time when you found no one to whom you could turn, when the darkness of quiet despair brooded over your soul, and you did not have the courage to let it go but would rather hang onto it and you even brooded once more over your despair? When heaven was shut for you, and the prayer died on your lips, or it became a shriek of anxiety that demanded an accounting from heaven, and yet you sometimes found within you a longing, an intimation to which you might ascribe meaning, but this was soon crushed by the thought that you were a nothing and your soul lost in infinite space?[30]

Extreme Weather

Blockages

Indeed, 2021 may be considered the year in which the nervous system of contemporary capitalism was laid bare, as we were forced to acknowledge the unglamorous reality of global "supply chains" rather than take them for granted, as we do our own vascular system. Suddenly we were learning just how delicate and complex the infrastructure is that has been enabling our "just in time" commercial compulsions, as the complex game of Tetris played on ports in China ran into logistical issues, creating a cascade of hiccups and full-blown blockages in Los Angeles and Rotterdam and elsewhere. (And vice versa.) The restrictions, and resulting labor shortages, around the pandemic led to a situation where thousands of ships were waiting off different shores, all over the world, to unload their cargo, with not enough people power in the ports to do the job. Crew members found themselves stranded at sea, suspended in a briny limbo, sometimes for weeks. Items previously taken for granted – from silicon chips to cream cheese – were suddenly impossible to find. Waiting lists for standard commodities ballooned, adding to the queasy liminality of lockdown life. Were we tasked with finding a "patient zero" for the supply chain crisis, we might nominate the *Ever Given*, a Taiwanese-Panamanian container vessel that became stuck in Egypt's vital Suez Canal in March, 2021. One of the world's biggest such ships – described by some as a horizontal sky-scraper – the *Ever Given* quickly symbolized a year that felt intensely *stuck*: trapped, as we all were, in the stale amber of an unprecedented socio-economic "pause." The entire world, so to say, had constipation. And we would evidently be suffering from side-effects of this lack of industrial peristalsis for a long time to come. Even today, it is unclear if ongoing supply problems will eventually resolve themselves, or if the continuing labor shortages and logistical crunches will create a feedback effect big enough to bring down the whole economic system.

Sequence 14

The Last Philosopher

You Were Here

In 2011, astronomers using NASA's Hubble Telescope revealed new data regarding a distant cluster of galaxies. Known as Abell 2261, this galaxy of galaxies was said to be approximately 1 million light years in diameter (one light year is equivalent to 6 trillion miles, roughly the diameter of the Milky Way).[1] In addition to this, in 2021 astronomers studying Abell 2261 noted one further thing: that at the center of Abell 2261 is a massive black hole, estimated to weigh approximately 10 million solar masses (one solar mass is equal to the weight of approximately 330,000 Earths).[2] However, a definitive detection of the black hole at the center of Abell 2261 has proven difficult, given that black holes so intensely absorb light, including the light emitted by the tools of astronomy. But, as the scientists note, it must be there. In a way, its absence points to its presence.

For many, discoveries such as those surrounding Abell 2261 continue to evoke a sense of awe and wonder. In such cases, to ask about "our place in the universe" would seem to be presumptuous, if not absurd. Of course, the astronomer can drop a pin and say "You are here." But does the sense – or senselessness – of that gesture change at the level of light years and solar masses? While "you are here" is useful and practical at the level of GoogleMaps, what is its effect at the level of galaxy clusters?

It's possible that our very ability to say "you are here" at such cosmic scales can have the dual effect of giving meaning to human life and rendering it utterly insignificant. For us non-scientists, part of this may certainly be due to our own ignorance about the technical details of astronomy. But it may also be due to that same technical information we're given – information that describes something that, for all intents and purposes, we can never actually experience "in person." In its own, abstract way, cosmological data provides a kind of vicarious thrill, as we make attempts to relate the vastness of a galaxy cluster with a black hole at its center to our own carbon-based, featherless, biped, like-and-subscribe Earth-bound sentience. Perhaps the very impossibility of the experience, along with its detection, is what makes it so – in Hollywood parlance – "mind-binding." In a way, scientific observations such as those of Abell 2261 lead us to a philosophical consideration, a consideration of granularity, of scale.

Cosmic View

A young woman sits with her cat on a lawn somewhere in the Netherlands. In another photo, we see the Milky Way, hinting at the infinite number of galaxies beyond. Between these is a series of pictures that take us, step by step, from the human level to that of galaxies and the cosmos itself. The lesson doesn't stop there, however. Going back to the girl and her cat, we then make the same step-by-step journey, only this time moving from the human level to the level of molecules and atoms.

Cosmic View is the title of a graphic book by the Dutch author Kees Boeke, first published in 1957. Boeke, a Quaker pacifist and educator, came up with the idea for the book as a way of allowing students to appreciate the humbling place of human beings within the universe. Since its publication, *Cosmic View* has had an impact not only in science education but in the design world, where the visual language of progressive scaling can be found in film versions of his book, such as *Cosmic Zoom* (1968), by the National Board of Canada, and *Powers of Ten*, produced by the design team Charles and Ray Eames, first released in 1968 and then again in 1977. Soon, versions for IMAX and various iPhone apps would follow. Its techniques of zooming in and zooming out contributing to a new ethos of "design optimism." Today, one can detect the visual techniques of *Cosmic View* in everything from advertising to internet memes.

At each step in *Cosmic View*, we move between macrocosm and microcosm, from the familiar, human scale of our sense perception of the world to the unfamiliar and largely hidden worlds of the atomic and cosmic. In each process, a kind of vanishing act takes place, as if the entirety of humanity itself suddenly evaporates once we simply zoom out or zoom in, entire worlds having dissipated in the simple shift of scale. In spite of its cheerful tone (or indeed because of it), there is a kind of melancholy to these shifts in scale, shifts that can have the effect of rendering the most meaningful things from the human perspective as nothing but momentary inflections of star-stuff. This is particularly evident as one pages through *Cosmic View*, a flip-book tinged with elegiac tones, as the human scale patiently recedes, step by step, into a background oblivion of galaxies and atoms. Yet we also understand the visual lesson, which is that human beings haven't gone anywhere; we are still "here."

We are still here, but there is also much, much more. We are in "the beyond" but also helplessly cut off from it, simply by virtue of being scale-bound organisms with a finite sense capacity. What goes for space follows for time. Suns, planets, and entire galaxies flare into and out of existence at time scales impossible for us to experience. Or are they? In roughly one trillion, trillion, trillion years, the continued expansion of the universe will eventually obliterate all matter, including galaxies, solar systems, and planets. In approximately 7.5 billion years the sun of our solar system will collapse, leaving behind cold and uninhabitable regions of space. In one billion years the Earth's oceans will dry out due to rising global temperatures. Projected increases in the planet's population and projected decreases in planetary resources could mean the extinction of the human species by the year 3000. The average human lifespan is eighty-six years. Next week, you have plans. At what point does "some day" and 7.5 billion years boil down to the same difference?

A simple but far-reaching intuition occurs: we as human beings understand the world in a way that is profoundly constrained by scale. At the level of subatomic particles or galaxy clusters, things are a little different. And yet, this relativity in scale is right here in front of us, all around us. Heat. Cold. Humidity. Wind. Rain. Sunshine. Daylight. Night. Cloudless blue skies, starry nights. Twilight haze. We might feel these in an everyday sense, but does this mean we are experiencing something as nebulous as "climate," let alone "climate change"? This weird sense of having a feeling without an experience.

Much of the data produced about global warming and climate change is the product of a vast array of planetary sensors, which themselves seem to envelop the Earth in a kind of meta-planetary cocoon. The results generated – graphs, charts, numbers, and elaborate info-graphic animations – are shot around via newsfeeds: human beings constitute 0.01 percent of the biomass of the planet, but we are responsible for the loss of 80 percent of all wildlife and 50 percent of all plant life; human-produced biomass such as plastic currently exceeds the biomass of the entire Earth; the "Great Pacific Garbage Patch" is approximately three times the size of France (or twice the size of Texas); the Earth can support a human population of 2.5 billion people (the current population is 8 billion people). A litany of graphs, charts, and numbers washes over us, producing a feeling, an affect, a disposition, a mood. Something at once abstract and concrete, personal and impersonal, deeply human yet utterly non-human, profoundly intimate and yet intractably estranged.

The Last Philosopher

It is no doubt with these considerations in mind that a young Friedrich Nietzsche wrote the following paragraph, sometime in the early 1870s:

> Once upon a time, in some out of the way corner of that universe which is dispersed into numberless twinkling solar systems, there was a star on which clever beasts invented knowing. That was the most arrogant and mendacious minute of "world history," but nevertheless, it was only a minute. After nature had drawn a few breaths, the star cooled and congealed, and the clever beasts had to die. – One might invent such a fable, and yet he still would not have adequately illustrated how miserable, how shadowy and transient, how aimless and arbitrary the human intellect looks within nature. There were eternities during which it did not exist. And when it is all over with the human intellect, nothing will have happened.[3]

Now an oft-quoted paragraph among Nietzsche aficionados, the essay would remain unpublished, soon eclipsed by the writing that would become his first book, *The Birth of Tragedy*. But the two projects are interrelated and point to Nietzsche's acute intuition regarding the new scope and scale of "the tragic impulse" in the modern world.

These and other writings from the period were part of a book that was never realized, which Nietzsche at one point titled *The Last Philosopher: Reflections on the Struggle Between Art and Knowledge*. At the core of the project was an issue that remains relevant today: "What the philosopher is seeking is not truth, but rather the metamorphosis of the world into men . . . He is satisfied when he has explained something anthropomorphically. Just as the astrologer regards the world as serving the single individual, the philosopher regards the world as a human being."[4]

A thinker with an omnivorous range of interests, Nietzsche was deeply immersed in the culture of classical Greece but equally taken by the then current trends of apocalyptic "last man" scenarios in nineteenth-century science fiction, itself influenced by developments in physics, cosmology, and the idea of the "heat death" of the solar system. As Nietzsche's notebooks reveal, *The Last Philosopher* project was to be taken quite literally, as a kind of philosophical parable. One imagines the extinction of humanity, or the collapse of the sun, or a "dying Earth," with the last philosopher remaining. What would the last philosopher think? What indeed would be the point of thinking at all? More importantly: what would philosophy have to become in order to think like "the last philosopher"?

One need not have the end actualized in order to entertain this idea. As the nineteenth century wore on, there were any number of indicators of an ending already taking place, from biological theories of extinction, to the Second Law of Thermodynamics (as energy decreases, entropy increases), to medical theories of degeneration, sociological theories of deviance and criminality, a burgeoning culture of "Decadence," and the incessant grinding of industrial capitalism's "Satanic mills." The end, it seemed, was everywhere; it was already happening. The philosopher in Nietzsche's time was already, as it were, looking back on the end of the world. Enlightenment is also anti-Enlightenment, humanism also anti-humanism.

This, for Nietzsche, is the "tragic insight": that there can never be anything but this limited, human-centric view. It's a lesson that Kant articulated (albeit in very different ways) a generation earlier. The rift between the world as it appears to us ("phenomena") and the necessity of a world in itself that we can never fully know ("noumena"), except by transforming it into the world for us and in relation to us. In this sense, it's no surprise that Nietzsche would find Greek tragedy both ancient and modern. The works of Aeschylus or Sophocles express an ongoing tension between human beings perpetually trying to outwit a cosmic order that is forever beyond the pale of their comprehension. Every move to outstep the human framework seems to result in its opposite, with the receding horizon of the non-human always just out of reach.

Writing in *Human, All Too Human*, Nietzsche notes: "'The dark times' is what people in Norway call those periods when the sun remains below the horizon for the entire day: under these conditions, the temperature falls in a slow, continuous way. – A beautiful image for all the thinkers for whom the sun of humanity's future has temporarily vanished."[5]

Help Less (a Eulogy for SN11)

On a foggy Tuesday in March of 2021, a 150 foot tall, stainless steel rocket stood erect in the hazy dawn of the Gulf of Mexico, on the southernmost tip of Texas. Dubbed SN11, it would reach a target altitude of approximately 32,000 feet before then descending towards a designated landing site nearby. From the beginning, however, the test launch was fraught with technical difficulties. While SN11 did reach its target altitude, the descent ended in an explosive array of charred rocket debris falling back to Earth. It was difficult not to see in the rise and fall of SN11, caught on the official SpaceX livestream as well as on amateur video, something at once absurd and tragic.

The official explanation of the crash came from Elon Musk himself: "Ascent phase, transition to horizontal & control during free fall were good. A (relatively) small CH4 leak led to fire on engine 2 & fried part of avionics, causing hard start attempting landing burn in CH4 turbopump." Journalists reporting the incident paraphrased Musk's wonderfully evasive techno-babble: "A plumbing leak."

The SN11 launch was part of a series of test launches centered around Starship, a prototype being developed by SpaceX. Along with Starlink – its continually expanding array of internet satellites around the Earth – the Starship project is part of SpaceX's larger agenda to move humanity (or at least some of humanity) "off world." Often referred to as a contemporary "Manhattan project" for space, Starship aims to make voyages to Mars not only feasible but necessary. At stake, one would suppose, is nothing less than the survival of the species – and at any cost.

While the SN11 crash video briefly made the rounds on the internet, there was little coverage of where all the rocket debris ended up. In the case of SN11, much of it ended up in the Rio Grande Valley National Wildlife Refuge, a 90,000 acre nature refuge located a stone's throw away from the Starlink production site and tracking station. Finding and removing the debris from the area required the coordinated efforts of Texas Parks and Wildlife, the US Fish and Wildlife Service, the National Wildlife Service, and representatives from SpaceX. A spokesperson from the clean up effort admitted that it's unlikely they will be able to recover all of the rocket debris. Added to their challenge is the disruptive effect that the sudden intrusion of humans (dressed in fluorescent green uniforms) will have on the nature refuge itself.

The SpaceX launch facility is also startlingly near several residential areas in the greater Boca Chica region, a concern that has been raised for years by activists and community leaders. But the concerns of the local residents were quickly eclipsed by political infighting between SpaceX and the US government. A day before the SN11 launch, the US House of Representatives reminded SpaceX that it was still under investigation for its launch of SN8 three months earlier – which also ended in an explosive crash landing. Just after the SN11 crash, the Federal Aviation Administration claimed SpaceX had launched without a license, failing to account for "far field blast pressure" (e.g., windows of residential homes shattering from the blast pressure). Indeed, some residents were not only able to capture video of the crash but in some cases claimed themselves to have recovered SN11 debris (which no doubt have found their way onto eBay for the space disaster connoisseur).

Put mildly, the underlying premise of SpaceX – that humanity should survive in perpetuity, and its best chance for doing so lies on another planet (with the asterisk, since we've destroyed this one) – bears further scrutiny, if not for its patent absurdity, then for its brazen entitlement. It seems to be the more reprehensible form of what philosophers sometimes call "effective altruism," the notion that science and technology provide us with the tools for helping the greatest number of people in the most direct way, shorn of all the window dressing of ideology, politics, and social media. While it may be true that the intersection of Big Data, sophisticated algorithms, and "program Earth" have transformed knowledge production, whether it is "helpful" seems open to debate. It's possible that the very concept of altruism has something of a species-specific presumption built within it. It not only presumes to know what is helpful, but it also presumes to advocate on behalf of those supposedly in need of help. The startling irony of SN11 is several-fold. A rocket launch to save humanity that threatens the safety of the local residents living near the launch site. A technological beacon of human superiority that, when it crashes and burns, rains its sorrowful debris across the placid and innocuous terrain of a nature reserve.

Altruism presumes that there is a definable boundary between being helpful and harmful, or between helpfulness and helplessness. But of course "helplessness" – learned or not – is one of those negative affects. It's a problem to solve, something broken to fix, an "issue" that we avoid or evade or outright deny. At the same time, there's no simply being on the side of helplessness. It can be debilitating. But it may also involve confrontation with issues of control and mastery. Maybe this also leads to letting go, relinquishing control, disavowing mastery. Maybe that in turn leads to resignation, or acceptance, or even humility. Maybe that turns into equanimity, detachment. Maybe a transformation takes place. Should we then say that helplessness is helpful? But what if that which is the most helpful for us as a species is the most harmful for the planet? In the case of a terrestrial-bound species going "off world," what would effective altruism be, if not a kind of species-level death drive, an aeronautical form of voluntary human extinction?

Meanwhile, SpaceX launches continue unabated by either political pushback or activist protesting. But videos of the SN11 crash also continue to have a strange, absurdist melancholy about them. They echo earlier attempts – and failures – to reach for the stars. The famous closing scene of *Koyaanisqatsi*, a long take of the 1962 Alpha-Centaur rocket explosion. The flaring debris reaches the peak of its arc and begins the long slow Icarus-like descent back to Earth, revealing something at once technological and mythical in the blind persistence of human finitude, the insatiable pursuit of human futility.

Eco-Ex

Established by the UN in the late 1980s with the specific mandate to study the impact of human activity on climate change, the Intergovernmental Panel on Climate Change (IPCC) released a key report in 2018 that analyzed the impact of an increase in global temperatures of 1.5 °C. The report describes worst-case scenarios over the next century that seem reflected in Hollywood disaster movies: densely populated cities with precarious infrastructure, waves of climate migration, global food shortages, uninhabitable coastal regions, and extreme weather events occurring on a regular basis.

In addition to the science research and policy recommendations, the IPCC report introduced a new vocabulary that pointed to the impact of climate change at the qualitative and not just the quantitative level. Hence its language of "climate crisis" and "climate emergency," while, at the same time, UN officials would likewise talk about the "existential threat" of climate change.

The shift in language is also a shift in thinking. Beneath the urgency of survival lies the deceptively simple question of how to live on, or how to live at all, or indeed what meaning human life would have, given the fundamental changes taking place to the planet itself. From the perspective of precarious humanity, climate change seems constantly to hover, much like the weather itself, between the apocalyptic and the post-apocalyptic.

It was not long before politicians, policy-makers, and the media took up the new vocabulary. That politicians are thinking about issues – any issues – at an existential level would seem to be promising. One imagines senators and congresspeople perusing their heavily dog-eared copies of *Being and Nothingness*, or *The Second Sex*, or *The Wretched of the Earth* in between meetings or sessions of Congress. While this doesn't seem to be the case, what is apparent is how the language of contemporary American politics – arguably its only substantive feature – has raised the stakes of the debate from the humdrum issues of "regular" politics to the "existential."

It goes without saying that phrases such as "existential crisis" remind us of existentialist philosophy itself, which, for a time, seemed to offer a way of posing the question "why?" for an epoch traumatized by world wars and the looming atomic age. Are we witnessing a new version of existentialism emerging within the climate change discourse (which we would most certainly have to call "eco-existentialism" or simply "Eco-Ex")? It's tempting to ask whether Camus & Co. would have anything to say about the current climate crisis and the ability (or inability) of human groups to do anything about it.

One can imagine Camus' Meursalt or Sartre's Roquentin over-intellectualizing the matter, painting themselves into a metaphysical corner: if it's going to happen anyway, what's the point in trying to fix it, or for that matter of doing anything at all? It's easy to see how the "big questions" of climate change elicit what Kierkegaard called "the absurd": the inability to make a decision combined with the necessity of deciding. There's nothing to do – and yet you can't do nothing. And even if, by some miracle of cooperative communitarianism, "we" do finally band together and turn it around (or at least make it less purgatorial), we then have to confront the science of extinction – if not now, then "someday." Too many people, not enough planet. And going off-world would seem only to exacerbate the condition by disseminating our species-specific insecurities onto other planets. In this sense, optimists and pessimists differ only on the end date.

If–When–Why

For many years, the default mode of climate change discussions has been "if. . . ." If we don't do this or make these changes, then things will get worse. If the nations of the world don't cut back on greenhouse gas emissions, then the atmosphere of the planet will continue to deteriorate, making it inhospitable for human life. The "if . . ." implies a basic relation of cause and effect with respect to human beings and the planet. It also implies a minimal awareness of the impact that human activity has had in shaping the planet itself (a basic tenet of the Anthropocene hypothesis). The "if . . ." therefore points to a difficult chain of associations: at what point does causality become technical instrumentality, at what point is instrumentality mastery, and when does mastery overreach its limit, producing the reverse – collapse?

At some point, perhaps around the turn of the millennium, the language changes. One could detect it not only in political rhetoric but also in documentaries, "news," and even popular culture. The shift from "if . . ." to "when . . ." When these things happen, we should do this or do that. When the polar ice caps melt and cause sea levels to rise, many inhabited coastal land masses will become inhabitable and will have to be evacuated. The "if . . ." allowed for a margin of error. There was still time. The future wasn't written. The "when . . ." is different. There may still be a slim margin of error, but it's best to assume the worst and prepare anyway. Start building the ark, start scouting off-world. The "when . . ." implies a point of no return (or at least a point of diminishing returns). More ominous in tone, "when . . ." is the withdrawal of possibility and a confrontation with fatality that can take on the mythic hues of tragedy. Whereas "if . . ." tackled both the promise and pitfalls of human industry and technological development, "when . . ." is largely reactive, a grappling with the runaway effects of centuries of mining the Earth in the name of human provenance. It is no accident that "when . . ." seamlessly joins together the most serious policy debates with the most frivolous, cathartic blockbuster movies. "When . . ." is the domain of threat, preparedness, adaptation, survival.

It would seem that the "when . . ." is the endgame of climate change – at least for the human species. But this belies another question we are perhaps just now witnessing. At some point, "when . . ." has turned into "why . . .?" In one sense, "why . . .?" is quite concrete. We know that fossil fuels are quickly running out, so why can't we shift to alternative energy sources? We have the technology for alternative energy, so why can't we implement it? Of course, behind such seemingly straightforward questions are questions that are not so straightforward, questions that bring back "big questions" concerning human nature, human culture, the rise and fall of civilizations, the death drive. The "why . . .?" becomes more abstract: Why is this happening? Why is this happening to *us*? Why can't we do anything about it?

Maybe this "why . . .?" deserves our attention in part because it may undermine the anxieties that already inhabit the "if . . ." and the "when . . ." Admittedly, asking "why?" is almost never helpful, in part because it's unending, as in the familiar (and irritating) children's game where the answer to every question is "why?," until one (usually a patronizing adult) either runs out of answers (due to their own ignorance) or becomes bored (the result of tedium). "Why?" is the most unwelcome of questions. Asking "how?" is much more practical and utilitarian, even technical. "How?" easily leads to "how to?" Traditionally, asking "why?" has been relegated to the disparaged corners of philosophy, if not to religion or poetry. "Why?" implies a question without an answer, or a question that simply leads to more questions, in a maddening downward spiral of uncertainty and doubt.

But, every so often, one encounters situations where asking "why?" becomes inescapable. Is the current "existential crisis" an indicator of a "why?" that lurks like a shadow behind every report on climate change, a subterranean current beneath all the data streams and interactive displays that detail to us just how inhospitable to human life the Earth has become?

The Gift of the Body

In the clear, brisk, early morning of April 14, 2018, what is left is a circular patch of burnt soil, scorched into one of the many greenspaces of Brooklyn's Prospect Park. A few hours previously, a man from the neighborhood had walked out onto the patch of grass. After clearing a modest circular area of soil in the grass, he sat down. With deliberate calm, he then set himself on fire. Witnesses called 911, and the police arrived shortly thereafter. Nearby a bag was discovered with his ID and a note apologizing "for the mess." Before leaving home, he had emailed a statement to several media outlets: "Most humans on the planet now breathe air made unhealthy by fossil fuels, and many die early deaths as a result – my early death by fossil fuel reflects what we are doing to ourselves."

The suicide of David Buckel seemed to many an extreme and even bizarre form of protest. A lawyer specializing in civil rights and climate justice, he had likely encountered the frustrating inertia if not outright denial surrounding the politics of climate change. Buckel's suicide was at once a personal expression of helplessness but also a political expression of hopelessness. Buckel's suicide dramatically points to a dilemma likely experienced by many who are conscious of the impacts of global climate change: the sense of a vast and hyper complex phenomenon in which we as human beings directly participate, but which we also feel unable (or unwilling) to change. The predictable fallout of Buckel's act – from headline-grabbing media coverage to the flurry of opinions on social media – belies the more far-reaching question his act poses. How should one comprehend a situation in which the very species that has developed the capacity to shape the world is also the same force which seems bent on its own destruction?

The practice of ritual self-immolation has a long and often conflicted history in world religions, particularly in Buddhism, where it is often connected to some form of protest. For many, the most well-known example is the self-immolation of Thích Quảng Đức, a Vietnamese Buddhist monk who set himself on fire in Saigon on June 11, 1963. The harrowing photos of a seated monk engulfed in flames, set against the backdrop of a busy urban intersection, have since become part of the visual iconography of an era, encapsulating the conflux of late twentieth-century geopolitics, colonial and post-colonial conditions, religious persecution, and the tragic costs of global capitalism. The brutal physicalism of the act itself is doubled by another, more ghostly body. A body in flames, a life wrapped in mortality, an allegory of human suffering.

Thích Quảng Đức's self-immolation, extreme though it seems, was part of a long tradition within Buddhism, one that has not been without its share of controversy. Practices of self-immolation are attested to in China as early as the fourth century, in which the influences of Mahāyāna Buddhism spread from northern India to China, where it mixed with variants of Taoism, producing a unique hybrid often referred to as Ch'an Buddhism. The practice of self-immolation seems to have been formalized early on, often taking place at a sacred site. A monk might swallow pieces of incense and then wrap their body in an oil-soaked cloth, in effect transforming themselves into a vehicle for fire, smoke, and ash. A sacred text such as *The Lotus Sutra* might be chanted during the burning itself, both acting as a focal point for the monk's attention while also serving as a kind of mystical purgation. It's not difficult to imagine the impact of such acts, a ritual conflagration rising in transient skies, a haunting reminder of everything that burns.

At its core, self-immolation is an extreme form of ascetic practice (to use the term "practice" here seems at once hallowed and absurd). The greatest act of shearing away all worldly attachments is to repudiate one's own, embodied, living self, an offering of "the gift of the body." Such protests could also be nested within more near-term, more politicized actions – a protest against the devastation of civil war, the political corruption of dynastic regimes, or the persecution of Buddhist monks themselves. Both government bureaucrats and religious institutions raise less elevated, more practical concerns that seem almost comical: if more and more monks practice self-immolation, who will be left to manage the temples? Someone has to check email, sweep the temple floor, take out the compost.

What burns. The elemental reduction to fire, air, ash, and bone. An act that culminates in the most intense form of suffering while also leading to the cessation of suffering, a stark reminder to those of us who remain behind of the transient cycles of life, death, mortality – for the individual as well as for the species.

Extinction without Death

It could be argued that, particularly in Western, technologically advanced cultures, death is no longer an existential concern. Medicine, neuroscience, pathology and a host of related fields have studied biological death in great detail, down to the last flicker of activity on an ECG. The death of the individual has become as much a technological event as it is an emotional, psychological, or religious one.

But this quality of death as an event is different from the nebulous, tenebrous awareness of death that inflects our consciousness (and subconscious) while we are alive. In a sense our individual lives are continually poised between what Heidegger called "perishing" and "death." For him, plants and animals "perish" whereas human beings "die," in part because we are endowed with or burdened with the awareness of our own mortality and the knowledge that we will, someday, die. The question, then, is how that awareness of our mortality (or its avoidance) impacts our life choices. The criteria for a meaningful life exist in this space between "perishing" and "death." Of course, we know we will die "someday," and more than one philosopher has noted how the business of our lives is, in a way, made up of techniques for infinitely deferring this basic acknowledgement. From the existential perspective, the human being both dies and perishes – though not necessarily at the same time (which would be both strange and haunting).

Is this also the predicament of human extinction? Can we say that death is to the individual what extinction is to the species? Technically extinction is the non-actuality of members of a set ("species"), but that isn't necessarily how it's experienced – especially by the members of that species that is or is about to become extinct. In spite of the wealth of scientific data on both speciation and extinction, there is a kind of lacunae in our ability to appreciate extinction as a unique kind of biological contingency, one that is as normal as living and dying itself – but which is never quite identical with it.

Thus, while we may be tempted to say that death is to the individual what extinction is to the species, we must immediately add Heidegger's caveat, that "death" is not the same as "perishing." Should we then say that perishing is to the individual what extinction is to the species? There is no shortage of data to show that extinction may be regarded as perishing on a mass scale, and over vast periods of time – the Fifth Mass Extinction, which included dinosaurs, is also the shortest, lasting a mere 2.5 million years. From the scientific perspective, perishing is as certain to species as it is to the individual organisms that make up those species.

And yet, the extinction of a species, however inevitable and even incidental it may be from the planetary perspective, doesn't take place in the same way as the biological perishing of the individual. The "species" – itself an abstract category that is the product of human knowledge – the species does not and cannot die in the way that individual organisms die.

The individual human being perishes. Our consciousness of this perishing is death. Comprehending the death of the individual is filled with a whole host of ambiguities, let alone the often under-appreciated mysteries of perishing and what happens to the body after death. If death and even perishing continue to lie at the limits of our understanding, how much more ambiguous is the cluster of moods associated with human extinction – particularly as the science reveals to us that human extinction may be an inevitability and not an anomaly?

Extinction is, perhaps, a different kind of limit. That you or I should die is difficult enough to accept. How implausible, how improbable, to accept that the entire species should no longer exist, for a species, unlike the forms of life that comprise a species, does not "die" in the usual sense. Instead, it vanishes, it disappears, it fades beneath the sedimented shrouds of geological deep time. We will not have died, we will simply no longer be here.

Cosmic Sacrifice

The earliest surviving chants – saturated in the ritual smoke of fire, oil, and golden milk – tell us of something revealed, something enigmatic and unknowable, something that is of the Earth but not reduced to it. There was "neither the realm of space nor the sky which is beyond."[6] What stirred, what rustled – and from where? There was "neither death nor immortality" and "no distinguishing sign of night nor day."[7] What emerged from the chthonic depths of caverns and ravines, from the unbreathable peaks of mountains or the cosmic depths of oceans? Everything is darkness because there is not yet darkness and no light. "Darkness was hidden by darkness in the beginning."[8] And yet, there is something, somehow. There is life, finitude, a world, and suffering both earthly and metaphysical. Again and again the question. "Whence is this creation?" "Whence was it produced?" "Who will proclaim it?"[9] What is this world, from what or whom has it emerged – and why?

Dated by most scholars to c.1500–1000 BCE (and by others as far back as c.1900 BCE), the collection of ritual texts known as the *Rig Veda* frequently return to a dilemma. On the one hand, a need to give meaning to the world and, by extension, human suffering. On the other hand, a no less urgent need to acknowledge the fundamental mystery or unknowability of the world, manifest in the *Rig Veda*'s creation myths. Something significant – something that must be significant – has revealed itself both *in* the sky and earth, and *as* sky and earth. Sacralization requires ritual, a ritual that acknowledges both the need for sacralization and the fundamental uncertainty that grounds it. "Who is the god whom we should worship with the oblation?"[10] A plea to an unknowable god, an invocation of elemental forces, the clearing of a space for sacralizing the planet. A system is developed, rituals performed, the mathematical specificity of precise gestures and intonations – all predicated on a deceptively straightforward idea. A world emerges, a planet is formed – and, at the same time, something of another order, something irretrievable, has been lost. Something is revealed, something else concealed. A condition of indistinctness at the horizon of human understanding gives way to existence and non-existence, life and death, the past and present and future.

But what has been lost also grounds what is revealed. Another ritual – a different one – takes place. A kind of primordial, anthropomorphized, cosmic being – the Purusha – that exists outside of our categories of space and time. The cosmic being is at once metaphysical and monstrous, "a thousand heads, a thousand eyes, a thousand feet," spread throughout the planet in every direction, and beyond it into the stars. The cosmic being is also parsed out into all the aspects of the world, infused into every living creature, "into that which eats and into that which does not eat."[11] At once stellar and earthbound, transcendent and immanent, the cosmic being's sole purpose: to be sacrificed. It is the ritual dismemberment of the cosmic being that creates not only the Earth and all of life but also the very possibility of a "world," an Earth made meaningful for us as human beings. The sacralization of the Earth necessitates a sacrifice. From the dismembered limbs a body politic arises. From the flesh and muscle and fat the animal world is formed. From the eyes the sun, from the moon, the mind. From the breath the wind, the clouds, the atmosphere. And from the voice, the ritual texts.

This need to render the Earth sacred reveals a further mystery. "With the sacrifice the gods sacrificed to the sacrifice."[12] The convoluted, evocative phrase occurs elsewhere in *The Rig Veda* and has puzzled scholars for centuries. Purusha, the cosmic being, seems to be at once subject and object, ritual executioner and ritual victim, at once that which is sacrificed and the divine being for whom the sacrifice is performed. *The Rig Veda* tells us the primordial sacrifice of the cosmic being is not performed by human beings – that will come later. Instead, it is gods who must perform this first sacrifice and who, in so doing, inaugurate the paradigm by which the Earth is rendered sacred. The sacrifice of the cosmic being is the creation of sacrifice itself.

Nevertheless, a shadow haunts this need for a sacred Earth. That is exactly the point of sacrifice as a practice, imbued with the otherwordly. The sacralization of the Earth is also an act of warding off its opposite, a desacralization in which the Earth is no longer an Earth but simply a planet, a potentially meaningless material accretion of mineral and mud, water and air. And what follows for the planet would follow for the tenuous human beings that are its temporary inhabitants. It is only by infusing every aspect of the Earth with meaning that the always hovering, tenebrous possibility of an insignificant Earth is avoided. A mantra from *The Rig Veda* contains the refrain "Sky and earth, guard us from the monstrous abyss."[13]

Sacred Conspiracy

The problem of unprovoked suffering, of meaningless suffering. A planet indifferent to the trespass of a species upon it. Cataclysms, plagues, floods, famine, and a vortex of planetary storms. These are planetary conditions for myth. Mircea Eliade: "If it was possible to tolerate such sufferings, it is precisely because they seemed neither gratuitous nor arbitrary."[14] Suffering before such vast, impersonal forces elicits a human response. For Eliade, "suffering is perturbing only insofar as its cause remains undiscovered. As soon as the sorcerer or priest discovers what is causing children or animals to die, drought to continue, rain to increase, game to disappear, the suffering begins to become tolerable; it has a meaning and a cause, hence it can be fitted into a system and explained."[15]

In the process, a transformation occurs: "The sacred tree, the sacred stone are not adored as stone or tree; they are worshiped precisely because they are *hierophanies*, because they show something that is no longer stone or tree but the *sacred*."[16] In the chaos of the impersonal, the sacred not only shows itself, but entire ritual systems are formed that guarantee this grounding of the world, a world arrayed around the crisis of unprovoked suffering.

But there is a counter-weight to this. The sacred affirms the human situated within the larger cosmic order. But, for Georges Bataille, it is precisely the sacred – via the act of ritual sacrifice – that negates the dominion of humanity above and over the world in which it lives and acts. For Bataille, that is, in a sense, what humanity is: the loss of a primordial "continuity" with all things that we are forever attempting to regain. "Divinity" is not up there, or out there, but immanent within "the insubordination of matter" on the Earth.

Such a view requires us to begin from a completely different vantage point, from "terrestrial activity regarded as a cosmic phenomenon."[17] Bataille's premise is that the "living organism, in a situation determined by the play of energy on the surface of the globe, ordinarily receives more energy than is necessary for maintaining life."[18] This excess energy can be utilized for growth and expansion, but it can also reach certain irrevocable limits: "if the excess cannot be completely absorbed in growth, it must necessarily be lost without profit; it must be spent, willingly or not, gloriously or catastrophically."[19]

Beyond the human, the planet. Beyond the planet, the sun. And it is in the sun that thinkers like Bataille detect another order of energetics, one predicated as much on expenditure as on accumulation, on excess rather than on scarcity, on waste as much as on utility. And beyond the sun? A conflagration spanning aeons seemingly without end. Light, heat, radiation engulfing the planets. An energy source. A technology. A theophany. The sudden constriction of human history into a momentary flare on a remote planet.

Sorrow that is subsumed in sacrifice. Perhaps these notions were behind Bataille's involvement with the secret society Acéphale in the 1930s, a group whose activities are still shrouded in mystery. There are texts, diagrams, rituals, "directions to the forest," vague but cataclysmic notions surrounding a cosmic sacrifice, a sacrificial act that would in some palpable if insignificant way respond to the ravages of war and genocide. But a sacrifice subsumed in a sorrow of a different order, at once mundane and cosmic, a sacrifice of a "planet congested by death and wealth," from which "a scream pierces the clouds."[20]

Today, it could be argued, we have re-entered cataclysmic time, neither quite linear nor quite cyclical, the existential insufficiency of scientific explanation matched only by the inadequacy of conventional religion, alternative spiritualities, and the like. Our awareness of the changes that have christened an entire planetary epoch – the Anthropocene – have also produced suspicions about the human incapacity to respond to such vast and impersonal shifts in climate, weather patterns, and geology.

Though the two may have been on opposite sides of the fence politically, Eliade, not unlike Bataille, expresses weariness regarding the voraciousness of our meaning-making systems, religious or otherwise: "The destruction of a harvest, drought, the sack of a city by an enemy, loss of freedom or life, any calamity (epidemics, earthquakes, and so on) – there is nothing that does not, in one way or another, find its explanation and justification in the transcendent, in the divine economy."[21]

And if human extinction is the final – if unintentional – act of sacrifice? If climate change is itself a hierophany, an interruption of the sacred into an anthropocentric world? We too are forced to acknowledge unprovoked suffering on an estranged planet. Who will give us reasons for it? Too cynical for faith, too weary for facts, the planet remains, reduced to the diligent documentation of a lost world, which has already, perhaps, entered the domain of myth.

Rare Earth

That the human species has evolved on the Earth is one thing. Whether it should have is another. Of course, both questions cannot but be proposed from the vantage point of those very same forms of life that are under consideration. The "Rare

Earth" hypothesis is the most recent approach to come out of the sciences which, in its own way, challenges long-held beliefs about the inevitability of life on any planet, let alone Earth.

Combining approaches from geology, evolutionary biology, paleontology, astrophysics, and other fields, the proposition of the Rare Earth hypothesis is fairly straightforward: that the emergence of complex, multicellular life forms on the Earth (to say nothing of consciousness and intelligence) was due to an improbable conflux of a multitude of highly specific conditions. Life as we know it is the product of largely happenstance conditions. Geological formations, atmospheric conditions, relative stability in temperatures, chemically appropriate environments, all of it – including being in the right galaxy, at the right time, at just the right orbital distance from the sun – all these conditions needed to occur so that multicellular life could evolve. It did happen, yes. But that doesn't mean it was destined to happen, much less that it was supposed to happen. In fact, some proponents of the Rare Earth idea go so far as to deduce that the high improbability of complex life on the Earth in turn implies the high improbability of complex life on any other planet.

Without explicitly saying so, the Rare Earth hypothesis bursts the bubble of human exceptionalism. It leans on the wonderfully named philosophical idea of the "principle of mediocrity": that it is precisely the unexceptional, mundane, "mediocre" quality of complex life forms that argue for its inevitability. If life was probable and even typical, then its existence on other planets might also be probable, if not typical. Extraterrestrial life must be out there; our mediocrity proves it.

The Rare Earth hypothesis contains its own irony by inverting the principle of mediocrity. Life is nothing special, precisely because it is exceptional. But it is one thing to be exceptional in the more analytical, quantitative sense (the right atmosphere, temperature, etc.) and another thing to be exceptional in an existential, qualitative sense (more significant, more meaningful). In a sense, the Rare Earth hypothesis is a variant on the fact–value distinction so intrinsic to the philosophy of science. Skeptics such as David Hume had long ago questioned the way in which philosophers often derive statements of value (good/bad) from statements of fact (is/isn't), and in a way such biases go back to the very foundations of philosophy – the preference for existence over nonexistence, presence over absence, life over death.

The Rare Earth hypothesis forces a wedge in the fact–value distinction. It leaves open the possibility that everything we deem significant about the evolution of complex life on the Earth – leading up to and including the entitled provenance of human beings – may simply be a by-product of a cluster of very specific accidents that makes the question of "our place in the universe" both laughable and absurd.

Another option is given by a philosopher like Schopenhauer, for whom life on Earth was nothing but a blind, impersonal, purposeless "Will-to-Live." It's only after the fact that we project meaning onto it, and it is likely that even this is a ruse of the Will-to-Live to perpetuate itself through us. The problem of suffering, so central to religious thinking around the world, is here given further proof in the fossilized strata of the planet. For Schopenhauer, something like the Rare Earth hypothesis would be less a threat to human exceptionalism and more like a dream vision, a fantasy, a parable:

> If we picture to ourselves roughly as far as we can the sum total of misery, pain, and suffering of every kind on which the sun shines in its course, we shall admit that it would have been much better if it had been just as impossible for the sun to produce the phenomenon of life on earth as on the moon, and the surface of the earth, like that of the moon, had still been in a crystalline state.[22]

It's as if the loftiest religious uncertainties are suddenly found to be rooted in astrophysics, suffering embedded in the very strata of rock, stone, and mineral of the planet, a kind of "geotrauma" that includes our rapacious capacity for incessantly unearthing the Earth through mining, drilling, and excavating. Through this lens, classics of twentieth-century existential psychology – from *The Trauma of Birth* to *Man's Search for Meaning* – might be re-read through the lens of a rare Earth and the way it binds suffering as invariably terrestrial.

We are left with a last option. That life is rare and, because of this, special. In fact, the most special. Perhaps even destined, written in the stars, gifted in the human provenance over a human world. The wild improbability of complex life – destined as it was, perhaps, to reach its pinnacle in human life – is itself evidence of its not being random or accidental. Part of a plan. Astronomy turns, with great subtlety, into astrology, and then into theology.

Its most concise expression is the twenty-first-century phenomenon of the "space selfie." While the first selfies from space can be traced back to the era of the space race itself, it more commonly refers to digital photography which is then circulated via social media. The astronaut Akihiko Hoshide, of the Japan Aerospace Exploration Agency, is often credited with the first space selfie in this sense. What began as a tongue-in-cheek gesture by an accomplished astronaut (a photo we might more accurately call a "sun selfie") captures not only the stark solitude of space but also the way in which all of us might rather turn the camera back on ourselves than face outward into the infinite blackness of deep space. (Yes, it did become a meme.)

Celestial Firmament

The idea of "first contact" is predicated on something that seems just steps away from faith. To posit the very possibility of first contact is to posit "that" and not "if," the stopgap between the assertion *that* intelligent life exists in outer space and the question of *if* intelligent life exists in outer space. The idea of first contact inhabits the interzone between the "if" and the "that." We're never quite sure, but we would like to think it's possible. A matter of preference. It's as if the negative affects associated with loneliness in the individual have been scaled up to the level of the species. The need for contact, the compulsion to communicate, the desire for community, the need to be seen, to be heard, to have one's existence ratified by some other being capable of recognizing our existence as significant, relevant, meaningful.

A world cast in the mold of the human being, fervently gazing out into space for a sign, any sign, that would in turn reflect back and verify everything human beings have ascertained about themselves. At stake are bigger, more grandiose issues: human exceptionalism, human provenance, human dominion. But also the most mundane of needs, needs that are at once selfish and selfless, the most self-centered and the most other-oriented. A labyrinthine game of glances ensues, an awkward dance of darting looks worthy of Hegel, Lacan, or twitchy teenagers. A planet shaped in our own image, according to our fears and desires, a planet both physical and metaphysical, the species solipsistic as a vortex of adolescent angst.

At its limit, the need for first contact has inadvertently produced its opposite – the impossibility of contact. Part of this is due to our seeming inability as human beings to relate to the other in any other way than by recuperating it as a part of the self. You are there, for me. But the impossibility of first contact may also be due to a very unphilosophical problem: that the Earth is currently arrayed by so many satellites and orbiting "space junk" that maneuvering large-scale spacecraft through all the debris has become increasingly difficult, a concern raised by NASA and off-world corporations such as SpaceX. In addition to the 7,500 satellites in low orbit, there are, by some estimates, approximately 27,000 pieces of space junk orbiting the Earth at any given time. Though the individual pieces of orbiting debris may be comparatively small, they can travel at speeds of up to 15,000 mph. A single piece of space junk traveling at such high speeds can easily damage any spacecraft carrying human passengers. In 2009 the abandoned Russian satellite Kosmos 2251 collided with Iridium 33, an active US commercial satellite. Kosmos had been decommissioned almost a decade earlier, left to its derelict fate in low orbit. The collision produced over 2,000 large chunks of space debris, now also in orbit. An anti-satellite test conducted in 2007 by the Chinese government had a more direct, if more provocative effect. In a test reminiscent of the vintage video game "Missile Command," the Chinese military launched a "kinetic kill vehicle" to intentionally destroy one of its own decoy satellites, generating over 150,000 pieces of small space debris. And, in a sardonic twist of fate worthy of Voltaire, there is the demise in 1996 of the Cerise ("Cherry"), a French military satellite that was fatally hit by a piece of the same model of rocket (the Ariane) that had originally launched it a year earlier. The very technology that has made space exploration possible has now, it seems, rendered it all but impossible. The irony is further compounded by the fact that many of these statistics are themselves generated by a host of planetary sensors, including those belonging to the US Space Surveillance Network (SSN).

But this too is perhaps symbolic. Thousands of satellites enveloping the Earth in a kind of solipsistic cocoon, thousands of discs covering the planet in a kind of meta-atmosphere, reflecting and refracting humanity back to itself in shimmering beams of data, a stellar form of narcissism that indexes the stunning human capacity for endless projecting itself onto every encounter. Every instance of an alien other a kaleidoscopic hall of mirrors that structures an anthropocentrism that runs so deep it forms the ground of the distinction between the world as it appears to us and the phantasmic notion of a world in itself.

Perhaps that's what humanity is, a kind of species-specific solipsism that "takes place," no matter the particularities of landscape, terrain, or atmosphere. It's reminiscent of the early notion of the Firmament, famously rendered by the astronomer and science fiction author Camille Flammarion, a picture of the Earth enclosed in a stellar canopy, beyond which only daring cosmologists might peek for a perhaps terrifying look beyond, before crouching back inside.

Extreme Weather

A Hero's Journey

A tiny flying mammal soared as never before. A female pipistrelle bat – no larger than a human thumb and weighing less than a third of an ounce – was found in the northwest of Russia, not far from the Baltic coast, after an epic journey of 1,200 miles. Residents of the small village of Molgino noticed that this leathery nomad had a tattoo on her shy and fuzzy wing, stating that the little creature was essentially the property of the London Zoo: an unprecedented journey for a bat of any size. While the bat clearly had more pluck than most, she came to a sad and sudden end when her rescuers left her alone just long enough to be eaten by a local cat.

Sequence 15

Solastalgia

Concern Team

Your internet goes down. This is always a rather unnerving experience, given how much you depend on our shared fiber-optic nervous system for work, entertainment, communication, information, provisions, and so on. As fate would have it, you were scheduled to teach a class on E. M. Forster's *The Machine Stops* later that afternoon. The irony would be lost on your students, however, if you can't zoom into the virtual classroom to let them know that your own machine had ceased to function. You say as much to the polite subcontinental gentleman on the other end of the phone, contracted by Verizon to reassure you that your first-rate Fios experience would be restored as soon as possible.

"I see there is an outage in your area," he informs you, "and we are working hard to remedy the situation. The current estimate for the return of full service is 6 pm."

"But I teach at four," you respond, restraining your frustration, in the knowledge that the man on the other end of the line has little to no influence on the current state of his employer's infrastructure.

"I understand," he says, in a convincingly sympathetic tone. "I will be sure to convey your concern to our Concern Team."

You are so thrown by this concept that you meekly thank him for his time and terminate the call. A concern team? How would such an assemblage operate? Do they have special uniforms? Do they act according to particular protocols? Are they themselves concerned all the time, frowning at each new concern as it arrives from the four corners of the nation, homeopathically absorbing the anxieties and grievances of each and every worried customer? Or are they especially Zen, hand-picked for their capacity to let other people's concerns flow off their unruffled feathers, like water off a duck's back? Should you, in turn – and according to the laws of reciprocal empathy – be concerned about the Concern Team?

In any case, you cannot be sure if this enigmatic cabal really was alerted to your own unremarkable concern. Nor could you have any tangible sense how they might respond, even if they were. You like to think, however, that your concern was delivered immediately, by ticker tape or carrier pigeon. And immediately upon receipt, the entire team gathered around a giant, suspended, pulsing crystal, into which they prayed for a speedy resolution to your own emotional dilemma. You also like to think this worked, since your internet service is restored half an hour before class is scheduled to begin.

Atlas Crunched

Spare a thought for the family of Lipetus and Clymene – two Titans from ancient Greek mythology, who must have made some questionable parenting choices somewhere along the way, since three of their four sons were severely punished by more powerful gods for various transgressions. Prometheus, for instance, was famously condemned to be chained to a rock until the end of time, while a punctual hungry eagle would arrive each morning to peck out his liver; that same organ regenerated overnight for him to suffer the same agony the next day, and so on, unto eternity. His crime? Stealing fire from the gods and introducing artifice and technology to the ambitious humans. (A fair sentence, in retrospect.) Prometheus' brother, Menoetius, didn't fare much better, although his punishment – for the more common crime of hubris – was much more quick and merciful: vaporized in an instant by a standard-issue bolt of lightning.

The third sibling, Epimetheus, lacked the brains and foresight of his brothers. In one highly fateful moment, he had been charged with the task of handing out specific qualities to all the creatures found on Earth. To the lion he gave courage, to the owl he gave wisdom, to the dog he gave loyalty, to the cat curiosity, to the gazelle grace, and so on. By the time Epimetheus came to dispense an exceptional quality to humans, however, his basket of attributes was empty. From our humble origins, then, humanity has been the animal without its own essence, doomed to make up for this originary lack with artifices and prostheses of all kinds. (Surely part of the general equation of our species' predilection for melancholia.)

Perhaps because he was known for being "slow," Epimetheus escaped the divine punishment of his brothers. Atlas, however, the last of the young men in the family, was not so lucky. For the crime of aligning with the losing side of the War of the Titans, Atlas – who had previously been hailed as the inventor of mathematics and astronomy – was condemned by the victorious Olympians to carry the Heavens around on his shoulders for eternity. (It is due to a long game of artistic and linguistic "telephone" that resulted in our understanding of Atlas holding up the Earth itself – a task which he apparently outsourced to turtles somewhere along the way.) Atlas has since become not only the patron saint of maps but also the totem of all those who feel they carry the world around upon their shoulders. (Including the notorious "mean girl," Ayn Rand, herself the guru of resentful go-getters the world over, all of whom fatuously believe they have transcended resentment.)

In any case, we can imagine the competitive conversations around the family dinner table on those rare occasions that Prometheus and Atlas were briefly released from their infinite toil, and thus in a position to compare scars and war stories. Prometheus would almost proudly show the scar on his stomach where his liver is pecked out every day, along with the pulpy wrists where the unbreakable chains have been nailed to the rocky cliff-face. In response, Atlas would hold up his hands for the rest of his family to see, pointing out all the burns and calluses received from straining against the stars and comets every night and day. ("The days are the worst," he might say, gulping down a cherished tankard of nectar. "The sun is so hot that it's like holding a glowing coal fresh from Hephaestus' furnace, multiplied to an ungodly degree.") At which point Lipetus and Clymene might smile to each other wanly and encourage their sons to look on the bright side – gesturing silently to the seat once reserved for their absent brother Menoetius. "You may be chained to a rock, or to the Milky Way, for the rest of time," their watery eyes seem to be saying. "But at least you're still here." For their part, Atlas and Prometheus know that no one else can fathom their agonies, except perhaps for that young buck Sisyphus, who also made some questionable choices along the way. (Most notably, thinking he was smarter than Zeus and temporarily outwitting death.)

Today, Sisyphus could be considered the godfather of modern exercise, since the task of staying fit is an endless one and usually involves some kind of seemingly pointless resistance work. (Indeed, it is surely only a matter of time before some enterprising Ayn Randian combines the futility of existence with the desire to have "rock-hard abs" into a patented Sisyphus Workout Plan.) Few places are indeed as sad as the gym, where panting, expressionless people climb electric stairs that go nowhere, or strain in landlocked row-boats, while staring at tiny screens showing gaudy home shopping bargains or fresh war footage from the Middle East. The gym is the exquisite apex of alienation from one's own body, as limbs and muscles tense for no discernible purpose beyond serving the gleaming machine for which this isolated movement was designed in the first place. Indeed, the Olympian gods are surely scratching their heads, looking down upon these mirrored spaces, wondering why humans have started assigning themselves seemingly endless punishments without any kind of vindictive divine intervention. (A question we would also do well to ask ourselves. What indeed *are* we running from . . . in one place . . . for an hour at a time? . . .

Actually, scratch that. The answer is pretty obvious when we pose the question so plainly.)

Sadness comes in many forms and can arrive drenched in endorphins, as well as a fugitive sense of accomplishment. For only a world designed around surveilled, encubicled inactivity would create special environments where people go to suddenly exert themselves for no reason beyond countering the stasis of their increasingly sedentary lifestyles. (The clicking of the mouse, its cursor hovering over different spreadsheet cells, being the modern, mental equivalent of the toil of Sisyphus.) Only a species that has lost its way would feel worthy of paying through the nose to do something that animals do all the time, as naturally as breathing. Exercise is a surreal invention by a creature that retreated from the natural motions of life; the quick-limbed gestures of simply being alive. (I suppose we can blame Epimetheus for that one – the brother who got off lightly.) To hold up heavy barbells or lumpy medicine balls, like a lycra-clad Atlas – or to push oneself elliptically up digitally rendered hills, like Sisyphus – is to make a Titanic effort to keep entropy at bay; to push back that fateful day our mortal bodies break down and we are obliged to cross the River Styx. There is thus something intrinsically demoralizing underlying the struggle to "stay motivated," since the end result is always the same.

There is indeed something both superfluous and inadequate about gym-based exercise – something too much about it, and yet not nearly enough. To speak in the terms favored by those punitive ancient Greeks, gyms are where *bios* (civilized life) goes to exhaust the *zoe* within, in order to sublimate the latter into more fuel to fight another working day. (*Zoe* being the shared "bare" or biological life of all creatures: a term consistent with the etymology of "gymnasium," which means to "exercise naked.") If, as Aristotle and other wise thinkers propose, the goal of human life is *ataraxis* – the *absence* of strain and stress – then the last place in which we should be spending time is the gym. (Granted, a fleeting and diminished form of *ataraxis* may immediately follow such exertions, but only as the dilation of a far greater social contraction.) For in these sweat-stained temples we *smell* the sadness of striving; and in the agonies of the swift-dropped dumbbell we *hear* the hernia sorrow of strain.

Indeed, we can only hope that such deep philosophical notions concerning the "proper life" were in the forefront of the copy-writers' minds when they proposed a recent slogan for Equinox gyms: "Life is the luxury."

Olympia

Watching the Winter Olympics in February, 2022, was a deflating experience, for both spectator and participant alike. The former are underwhelmed by the lack of atmosphere, given the fact that the Chinese authorities – still clinging to the possibility of "Covid zero" – banned all spectators from all events, resulting in empty stadia, lonely routines, and uncannily quiet feats of gravity-assisted kinetics. The participants themselves – who have been working towards this moment every day for the past several years – appear visibly robbed of the chance of grasping the golden crown of triumph in front of a cheering crowd.

The mountains around Beijing, covered in artificial snow, appear empty and listless on screen; as if a few vacationing stragglers were trying to steal one more hour on the piste before an avalanche warning comes officially into effect. My heart goes out most, however, to the ice dancers, who have been weaned on noisy adulation and, for the top-tier athletes, even cultish fandom. Now they perform in the middle of an echoing hall, the schmaltzy music unmuffled by the soft and sentimental bodies of fans and family. Even the most graceful twirl and elegant leap is met with silent indifference, and no flowers or teddy bears are thrown on the ice immediately following the performance. Panting and grimacing at the end of their routine, the ice dancers acknowledge the judges – those (now-masked) stony-eyed jurors of their fate – before turning to the four cardinal points, to bow or curtsy – depending on their gender – towards rows upon rows of empty seats. Who knew the absence of applause could be so deafening?

Who could have anticipated such an eventless event, where the competition goes on, for the sake of itself, forsaken? Who really understood the importance of live spectators to the spectacle? (Other than the officials who, in less prudish parts of the world, have been stacking empty stadiums with reconfigured blow-up dolls or hastily dressed mannequins, to at least simulate a sense of collective embodied attention.)

In these Winter Olympics, the proceedings are quiet enough to practically hear a universal mantra – spoken in over a hundred languages – all translating into English as, "Is that all there is to glory?" The eyes of the athletes seem both disappointed and restless, seeking to at least catch the eye of the camera: a now rather sinister machine which has apparently kidnapped humanity and trapped all their potential fans and well-wishers in a kind of compressed, yet distributed, sardine can. Indeed, I cannot be sure if it was my own pandemic fatigue, a bad real-time translation, or the effect of the competitor's mask – or indeed a combination of all three – that made me mishear the winner of the women's luge. When asked a general question about how she feels, with her dream of an Olympic gold medal now accomplished, the newly minted champion responded: "How do I feel? . . . You ask me how I feel? . . . I feel my victory is as hollow as a tree that has fallen in a forsaken forest, bereft of even the dignity of a witness. Mount Olympus itself is abandoned. Yet who can blame them? . . . And so we compete in the vacuum left behind by bored and indifferent gods. A vacuum I will now take home with me, and live with the rest of my life, as surely as the medal which I can affix as a kitsch trinket to the meaninglessness I carry in my breast."

Long After the Thrill

Despite the imaginary people in commercials and the image-conscious people on Instagram, everyone is sad. No matter our station in life, we all compose whatever melodies our characters can conjure over – and usually despite – the morose tones of our own private pulse. (Our shared heritage of sorrow being, as covered already, a combination of existential, evolutionary, spiritual, political, economic, social, cultural, psychological, environmental, and chemical factors.)

Your parents? Sad.

Your sibling? Sad.

Your romantic partner? Sad.

Your business partner? Sad.

Your old teachers? Sad.

Your best friend? Sad.

Your kids? Sad. (Not entirely your fault.)

Your boss? Sad. (Probably your fault.)

Your Uber driver? Sad.

The guy who works at the deli who always gives you a friendly wink when you order your usual sandwich for lunch? Sad.

Your dentist? Especially sad. (With the morbid statistics to prove it.)

Yo Yo Ma? Sad.

Adam Sandler? Sad.

Jeff Goldblum? . . . well? . . . Sometimes, sad? . . . At least.

The King of England? Sad.

Lana del Rey? Very sad. (Obviously.)

Everyone? Sad!

. . .

And yet.

And yet children and baby animals play, frolic, cavort. Occasionally we do too, under the right conditions. It's almost as if happiness is like one of those unexpected zephyrs, or warm patches of water, that one encounters randomly, among the prevailing cold winds or chilly currents of life. Certainly, kids and young animals can be very playful. Adults, whether estate agents or elephants, not so much. This is in itself a truism suggesting that life becomes bored with itself at some point. As that moody German philosopher Martin Heidegger may have said: "The facticity of ontology continues beyond the enthusiasm of any ontic individual experience." Or as John Cougar Mellencamp put it: "Oh yeah, life goes on, long after the thrill of living is gone."

This hypothesis – let us call it the Mellencamp doctrine – in itself suggests that there is a stable and finite amount of happiness in the universe, perhaps even present in the Big Bang, in trace amounts – like lithium and beryllium – and now extending its merry way through the sad, inky void, like a stream of happy-go-lucky antimatter. Indeed, like energy itself, there is likely even a physics of happiness, so that more *over here* means less *over there*. Happiness is thus forever leaking out of happy moments and places, like heat trickling out of a warm room, the speed of its loss dependent on the emotional insulation present. A case of affective entropy.

Out of sheer necessity, then, we humans have invented some negentropic technologies in a bid to counter the intrinsic entropic effects of happiness: art, alcohol, Alprazolam, apple strudel, and so on. We have learned to make at least a fleeting form of happiness readily available in a convenient portable form: chocolate bars, wine bottles, jewelry, edibles, novels, maracas, kisses, corgis. On the other hand, humans are such perverse animals that we have even learned to be happy about having our happiness consistently thwarted. So often we seem to fear that attaining happiness will leave us unsatisfied, since we also secretly suspect that it is the striving for happiness – forever just out of reach – that makes us really happy. (Or at least motivates us to do the stuff that we believe will one day make us happy.) Like a mirage, the closer it seems, the more we can ascertain its illusory seduction.

Or so we tell ourselves. Until we see viral videos of baby bears cavorting near a river, or toddlers laughing with glee having torn open the family beanbag. Happiness is patently available, to some, at least. It laughs, and by virtue of this, it exists. (Even rats, scientists have now discovered, giggle when tickled. Indeed, they even giggle at the *prospect* of being tickled, as when they recognize the visage of one of their tickle-happy humans.) A large measure of sadness is our lot in life, when the toys are taken away and the serious business of "making a living" (and indeed making a life) pulls us away from our ludic instincts by the ear lobe. By what esoteric alchemy can the leaden base of sadness be transformed back into the glittering gold of its opposite, once we have been exiled from the Arcadia of play into the heavy cares of adulthood?

This question is complicated by the social value placed on at least *appearing* happy much of the time, along with the taboo against expressing sadness or negativity of any kind. Add to this the "gamification" of many industries and activities and, in many ways, we are being increasingly infantilized as a strategy to make us *feel* like we're playing – like we're having fun – even as we're being exploited in unprecedented ways (so the rich can buy yet more exotic toys with which to fill the vacuum of their unhappy souls). Affective entropy is a global given, and it is an irony of our age that the more we try to *produce* or *engineer* happiness – whether it be through pills, or new TV shows, or curated experiences – the more we crash up against the fact that there is only a finite amount of the good stuff to go around. Our current obsession with boosting serotonin levels, and courting endorphins, is the flipside of our hyper-consciousness of anxiety and dejection. But when society's communication mechanisms are wired to constantly transmit the message that being happy – or at least being in a state of feverishly *chasing* happiness – is practically an obligation, the embrace of its opposite by renegades and outliers can be a liberating heresy.

Sadness as the pathway to something beyond itself.

Such is the heavy-feathered promise of the dark angel, who carries a vial of black bile beneath her black robe.

Sad Girls

In the midst of the aughts, a new cultural type emerged from the digital lily ponds of the internet – the so-called sad girl. Of course girls, of every stripe and station, have experienced sadness since time immemorial. This particular variation on the theme, however, concentrated around the image-sharing platform Tumblr and was a new opportunity for teenage girls especially to share their sadness via the *mise-en-scène* of melancholia, as represented by the flotsam and jetsam of the

Spectacle: from paintings of Ophelia drowning in a lake, to looped gifs of Anna Karina weeping in a Paris café, to manga renderings of Wednesday Addams holding aloft a lit match, to photographs of Lana Del Rey – the contemporary patron saint for this particular aesthetic – simpering in some kind of vaguely Nabokovian scenario, most likely outside a retro motel somewhere in the California desert. Sad girls were all about leaning into the sorrowful nature of existence and creating infinite mood boards around their still inchoate sense of loss, alienation, rejection, self-pity, and ambient ennui. Any given sad girl Tumblr page might feature images of retro supermodels from the 1990s (for "thinspiration"), photos of aspirational pharmaceutical cabinets (featuring name-brand medications for anxiety and depression), pictures of poeticized forms of self-harm (especially a kind of ceremonial cutting), and anti-motivational slogans plastered ironically over romantic sunsets, pointing to the futility of hopes or dreams (in a kind of stylized and ultra-hip nihilism). Sad girls – who, it shouldn't be necessary to note, were not always "girls" according to any conventional definition – liked to get high on the feeling of being low and would huff on the fumes of other people's trauma and distress in order to keep that feeling going. As my students never tire of explaining to me, back in 2010, it was almost mandatory for teenage girls to imbibe the sad girl affect, even if they would happily play silly video games or go on a wholesome bike ride to buy cookies only minutes after posting selfies of themselves crying over some imaginary break up, or scribbling some cryptic note which may or may not show evidence of suicidal ideation. (Which is not to say that a certain percentage of sad girls were often genuinely depressed and in need of help. Just that there was also a sense of coercion and conformity involved when it came to the online subculture as a collective entity – as if being upbeat were automatically to be tainted with "toxic positivity.")

In her article analyzing the phenomenon, Fredrika Thelandersson argues that, while we may be tempted to make fun of young soon-to-be-women, performing their own sorrows on social media, there is something genuinely (albeit latently) resistant or transgressive about the refusal to go with the flow of neoliberal optimism. Negation, even in potentially cynical or pre-commodified forms, Thelandersson insists, is still negation, and it nurtures a spirit of refusal, skepticism, and self-determination. From such a perspective, all these girls with sulky faces and wispy baby-doll dresses are so many radicalized she-Bartlebys, telling the world they would simply "prefer not to." To what extent this particular form of gendered sadness is related to other contemporary crises – such as climate anxiety, economic precarity, and social dysfunction – is hard to gauge. But surely there is a strong and suggestive correlation between the figures relating to everything from the medicalization of mood, to the evaporation of jobs (and the sense of vocation attached to them), to the mass extinction of other animals (which were, after all, our intimate companions in being), to the ongoing violent and reactionary spasms of the patriarchy against a feckless kind of feminism.

In more recent years, the sad girl – who represents the other side of the coin to "the manic pixie dream girl" – has seemingly ceded much ground to three emerging essential types: the "girl boss" (a young woman who embodies a kick-ass kind of dominating agency), the "basic bitch" (who represents sheep-like conformity to the zeitgeist), and the "e-girl" (an "extremely online" caricature of a persona that blends together mall-goth aesthetics with anime kink and video-game accouterments). Moreover, the curatorial narcissism of Tumblr has given way to the literal performativity of Instagram and TikTok, partly as an effect of young women attempting to monetize their physical assets. Who has time for sadness when you need to hustle simps to your OnlyFans page in order to pay rent?

Thus we are confronted with another cultural paradox, where today's online content, produced by young people, is far more upbeat than the mood of the times, and far more optimistic than the current situation might warrant. Even during Covid, we might note, social media that skews youthful was more about raising morale than indulging dark, romantic phantasms. It was more about being plucky than being resigned. Indeed, it's strange to look back over the past few decades and think how the punks screeched "no future!" all those decades ago – in a previous century in fact. And yet today, when the UN warns of a possible "global collapse scenario" within existing lifetimes, the kids are wiggling their hips, smiling cheer-leader smiles, and essentially singing "hooray for everything!" into the anonymous eye of their unblinking webcams.

Nine of Swords

As only the most recent off-shoot of the evergreen legacy of the early nineteenth-century Romantic movement, sad girls are interested in the esoteric, the irrational, and the occult. Dabbling in astrology or tarot is considered no longer the symptom of a soft mind but, rather, a post-ironic openness to oblique semiotic signals from the universe. Even if we don't sincerely *believe* in such ancient techniques for orienting ourselves in this perplexing existence, we respect the suggestive integrity of their own terms, as well as their own formalized attempts to reveal, as much as conceal. (Indeed, it is only us hypermoderns that are inclined to be skeptical that our moods and fates are dependent on the movements, and constellations, of heavenly bodies.) Astrology and tarot cards help remind us that we are not isolated individuals but part of much wider webs of cosmic connection and influence – even if such diagrams are difficult to trace with any kind of certainty.

Sad girls (and we are *all* sad girls these days; at least when we allow ourselves to listen to what lies beneath the static of our own irradiated souls) both understand and appreciate this reminder. As such, they are especially attuned to periods where such connections are threatened or at risk: times of enhanced trouble, disharmony, and miscommunication. "How to Survive Mercury in Retrograde," announce a thousand click-bait web pages. The answers may be trite, but the question rests on a much longer tradition of situating the body–mind–soul nexus on a vertical axis connecting the Earth with the heavens via the four key humors (blood, phlegm, yellow bile, and black bile). Such literal spheres of influence may not be verifiable in a scientific sense, but even to give some credence to the possibility of astrological interconnection is a somewhat self-fulfilling prophecy, since it places the self in an expanded context and breaks the atomic, and purely mechanical, paradigm of the pharmaceutical–medical complex. Sad girls instinctively understand, through the obscure truth of the body, that mood is connected to much larger bodies than our own: the sun, the cycles of the moon, the spin of the rings of Saturn. Menstrual blood, after all, is pulled by lunar phases, just as the tides of the vast oceans are. Why would one vital liquid be immune, simply because its vessel has been given a proper name? Perhaps this is the lesson hidden within the zodiac that Adorno couldn't see. Our star sign reminds us that we are indeed star-stuff. And even the scientists are happy to sign off on that one.

The Waning of Affect

Fredric Jameson famously described postmodernism as "the cultural logic of late capitalism": a structure of feeling shaped by voracious economics, on the one hand, and exhausted aesthetics, on the other. The postmodern era itself, and the cultural artifacts that it produced, Jameson argued, exhibited a novel kind of "depthlessness" evident in artistic expression and everyday interactions. This "waning of affect" could be seen as a flat pastiche of former modes of emotional synchronicity, leading to the kind of blank exchanges that we find in the proto mumblecore films of Hal Hartley or the hyper-alienated novels of J. G. Ballard. Looking back on this diagnosis from the new millennium, it is increasingly clear that such a claim was premature, if not outright mistaken. (As indeed may be the implicit optimism embedded in the very term "late capitalism.") Today, affect is the dominant mode of being, and we are increasingly obliged to "read the room," demonstrate our moods, amplify our temperaments, index our emotions, and verify our embodied responses to any given situation. This new regime even has its own mode of work – "affective labor" – a type of obligatory mood-management, or vibe-curation, that dovetails neatly with "the experience economy." (That is to say, a market based on little more than the emotionally toned memories it creates.) So to say, we are all subject – sometimes as producers and other times as consumers – to the new tyrannical mode of this *structure of feelz*.

Far from the kind of deadpan communication that we used to fear would be a signature of a flat, matte dystopian future, our own dystopia is notable for its bright colors, solicitous gestures, didactic voices, and rather hysterical behaviors. While our forebears feared a more automated society would lead to more robotic humans, we have over-compensated for such fears by becoming a race of Reality TV hysterics: performative, demonstrative, parodic. People who don't *feel* – intensely and often – are considered suspicious and "inauthentic": they are clearly hiding something. Moreover, the current structure of feeling seems to be *producing* identities directly, to service just such a structure, rather than the former scenario, where somewhat independent individuals would merely be influenced by different emotional epochs. In other words, today's personalities are little more than condensations of affect – vectors of emotional intensities – that bypass the now largely unnecessary filter of personhood. We are but occasions for feelings and for the communication of such feelings to others. Mood is a virus, and contagion is not only obligatory but desirable, since it is the key sign of belonging to the group. (And, given the ecological nature of this effusion of affect, collective moods can now be tracked – especially through social media – in the same way we follow the formation and movement of weather systems.) Where the diva used to be the *source* of a certain kind of disciplined hysteria, she is now the puppet-like effect of its atmospheric ubiquity. Emotion is now untethered from identity – even from subjectivity itself, or direct experience. *I feel therefore I am.*

Hiding the Pain

Silent movies can seem ridiculous to us today, with their mute, exaggerated, theatrical gestures and leering, yearning, wide-eyed faces. They seem to emote *too much*, as we retroactively ascribe to them the need to compensate for the lack of audible speech, which would arrive a few decades later. *More is more*, early cinema appears to tell us; and we congratulate ourselves on being more subtle. And yet, today's superhero movies and Pixar's mugging animated faces suggest otherwise. (Not to mention the exaggerated movements and expression of your common-garden thirst trap on TikTok.) We are still strutting on this worldly stage, hamming it up for the camera, and each other.

Somewhere around the 1930s and 1940s, when sound and image synchronization was smoothed out by the Hollywood studios, affect was recalibrated to produce a new kind of face: no longer beset by twitches and ticks, but displaying a powerful kind of totemic, or archetypal, passivity, like a landscape illuminated by the moon. Epitomized by Marlene Dietrich and Greta Garbo, this new visage helped to cool the general affect and slowed down the pulse of the film-going public after the hot-blooded freneticism of the 1920s. Just as the world was tipping towards one of its darkest chapters yet, cinema was exhibiting a kind of preemptive sadness and impersonal world-weariness. As Roland Barthes famously noted: "Garbo still belongs to that moment in cinema when capturing the human face still plunged audiences into the deepest ecstasy, when one literally lost oneself in a human image as one would in a philtre, when the face represented a kind of absolute state of the flesh, which could be neither reached nor renounced."[1] This, in contrast to the more "modern" individualization of faces, as found in Audrey Hepburn, for instance, who – for Barthes, at least – represents nothing, or no one, beyond herself. Nothing more than a *specific* form of beguiling femininity.

While cinema certainly featured some subtle, sad faces before the arrival of the talkies – Buster Keaton especially comes to mind – it wasn't until the golden age of Hollywood that the expert fetish of the sorrowful visage burnt itself into our collective psyche. Who had the saddest face in movies? Candidates include Barbara Stanwyck, Peter Lorre, and Judy Garland. Strangely, however, the more the movies attempt to aggressively squeeze the tears from us – that is, through melodrama and "weepies" – the more a part of us resists. (Depending on our mood, situation, and hormonal cycles, of course.) So to say, there is something *obscene* about depicting naked sadness on screen, just as there is about depicting naked bodies. Melodrama and pornography may both be successful – when it comes to wringing (different) bodily fluids from us – but the operation seems too cynical, too efficient – too calculated. Better those poignant, nuanced moments that reverberate all the more powerfully for being fleeting and almost imperceptible. The flicker of an eyebrow in Cassevetes. The angle of a wrist in Ray. The timing of a sigh in Varda. The pursing of the lips in Ozu. Or the shaking of the shoulders in Wong Kar-wai. We are thus tempted to conclude that sadness, like horror, is most effective when largely left off-screen, out of frame; that is to say, left to the imagination, which is now free to actively fill in the blanks.

Today, however, film culture contends with a belligerent new scopic form – that of the meme. And memes are nothing if not crystallized moments of reactive affect: images congealed by political anger, economic frustration, sexual angst, generalized boredom, and so on. When one particular image is so versatile that it becomes a common, recognizable icon, it is given the exalted status of named meme template. One such ur-image from the past few years is called "Hide the Pain Harold" and features the heart-tugging grimace of a middle-aged man, sitting in front of a computer and holding a cup of coffee. The pained face of Harold actually belongs to András Arató, a septuagenarian Hungarian electrical engineer. Though Hide the Pain Harold began life as a stock photo model, his unconvincing smile has elevated him into the new online collective unconscious, representing a boomer whose life apparently didn't turn out the way he hoped (indeed, in a rather charming TED Talk, Arató notes: "it's a role given to me by the internet people"). Again, sadness is best digested in a diluted form, lest the senses flood and shut down. Something about the cognitive umami of laughing *at* Harold, while inwardly crying *with* him, speaks to the high-strung, neurotic complexities of our shockingly stupid and simple age.

Bitter Lemonade

Students increasingly tend to expect their reading material to be uplifting or inspiring. If a character encounters trouble – sadness, trauma, disappointment, or danger – they are expected to overcome it. They are obliged to turn lemons into lemonade. Indeed, this younger generation, as a general proposition (and weaned on plucky YA novellas), seems perplexed when encountering writers who offer no redemption or silver lining – Kafka, Rhys, Bachmann, Barnes, Comyns, Lispector, Acker, Houellebecq, and so on – as if negative affect could exist only as a pretext for its own transcendence.

Of course, there is a long history of impatience with any prolonged sign of disaffection. And what, in previous centuries, was experienced as merely tiresome or frustrating, for those not seized by the enervating grip of melancholia, has now prompted an elaborate diagnostic apparatus to be assembled around sighing, weeping, frowning bodies. The more the world becomes one vast and ingenious occasion for sorrow, the more we are exhorted by experts and friends alike to fight against it, rise above it, and reconnect with the joy within. (As if happiness were a factory setting of the human. As if we weren't born shrieking.)

We are also told by neurologists that, if we force our mouth muscles to smile – in an effort (literally, physically) to "turn our frown upside down" – then we can fool our brain into thinking we're happy and releasing those precious chemicals (serotonin, endorphins) that make us feel at least some sense of well-being. But the forced smile can only fool the brain for so long. Hence the useful phrase "toxic positivity" to describe all the wellness ideologies, programs, and subtle pressures that attempt to fill the void created by (or rather, *exacerbated* by) the cold capitulations of capitalism. "Leaning in" to the misery of it all – as a writer like Anna Kavan does in her singular novel *Ice* – challenges the current moral(istic) imperative to resist the seductions of negativity, no matter how much the cosmos stacks the cards against us. Kavan does not exactly offer catharsis or solace in her bleak vision of a world besieged by gathering glaciers, but the plight of her "pale girl" does suggest the deliberate choice of aesthetic negativity over and against the toxic positivity that Kavan herself no doubt noticed crystallizing in the Western capitals of the mid-1960s.

The Ashes

While the plight of endangered species is something we are familiar with, the idea of an endangered *activity* is generally considered to be less urgent and more difficult to track. Nonetheless, cultural rituals that once formed the rhythm and structure of everyday life – from barn dances to siestas to the evening pint at the pub – have, one by one, ceded their time and authority to TV, social media, and the hustle and grind. One such endangered activity – at least in the Commonwealth countries – is the game of test cricket: a mystifying ceremony, to the uninitiated, and a holdover from a more leisurely age, when it seemed fitting and proper that a single match last for five full days (including breaks for lunch and afternoon tea). Even at the end of such an elongated encounter, the result would just as often be a draw as a clear result. Today, test cricket is besieged on several fronts – shorter, flashier versions of the game, finished in less than five hours; shorter attention spans (as much of the players as of the dwindling spectators); waning interest; and even the challenge of climate change, which has resulted in drier pitches that crack and crumble long before the fifth day.

But just as there is something inherently sad about the English themselves, there is something naturally melancholic about the national game – especially in these accelerated times, and in an age with no patience for the gentle pace of a sport that somehow appears *less* strenuous than your average picnic. Test cricket is associated with a surfeit of standing around in white cotton clothing doing apparently nothing; the meditative sound of "leather on willow" (that is, the sound of the leather ball striking the sprung willow timber of the bat); the scattered applause of the drowsy spectators, half-snoozing off the gin and tonic that accompanied lunch, when someone finally manages to score a run; as well as the on-field mantra "well left" (a form of praise reserved for the batsmen who judiciously refuse to play any shot whatever).

The most prestigious trophy in world cricket is also the oldest and symbolizes the melancholic roots of the game. Known as The Ashes, this prize has a singular origin story, emerging from the English popular press immediately after Australia defeated England in 1882 – the first time they had managed to do so away from home. The *Sporting Times*, in the sting of such an unexpected loss, felt compelled to publish an "obituary" for English cricket, now that the wild colonial upstarts had beaten them at their own game and on their own lush wickets. English cricket was dead, they decried, tongue somewhat in cheek – now reduced to ashes. The next series – always a best of five matches (adding up to twenty-five days in all) – was to be played down under; not a small matter, given that Sydney was a green-gilled three-month journey by steamship in those days. Such a journey, as befits an epic undertaking, became known as "the quest to regain the ashes." Today, Australia and England assemble every four years for the right to boast of possession of these hidden cinders, which are said to be the cremated remains of a bail – that is to say, one of the little pieces of wood that teeters on top of the stumps forming the target of the bowler and rest in the safekeeping of the batsman: the cinders are now kept in a surprisingly diminutive urn at Lord's Cricket Ground in London (the spiritual home of the game).

And while the players who triumph in these contests are all smiles and champagne stains, there is something poignant about a sport symbolically organized around its own funeral, as if the Spirit of Cricket itself knew – nearly a century and a half ago – that it was destined to be wiped out by the lurching impatience of modern life. For just as the British Empire rendered extinct so many traditional lifeways, languages, and ways of being – all around the world – it also exported a surprisingly humane game to colonies that would soon excel at the same, often beating the English as soundly as the Australians did. Today, however, especially in India – the new home of cricket – the game looks more like baseball on steroids and is over before it seemingly begins. The players wear garish colors, and no one can hear the sound of leather on willow over the shrieking fans, sponsored announcements, smoke machines, and techno-Bollypop music. Whether an unlikely phoenix will rise from these ashes remains to be seen. But, either way, cricket will always be something closer to a ritual than a sport and, as such, carry the whiff of incense that accompanies sacred anachronisms, holy relics, and forsaken martyrs. The almost forgotten game of a forgetful people.

Back in the Saddle

Along with millions of others – most of whom currently seem to be in this self-same airport check-in line – you decide it's finally time to travel again, now that Covid seems to be ever so slowly transitioning from looming menace to ambient risk. The airlines, however, are not prepared for this post-lockdown summer surge, and there seems to be only one person, looking harassed and sweaty, processing an entire 747-worth of passengers all on his own. It must be said that the merchants visiting from Dakar, with several giant suitcases each – yet arguing about the overweight charges policy – are not helping the flow. Some travelers smattered around the airport are still wearing masks, but most are flagrantly displaying their naked faces. Seeing all those orifices open to the world still looks promiscuous, if no longer downright obscene. The inevitable sneezes and coughs that punctuate the stale air, already thickened by impatience and boredom, still tighten nearby sphincters but no longer threaten to spark public confrontations. Children run rampant, oblivious of the lingering anxieties of the older folk.

As you line up in "Zone 4" you hear a crash to your right, followed by a gasping silence. A middle-aged man has collapsed onto the polished concrete like a felled tree, smashing his glasses and sending his book sliding across the waiting gate. For a few long seconds, no one can be sure if he's alive or dead. But then the spell is broken when someone rushes for some ice, and other people start to yell for help. He stirs a little, and moans. A few minutes later, and the man – his nose smashed and bloodied – is sitting groggily and waving away surplus attention, insisting he is still OK to travel. Shaken, you can't help wonder if the man has Covid and is trying to get home to France in order to avoid astronomical medical bills. People return to staring at their phones and shifting their weight from one leg to the other. As the more privileged zones finally begin to board, an American man starts yelling at one of the Air France employees. Apparently she was less than civil to his rambunctious brat, and he decided to spasm into a fit of "air rage" before even leaving the ground. The employee blinks under his verbal assault and aggressively wagging finger, an inch from her face. Surprisingly, he and his family are still allowed to board the aircraft rather than being hauled away by JFK security. You begin to wonder if these are all omens encouraging you to turn around and return home, where things are easier and less stressful. But then you remember your bags are already on the airplane.

Eventually finding yourself inside the cabin, you note that it is both familiar and uncanny. Indeed, you weren't sure – in the midst of rolling lockdowns, border closures, elaborate visa requirements, and a mild case of agoraphobia – if you would ever be able to travel again. You'd like to relax and let go of more than two years of "unprecedented" tension. The vibe, however, is still too tense. We don't get past a global trauma like that so easily, either as an individual or as society. Besides, the person in front of you is reading a new magazine bearing the headline "Will Monkeypox Be the Next Covid?" You note that experts seem to take a bitter pleasure in informing us that rapid deforestation and warming temperatures will surely release worse microscopic, zoonotic foes in the near future – to the extent where we'll probably be positively nostalgic for the coronavirus.

The transatlantic flight is bumpy all the way, to the point where you start to get air-sickness. The planet is getting windier, you remember hearing somewhere – again, thanks to climate change – meaning that the nerves of jittery fliers, like yourself, will be tested more than ever. You arrive in one piece, however, and attempt to remember what it's like to be a carefree tourist in the Old World. You buy cheeses, fruit, vegetables, and wine at a local market. You make a decent dinner and eat it outside, in the garden of the 500-year-old farmhouse in the Dordogne that you found on Airbnb. The mosquitoes are so vicious, however, that you are driven inside again before dessert. The size of the bites, and the stealth attack of the tiny assailants, means that the likely culprit is the tiger mosquito: a relatively recent immigrant to the continent, having flown up from Africa following the new Saharan weather patterns as they plume further north. (A kind of "yin" to the "yang" of the polar vortex that now balloons down to lower latitudes during the winter months.) These tiny vampires of course bring with them diseases previously unknown to the area. Perhaps summer al fresco dining can only happen in Pinterest photos from now on. Nevertheless, you are determined to enjoy your holiday.

More challenges arise, however. A heatwave soon arrives, with record breaking temperatures. Even soggy old England breaks the 40-degree barrier. Unthinkable just a few years before, but now a likely routine going forward. A story circulating on social media – that a hospital in Blackpool was forced to open the doors and windows in an attempt to counter the oven-like heat, only to allow dozens of ravenous seagulls to invade the place and steal chips out of the spittle-flecked mouths of moaning patients – was confirmed by a local journalist. Clearly Europe is not ready for such extremes, with few houses or institutions equipped with air-conditioning. Then again, if the continent does begin to "catch up" with the US, the problem will become exponentially worse. In this region of France – famous for castles, walnuts, and tortured geese with delicious livers – the temperature "feels like" 43 degrees. Your Airbnb host, who used to be a science teacher, explains – while mopping his brow – that the Earth is less luminous than it used to be when seen from space. And this reduction in reflection, caused by pollution in our oceans, means that yet more heat is being stored in the atmosphere. The old farmhouse you are currently renting certainly isn't air-conditioned, so you must rely on the ancient technology of wooden shutters to keep out the sun during the day and hide inside – like one of those anonymous cave-dwellers who drew such vivid portraits of bison on the walls of Lascaux nearby – nearly 17,000 years ago. You can now understand what led them to such artistic accomplishments in the first place, given the dangers lurking outside in the sunlight. (In their case, wild cats and other hostile *Homo sapiens*, rather than temperatures that make your eyeballs feel like they are broiling in your sockets.)

The news on the radio is full of reports of wildfires in Spain and Western France. And, sure enough, a couple of days later you wake to an apocalyptic sunrise, choked with smoke. Again, you must cower inside with all the windows shut; this time for fear of breathing in live cinders, along with the strong blanket of ozone that smells like a thousand jet engines. You click around the news headlines on your cell phone, only to discover that people are being discouraged from visiting Mont Blanc because of dangerous rock falls caused by "exceptional climatic conditions" and "drought." This warning has an increased urgency after eleven people recently lost their lives in the Italian Alps when the country's biggest glacier gave way, melting under the incessant barrage of the sun. Indeed, there is not a trace of rain in the month-long forecast. You decide to head south, to the Côte d'Azur, where you hope some sea breezes will take the edge off the infernal temperatures. You forget about the humidity, however. Indeed, the water is nearly 30 degrees centigrade, as the Mediterranean suffers an extreme – and, yes, *unprecedented* – "marine heatwave." ("You can eat the fish already cooked from the ocean," jokes the taxi driver.) There is no relief to be gleaned from jumping into the sea. It feels like a giant soupy bath, filled with the sweat and urine of tourists and the dirty sump oil of the giant ferries that carry these same freshly vaccinated bodies hither and thither across the nearly stagnant sea. In a concerted attempt to find the glass half full, you note that there are not as many "medusa" as one might expect, given the conducive conditions for jellyfish. (Box jellyfish, you recall reading somewhere, have "an apparently unique form of venom whose recorded symptoms include 'a sensation of impending doom.'")

So you find yourself in the surreal situation of praying for rain during your vacation, just to bring the ambient temperature of the concrete streets down, as well as the core temperature of your own body. You can't even have a cold shower because the water out of the sulfurous pipes remains a maddeningly tepid lukewarm. As you sip a glass of Perrier from the struggling refrigerator, you read that the Loire river is now barely a trickle and easily crossed by foot. The Rhine too is running dry, with barges stuck fast in the silt. You daydream of a rustic rain tank, catching pure water to slake your chronic thirst, but, once again, the experts caution that we have crossed yet another threshold, and all rainwater – no matter how remote – is now unsafe to drink. The fluffy clouds, drifting innocently overhead, are full of "forever chemicals" – even in places previously considered pristine, such as Scandinavia or the Arctic. And so you switch to sipping a local wine as you fry up a fish that was no doubt imported from Madagascar or Australia. But this only prompts you to wonder what kind of "notes" such conditions will leave on the grapes of the next vintage.

Enough is enough. You head back to the airport, realizing that travel will never be "the same" again. (Also mindful that your jaunt across the sky helped exacerbate the problem in a measurable way.) The plane must be changed at the last minute, due to mechanical issues, due to a lack of mechanics. When you finally land back home, you realize they have lost your bag due to the lack of baggage-handlers. Meanwhile, profits for the airline companies are sky high, bouncing back with a vertiginous spike from the Covid-inspired travel bans. You can't help but feel that you are part of a planet-wide experiment concerning just how bad the experience can be before people give up traveling altogether. It's a fine line, since the companies still want you to buy the tickets, but they don't want to provide the twentieth-century "niceties" that one might still expect. (Like a reserved seat, a vaguely palatable meal, flight attendants, or a functioning plane.)

When you finally find a cab and get back to your apartment you are too jet-lagged to acknowledge the fact that all your indoor plants, despite an improvised watering system involving gravity-assisted soda bottles and slow-release nozzles, have perished in your absence.

Solastalgia

As the news headlines become increasingly shrill, "climate anxiety" is swiftly moving from an amorphous global mood to an official diagnosable condition. In a recent global survey, nearly eight out of ten young people, aged sixteen to twenty-five, agreed with the statement that "the future is frightening." Over half of those polled (56 percent) believe that "humanity is doomed" – a somber conviction consistent with a UN report, released almost in tandem with the survey (in April 2022), concluding that "the Earth is firmly on track toward an unlivable world." One striking finding of the survey was that "mental distress increases with hotter temperatures," prompting experts to anticipate an increase in suicides over the coming years. Meanwhile, Google reports that searches for "climate anxiety" surged by 565 percent over the previous twelve months, suggesting that people are finally acknowledging the existential stakes of our predicament, even as there are no easy answers to hand. Psychotherapists are scrambling to address the wave of "eco-anxiety" increasingly exhibited by their patients: a condition defined less by personal neuroses than by a collective metaphysics of despair. A full sixty years after Rachel Carson first sounded the environmental alarm in her bleak best-seller *Silent Spring*, the general population is only just beginning to at least *feel* the consequences – if not directly *face* them.

A new feeling requires a new word to describe it. And, in 2005, the Australian environmental philosopher Glenn Albrecht proposed the term "solastalgia" for a specific kind of ecologically inflected depression: specifically "the homesickness you have when you are still at home."[2] Solastalgia literally translates as "comfort grief" but, more specifically, describes the painful experience of no longer being able to recognize, or relate to, the place where one grew up. Solastalgia is thus the flipside of the more familiar experience of nostalgia, and, as such, it is even more distressing, since the sufferer of this syndrome cannot even fantasize, or hope for, a return to familiar surroundings. (Though the more we interrogate the idea, the more nostalgia and solastalgia tend to blur, given that the former was always concerned with a kind of environmental abandonment – an exile from Eden.)[3] As Albrecht writes in a follow-up article, "[a]s human impacts on the planet increase, it should come as no surprise that in addition to biophysiological pathology induced by environmental pollution, there should be psychological illness linked to a negative relationship between humans and their support environment."[4] You don't say! Indeed, the only real surprise here is that it took so long for the medical community to acknowledge the importance of "negative environmental factors" on mental health: factors like drought, flooding, deforestation, salinization, pollution, erosion, and so on, as well as their complex repercussions in our daily lives. Many people in the Pacific islands, for instance, have already watched their homes – their islands, even – literally sink under rising seas (merely a taste of the 50 meter rise now anticipated in the next hundred years or so).

As is usually the case, literature, philosophy, and the social sciences register such symptoms with more subtlety than – and many years in advance of – the so-called hard sciences. (Or rather, the hard-of-hearing sciences.) Blake, for instance, famously shivered in the shadows of the "dark Satanic mills" forged by the silk-frocked minions of the Industrial Revolution. Charles Fourier was so horrified at the mountain-top mining he witnessed in Virginia that he decided to design and promote a global utopia to avoid such horrors in the future. Henri Lefebvre lamented the life-sapping artifice of "the new town," despite the best intentions of mid-century technocrats and urban developers. "The bourgeois mentality," he writes, "has dismembered everything which had hitherto been organically united: nature and the social man, being and thought, work, actions, activities, generations, ideas, feelings, functions, forms." The traditional village, by contrast, was an organic place of convivial association – something like a human sea-shell – whereas the new town is reduced to efficient function, and the angular, alienating forms these produce. ("The expiring seashell lies shattered and open to the skies," Lefebvre adds. "The surviving shopkeepers are little more than managers.") More recently, in her original crime novel, *Drive Your Plow Over the Bones of the Dead*, Olga Tokarczuk uses similar imagery. "For people of my age," she writes,

> the places that they truly and to which they once belonged are no longer there. The places of their childhood and youth have ceased to exist. The villages where they went on vacation, the parks with uncomfortable benches where their first love blossomed, the cities, cafés and houses of their past. And if their outer form has been preserved it's all the more painful, like a shell with nothing inside it.[5]

In fact, this accumulative estrangement could simply be a synonym for "modernity": the name given to our violent historical lurch into an unprecedented situation where people now leave a world notably different from the one they were born into. (In contrast to the majority of human experience, pre-1400 or so.)

Solastalgia is thus a belated tail or footnote to much larger and deeper forces that have propelled modernity for the past half-millennium – most notably colonialism and capitalism. Certainly, captured slaves who survived the Middle Passage suffered from nostalgia, if they ever had a moment to feel anything other than hunger, strife, grief, and toil. But those who weren't kidnapped onto ghoulish ships were left to watch their homes rapidly transform, just as indigenous people around the world had to contend with an invading race who saw not someone else's home but, rather, a stockpile of natural resources ready to be converted into a distant and abstract – yet also brutally consequential – form of wealth. Solastalgia thus describes the belated era when such vulture-beaked chickens necessarily come home to roost, and the rapacious logic of colonial exploitation is now applied to the "home" of the white folks themselves. (And perhaps the reason that solastalgia hasn't become a household word – despite its global applicability – is the fact that the majority of the world's population are no longer in the comfortable position of equating their current housing situation with home; nor do they stay in one place long enough to register such changes at the level of personal biography.)

Soon enough we will need ever more nuanced words to describe each turn of the screw when it comes to the profound lack of rootedness, belonging – or even orientation – whether that be a drifting in space or in time. Nostalgia, they say, ain't what it used to be. And, indeed, we may need a different term to explain the nostalgia we have for former time periods that we didn't even experience directly ourselves. (The premise for some of the most popular TV shows on Netflix, of course.) Similarly, solastalgia may be a transitional term for a species that has abandoned the stable idea of home almost completely. For some, this may in fact be a potentially progressive step, given the historical fetish for "blood and soil" and the various belligerent nationalisms that still plague the world. As any foster child can tell you, however, it is challenging (to say the least) to navigate life with no stable sense of home, kin, or place. Our long natality as an exceptionally helpless mammal is an evolutionary proof of the extent to which we need some kind of stable protection and apprenticeship in life: a process that necessarily involves familiarity, habit, consistency, predictability, and so on. Given the climate-aggravated chaos that has started to visit large swathes of the world, forcing mass migrations and ongoing displacement, we also need a word that captures the homesickness one feels when "home" is something one has yet to even experience, when it is beckoning from the horizon, like a sun forever setting on the half-buried ruins of the British Empire.

Moving Home

The idea of *home* can be confused or complicated in many ways. As with nostalgia, home may be a place now located primarily in the memory, with no immediate physical trace of itself. Or, as with solastalgia, home may be identified with the same dwelling in which you were born, but the surrounding environment has changed so radically that it can no longer be considered a comforting *habitus* in the same way. Freud famously deployed the term *unheimlich* to describe the uncanny sensations evoked by weird dreams and gothic literature, whereby *home* is suddenly estranged, or rendered unfamiliar – vulnerable and besieged. The perverse appetite for dark tales that inspire such queasy emotions suggests that we have mixed feelings about the notion of home, along with all those factors – economic, social, familial, and so on – that go into making and sustaining such a nurturing base. The long history of gothic stories also suggests that we have felt a sense of unease regarding the domestic front for many generations. These tales witness the fact that we can sometimes suffer the experience of exile within our own kitchens, or feel "unhomed" under the same roof under which we first learned to walk.

In the case of the Swedish town Kiruna – located 200 miles above the Arctic Circle – the question of home has recently been given a further twist, since the decision was made to move the entire municipality 3 kilometers to the east. This decision was taken after engineers confirmed that the large iron-ore mine – the same which had formed the open heart of the community for nearly a century and a half – is on the brink of turning the town into a giant sinkhole. As it happens, there is still plenty of iron buried in the ground. It will mean tunneling under the current buildings, however, in order to access it. And so, in a very Scandinavian and literal interpretation of the *unheimlich*, thousands of residents are currently being relocated in a logistical challenge that evokes the whimsical fables of Borges as reimagined by the minds that brought us the Ikea flat-pack.

No doubt town planners around the world are watching very closely, in the age of the Anthropocene, wondering if something similar could be achieved on a much larger scale – if, for instance, Mexico City ran out of water or Genoa started to flood. Could it be feasible to disassemble, transport, and then reassemble an entire megalopolis in a more conducive environment? (The answer, we suspect, is absolutely not. Relentless rationalized optimism, however, has always been the hallmark of hubristic city planners and ambitious technocrats.) During Kiruna's relocation process – scheduled for completion in 2035 – one hopes that sociologists and psychologists are also watching closely, armed with relevant questions for tracking the consequences of a communal move that is too short to be *fully* uprooting but is surely too far to have no discernible impact on the citizens' sense of place. Will the inhabitants have the same civic pride towards a town that has shifted a good 40-minute walk along this Arctic latitude? Will they feel the same sense of belonging to a community, or the same sense of domestic continuity, if their church now sits on a different kind of outcrop, or if their bedroom window now looks out on a different vista? How local *is* the local, when it comes to the intimacy between identity and geography? One kilometer? Ten? Moreover, can materialized memories be placed on a flatbed truck, and delivered just down the road, without changing them, without reshaping them in transit?

In our age of deliberate "disruption," this kind of compromise between abandonment and staying put sheds a new light on the solastalgia to which we all fall prey to differing degrees. There is something ironic and allegorical about a town that obligingly moves itself a little to the left in order to allow the business of mineral extraction to continue. It suggests we might entertain larger, almost cartoon-like, solutions to environmental problems. Home, they say, is where you find your heart, your hearth, or – in the case of the more restless – your hat. (Though perhaps it should be noted that Plutarch described the wandering Earth itself as "Hearthless and homeless" – "borne across an infinite void towards nothing which it can call its own.")[6] Such cosmic exile notwithstanding, there is indeed something comforting about the idea of being able to take *home* around the world with you, like *Howl's Moving Castle*. But climate chaos means that homes are far more likely to be burnt to a crisp or washed away in a mud-slide than maneuvered out of harm's way by a nice Swedish man with a clipboard and a hard hat. And, as the twenty-first century unfolds, the urgently pragmatic question of shelter will eclipse the romantic, and ultimately privileged, ambivalences of home. So to say, we may not – as a global species – worry so much about twinges of nostalgia or solastalgia in our hearts, so long as we have a roof of some unleaking description over our heads.

The Lucky Country

It is no coincidence that an Australian dreamed up the concept of solastalgia. Indeed, Glenn Albrecht did not have to look far for examples of "homesickness while still at home," writing about the Hunter Valley, among other similar places, which have been swiftly transformed by the mining industries that hold much of that nation to ransom. What is frequently referred to as "the lucky country" by its own inhabitants – and depicted as a laid-back paradise by visitors – has been, since European invasion, firmly on the vanguard of self-exploitation and self-inflicted environmental damage. Through a combination of fossil-fueled greed, relentless mineral extraction, unsustainable farming, egregious political neglect of the environment, and personal irresponsibility, Australia is today one of the most distressed canaries in the coal mine of world affairs. And while an upbeat fetish of "the lifestyle" persists in the cafés of Melbourne and on the beaches of Sydney, the rest of the country – most notably its surviving indigenous inhabitants – have been contending with the legacy of this accelerated, heedless experiment in "crapping where one eats" (to use a suitably charming antipodean expression).

Australian culture has, from its humble inception, struggled with the burden of its violent colonial roots, as well as with its legacy as a kind of neo-Victorian science-fiction penal colony. (It is a little-known fact that H. G. Wells based his famous novel of Martian invasion, *War of the Worlds*, on the genocidal "campaign" against the aborigines in Tasmania.) The bad conscience of white Australia, compounded by the resentment of being the progeny of the unwanted and unwashed of the British Empire, flashed into unprecedented visibility during the most celebrated era of its film history: the 1970s and 1980s. It was around this time – when the government was tentatively beginning to acknowledge the atrocities on which the country was based – that Australians were also watching movies that at least elliptically admitted to the *unheimlich* history of this troubled nation.

Picnic at Hanging Rock (1975), for instance, struck a chord even above the equator, with its romantic, hazily gothic story of a group of Edwardian schoolgirls who embark on a day-trip to the country but who encounter a mysterious and distressing force, seemingly emanating from the rock formations under which they sought shade. The class and their chaperones eventually return to their school, hysterical, and missing several of their classmates, for reasons unknown. The menace is not named or identified, but most critics felt compelled to interpret the film – based on a novel by Joan Lindsay written a few years earlier – on the ambient sense of guilt that Australians spend much of their lives disavowing: the guilt spawned from commandeering an entire continent from its original owners. (Or we should rather say "stewards," since there was no sense of "ownership," as we think of it, in pre-contact Australia.) Take note, the film seemed to be saying, because now the white folks are suffering the karmic consequences of their own history. (A trope also found in North American films of the same era, featuring the revenge of spirits emerging from "an Indian burial ground.")

Around the same time, *Mad Max* (1979) – and especially its sequel, *Mad Max 2* (1981) – spawned an entirely new genre: the anarchic, deserted, desertified, post-apocalyptic world, along with the almost feral outback-ochred people who still eked out a wild existence therein. This franchise, resuscitated more recently with *Fury Road*, creates a rather incoherent new mythology in which the white population manage to cosplay a novel kind of indigeneity, effectively white-washing the original inhabitants, while also visiting all sorts of punishments on those who remain, as a kind of confused morality tale for more liberal, postcolonial times. *Mad Max*, in other words, both acknowledged and denied the crimes of the invaders, riding the rusty metal Trojan horse of a new aesthetic: one that has only become more seductive and viable over time. (To the extent that the whole "Road Warrior" series could soon be viewed as prophetic neo-realism.)

A much more obscure film, even in its native Australia – but dating from the same era – is *Long Weekend* (1978): a low-budget gem that borrows some of the uncanny, environmental dread of *Picnic at Hanging Rock* but sheds all the Merchant Ivory trappings, offering instead a wincingly pitiless portrait of a lower middle-class marriage on the skids. (We might give the simplified pitch as *Crocodile Dundee* meets *The Birds*.) Most of Australian culture's more problematic traits are embodied in the main character of Peter (played by John Hargreaves), who is macho, chauvinistic, arrogant, uncouth, and negligent. Peter seems to be as unconcerned with his wife's many grievances as he is of the respect that should be afforded to the natural world when camping on a hidden clearing where the forest meets the sea. (The movie's tagline is: "Their crime was against nature – nature found them guilty.") Certainly, Australian nature – "the bush" – is not the same as its bucolic European equivalent, as the new "settlers" learned the hard way. In the southern hemisphere, the local fauna and flora are evidently more poisonous, aggressive, and hostile – at least to those who are ignorant about how to live among them and appreciate their alien ways. Instead of the idyllic forests of England's "green and pleasant lands," those transported to Australia found themselves surrounded by a "brown and harsh" terrain – terrain that only the enigmatic aboriginals knew how to navigate without being stung, bitten, scratched, or even eaten alive. (This contrast was indeed so powerful that early paintings of Australia depict landscapes much more evocative of Shropshire or Sussex than the initially unsettling ghost gums of this so-called *terra nullius*. These painters simply could not bring themselves to *see*, or at least *represent*, the unfamiliar environment that they were looking at.)

Long Weekend was filmed a few generations after this initial disorientation was captured on the canvas of the newly arrived colonists, but it evinces an ongoing alienation from the natural surround, even by "modern Australians." As such, it is a neglected classic of early ecological anxiety and deserves to be rediscovered as such, since it combines the eerie atmosphere of a classic horror movie with the fateful momentum of a gritty revenge flick. (In this case, however, the "person" inflicting vengeance is not Charles Bronson but Mother Nature herself.) The natural world is clearly offended by these interlopers, especially by the man, who runs roughshod over everything – hitting a kangaroo with his car and chopping down trees – with no understanding that he is in fact the guest in this world, and one who needs to respect the rules of his host. Various critters begin to make their feelings known in increasingly unsettling – and ultimately violent – ways. Bull ants swarm over their provisions. An eagle attacks Peter's head. A possum bites his hand. (It is guaranteed that, after watching this film, the viewer will never think of a dugong the same way again.) The couple become increasingly panicked, as spiders and snakes prevent them from leaving the camping site. In the end, a harsh poetic justice prevails, and neither Peter nor his wife ever return home. Their fate may soon be shared across the country, however, as news reports glimpsed at the beginning of the film tell of strange bird attacks increasing even in the city center.

The list of ecologically unnerving films from Down Under towards the end of the last century goes on. It is notable, however, that, even as the question is starting to be asked – "can humans continue to live in Australia for much longer, given the massive water shortages and extreme conditions forecast?" – its books and films have largely retreated from such large-scale environmental concerns and returned to more intimate, intersubjective human stories. The inhabitants of the Great Southern Land – whether of European or indigenous descent (or from the hundreds of other countries that make up the truly multicultural population of today) – would do well collectively, and more consciously, to fashion a new creative language beyond the now tired iconography of *Mad Max* – as well as the revealing, but symptomatic, dead end of *Long Weekend* – to face the challenges of a society still tethered to an economy based primarily on rapacious resource extraction.

Shipping Eden

Werner Herzog's film *Where the Green Ants Dream* (1984) depicts Australia from the perspective of a European long obsessed with margins, eccentrics, and colonialist follies. In one particularly memorable scene, a group of aborigines sit in a circle, their heads bowed in silence, in the middle of a brightly lit supermarket. At first, this seems like surrealism. But we soon learn that these indigenous folks are honoring a sacred tree that had been chopped down by the local mining company in order to clear the way for this supermarket, built for the convenience of its employees. This image succinctly captures the havoc that time can inflict on space – being in the right place, but now too late. The hundreds of different aboriginal languages that existed during the time of the First Fleet surely had their own equivalent for *solastalgia*, long before white Australians felt the need to affix an official term to their historical and existential discomfort. How could they not, given how quickly and thoughtlessly the land with which they lived was fenced in, ransacked, and transformed?

Had the original European invaders been Swedish, however, rather than British, we might imagine a scenario where the aborigines in Herzog's film did not need to mourn a now vanished tree, for the simple reason that it had been moved 3 kilometers east, like the town of Kiruna. But would this be any better? Such a "compromise" would still be very much to prioritize the mine and oblige the original population to contend with a kind of deracinated sacrality, uprooted from the particular place in which the source of spiritual nourishment first flourished. We may also note that sacred trees are not as easy to relocate as sacred buildings – such as the churches being transported on giant trucks to their new location in the Arctic Circle – since the former are living things, liable to die during the journey, or expire soon after because their new environment lacks something essential they need.

Such a concern, we might also note, did not stop the Georgian billionaire Bidzina Ivanishvili from transporting hundreds of giant, hundred-year-old trees from the coast of his native land to his lavish compound-cum-estate, as detailed in the mesmerizing documentary *Taming the Garden*. Ivanishvili claims that only one tree died during the enforced "resettlement," and that thousands of Georgians can now enjoy these beautiful trees in his carefully sculpted park, open to the public. There is certainly something typical of the modern human spirit in seeking to create an arboreal paradise by essentially kidnapping hundreds of trees and shepherding them together in a new and alien setting. Trees, we now know, are social and symbiotic beings. They are not merely individuals, standing tall in the landscape, but collective sentient entities, in constant tactile communication with mycelium and other multispecies networks. Simply to tear a tree out of the ground, and assume it will make new friends in a new environment, is presuming a great deal. It is one of our common egotistic liberties. And the film documenting the process conveys the inconvenient pathos underwriting the project, especially in shots of lone trees, tied on to large flat boats, sailing around the coast of the Black Sea.

We have taken forests for granted, of course, for hundreds of years. The Industrial Revolution would not have occurred were it not for the stripped timber that allowed all those ships to go and pillage the four corners of the Earth. Old growth forests – that is to say, trees that pre-date the human urge to wield the ax – currently cover only 3 percent of the European Union. Moving trees in order to save them may soon become not just the whim of a Georgian billionaire but the tactic of environmental activists forced to contend with corrupt governments, impatient shareholders, and trigger-happy chainsaw operators. Even so, the goal of "protection" is debatable – akin to "rescuing" indigenous artifacts by putting them in a museum.

Such was the poignant contradiction at the heart of the ecologically minded sci-fi movie *Silent Running* (1972), in which the world's last remaining forests are moved on to specially designed spaceships, carrying large climate-controlled domes, to hover around the solar system. Here they glide around the Earth until such time that humans get their act together enough to clean up the planet and bring the trees back home. Of course, such a task is beyond our species, and the decision is eventually made to hit the self-destruct button on these magnificent forest-ships, after bringing the caretakers back home safely. Aghast at this news, the project's resident botanist – the unsubtly named Freeman Lowell – does some ethical calculus in his head and decides it's more justified to murder his three dutiful colleagues in order to save the lives of the hundreds of plant species that he has been tending for years. As orders continue to be barked through the intercom from Mission Control, Lowell goes increasingly rogue. He sets new coordinates for the ship. Things go awry – as they so often do in space – and by the end of the film only one englobed forest survives, tended by a rather adorable robot with a watering can and a new program coded to maximize its rusty green thumb.

This kind of pessimistic scenario may, however, be underestimating the extent to which plant life can survive, adapt, and regrow, no matter what kinds of technologies and toxins we throw at them. On the other hand, it cannot be denied that, if we continue to pave paradise, to put up yet more parking lots, then trees may become as rare as pandas or rhinos today. Billionaires will no doubt continue to buy up the remaining ones and transport them as status symbols, to complete the holistic visions of their overpaid landscape designers. Like the doomsday preparations of the elite, *Silent Running* does not explain how humans might continue to exist without trees to produce oxygen, and to scrub at least some of the carbon we produce that is polluting the atmosphere. But you can be sure that silicone-pilled technocrats are trying to figure out if such a feat can be accomplished.

One wonders, however, if computer modeling, no matter how sophisticated, can really crunch the numbers when it comes to the dark and composted world fermenting under the soles of our shoes.

The Two Willow Trees (a Lachrymose Children's Story)

For more sunsets than anyone could count, the two willow trees stood side by side.

They stood together, close enough so that their leaves, in summer, would sometimes caress in the breeze.

And they stood far enough apart to contemplate their own slightly different views on the lake which rippled beneath them. (Twin perspectives, ever so slightly different, as when we close one eye to look at something and then switch to the other eye.)

The two willow trees were unconcerned by the steady stream of tourists who visited the park from all over the world, many of whom stopped to photograph the trees together, standing side by side, like the proscenium arch of an enchanted play, with the bow bridge painted by sunlight in the background, and several celebrated buildings completing the scenery further behind.

The two willow trees were similarly unheedful of the tourists who took to the water, floundering in row boats, rented by the hour from sun-burnt, gum-chewing locals. The two willow trees existed at a different speed and rhythm to these ungainly creatures, who were dimly perceived as a kind of blur or hum – a parade of clumsy, pasty will-o-the-wisps, barely distinguishable from the honk of the geese, the leap of the squirrel, or the thrashing of the muddy carp.

The two willow trees were the bookends of an infinite and invisible library that grew up between them: an entire catalog of sensations, perceptions, and cogitations. Sometimes they shared a single thought that stretched for over a decade in human years, and beneath which pulsed a multitude of subthoughts, like the slow churn of a mute symphony orchestra.

To say the two willows sometimes quarreled would be to smuggle human foibles inside their gnarled trunks. To say they sometimes canoodled would similarly be a misunderstanding of matters arboreal.

But they thrilled in their way. They brooded. They reharmonized. They sang together, silently. They danced, without moving from the one spot, allowing the scented zephyrs to choreograph their limbs.

When autumn came, on the breath of the north wind, their leaves turned a rusty orange, and they succumbed to a dual melancholia. As the gusts turned stronger and colder, they relinquished their leaves altogether and shivered together, naked in the face of oncoming snow storms.

But they understood this was the wisdom of the seasons, and they did not hold any bitterness in their pulpy hearts. Rather they withdrew their fibrous minds into their roots, where the soil was still warm and moist. Here, below ground, they meditated together, sharing a shapeless mantra all winter, as the skittish squirrels foraged among their dry branches.

When spring began to uncoil itself through the park, the willow trees were among the first to bud. Their consciousness began to rise back up through the roots, into the trunk, and up into the branches. The feeling of new leaves – new life – was like thousands of butterflies made of light, fluttering and perching all over their barkish skin.

As the turtles emerged from the subterranean mud and basked on the warm rocks, the two willows trailed their lovely locks over the brackish shore, like two twin ladies of the lake. But as the warmer air began to triumph over the remaining cold fronts, storms brewed in the distance, and winds gathered a terrible force.

Many gales they had weathered together, not always without fear, or at least apprehension. But they would sing to each other over the howling sounds and give each other courage as Mother Nature pulled at their arms, in unprovoked maternal wrath. At such times, the two willow trees were grateful for the depth of their roots, as the wind tried to tie their billowing locks into knots.

But one day the roots could hang on no longer, and one of the willow trees – the one slightly to the north – was wrenched out of the ground and fell backwards into its own horizontal end.

The remaining willow tree – true to its name, and now with good cause – wept.

And wept.

And wept.

Its companion was swiftly removed by the human stewards of the park, without ceremony or sympathy, beyond a kind of aesthetic regret that one of the most photogenic views of the area was now so compromised.

The remaining willow tree was distraught and disoriented, but not in any way that you or I could understand or intuit. The sadness spread through the sap slowly, from the tips of the branches, which could sense the changes above ground, to the very base of its roots, which only knew the ways of the clay.

The tourists still took photographs, but even the ones who were visiting the park for the first time could sense something amiss. Or something missing, rather.

The remaining willow tree persisted, however.

And when strong winds began to blow, it no longer felt fear. Indeed, it felt a kind of yearning, or hope.

Spring after spring . . . summer after summer . . . the willow tree continued, willowing.

But it never adapted to its solitude, its now on its ownness.

Some humans who used the willow tree for shade read

books about grief and about the healing passage of time. But this was nothing but mammalian superstition to the willow tree.

Instead, there is passage; there is stationary unfolding; there is a constant reckoning with a looming no-longer-there.

After years passed this way, almost no humans remained who could recall the fact that this was a site of two willow trees rather than one.

But for the remaining willow tree, there had been no assenting to events, which tumble into the world wearing the garments of fate.

Instead the willow tree simply bowed its head.

And wept.

And wept.

And wept.

Extreme Weather

Shine Off You Crazy Diamond

The Earth is "losing its shine," according to new research published in 2021. Even as we like to think of our planet as glowing a bright and conspicuous blue amidst the cosmic darkness, scientists now tell us that the Earth's brilliance has dimmed measurably over the past few years. (Down by about half a percent since 2018.) Reflecting approximately 30 percent of the sun's rays is an important way our planet avoids overheating, so any lessening of this capacity is concerning. Even more concerning, experts explain, "this change in captured light 'is of the same magnitude' as the total impact people have had on climate over the last two decades." Perhaps there is a dark irony here, or unfortunate poetic connection. The duller humans become, in their glazed and hypnotized state, the less brilliant the Earth itself also becomes, muddied and baked by oceans now too polluted to function as vast, shimmering, liquid crystal mirrors.

Sequence 16

The Clever Beasts

The Machine Stops

E. M. Forster's science-fiction short story *The Machine Stops* – first published in 1919 – should be required reading today: an age in which being "extremely online" is swiftly becoming the default mode. Indeed, this tale only becomes more and more relevant in the decades since it was written, even if the style retains its early twentieth-century dustiness. In Forster's future scenario, the Earth has become a sad planet indeed, as humans are now obliged to live deep underground due to the ruinous effects of runaway global industrialization. People no longer interact in person but remain "socially distant" while using "the machine" to cater to all their needs, from temperature control to food to entertainment to work to communication. (Sound familiar?) The two main characters are a mother (Vashti) and son (Kuno) who clash over the omniscience of the Machine after the young man becomes disenchanted with living completely within the cybernetic womb and hatches an escape plan. Vashti, for her part, has lived her whole life according to the dictates and beneficence of the Machine; she finds her son's attitude not only ungrateful but heretical and dangerous. It is therefore not a stretch to describe *The Machine Stops* as an Edwardian precursor to *The Matrix*. (A mediocre film that nevertheless struck a nerve in the cultural imagination, precisely for its allegorical update of Plato's Cave for a time in which the internet was starting to really spread its digital tentacles around the globe for the first time.)

Forster's story explores the question as to what happens to humanity when we start to rely on our machines more than they rely on us. The answer it provides is that we become helpless: simultaneously posthuman and subhuman. For while it is true that we may still present sophisticated papers on scholarly topics to a curious audience, scattered throughout the subterranean world, via the Machine, we are also pale, hunched, cowed, isolated, and hyper-dependent on the infrastructure on which our lives literally depend, wriggling around in a confined space, like well-educated larvae.

When, at her son's feverish insistence, Vashti reluctantly leaves her domestic pod, she feels lost and strange. Boarding a zeppelin that ferries the occasional passenger from one place to another, she looks down on the unfamiliar ground and then up to the equally uncanny sky. In sharp contrast to the transcendent sense of wonder that humans have historically described when pondering the sublimity of the stars – or indeed when reflecting back on our home planet from the weightlessness of space – Vashti is repelled. "I dislike seeing the horrible brown earth," she admits, "and the sea, and the stars when it is dark. I get no ideas in an air-ship." For this middle-aged woman, who has spent her whole life in the amniotic embrace of the Machine, even the prospect of seeing her son – her own flesh and blood – in person, is not enough to dispel feelings of unease, dislocation, and agoraphobia.

The title Forster gave to his story is itself a spoiler, as the Machine succumbs to an accelerated kind of entropy. What begins as seemingly minor glitches in the system – strange, unsettling sounds interrupting streamed music; moldy food; dirty bathwater – soon snowballs into full-scale meltdown, and the humans are left without oxygen, wriggling around like panicked grubs, until they expire. A pessimistic portrait of our future, to be sure, and a cautionary tale to challenge all those upbeat narratives hatched in Silicon Valley where the answer to the woes created by our hyper-technological world is *yet more technology*. (I write these lines on the same day that Mark Zuckerberg plays the huckster for a new fully immersive "experience" called the Metaverse: the latest attempt to realize Forster's dystopian scenario through virtual reality technology, and to sell it to us as Life 2.0.)

In many ways, it feels like the Machine is starting to stop in our own time. (In this case, the machine of the global neoliberal techno-economic system.) Covid-19 seems to have accelerated the stuttering collapse of a "just in time" system that was designed to make the maximum amount of money with the minimum amount of resilience to unforeseen shocks. In this case, a microscopic pathogen has challenged the house of cards in which we live. Moreover, it remains to be seen whether the supply issues will eventually resolve themselves or if they also augur the beginning of the end – of everything crashing down.

Collapsology

One group that wagers we are witnessing the latter is a loose collective of environmentalists who have crystallized around the new para-science of "collapsology": an approach to the world that aims to document, anticipate – and hopefully mitigate – the inevitable downfall of the modern world. The collapsologists take Paul Virilio's observation that the more sophisticated the object or system, the more catastrophic its collapse, as an article of faith. (A neat example of which can be found in the philosophical documentary *The Ister*, when an architect points out that ancient Roman bridges in Croatia are still standing after the war of the 1990s, while much more modern ones have fallen into history.) The collapsologists are especially attentive to certain thresholds, tipping points, or feedback loops that will lead to an inevitable cascade into social and ecological disaster. (For instance, the famous example of the Gulf Stream essentially "switching off" and causing almost instantaneous climate chaos in the process.) Indeed, if this movement is correct about the imminent demise of modernity itself, every present human endeavor can only be considered through the prism of unsustainability, or even hubris. Late capitalism is viewed as little more than an almost infinite series of spinning plates. And, no matter how many humans we produce, we cannot coordinate our efforts to keep these plates from eventually – or indeed imminently – crashing to the ground.

Zoom Fatigue

1977 was too late to still be surfing the wave of optimism that followed the Second World War in the US. Nevertheless, Charles and Ray Eames summoned up enough of that residual gumption to make the now celebrated short film *Powers of Ten*, commissioned by IBM to showcase the power of their computer's processors and also designed to initiate a new generation into the marvelous world of scientific scale. The film opens with a scene of an attractive young white couple, picnicking by Lake Michigan in Chicago. We thus begin within the scale of the human – easily represented, and just as easily understood. The camera begins at a distance of 1 meter, and the narrator explains the conceit right off the bat: the shot will zoom out by the power of ten every ten seconds. "Our picture will center on the picnickers even after they've been lost to sight." In a smooth motion now familiar to our image-saturated minds (especially after the invention of Google Earth), the film pulls back and back, revealing more of the planet as it goes. The picnic blanket soon gives way to the city, which in turn gives way to the state, which in turn gives way to the country, and soon enough the Earth as a whole. The film doesn't stop there, however, as computer graphics step in where analog filmic technology can no longer reach, and the "picture" continues rather seamlessly to zoom out to reveal the solar system (". . . our sun is plainly now only one among the stars"), the Milky Way, and various galaxy clusters. At the scale of 100 million light years, this simulated cosmic journey slows down, and the narrator notes, "as we approach the limit of our vision, we pause to start back home." (The limit of our vision being dictated more by the astronomical models of the time than the possibilities for animation and rendering.) The film pauses to note: "This lonely scene – the galaxies like dust – is what most of space looks like. This emptiness is normal. The richness of our own neighborhood is the exception."

Having emphasized the defining mystery of our own terrestrial anomaly, the "camera" then begins zooming back through the nebulae and cosmic dust clouds to the sunny Chicago shoreline, before focusing on the now sleeping man's hand. Now we switch from macrocosm to microcosm, as the "camera" burrows down into the body, according to a different scale of powers of ten, adapted to the *inner* universe it is exploring. The picture penetrates the oblivious skin to reveal blood vessels, followed swiftly by "felty collagen," the capillary, a single white cell, the nucleus, the DNA helix, and then – shifting into the atomic scale – the carbon atom itself, electrons in quantum motion, inner electrons, the atom's attracting center ("a vast inner space"), the carbon nucleus, and, finally, "six protons and six neutrons." The narrator now explains, "We are in the domain of universal modules . . . and as a single proton fills our scene, we reach the edge of present understanding."

It is notable that the film simply ends here, without zooming back "up" or "out" to the couple snoozing by the lake shore. As an audience, we are given a kind of metaphysical whiplash after lurching from the infinitely distant edges of the universe to the uncanny, lonely voids deep inside our every cell. Indeed, we are simply stranded in the latter, as if the rollercoaster journey from physics into biology provided enough vertigo to last a lifetime. (Though a strange and intimate continuity between the macroverse and the microverse can be salvaged, if we remember Carl Sagan's mantra that "we are star-stuff." In other words, the carbon atoms that make up our own lithe young bodies are in fact 13.8 billion years old, dating back to the Big Bang itself. No wonder we feel so exhausted!)

Powers of Ten evokes a scientifically produced sublime, in sharp contrast to the traditional, or even "natural" kin, favored by the Enlightenment philosophers such as Burke and Kant. Where the latter points to an unmediated sense of awe or dread in the face of natural forces – or the proximity of a numinous presence – that dwarf our powers of perception, the Eames brothers ramp up the inhumane scale exponentially. The mind cannot contain such magnitudes, except in the abstract, aided by visual approximations. This secular rendering of the sublime nevertheless has a similar effect in the human mind or heart: a sense of radical irrelevance, of dizzying awe, of unprocessable experience, of cognitive or affective overflow, and/or a quasi-religious sense of cosmic connection or universal coherence.

Just as "man is the astronomer," in this case, man – or, rather, a man and a woman (Charles and Ray Eames) – consciously *produce* a sense of the sublime in the viewer according to mathematical principles. In this sense, something previously considered immeasurable can now be codified and represented. Something as elusive and abstract as sublime experience is "enframed" by the grid of the screen, as well as the framework of decimal logic. The net effect – as much aesthetic as rationalistic – reinforces the notion of Man as the measurer, if not the measure. It uses technology and special effects to create a kind of God effect – or an Archimedean point – even as it acknowledges significant gaps in our own knowledge of The Way Things Are. *Powers of Ten* is such an enduring document because it continues to suggest that the human is the species that can transcend its cosmic parochialism through the earnest application of its own tools. We are the animal that can embrace its own exceptional destiny as "prosthetic gods" (to quote Freud).

Cosmographs

But what happens when we realize that even our most sophisticated maps are woefully inadequate? How do we rationalize the fact that any representation we make – especially of something as vast as the universe – is bound to be anything but "lossless" (to adapt a concept from the sonic realm)? In the age of the Hubble and James Webb telescopes, have we really progressed beyond those old cartographic tricks of simply filling in the blanks by speculating "here be dragons"?

One popular image, of unconfirmed origin, circulating through nerdy networks online is an "observable universe map in logarithmic scale." This image is unabashedly heliocentric, as if our own solar system were in the middle of a strong fisheye lens, and the overall optical effect is that the universe itself looks uncannily like a human eye. (A detail or conceit that Stanley Kubrick would no doubt appreciate, given his own investment in the figure of the "cosmic human witness" . . . in this case, suggesting a rather flattering notion that the universe is looking back at us!) The endless quest for increasingly detailed and comprehensive maps – even of spaces and places where no human will ever come close to setting foot – has a long history. The historian of science John Tresch has studied the history of maps whose ambitions are nothing less than representing the entire known universe.[1] "Cosmograms," as they are called, not only "convey relations among human, natural, and divine realms" but can also "serve as propositions for how the world might be, with utopian, eschatological, or simply conciliatory aims." More often, however, "they serve didactic, dogmatic, propagandistic ends." In other words, such maps tell us more about the time in which they were being created – and the minds that made them – than anything objective about a geo-cosmic "reality" that they claim to index. They thus tautologically represent the visual legacy of our "will to represent," as well as our drive towards an omniscient comprehension.

Today we have largely abandoned the naïve quest to produce One True Map of Everything. Instead, we multiply diagrams, charts, renderings, data, and data visualization models in a kind of collective faith that they will all add up, eventually, to essentially the same thing. (Even as no one single mind will ever be able to perceive the result, save for some kind of supreme computational Singularity.) The totalizing spirit of the Age of the World Picture continues, albeit in a billion different refresh screens, none of which can communicate with the others in any kind of coherent or coordinated way. (As much as the CIA dreams of such.) As Tresch himself notes, "The planet is now shattered into an array of 'planetarities': the globe of free trade, the calculable systems of earth science, the spiritual or indigenous nature beneath the pavement, a geopolitics redrawn by industrial powers outside the West, the elusive and unpredictable Gaia." Humans, so to say, dream of nice, simple tree diagrams, while encouraging the conditions to exponentially multiply the rhizomes which entangle our attempts to locate and fix our own place in the universe. ("You are here!")

Cosmographs are thus a quintessential example of what Nietzsche famously critiques as an *exclusively human* truth (and, thus, not a very impressive truth at all): the *Homo sapiens* urge to confuse metaphors, analogies, allegories, ideas, and concepts for the Real Itself. Human minds, to Nietzsche's own way of thinking, are portable planetaria, designed to project cultural patterns, stories, definitions, perspectives, interpretations, and so on, *on* to the natural world, or given order of things. We are thus mesmerized by our own symbolic filtering of reality. (An inevitable "translation" program that also stymied Kant, who believed we could never hope to have unmediated access to Things-in-Themselves but must be satisfied with our facility and familiarity with the second-order phenomena, once it has passed through the organic parsing operation of our perceptual faculties and the cultural processing of conceptual grids.)

The Clever Beasts

It's worth returning again to the opening lines of Nietzsche's essay "On Truth and Lies in a Nonmoral Sense," which could indeed be mistaken for the most depressing children's book ever:

> Once upon a time, in some out of the way corner of that universe which is dispersed into numberless twinkling solar systems, there was a star upon which clever beasts invented knowing. That was the most arrogant and mendacious minute of 'world history,' but nevertheless, it was only a minute. After

> nature had drawn a few breaths, the star cooled and congealed, and the clever beasts had to die.[2]

For the skeptical German philosopher, humans are alienated from the world in which they emerged to the same degree that they believe they have some kind of intellectual key to its purpose or workings. (Often conflated as the same thing.) "One might invent such a fable," Nietzsche writes, "and yet he still would not have adequately illustrated how miserable, how shadowy and transient, how aimless and arbitrary the human intellect looks within nature." This is indeed a shrewd, comic move: depicting the human as the equivalent of the insufferable young man in the second-year philosophy class, who arrogantly presumes to have understood everything but is in fact chasing the phantom tail of profound ignorance.

Nietzsche's rather insulting portrait of his own species was indeed a philosophical call back to Copernicus, only now tailored to ridicule the academic reflex of placing the human as the unquestioned center of things, even in the high scientific age. Nietzsche had little patience with anyone who sought to place humanity as the cosmic protagonist (though he would go on to ask what we would have to change before deserving to reaudition for such a role). His writings therefore expose the arrogance – even delusion – behind such philosophical riddles as, "If a tree falls in the forest, and there is no one there to hear it, does it make a sound?" From the Nietzschean perspective, such a koan is the height of unabashed humanism. (Unless we count birds, squirrels, and beavers as a person, which well we might. Not even to mention the status of the tree itself!)

Of course, a modern physicist would be less likely to pose the question in such a way. Indeed, why should an effect – any shift or intensification in mass or energy – be somehow *witnessed* or registered by a "rational animal" for it to have occurred, for it to have ontological validity? The idea is preposterous from the perspective of "science." And yet there is still the residual sense that the scientist, him- or herself, is somehow *bequeathing* added reality on to the changing face of

Nature by virtue of observations and registrations. A romance continues, albeit in a minor key, where the human is still witness, created *by the universe itself* (rather than God) in order to validate itself. (A flattering scenario we see most often in popular science books or articles, even today.) The human as self-appointed Big Other. The human as glorified parking validation mechanism. For Nietzsche, however, we should not feel too cocky about our place in the supposed great chain of being. After all, "when it is all over with the human intellect, nothing will have happened." Why not? Well, primarily because "this intellect has no additional mission which would lead it beyond human life. Rather, it is human, and only its possessor and begetter takes it so solemnly – as though the world's axis turned within it."

Granted, anthropocentrism is a hard lesson to unlearn, especially on an *affective* level, since we *feel* so central, so very indispensable. After all, we are the animal that invented an entire "science" – astrology – that rests on the premise that our tiny, meaningless, insignificant lives are somehow "written in the stars" and reflected in heavenly bodies. (A conceit that would really be justified only if every and any entity whatever was similarly pre-inscribed via celestial fates.) Even after Copernicus, Darwin, Freud, Deep Blue, and Donald Trump, we still stubbornly insist – deep down in our viscera – that there's something special about humans: "a continuous fluttering around the *solitary* flame of vanity." Indeed, most of us are closet human supremacists, with all the sense of existential entitlement that comes with it, despite the abundant evidence to the contrary. (Further evidence for Nietzscheans that we are "most unfortunate, delicate, and ephemeral beings," lost in "the land of ghostly schemata.")

How to account for this cognitive dissonance? How to explain the fact that we now *know* how irrelevant we are, cosmically speaking, and yet we continue to claim some kind of ontological privilege or exceptionalism? Why is it that we still like to depict ourselves as bringers of enlightenment when we are literally in the dark about 99.99 percent of existence? Indeed, as Nietzsche reminds us, we are a black box even to ourselves. When it comes to Man, "[d]oes nature not conceal most things from him – even concerning his own body – in order to confine and lock him within a proud, deceptive consciousness, aloof from the coils of the bowels, the rapid flow of the blood stream, and the intricate quivering of the fibers!"[3]

But, as unflinchingly perceptive as he is, Nietzsche perhaps unwittingly outs himself as a human exceptionalist, albeit in a negative sense. "Everything which distinguishes man from the animals," he writes, "depends upon this ability to volatilize perceptual metaphors in a schema, and thus to dissolve an image into a concept." Humans are, in other words, the animals that allowed themselves to get lost in a mental fog; concepts forming new scales on our eyes, allowing us to only see through a glass darkly. We are thus the metaphorical animal, the inessential animal.

There is, however, even more to the story. "That which makes us human is something totally *subjective*. It is the accumulated ancestral estate in which everyone has a share." Nietzsche here is alluding to a kind of collective subjectivity: what Jean-Luc Nancy called "being singular plural," or what Gilbert Simondon called "transindividuation." This is another way in which humans can perhaps lay claim to an exceptional condition, being the animal that has learned to forge an objective form of memory – through our writings, artifacts, artworks, tools, media, and so on. Where other animals proceed through the world, seemingly leaving no trace beyond ripples, footprints, feathers, and – eventually – bones, humans leave wills, instructions, memoirs, blueprints, plans, machines, record collections, and of course maps. And it is this *third* type of memory – beyond the biology and biography of other individual creatures – that really makes us human (for better or for worse). Hence one of the central paradoxes of humanity: our sense of self is largely a temporary coalescence of *pre*-personal affects and *im*personal ideas. What we think of as our most precious and intimate "personality" turns out to be little more than the echoes and residues of our forebears. Our own soul is revealed as a case of existential photocopying, or even plagiarism.

All of which is to say: Nietzsche is one of the patron saints of "sad planets" since he is one of the most attuned figures to the absurdity of our cosmic predicament. (Even as he attempted to turn this absurdity into an opportunity to "get over ourselves" and become something more impressive and less deluded. Something deserving of the accolades we already give ourselves.) It makes sense, then, that Nietzsche – who on more than one occasion seemed to relish a kind of egoistic callousness towards the suffering of others – famously broke down while witnessing the beating of a horse in a square in Turin: a breakdown from which he never recovered. For while his name is associated with the *Übermensch*, or superman – and the creation and practice of a "joyful" science – Nietzsche was ultimately a melancholic who suffered powerful and frequent bouts of *acedia*.

Like many of our other sorrowful saints, this amoral genealogist understood that we live in a dark "out of the way corner of the universe." Moreover, he felt in his bones that "the clever animals had to die." What to do with a life that is both spatially forsaken and temporally doomed? *This* is the modern philosophical question par excellence. Intellectually, Nietzsche understood the dark irony that the stars above – those glittering, awe-inspiring pinpricks in the heavens – are quite likely to be already extinguished, given how long it takes for such light to reach the Earth. But even he could not resist placing some kind of hope – or at least some kind of alien redemptive integrity – in the figure of the star.

As he writes, in poet mode, in a prelude to *The Joyful Science*:

Ordained to move as planets do,
What matters, star, the dark to you?
Roll blithely through our human time!
Beyond its wretched mis'ry climb!
The furthest world deserves your shine:
For you compassion is a crime!
One law applies to you: be thine![4]

Objective Allegories

Some ironies go beyond embodying a sly or paradoxical cultural lesson and crystallize into something profound – more ineluctable – about the world itself, in all its brute and stupid facticity. (That is to say, in all its negotiations with human obscenity.) Take for instance the photos of people recharging their Tesla electric cars with highly polluting generators because power grids are down. Or consider the significant spike in carbon release required for all the participants in the United Nations Climate Change conference, hosted in Glasgow in 2021. (Not to mention all the protestors, who also felt the imperative to be there.)

But even more potent than examples of what Jean Baudrillard would call "objective ironies" are the flurry of objective allegories that the current news-scape is serving up for our bleak delectation. Consider the infamous Fyre Festival of 2018: a debacle so resonant that it required *two* high-profile documentaries to capture the chaos that so clearly and closely mimicked – in perfect microcosm – the false promises of late-stage, proto-collapse capitalism. (Especially as it sells itself in the guise of the experience-based economy, as filtered through the pleasure-by-proxy prisms of social media.) Consider also the ill-fated cruise ship, in the very first weeks of the Covid pandemic, drifting on the ocean, carrying corpses from port to port, in a vain search for a country willing to take the infected human cargo. Few people, when encountering this story, would not realize in their bones that *the whole world* was now this cruise ship: the planet abandoned to its fate, as the buffet dwindled to nothing, the plumbing system filled with feverish excreta – the gills of the population, green with fear and nausea – with no exit on the horizon. Or consider the latest candidate for perfect objective allegory: the container ship in 2022 on fire in the Atlantic, with all crew winched to safety, but now burdened with hundreds of luxury cars burning, bubbling, and blistering in the hold. So many dreams of high-octane freedom – so many solvent solutions to mid-life crises – now going up in flames: 1,100 brand-new Porsches and 189 Bentleys providing toxic kindling to a massive bonfire of the vanities, adrift in the ocean, as much as in the wave-tossed nightmares of the insurance underwriters. One can't help but wonder if one Porsche's car horn started sounding in alarm as the temperatures became unbearable, causing panic to sweep through the hold; each separate luxury vehicle picking up the terrified refrain, its leather interiors blistering, and its sleek horse power now stampeding in a lost, shrill chorus, shrieking into the blazing night.

Exhibit D

Objective allegory is not especially new, however. Take for instance the canary resuscitator: a rather gothic object, used in late nineteenth-century mining operations, that would attempt to breathe life back into an ailing canary in a hazardous coal mine. Indeed, so many of our technologies today could be considered simply newfangled iterations of the canary resuscitator – treating the symptom rather than the disease.

Global Happiness Index

Once a year, news outlets report the findings of the Global Happiness Index – a well-meaning, but surely misguided, attempt to measure something as intangible as happiness. The index – created in collaboration with sociologists, psychologists, economists, and other such diviners of human souls from external indicators – takes into account an entire mesh of psycho-social factors, including average income, social services, support networks, functional infrastructure, self-reported satisfaction surveys, as well as daily lives relatively untainted by pollution or unravaged by war. As to be expected, the richer nations sit on top of the rankings – with Finland, Denmark, and Switzerland taking the top three places in 2020. (Though having myself lived in Switzerland for two years, I would quibble with the description of their collective state of mind as "happy.") Of course, if we flip the index from top to bottom, then we also get a Global Sadness Index. There are, again, no surprises to see countries such as Afghanistan, Rwanda, and Haiti down at the bottom of the scale.

The idea of quantifying a nebulous affect like "happiness" is patently absurd, even if it does correlate with important human values – healthcare, education, and freedom of movement and association. Given that the Constitution of the United States guarantees the freedom to engage in "the pursuit of happiness," it also makes a strange kind of sense that social scientists would eventually decide to figure out an instrument that measures such a state. The language of the Constitution, however, places happiness more in the position of a goal than a condition – or even a type of quarry. The codified assumption is that we should be free to *pursue* happiness, even as such a promise is likely to be forever out of reach, like a will-o'-the-wisp or greased piglet.

A Global Sadness Index – taking people's innermost hearts more than objective metrics into account – would no doubt yield a less predictable ranking than the one that so clearly mirrors over-determined factors such as GDP and tax bracket. The stereotype of poor but happy villagers is no doubt offensive and inaccurate. And yet sadness is not only the curse of low-income people. And the old cliché "money doesn't buy happiness" holds more than a grain of truth. (Though money *does*, to be sure, afford a much better class of misery.)

The most interesting aspect of a pseudo-scientific "index," for any affect whatever, is the way it attempts to trace the mobius strip between the self and the social, the individual and the collective. It's perfectly possible to find oneself the solitary "glum bum" in a generally merry group, just as it's conversely feasible to be strangely giddy among a group of sad sacks. But, on the whole, affect is shared and infectious – at least when it is spontaneous and genuine rather than obliged or expected. "Misery loves company," notes the old saying, to the extent that it will actively enlist others in such a state of mind (cf. the increasingly exquisite art of passive aggression). Sadness is hard to contain and billows out into the room like soot blown back down the chimney. Freud, of course, understood that some of the most outwardly jovial people are merely masking an especially deep melancholy, to the extent where they themselves may not even know their own condition and are instead trying to outsource their own sadness to others. Spinoza also understood the extent to which the sad passions communicate themselves between people, not unlike a contagion or virus. (Though as the Earl of Shaftesbury also noted, enthusiasm is a self-perpetuating emotion, often prompting us to become excited before we even know the occasion for such – something dogs absolutely excel at.)

Sadness is such a slick and slippery thing to grasp because it can be intensely personal: an icy, grimacing eel, curled up in the heart, that no one else can see or slay. But it can also be ambient, atmospheric – absolutely *im*personal: the troubling cosmic ripples of Mercury in retrograde. Sorrow can be a cloud one carries over one's own head, or a vast weather-front, menacing the entire continent. What's more, these different scales of sadness swirl together, like differently textured black paints on the messy and mottled palette of human feeling.

Indexicality

The idea of an *index* evokes the semiotic concept of "indexicality": a rather fancy word, meaning the real-world impression left by someone, or something, on its surroundings. An "indexical sign" consists of a physical trace, like a stain, scratch, bullet, or footprint. (In contrast to a symbolic sign, which has no real-world connection to the thing that it is signifying but, rather, is figured through cultural association.) The very existence of a Global Happiness Index, however, begs a related question: what are some *indexical* signs of happiness? An ice cream on the ground? Surely not! That would be a tangible sign of recent tears or tantrums. A balloon stuck in a tree? Also uncertain, as this could be just as much the evidence of a disappointing party than a fun-filled one. A lone sandcastle on the beach? Again, perhaps not. Perhaps this sea-shell-studded fortification was assembled out of a heavy sense of obligation to an overly solicitous parent, and soon washed away by the waves, in any case. What about a polaroid of a honeymoon, then? Surely *this* is a material index of happiness. Well, it may indeed be true that the obedient chemicals on Polaroid's patented surface were imprinted with smile-infused photons, which themselves happened to have the good fortune to convey, and subsequently capture, a genuinely happy moment. The ghostly persistence of the image, however, now hidden away between the moldering covers of a seldom-touched photograph album – or, alternatively, displayed so prominently that it has now been rendered invisible by the sheer over-familiarity of its domestic presence – now works diligently backwards through time, hollowing out the original innocence and immediacy of the happy occasion through sheer, stubborn duration. Lipstick on a collar? Well, this classic example may indeed betray a material trace of an ecstatic moment. But its inevitable discovery will soon excite paranoia, anger, jealousy, defensiveness, and so on.

In fact, the more we try to itemize objects, souvenirs, or other remnants of pleasure, the more a sense of pathos muscles morosely into the picture. The temporal element – the passing of time – seems to scrub happiness of its spontaneous warmth, leaving only remains or residues. Sadness, on the other hand, when leaving its impression upon the world, exhibits no such ambivalence. Gravestones, broken bottles, ripped tickets, burst balloons, unworn clothes, discarded pill dispensers, yellowed Dear John letters – they all fit into the environment more organically than the flotsam of fun. No doubt, this is partly because sadness is easier to sustain: an extended symphony rather than a passing pop song. But it is also because sorrow is a more "natural" fit with the environment – especially the *human* environment – since both stem from what Georges Bataille called our fundamental "discontinuity" with the universe at large. Since we find ourselves unceremoniously thrown into this world – and, what's more, mentally equipped to register the extent of our existential estrangement from the rest of the cosmic ballet – it makes perfect sense that the tangible record of our passage through life – all these artificial fossils we leave behind in the brief, warm window between inanimacies – would combine to form the general shape of what Freud called "the nostalgia for returning to brute matter."

In short, there is something about happiness that refuses to be pinned down, memorialized – *indexed*. Sadness, on the other hand, is only too happy to oblige, forever leaving evidence of itself around the scene of the existential crime. (That is to say, the crime of existing at all.)

Sad Things (a Partial Inventory)

- broken dreams
- dashed hopes
- enthusiasm
- unrequited love
- squandered opportunities
- wasted efforts
- unrealized talents
- injured animals
- homemade lost dog signs
- an empty restaurant next to a bustling one
- a moth-eaten teddy bear missing one button-eye
- the certitude of youth (at any age)
- old, unread love letters
- new, just read rejection letters
- music composed in the key of D
- coach terminals after sundown
- nursing homes after, and before, sundown
- abandoned fun parks
- a pet after its owner has died
- Soviet-era playgrounds
- pawn shops
- porn shows
- underwear with holes, still in rotation
- underfunded orphanages

- meals prepared without love
- meaningless sentience
- sparsely attended book parties
- the photos of Jacob Riis
- a tied-up dog sitting patiently outside a convenience store – it starts to rain
- the paintings of Edward Hopper
- a new business, opened by a recently arrived middle-aged immigrant couple, but one that is not a good fit for the neighborhood
- an outdoor wedding party during a torrential rainstorm
- that moment in *Highlander* when Connor MacLeod's wife appears on screen, suddenly aged decades older than him (for he is immortal)
- a senior citizen caught in a closing bus door because he's too slow to get off at his stop
- a woman on a blind date waiting in vain for her companion to come back from "the bathroom"
- a humble farmer in an old black-and-white movie wearing a borrowed suit and holding his hat in his hands like a shabby steering wheel made of felt
- waking up
- dawn

No More Happy Returns

We began this sad, planetary journey with the Mars Opportunity Rover: a plucky NASA robot on wheels, worthy of its own Pixar franchise. This all-terrain off-world probe, affectionately known as "Oppy," spent fourteen years, from 2004 to 2018, collecting samples, taking photos, and sending gigabytes of information back to scientists on Earth. Since the Rover was given an official serial number in 2003 (SATCAT-27849), we can say that Oppy was fifteen years old when it either died or simply ceased to function (the preferred phrase depending on your own particular investment in anthropomorphizing conscientious machines). Five years before Oppy's battery "died," another Rover arrived to help explore the surface of the red planet: the Curiosity Rover. This veteran workhorse has been mapping the alien landscape – taking climate measurements and performing other related tasks – since 2013. At the time of writing (in the fall of 2022), Curiosity is still officially curious, way up there on Mars. (Perhaps, like a cat, this rover has nine lives.)

To celebrate the first successful year of Curiosity's mission, NASA engineers playfully reprogrammed the robot to "sing" "Happy Birthday" to itself. (In truth closer to a kind of humming, like an old dot-matrix printer.) Sadly, Oppy could not share in the celebrations, since the two droids were approximately 8,400 kilometers apart from each other. As a result, a journalist from *The Atlantic* magazine called this moment "perhaps the loneliest birthday in the galaxy." This same writer learned that the whimsical occasion in fact happened only once. And so she decided to contact the space agency to find out why they did not feel the need to repeat it. The answer, from the deputy chief technologist at NASA's Science Mission Directorate, sounded rather cold: "In a nutshell, there is no scientific gain from the rover playing music or singing 'Happy Birthday' on Mars." Clearly, scientists are not infected by the bug that encourages many of us to personalize machines. But as one user on Twitter noted, "It's literally an inanimate object. Why am I still crying?" Why indeed.

Two robots, toiling thousands of miles apart, one eventually succumbing to a strong dust storm – and communicating no more – and the other still working diligently, even as its nuclear battery might, at any moment, run out. (And even as it is now denied a micro-break from its 24/7 schedule to sing itself "Happy Birthday" once a year.)

Is this – in any way, from any angle, by any stretch of the imagination – objectively sad? Or is it just yet another insentient opportunity for us to project our melancholia into the firmament – an alibi for smearing our own sorrow across the solar system?

The answer, we submit, is somewhere in between. For where did that sorrow come from in the first place, if not from the cosmos in which we also float and toil and sing ourselves little songs, and eventually expire?

"Why am I still crying?"

Why indeed.

Notes

Sequence 1

1 Margolis.
2 Bataille, 1989, p. 19.
3 Nietzsche, 1974, Bk 3, #224.
4 "The Death of Stars."
5 *New Revised Standard Version Bible*, Catholic edn. Nashville: Thomas Nelson, 1993.
6 Sagan, pp. 12–13.
7 Milman.
8 Turkina.
9 Bradbury, p. 26.

Sequence 2

1 Huygens, pp. 299–300, translation ours.
2 Greene, p. 45.
3 Ibid., p. 41.
4 Ficino, 1997, p. 160.
5 Ibid.
6 Ibid.
7 Ficino, 2019, p. 115.
8 Kilbansky et al., pp. 331–2.
9 Ficino, 2019, III: xxii, p. 365.
10 Kilbansky et al. pp. 359–60.
11 *Hamlet*, I, ii, 129–30.
12 Shakespeare, Sonnet no. 73, 5–8.
13 Petrarch, Sonnet no. 312, 1; no. 329, 6; no. 329, 2.
14 Stampa, Sonnet no. 213, 169.
15 Góngora, I, pp. 681–3.
16 Milton, *Il Penseroso*, 13–16.

17 Verlaine, pp. 19–20.
18 Nietzsche, 1966, "The Drunken Song," p. 323.
19 Macrobius, p. 65.
20 Ibid., p. 64.
21 Voltaire, p. 9.
22 Ibid., p. 10.
23 Sebald, pp. 90–1.
24 Ibid., p. 181.
25 Ibid., p. 52.
26 Ibid., p. 31.
27 Benjamin, p. 190.
28 Ibid., p. 188.
29 Ibid., p. 140.
30 Sebald, p. 237.

Sequence 3

1 Liu, p. 175.
2 Ibid., p. 324.
3 Ibid., p. 253.
4 Buchanan.
5 Cicero, p. 55.
6 Cavazzoni, pp. 29–31.
7 Flusser, 2013, p. 71.

Sequence 4

1 Tarlach.
2 Endicott.
3 Fanon, p. 251.
4 Sun Ra, 2011, p. 5.
5 Sun Ra, 2014, pp. 88–9.
6 Ibid.
7 Sun Ra, 2011, p. 18.
8 Ibid., p. 56.

Sequence 5

1 Byron, "Darkness," ll. 2–5.
2 Ibid., ll. 24–30.
3 Ibid., ll. 69, 72.
4 Cuvier, p. 3.
5 Ibid.

6 "Milestone for humanity."
7 Morselli, p. 9.
8 Ibid., p. 21.
9 Ibid., p. 40.
10 Nietzsche, 2012, p. 159.
11 Morselli, p. 75.
12 Defoe, p. 51.
13 Ibid., p. 90.
14 Ibid., p. 91.
15 Ibid., p. 111.
16 Haushofer, p. 209.
17 James, p. 161.
18 Haushofer, p. 210.
19 Athanasius, pp. 42–3.
20 Abe, p. 14.
21 Benedicta Ward, p. 8.
22 Ibid., p. 10.
23 Ibid., p. 173.
24 Ibid., p. 11.
25 Turgenev, 1920, pp. 254–5.
26 Ibid., p. 255.
27 Ibid.
28 Ibid., p. 256.
29 Ibid., pp. 256–7.
30 Turgenev, 1999, p. 90.
31 Yi Sang, p. 135.
32 Ibid., p. 136.

Sequence 6

1 Blackwood, 1924, p. 37.
2 Blackwood, 1901, p. 354.
3 Ibid., p. 426.
4 Ibid.
5 Ibid., p. 354.
6 Blackwood, 2002, p. 52.
7 McSweeney, p. 15.
8 Kyōka, p. 175.
9 Ibid., p. 37.
10 Ibid.
11 Le Guin, p. 124.
12 Ibid., p. 125.
13 Ibid., p. 128.
14 Blackwood, 2002, p. 51.
15 Wilk, p. 4.

16 Ibid., p. 9.
17 Burnet, p. xiii.
18 Ibid., p. 68.
19 Ibid.
20 Kyōka, p. 43.
21 Ruskin, p. 152.
22 Ibid., pp. 152–3.
23 Ibid., p. 154.
24 Ibid., p. 155.
25 Ibid.
26 Ibid.
27 Blair, pp. 1–2.
28 Ruskin, p. 158.
29 Ibid., p. 159.
30 Ibid.
31 Raffles, p. 78.
32 Ibid., p. 80.

Sequence 7

1 Lévi-Strauss, p. 38.
2 Ibid., p. 23.
3 Ibid., p. 413.
4 Ibid., p. 414.
5 Ibid., p. 415.
6 Ibid., p. 413.
7 Strickland and Harris.
8 Cioran, p. 59.
9 Ibid., pp. 58–60.
10 Ibid., p. 60.
11 Ibid., pp. 34–5.
12 Ibid., pp. 57–8.
13 Ibid., p. 122.
14 Ibid., p. 92.
15 Bunch, pp. 29–30.
16 Baumer, p. 81.
17 Ibid., I.
18 Ibid., III.

Sequence 8

1 Sontag, p. 390.
2 Flammarion, p. 285.
3 Wells, 1899, p. 57.

4 McGinn, p. 7.
5 Rumi, p. 168.
6 *The Mirror of My Heart*, p. 247.
7 Tang Yaping, p. 137.
8 de Camp, p. 287.
9 Ibid.
10 Wall, 21 December 2017.
11 Chuang Tzu, p. 327.
12 Browne, p. 263.
13 Rosny aîné, 2018, p. 18, translation ours.
14 Ibid., p. 29.
15 Ibid., p. 30.
16 Ibid.
17 Rampino et al.
18 Kant, 1996, p. 221.
19 Ibid.
20 Ibid., p. 225.
21 Ibid., p. 224.
22 Ibid.

Sequence 9

1 Lem, p. 176.
2 Ibid., pp. 17–18.
3 Ibid., p. 116.
4 Ibid., p. 119.
5 Ibid., p. 117.
6 Ibid., pp. 120–1.
7 Ibid., p. 72.
8 Ibid.
9 Lenau, p. 20.
10 Kant, 2000, p. 140.
11 Radcliffe, pp. 148, 149.
12 Kant, 2000, p. 158.

Sequence 10

1 Sturgeon, pp. 180–2.
2 Barnes, p. 98.
3 "Greta Thunberg's speech."
4 See Grebowicz.
5 See Graeber and Wengrow.
6 Flusser, 2012, p. 49.
7 Ibid., p. 50.

8 Ibid., p. 63.
9 Ibid., pp. 63–4.
10 Ibid., pp. 66–7.
11 See Lewis.
12 McMenamin and McMenamin, p. xiii.
13 See Pettman.
14 McMenamin and McMenamin, p. 4.
15 Ibid.
16 Ibid., p. 5.
17 Ibid., p. 6.
18 Ibid., p. 4.
19 Coccia, p. 35.
20 See Thacker.
21 Lingis, p. 2.
22 "The Death of Stars."

Sequence 11

1 Kavan, p. 142.
2 Ibid.
3 Ibid., p. 117.
4 Ibid., pp. 122–3.
5 Ballard, 2005, p. 78.
6 Ibid., p. 76.
7 Rosny aîné, 1968, p. 112.
8 Stifter, pp. 46–7.
9 Ibid., pp. 60–1.

Sequence 12

1 Baudelaire, p. 90.
2 Ibid., p. 91.
3 Ibid., p. 92.
4 Hippocrates, *Aphorisms*, LVI, p. 193
5 Foucault, p. 122.
6 Ibid.
7 Leopardi, pp. 170–1.
8 Ibid., pp. 162–6.
9 Nietzsche, 2012, p. 155.
10 Burton, p. 237.
11 Ibid.
12 Ibid., p. 16.
13 Ibid., p. 332.
14 Keats, pp.11–12.

15 Burton, p. 237.
16 Ibid.
17 Ibid., p. 148.
18 Ibid., p. 39.
19 Ibid., p. 43.
20 Ibid.
21 Rosenthal, p. 4.
22 Ibid., p. 6.
23 Watsuji, p. 2.
24 Ibid., p. 3.

Sequence 13

1 Martinson, #102, p. 148.
2 Ibid., #10, p. 44.
3 Ibid., #74, pp. 123–4.
4 Ibid., #103, p. 149.
5 Ibid., #103, p. 148.
6 Berg, p. 25.
7 Ibid., p. 27.
8 Ibid.
9 Ibid., p. viii.
10 Ibid.
11 Ibid., p. 105.
12 Kierkegaard, 1996, p. 413.
13 Ibid., p. 13.
14 Margulis, p. 145.
15 Peter Ward, p. 35.
16 Euripides, 258–63.
17 Nietzsche, 2012, p. 159.
18 Ibid.
19 Ibid.
20 Ibid., p. 158.
21 Ballard, 2010, p. 2375.
22 Ibid.
23 Ibid.
24 Ibid.
25 Pascal, p. 60.
26 Ibid.
27 Ibid., p. 61.
28 Ibid.
29 Ibid., p. 60.
30 Kierkegaard, 1983, p. xii.

Sequence 14

1 "Brightest galaxy in Abell 2261."
2 Wall, 1 January 2021.
3 Nietzsche, 2000, p. 79.
4 Ibid., p. 52.
5 Nietzsche, 2012, p. 236.
6 *Rig Veda*, 10.129, p. 25.
7 Ibid.
8 Ibid.
9 Ibid.
10 Ibid., 10.121, p. 27.
11 Ibid., 10.90, p. 30.
12 Ibid., p. 31.
13 Ibid., 1.185, p. 204.
14 Eliade, 1971, p. 96.
15 Ibid., p. 98.
16 Eliade, 1987, p. 12.
17 Bataille, 1988, p. 20.
18 Ibid., p. 21.
19 Ibid.
20 Bataille, 2004, p. 221.
21 Eliade, 1971, p. 100.
22 Schopenhauer, p. 114.

Sequence 15

1 Barthes, p. 56.
2 Albrecht, 2019, p. 200.
3 See Dodson.
4 Albrecht et al., 2007, p. S95.
5 Tokarczuk, pp. 162–3.
6 Danielson, p. 62.

Sequence 16

1 Tresch.
2 Nietzsche, 2000, p. 79.
3 Ibid., p. 80.
4 Nietzsche, 2023, pp. 33, 35.

References

Abe, Kōbō, *Woman in the Dunes*, trans. E. Dale Saunders. Rutland, VT: Tuttle, [1962] 1967.

Albrecht, Glenn, *Earth Emotions*. Ithaca, NY: Cornell University Press, 2019.

Albrecht, Glenn, et al., "Solastalgia: the distress caused by environmental change," *Australasian Psychiatry*, 15 (2007), suppl.

Athanasius, *The Life of Antony and the Letter to Marcellus*, trans. Robert Gregg. Mahwah, NJ: Paulist Press, 1972.

Auerbach-Baidani, Emanuel Jakob, *Astroloetheia*. Privately pubd, 2022.

Ballard, J. G., *The Crystal World*. London: HarperPerennial, 2005.

—— "Report on an Unidentified Space Station," in *The Complete Short Stories of J. G. Ballard*. New York: W. W. Norton, 2010.

Barnes, Julian, *Staring at the Sun*. New York: Knopf Doubleday, 1993.

Barthes, Roland, *Mythologies*, trans. Annette Lavers. New York: Noonday Press, 1991.

Bataille, Georges, *The Accursed Share: An Essay on General Economy*, Vol. I, trans. Robert Hurley. New York: Zone Books, 1988.

—— *Theory of Religion*, trans. Robert Huxley. New York: Zone Books, 1989.

—— "The congested planet," in *The Unfinished System of Non-Knowledge*, trans. Michelle Kendall and Stuart Kendall. Minneapolis: University of Minnesota Press, 2004.

Baudelaire, Charles, *The Flowers of Evil*, trans. Marthiel Mathews and Jackson Mathews. New York: New Directions, 1989.

Baumer, Mark, *The One on Earth: The Selected Works of Mark Baumer*, ed. Blake Butler and Shane Jones. Hudson, NY: Fence Books, 2021.

Benjamin, Walter, *The Origin of the German Trauerspiel*, trans. Howard Elland. Cambridge, MA: Harvard University Press, 2019.

Berg, Aase, *Dark Matter*, trans. Johannes Göransson. Boston: Black Ocean, 2013.

Blackwood, Algernon, "Down the Danube in a Canadian canoe," *Macmillan's Magazine*, LXXXIV (1901), pp. 350–8, 418–29.

—— *Episodes Before Thirty*. London: E. P. Dutton, 1924.
—— "The Willows," in *Ancient Sorceries and Other Weird Stories*, ed. S. T. Joshi. London: Penguin, [1907] 2002.
Blair, Robert, *The Grave: A Poem. With Illustrations, from Designs by William Blake*. London, 1847.
Boeke, Kees, *Cosmic View: The Universe in 40 Jumps*. New York: John Day, 1957.
Bradbury, Ray, "Kaleidoscope," in *The Illustrated Man*. New York: Bantam, 1972.
Browne, Thomas, *The Major Works: Religio Medici, Hydriotaphia, The Garden of Cyprus, A Letter to a Friend, and Christian Morals*, ed. C. A. Patrides. Harmondsworth: Penguin, 1977.
Bunch, David R., *Moderan*. New York: New York Review Books, 2018.
Burnet, Thomas, *The Sacred Theory of the Earth*. Glasgow: R. Urie, [1684] 1753.
Burton, Robert, *The Anatomy of Melancholy*, ed. Floyd Dell and Paul Jordan-Smith. New York: Tudor, [1621] 1927.
Byron, George Gordon, *Selected Poems*, ed. Susan J. Wolfson and Peter J. Manning. London: Penguin, 2006.
Cavazzoni, Ermanno, *Brief Lives of Idiots*. Cambridge, MA: Wakefield Press, 2021.
Chōmei and Kenkō, *Essays in Idleness and Hōjōki*, trans. Meredith McKinney. London: Penguin, 2014.
Chuang Tzu, *The Complete Works of Chuang Tzu*, trans. Burton Watson. New York: Columbia University Press, 1968.
Cicero, *The Nature of the Gods*, trans. P. G. Walsh. Oxford: Oxford University Press, 2008.
Cioran, E. M., *Drawn and Quartered*, trans. Richard Howard. New York: Arcade, 2012.
Coccia, Emmanuel, *The Life of Plants: A Metaphysics of Mixture*. Cambridge: Polity, 2018.
Cuvier, Georges, *Essay on the Theory of the Earth*, trans. Robert Jameson. Edinburgh: Blackwood, [1813] 1827.
Danielson, Dennis (ed.), *The Book of the Cosmos: Imagining the Universe from Heraclitus to Hawking*. New York: Basic Books, 2002.
de Camp, L. Sprague, *Lost Continents: The Atlantis Theme*. New York: Ballantine Books, 1970.
Defoe, Daniel, *Robinson Crusoe*, ed. John Richetti. London: Penguin, 2003.
Dodson, Thomas, *What Nostalgia Was: War, Empire, and the Time of a Deadly Emotion*. Chicago: University of Chicago Press, 2018.
Dostoevsky, Fyodor, "The Dream of a Ridiculous Man," in *A Writer's Diary*, Vol. 2: *1877–1881*, trans. Kenneth Lantz. Evanston, IL: Northwestern University Press, 1994.
Du Bois, W. E. B., "The Comet," in *Dark Matter: A Century of Speculative*

Fiction from the African Diaspora, ed. Sheree R. Thomas. New York: Warner, [1920] 2000.
Eliade, Mircea, *The Myth of the Eternal Return; or, Cosmos and History*, trans. Willard Trask. Princeton, NJ: Princeton University Press, 1971.
—— *The Sacred and the Profane: The Nature of Religion*, trans. Willard Trask. San Diego: Harcourt, 1987.
Endicott, Clara, *Days of Delusion: A Strange Bit of History*. Boston: Houghton-Mifflin, 1924.
Euripides, *Medea and Other Plays*, trans. Diane Arnson Svarlien. Indianapolis: Hackett, 2008.
Fanon, Frantz, *The Wretched of the Earth*, trans. Constance Farrington. New York: Grove Press, 1963.
Ficino, Marsilio, *Meditations on the Soul: Selected Letters*, ed. Clement Salaman. Rochester, VT: Inner Traditions, 1997.
—— *Three Books on Life: A Critical Edition and Translation*, ed. Carol Kaske. Tempe, AZ: ACMRS Press, 2019.
Flammarion, Camille, *Omega: The Last Days of the World*. New York: Cosmopolitan, 1894.
Flusser, Vilém, *Vampyroteuthis Infernalis*. Minneapolis: University of Minnesota Press, 2012.
—— "The Moon," in *Natural:Mind*. Minneapolis: Univocal, 2013.
Forster, E. M., *The Machine Stops*. Flugschriften, 2021.
Foucault, Michel, *Madness and Civilization*, trans. Richard Howard. New York: Vintage, 1988.
Góngora, Luis, *The Solitudes*, trans. Edith Grossman. London: Penguin, 2012.
Graeber, David, and David Wengrow, *The Dawn of Everything: A New History of Humanity*. Toronto, CA: Signal, 2023.
Grebowicz, Margret, *Whale Song*. New York: Bloomsbury, 2017.
Greene, Robert, *Planetomachia*, in *The Life and Complete Works in Prose and Verse of Robert Greene*, Vol. V, ed. Alexander Grosart. Leopold Classic Library, [1585] 1881–3.
Haushofer, Marlen, *The Wall*, trans. Shaun Whiteside. New York: New Directions, 2022.
Heidegger, Martin, "The Age of the World Picture," in *Off the Beaten Track*, ed. and trans. Julian Young and Kenneth Haynes. New York: Cambridge University Press, 2002.
Hippocrates, *Volume IV – Aphorisms*, trans. W. H. S. Jones. Cambridge, MA: Harvard University Press, 1931.
Huygens, Christiaan, *Systema Saturnium*, in *Oeuvres Complètes de Christiaan Huygens*, Vol. XV. The Hague: Martinus Nijhoff, [1659] 1925.
Intergovernmental Panel on Climate Change (IPCC), *IPCC Special Report on Impacts of Global Warming of 1.5°C above Pre-industrial Levels in the Context of Strengthening Response to Climate Change, Sustainable Development, and Efforts to Eradicate Poverty*. Cambridge: Cambridge University Press, 2022.

James, William, *Essays in Radical Empiricism*. London: Longmans, Green, 1912.

Jansson, Tove, "The Wolf," in *The Woman Who Borrowed Memories: Selected Stories*, trans. Thomas Teal and Silvester Mazzarella. New York: New York Review Books, 2014.

Kant, Immanuel, "The End of All Things," in *Religion and Rational Theology*, ed. and trans. Allan Wood and George di Giovanni. New York: Cambridge University Press, 1996.

—— *Critique of the Power of Judgment*, trans. Paul Guyer and Eric Matthews. Cambridge: Cambridge University Press, 2000.

Kavan, Anna, *Ice*. London: Peter Owen, 2006.

Keats, John, *The Complete Poems*, ed. John Barnard. London: Penguin, 1977.

Kilbansky, Raymond, Erwin Panofsky, and Fritz Saxl, *Saturn and Melancholy: Studies in the History of Natural Philosophy, Religion, and Art*. Montreal: McGill–Queen's University Press, 2019.

Kierkegaard, Søren, *The Sickness unto Death*, ed. and trans. Howard V. Hong and Edna H. Hong. Princeton, NJ: Princeton UP, 1983.

—— *Papers and Journals: A Selection*, ed. Alastair Hannay. London: Penguin, 1996.

Komatsu, Sakyo, *Japan Sinks*, trans. Michael Gallagher. New York: Harper & Row, 1976.

Kyōka, Izumi, *Japanese Gothic Tales*, trans. Charles Shirō Inouye. Honolulu: University of Hawai'i Press, 1999.

Le Guin, Ursula, "Vaster Than Empires and More Slow," in *The Wind's Twelve Quarters*. New York: Harper Perennial, 2004.

Lefebvre, Henri, "Notes on the New Town," in *Introduction to Modernity*, trans. John Moore. New York: Verso, 1995.

Lem, Stanisław, *Solaris*, trans. Joanna Kilmartin. New York: Berkeley, 1971.

Lenau, Nikolaus, *The Poems and Letters of Nikolaus Lenau*, ed. and trans. Winthrop H. Root. New York: Frederick Ungar, 1964.

Leopardi, Giacomo, *Canti*, trans. Jonathan Galassi. London: Penguin, 2010.

Lévi-Strauss, Claude, *Tristes Tropiques*. London: Penguin, 1992.

Lewis, Sophie, "My octopus girlfriend," *N+1*, no. 39 (2021), https://nplusonemag.com/issue-39/reviews/my-octopus-girlfriend/.

Lingis, Alphonso, *The Imperative*. Bloomington: Indiana University Press, 1998.

Liu, Cixin, *The Three-Body Problem*, trans. Ken Liu. New York: Tor, 2014.

Lovelock, James, *Gaia: A New Look at Life on Earth*. New York: Oxford University Press, 1979.

Macrobius, *Saturnalia, Books I–II*, trans. Robert Kaster. Cambridge, MA: Harvard University Press, 2011.

—— *Saturnalia, Books III–V*, trans. Robert Kaster. Cambridge, MA: Harvard University Press, 2011.

Margulis, Lynn, *Symbiotic Planet*. London: Trafalgar Square, 1999.
Martin, Nastassja, *In the Eye of the Wild*. New York: New York Review Books, 2021.
Martinson, Harry, *Aniara: An Epic Science Fiction Poem*, trans. Stephen Klass and Leif Sjöberg. Brownsville, OR: Story Line Press, 1998.
McGinn, Bernard, *Visions of the End: Apocalyptic Traditions in the Middle Ages*. New York: Columbia University Press, 1998.
McMenamin, Mark, and Dianna McMenamin, *Hypersea*. New York: Columbia University Press, 1996.
McSweeney, Joyelle, *The Necropastoral: Poetry, Media, Occults*. Ann Arbor: University of Michigan Press, 2015.
Milton, John, *The Complete Poems*, ed. John Leonard. London: Penguin, 1999.
The Mirror of My Heart: A Thousand Years of Persian Poetry by Women, ed. and trans. Dick Davis. London: Penguin Classics, 2021.
Moebius [Jean Giraud], *40 Days Dans Le Desert 'B'*. Paris: Moebius Production, 1999.
Morselli, Guido, *Dissipatio H.G. – The Vanishing*, trans. Frederika Randall. New York: New York Review Books, 2020.
Moynihan, Thomas, *X-Risk: How Humanity Discovered its Own Extinction*. London: Urbanonic, 2020.
National Institute of Mental Health (NIMH), "Seasonal Affective Disorder," Publication no. 20-MH-8138.
Nietzsche, Friedrich, *Thus Spoke Zarathustra*, trans. Walter Kaufmann. New York: Viking, 1966.
—— "On Truth and Lies in a Nonmoral Sense," *Philosophy and Truth: Selections from Nietzsche's Notebooks of the Early 1870s*, ed. and trans. Daniel Breazeale. New York: Humanity Books, 2000.
—— *Human, All Too Human II*, ed. and trans. Gary Handwerk. Redwood City, CA: Stanford University Press, 2012.
—— *The Joyful Science, Idylls from Messina, Unpublished Fragments*, trans. Adrian Del Caro. Stanford, CA: Stanford University Press, 2023.
Orozco, Olga, *La oscuridad es otro sol*. Buenos Aires: Editorial Losada, 1967.
Pascal, Blaise, *Pensées*, trans. A. J. Krailsheimer. London: Penguin, 1995.
Petrarcha, Francesco, *The Canzoniere*, trans. Mark Musa. Bloomington: Indiana University Press, 1996.
Pettman, Dominic, *Peak Libido: Sex, Ecology, and the Collapse of Desire*. Cambridge: Polity, 2021.
Poe, Edgar Allan, *The Narrative of Arthur Gordon Pym of Nantucket*, ed. Richard Kopley. London: Penguin, 1999.
Radcliffe, Ann, "On the supernatural in poetry," *New Monthly Magazine and Literary Journal*, 16/1 (1826).
Raffles, Hugh, *The Book of Unconformities*. New York: Pantheon, 2022.
The Rig Veda, trans. Wendy Doniger. London: Penguin, 2005.
Robinson, Kim Stanley, *Aurora*. London: Orbit, 2016.

Rosenthal, Norman, *Winter Blues: Everything You Need to Know to Beat Seasonal Affective Disorder*. New York: Guilford Press, 2006.

Rosny aîné, J.-H., "The Shapes," trans. Damon Knight, *Magazine of Fantasy and Science Fiction* (March 1968).

—— *La Mort de la terre*. Paris: Librairie Plon, 2018.

Rumi, *Selected Poems*, ed. and trans. Coleman Barks. London: Penguin, 2004.

Ruskin, John, *Modern Painters*, Vol. III. London: Smith, Elder, 1856.

Sagan, Carl, *The Pale Blue Dot: A Vision of the Human Future in Space*. New York: Ballantine, 1997.

Saigyō, *Poems of a Mountain Home*, trans. Burton Watson. New York: Columbia University Press, 1991.

Schopenhauer, Arthur, *On the Suffering of the World*, ed. Eugene Thacker, trans. E. F. J. Payne. London: Repeater, 2020.

Sebald, W. G., *The Rings of Saturn*, trans. Michael Hulse. New York: New Directions, 2016.

Shakespeare, William, *Hamlet: The Texts of 1603 and 1623*, ed. Ann Thompson and Neil Taylor. London: Bloomsbury, 2007.

—— *Shakespeare's Sonnets*, ed. Katherine Duncan-Jones. London: Bloomsbury, 2010.

Sontag, Susan, "The Imagination of Disaster," in *Against Interpretation and Other Essays*. New York: Picador, 2001.

Stampa, Gaspara, *Selected Poems*, ed. and trans. Laura Anna Stortoni and Mary Prentice Little. New York: Italica Press, 2008.

Stifter, Adalbert, *Rock Crystal*, trans. Elizabeth Meyer and Marianne Moore. New York: New York Review Books, 2015.

Sturgeon, Theodore, "Galaxy's 5 star shelf," *Galaxy Science Fiction* (August 1963).

Sun Ra, *This Planet Is Doomed*. New York: Kicks Books, 2011.

—— *Prophetika, Book One*. New York: Kicks Books, 2014.

Tang Yaping, "Black Desert," in *Out of the Howling Storm: The New Chinese Poetry*, ed. Tony Barnstone. Middletown, CT: Wesleyan University Press, 1993.

Taylor, Leila, *Darkly*. London: Repeater, 2018.

Thacker, Eugene, *After Life*. Chicago: University of Chicago Press, 2010.

Thelandersson, Fredrika, "Social media sad girls and the normalization of sad states of being," *Capacious: Journal for Emerging Affect Inquiry*, 1/2 (2017); https://capaciousjournal.com/cms/wp-content/uploads/2017/04/capacious-therlandersson-sad-girls.pdf.

Thoreau, Henry David, *Walden*. London: Signet, 2012.

Tokarczuk, Olga, *Drive Your Plow Over the Bones of the Dead*. New York: Riverhead Books, 2018.

Tresch, John, "Cosmic terrains (of the Sun King, Son of Heaven, and Sovereign of the Seas)," *e-flux*, no. 114 (2020); www.e-flux.com/journal/114/364980/cosmic-terrains-of-the-sun-king-son-of-heaven-and-sovereign-of-the-seas/.

Turgenev, Ivan, "The End of the World: A Dream," in *Dream Tales and Prose Poems*, trans. Constance Garnett. New York: Macmillan, 1920.
—— *Diary of a Superfluous Man*, trans. David Patterson. New York: W. W. Norton, 1999.
Turkina, Olesya, *Soviet Space Dogs*. London: Fuel, 2014.
Verlaine, Paul, *Paul Verlaine: A Bilingual Selection of His Verse*, trans. Samuel H. Rosenberg. University Park: Pennsylvania State University Press, 2019.
Voltaire [François-Marie Arouet], *Micromégas and Other Short Fictions*, ed. Haydn Mason, trans. Theo Cuffe. London: Penguin, 2002.
Ward, Benedicta (ed. and trans.), *The Desert Fathers: Sayings of the Early Christian Monks*. London: Penguin, 2003.
Ward, Peter, *The Medea Hypothesis: Is Life on Earth Ultimately Self-Destructive?* Princeton, NJ: Princeton University Press, 2009.
Watsuji, Tetsuro, *A Climate: A Philosophical Study*, trans. Geoffrey Bownas. Tokyo: Japanese Ministry of Education, 1961.
Wells, H. G., "The Extinction of Man," *Pall Mall Gazette*, no. 59 (1894).
—— "The Star," in *Tales of Time and Space*. London: Doubleday & McLure, 1899.
—— *In the Days of the Comet*. London: Fontana/Collins, 1906.
Wilk, Elvia, *Death by Landscape*. New York: Soft Skull, 2022.
Wyndham, John, *The Day of the Triffids*. New York: Modern Library, 2003.
Yi Sang, "Ennui," trans. Jack Jung, in *Yi Sang: Selected Works*, ed. Don Mee Choi. Seattle, WA: Wave Books, 2020.

Films / TV

Aniara, dir. Pella Kågerman, and Hugo Lilja, 2018.
The Day of the Triffids, dir. Steve Sekely and Freddie Francis, 1962.
Don't Look Up, dir. Adam McKay, 2021.
Encounters at the End of the World, dir. Werner Herzog, 2007.
E.T. the Extra-Terrestrial, dir. Steven Spielberg, 1982.
Fireball: Visitors from Darker Worlds, dir. Werner Herzog, 2020.
The Hole, dir. Tsai Ming-liang, 1998.
Into the Inferno, dir. Werner Herzog, 2016.
The Ister, dir. David Barison and Daniel Ross, 2004.
Japan Sinks, dir. Shirō Moritani, 1973.
Lessons of Darkness, dir. Werner Herzog, 1992.
Letters from a Dead Man, dir. Konstantin Lopushansky, 1986.
Long Weekend, dir. Colin Eggleston, 1978.
The Man Who Fell to Earth, dir. Nicolas Roeg, 1976.
Melancholia, dir. Lars von Trier, 2011.
My Octopus Teacher, dir. James Reed and Pippa Ehrlich, 2020.
The Outer Limits, "The Architects of Fear" (TV), 1963.
Powers of Ten, dir. Charles and Ray Eames, 1968/1977.

Silent Running, dir. Douglas Trumbull, 1972.
Solaris, dir. Andrei Tarkovsky, 1972.
Space Is the Place, dir. John Coney, 1974.
Star Trek IV: The Voyage Home, dir. Leonard Nimoy, 1986.
Taming the Garden, dir. Salomé Jashi, 2022.
The Thing, dir. John Carpenter, 1982.
Under the Skin, dir. Jonathan Glazer, 2013.
Where the Green Ants Dream, dir. Werner Herzog, 1984.
The World, the Flesh, and the Devil, dir. MacDougall, 1959.

News Articles

"Brightest galaxy in Abell 2261," European Space Agency, 25 October 2012; https://esahubble.org/images/heic1216a.

Buchanan, Mark, "Contacting aliens could end all life on Earth. Let's stop trying," *Washington Post*, 10 June 2021; www.washingtonpost.com/outlook/ufo-report-aliens-seti/2021/06/09/1402f6a8-c899-11eb-81b1-34796c7393af_story.html.

"The Death of Stars," *In Our Time*, BBC Sounds, Radio 4, June 2022; www.bbc.co.uk/programmes/m0018128.

"Greta Thunberg's speech at the UN Climate Action Summit," 23 September 2019; www.npr.org/2019/09/23/763452863/transcript-greta-thunbergs-speech-at-the-u-n-climate-action-summit.

Margolis, Jacob, "How a tweet about the Mars rover dying blew up on the internet and made people cry," *LAist*, 16 February 2019; https://laist.com/2019/02/16/jpl_mars_rover_opportunity_battery_is_low_and_its_getting_dark.php

"'Milestone for humanity' as UN celebrates 8 billionth birth," *United Nations News*, 15 November 2022; https://news.un.org/en/story/2022/11/1130632.

Milman, Oliver, "Revealed: all 27 monkeys held at Nasa research center killed on single day in 2019," *The Guardian*, December 22, 2020; www.theguardian.com/world/2020/dec/22/nasa-killed-all-monkeys-on-single-day.

Navarro, Adriana, "Gulf of Mexico 'dead zone' has grown larger than Connecticut," *AccuWeather*, 9 August 2021; www.accuweather.com/en/weather-news/gulf-of-mexico-dead-zone-has-grown-larger-than-connecticut/994180.

Rampino, Michael R., et al., "A pulse of the Earth: a 27.5-Myr underlying cycle in coordinated geological events over the last 260 Myr," *Geoscience Frontiers*, 12/6 (2021); www.sciencedirect.com/science/article/pii/S1674987121001092/.

Strickland, Eliza, and Mark Harris, "Their bionic eyes are now obsolete and unsupported," *IEEE Spectrum*, 15 February 2022; https://spectrum.ieee.org/bionic-eye-obsolete.

Tarlach, Gemma, "Did the dinosaurs die on a pleasant North Dakota spring day?" *Atlas Obscura*, 23 February 2022; www.atlasobscura.com /articles/dinosaur-extinction-spring.
Wall, Mike, "A giant black hole keeps evading detection and scientists can't explain it," *Space.com*, 1 January 2021; www.space.com/abell-22 61-supermassive-black-hole-missing/.
—— "Haunted again: skull-faced 'Halloween Asteroid' returns in 2018," *Space.com*, 21 December 2017; www.space.com/39173-hallow een-asteroid-2015-tb145-returns-2018.html.